PENGUIN BOOKS

THE SOCIAL PSYCHOLOGY OF WORK

Michael Argyle, D.Sc., D.Litt., Hon., D.Sc. Psych., is Emeritus Reader in Social Psychology and Fellow of Wolfson College, and Emeritus Professor of Psychology of Oxford Brookes University. He was born in 1925, went to Nottingham High School and Emmanuel College, Cambridge, and was a navigator in the RAF. He has been teaching social psychology at Oxford since 1952. He has been engaged in research in various aspects of social psychology and is particularly interested in the experimental study of social interaction and its application to wider social problems. He has been a visiting professor at a number of universities in the USA, Canada and Australia, and has lectured in thirty-four countries. He established the Oxford Social Psychology group, which has so far produced sixty-eight D.Phils, some of them now professors elsewhere.

His recent books have been *Psychology and Social Class*, *The Social Psychology of Everyday Life*, *The Psychology of Happiness*, *The Anatomy of Relationships* (with Monika Henderson) and new editions of *Bodily Communication*, *The Social Psychology of Work* and *The Psychology of Interpersonal Behaviour*. He has written numerous articles in British, American and European journals. He helped to found the *British Journal of Social and Clinical Psychology* and was Social Psychology editor (1961–7). He was editor of the Pergamon Press *International Studies in Experimental Social Psychology* and Chairman of the Social Psychology Section of the British Psychological Society (1964–7 and 1972–4).

He is married and has four children; his hobbies are travel, interpersonal behaviour, Scottish country dancing, Utopian speculation, theological disputation and playing the goat.

THE SOCIAL PSYCHOLOGY OF WORK

SECOND EDITION

MICHAEL ARGYLE

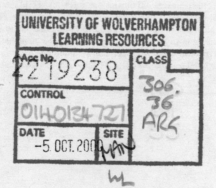

PENGUIN BOOKS

PENGUIN BOOKS

Published by the Penguin Group
Penguin Books Ltd, 27 Wrights Lane, London W8 5TZ, England
Penguin Books USA Inc., 375 Hudson Street, New York, New York 10014, USA
Penguin Books Australia Ltd, Ringwood, Victoria, Australia
Penguin Books Canada Ltd, 10 Alcorn Avenue, Toronto, Ontario, Canada M4V 3B2
Penguin Books (NZ) Ltd, 182–190 Wairau Road, Auckland 10, New Zealand

Penguin Books Ltd, Registered Offices: Harmondsworth, Middlesex, England

First published by Allen Lane The Penguin Press 1972
Published in Pelican Books 1974
Second edition 1989
Reprinted in Penguin Books 1990
3 5 7 9 10 8 6 4

Printed in England by Clays Ltd, St Ives plc
Filmset in Monophoto Photina

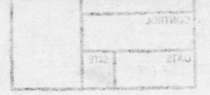

FOR MIRANDA

CONTENTS

Preface   ix

1   The Social Problems of Working Organizations   1
2   The History of Work   7
3   Technology and Job Design   29
4   Personality and Work   52
5   The Motivation to Work   86
6   Working Groups and Relationships   114
7   Social Skills and Work   148
8   Working in Organizations   197
    Appendix: Industrial Democracy   222
9   Job Satisfaction, Absenteeism and Labour Turnover   233
10 Stress, Health and Mental Health at Work   260
11 Unemployment and Retirement   285
12 The Future of Work   307

    Appendix: The Japanese Method of Working   328
    Acknowledgements   336
    References   339
    Author Index   381
    Subject Index   393

PREFACE TO THE SECOND EDITION

This book is intended for those who work and would like to understand it better, and for those who organize work and would like to organize it better. There are a number of pressing problems of work in modern countries: widespread discontent and alienation; high levels of stress and resultant illness; low motivation and lack of cooperation; conflict between management and unions, and between other groups; and difficulties with introducing new technologies, leading to a slow rate of economic growth in Britain and other countries.

These problems are becoming more acute as we move into a period of automation and post-industrial society, and are faced with the decline of the Protestant Work Ethic. An immense amount of research has been carried out in recent years in the field of industrial psychology and sociology. The study of social behaviour at work constitutes a further dimension not covered by industrial relations, management techniques or work-study, though it has implications for all these. Most work involves co-operation in groups, leadership and organization, the use of social skills and a number of different kinds of social relationship. Social psychology is concerned with the social interaction and social relationships involved, and their effect on work efficiency and satisfaction.

I have had two groups of readers particularly in mind.

Managers, trade unionists, and others involved with work. There is now a great deal of information about motivation, groups, skills, and other aspects of social psychology relevant to the enhancement of efficiency and satisfaction with work. A number of popular theories and packages will be evaluated and many of them found to be wrong. I shall try to evaluate these approaches in the light of the mounting mass of empirical evidence. We shall look at work as it is done in some other countries today in order to obtain a wider perspective. There is considerable agreement over the empirical facts in this field, and they point clearly to a set of optimum conditions for work.

Social psychologists. Work is one of the central activities of life, and social behaviour at work is one of the most important and interesting forms of social behaviour. Research on work extends our vision of social behaviour by drawing attention to factors which are not found inside laboratories – the effects of technology and of social structures, the historical development in the culture of social relationships, the effects on behaviour of socialization for roles and of powerful motivations, the performance of professional social skills.

I have tried to produce a book that is both popular and scholarly; popular in that it is intended to be of use to a wide audience, scholarly in that all the assertions in it are based on good evidence and some of the main sources are given.

Since the first edition of *The Social Psychology of Work* was published in 1972, there has been such an explosion of empirical knowledge in this field that the book has had to be rewritten. On a number of important topics there are now so many studies that meta-analyses have been published to show the overall findings from a hundred or more of them. I have added two chapters, 'Stress, Health and Mental Health at Work' and 'Unemployment and Retirement', both areas in which much recent research has been carried out.

I am grateful for the help, suggestions or collaboration in research from Margaret Ackrill, Donald Broadbent, Naomi Clifton, Adrian Furnham, Monika Henderson, Roger Lamb and Kathy Parkes. While I have drawn heavily on American work, among the research workers in Britain I am particularly indebted to the work and ideas of Peter Warr, Toby Wall and others at Sheffield, and to Cary Cooper, Charles Handy and J. E. Kelly. The librarians of Templeton College, the Radcliffe Science Library, and the Oxford

Polytechnic Library have been most helpful. Once again Ann McKendry did a marvellous job of typing the manuscript.

Michael Argyle
September 1987
Department of Experimental Psychology, Oxford

I

THE SOCIAL PROBLEMS OF WORKING ORGANIZATIONS

Work has to be done; sometimes it is enjoyable, sometimes it is not. It has to be done to provide food, clothes, shelter, protection from enemies without and disruptive elements within, care, protection and education of children, and all the elaborate arrangements for entertainment, travel, etc., to which we have become accustomed. Animals work, too, for some of these reasons, and do so largely through instinctive patterns of behaviour, which are the product of evolutionary processes. It is not clear whether man has innate patterns of work behaviour or not; it is possible that man's capacity for learned, persistent, goal-directed behaviour in groups is such an innate pattern; it is certainly very well suited to man's extensive material needs for clothes and shelter for example. The carrying out of these persistent patterns of behaviour (whether they are called work or leisure) gives men a sense of identity and purpose, and may be necessary for mental health. By far the greater part of our behaviour at work is the product of cultural factors; through historical processes a society develops certain attitudes to work and ways of working, and these are passed on to children in the course of education and other kinds of socialization. We shall see in later chapters that different civilizations in the past, and different nations in the contemporary world, have evolved very different attitudes to work and very different types of working organization. The Romans thought work was only fit for slaves, while feudal serfs worked because of a sworn obligation to their overlord; Yugoslav factories are owned by the state and controlled by the workers, while Japanese factories are paternalistic and hierarchical. In addition, we have recently entered a new epoch for work, with the explosive development of microelectronics and automation. This has had an impact both on the way work is done, and on the amount of work to be done – it has created much unemployment.

Social psychologists have been studying social behaviour at work since the early 1930s. They have studied such things as behaviour in working groups, the relations between managers and supervisors and those supervised, and the organizational structures associated with work. This has been one of the main spheres of research by social psychologists outside the laboratory – social behaviour at work is affected by many factors not found in the laboratory. It is for this reason that the social psychology of work is important for social psychology as a branch of science. Most of the research was carried out in the USA, Britain and western Europe, i.e. within a particular cultural setting, with a particular set of attitudes to work. We shall try to broaden the generality of the findings by keeping an eye on other historical periods and other countries.

Psychologists have often been asked to identify the conditions which result in high productivity, measured, for example, in terms of amount of useful output per man-hour. They have also studied the conditions which result in the greatest job satisfaction. It is an important empirical question how far high output and high job satisfaction are compatible goals. The evidence on this will be discussed later. Social psychologists have also studied the conditions under which absenteeism and labour turnover are lowest; these are found to be low when job satisfaction is high, and when they are low, overall productivity is high and labour costs low.

The social psychology of work really began with the Hawthorne studies in the 1930s, which showed the importance of interaction within working groups. The Human Relations movement demonstrated in numerous studies how the style of supervision and composition of different groups affected their work performance and satisfaction. The Tavistock Institute of Human Relations showed the importance of linking work groups to technology in the best way. Industrial sociologists have studied the operation of different kinds of working organization, and vocational guidance and selection psychologists have shown how people of different abilities and personalities can be placed in the most suitable jobs.

The early theories of behaviour at work are now known to have been mistaken and misleading. Classical organization theory, for example, left out any reference to groups, had an inadequate view of motivation, and led to boring, repetitive jobs, while some social psychological theories omitted the organization or the design of jobs. More recent theories have done better and a number of them – those of Fiedler, Herzberg, McGregor and Maslow, for example – have been popular with managers. However, there is now so much empirical research that there are meta-analyses of most of the main empirical issues. Some famous theories are now known to be wrong; in other cases the situation is much more complex than had been expected.

The Social Problems of Work

There are a number of very important social problems in industry today which fall into the sphere of the social psychologist.

Alienation and low job satisfaction. In modern industry a considerable proportion of workers do not really enjoy their work. In one survey it was found that only 16 per cent of unskilled steel workers said that they would choose the same kind of work if they were beginning their career again, as compared, for example, with 91 per cent of mathematicians (Table 20). Many are *alienated* in the sense that they feel that they have no control over the work process, that the work is meaningless to them, that they do not belong to the work community, and that the work is not an important part of their personalities or lives. Work also affects mental and physical health; many people suffer from high blood pressure, ulcers, heart disease, anxiety and other signs of bodily or mental stress as a result of their work.

These various aspects of unhappiness at work are most common in the lowest ranks of industry, though manual workers can enjoy their work very much if the conditions are right. Dissatisfaction is greatest in the most repetitive, machine-controlled jobs, such as assembly-line work. An important source of job satisfaction is membership of properly designed working groups; another is the matching of the person and the job, which can be enhanced by good selection and guidance; another is the social skill of supervisors.

Low motivation and productivity. A problem in many British firms has been low productivity and slow economic growth. This is no doubt partly due to slow introduction of new technology, poor management skills and trade union resistance to change. It is also due to low motivation.

In earlier historical periods people worked because they needed clothes, food, etc. Much work today is not so directly linked to the satisfaction of material needs, and direct motivation has been replaced by economic motivation. Economic incentives are important here, but their effects may be limited and may merely produce unwilling compliance. It is now realized that many people, especially those doing more interesting jobs, work because they enjoy the work itself, because they can exercise and develop their skills and abilities, because they want to achieve something, or because they are committed to the goals of the organization. Could these forms of motivation be extended to alienated workers, or to those individuals with no great desire to work?

Several social factors are important in the motivation of work, such as the social skills of supervisors; the more specialized skills of interviewers, negotiators and salesmen are also important. The design of working groups is important for productivity, as well as for job satisfaction.

Organizational problems. For many years the design of working organizations was a matter of trial and error, but it was also affected by *ideas*, for example those of classical organization theory (see p. 204ff). Another problem was that those at the bottom became discontented and alienated. Role conflict was common and some people were exposed to conflicting expectations and pressures. However, a lot is now known about working organizations, and how they can be designed best for particular conditions.

There are alternative ways of running working organizations. One is the development of autonomous, leaderless groups. A more radical alternative is the Japanese factory, with its lifelong employment and deep commitment to the firm.

Industrial conflict. The conflict between management and labour is institutionalized for Western capitalism in the form of collective bargaining. The unions want to get better pay and working conditions for their members; management may resist because this will add to the cost of the product and make it less competitive. There is also a harmony of interests – the unions do not want to drive the firm out of business, and management does not want an undue level of labour turnover, absenteeism, or other manifestations of dissatisfaction. Much is known about how strikes and stoppages come about, along with some of the ways of averting or resolving them.

However, it can be argued that preserving the management–union conflict in an institutionalized form places too much emphasis on conflict, and not enough on cooperation. An alternative way of dealing with the same problems is to arrange worker participation in some kind of industrial democracy. A number of different forms have been tried out, some of which appear to have been very successful. The unions may play an active role as in the West German system, or a much diminished one as in Yugoslavia.

Problems of technological change. The nature of work has been changing fast. The early factories introduced time-and-motion study, assembly lines, and boring, repetitive work. Discontent with this led to various forms of job enlargement, but these have been overtaken by the revolution in microelectronics and the extensive development of automation. Job design should not be left to engineers and accountants, as it is a major source of intrinsic motivation, satisfaction and stress. Sometimes these technological changes make life and work more agreeable, but they can also result in isolation, a loss of skills and unemployment. It may be argued that such changes should not be considered solely in an economic context, but in terms of their total effect on life in society. It should be a common goal of management and workers' representatives to plan the next step in industrial technology, not only in the pursuit of greater profits or wages, but also to create an optimum working community.

The situation has, however, changed radically in one important respect. There is now a great deal of empirical knowledge about these matters and about how to create conditions for maximum satisfaction, cooperation and effectiveness. There is still a lot of detailed research to be done, but the most important generalizations are probably now known. While some of these research findings apply only to a particular industry, country or historical period, others appear to be of much wider application. While some of this research has been done from the point of view of management and directed towards productivity, much has been more concerned with the happiness of workers. Fortunately it seems possible to aim for the two goals at the same time; we shall consider the welfare of the whole working organization, and emphasize measures which are in the interest of all. Research is neither pro management nor pro anyone else, but may point to designs for working organizations which are most satisfactory from various points of view.

We are bound to wonder how work will develop in the future, and should attempt to choose between the alternatives. Should work be decentralized, with many people working at home with a video or computer link? Will jobs become more or less skilled, more isolated? If 10 per cent of the population could satisfy our material needs, as has been estimated, what will the others do? Should there be work-sharing, or a large 'leisure class'? Could leisure be made more serious, more like work? Should the informal, unpaid economy be expanded? Should we cease to value work so highly and value leisure more?

2

THE HISTORY OF WORK

The Evolutionary Origins of Work

The concept of work is not generally used in accounts of animal behaviour. Nevertheless, the antecedents of work can be seen in all species: they have to find food by hunting or gathering ('agriculture'), build nests or other forms of shelter ('building'), look after their young ('child-rearing' and 'education'), and repel their enemies ('defence'). All these activities are necessary for the survival of particular groups, and the survival of the species. The patterns of work behaviour in a particular species are largely, and in some cases entirely, innate. In the course of evolution there is selection for survival of those members of a species who are best equipped for life in their particular environment. Evolutionary processes result in changes and development both of bodily features, such as antlers and skin colour, and also of patterns of behaviour. These include forms of 'work' behaviour such as nest-building, and forms of social behaviour such as cooperation over nest-building, organization of social groups and means of communication.

Forms of work and social behaviour similar to those of humans are found in higher mammals and birds. Work among apes and monkeys is in fact remarkably similar to work in the most primitive human societies, suggesting that there may be innate factors in human work-patterns also.

The non-human primates, the monkeys and apes, are of particular interest, since they are the animals most similar to humans on the evolutionary scale. Compared with lower mammals the primates have more highly developed and sensitive hands, which grasp and have a larger area of the brain associated with them; they have a weaker sense of smell but better vision, which is stereoscopic, again with a larger associated brain area; by standing upright they can see further and free their hands for manipulating objects; they can communicate by a range of noises, gestures and facial expressions, but cannot use symbols (unless taught to do so by humans); chimpanzees, gorillas and orang-utans can make some use of tools; there is a longer period of infant dependence, and males are regular members of the social group and protect the young, although they do not recognize their own children. They live in the jungle (e.g. chimpanzees) or in open grassland (e.g. baboons). In either case their main diet is vegetarian – fruit, nuts, leaves or roots, which are usually in plentiful supply. They also eat insects, while baboons eat lizards, scorpions, crabs and mussels as well. Chimpanzees use a simple tool to eat ants; they poke a stick into the nest until it is covered with ants and then lick them off. The collecting of food is an individual activity, but the group keeps together, the dominant males deciding where the group shall go to feed.

Most apes and monkeys construct simple nests to sleep in at night, high up in the trees away from predators. Exceptions are baboons, which live in open country and may sleep on ledges or in caves, and gorillas, which sleep in nests or on the ground – they are not afraid of other animals. Nests are very simple, made by bending branches, and are constructed in a few minutes. Most animals sleep alone in private nests, although infants sleep with their mothers, males may sleep together, and members of a group make their nests close together. It is thought that the animals probably learn how to make nests rather than knowing innately.

Humans descended from a branch of the primate family which is now extinct. The earliest remains of primitive humans date from about two million BC. These people made tools, stood more upright than the apes, had smaller canines, but brains no larger than those of apes. During the next two million years the primitive human evolved further, and succeeded in adapting genetically and culturally to a variety of climates and habitats, and to the Ice

Age. Several important evolutionary developments occurred during this period affecting work and social behaviour.

However, changes during the last 4,000 years are much more the result of cultural development – the gradual accumulation of new patterns of behaviour introduced by innovations diffused through a social group, and taught to children. Evolution proceeds by selecting those species with the greatest survival value; cultural development operates by selecting those ways of life which are found to be most satisfactory, biologically and otherwise. However, culture is passed on by learning, while evolutionary developments are passed on genetically. Learning from the culture has become important as a direct result of the evolutionary development of the larger brain, speech and the prolonged period of childhood dependence. Human beings with the same physiological equipment are capable of learning to live in a great variety of different styles.

Humans live in communities, and each community has its own culture. Cultures are 'historically created designs for living, explicit and implicit, rational, irrational and non-rational, which exist at any given time as potential guides for the conduct of man' (Kluckhohn, 1954). Culture is learnt, though it may also reflect innate dispositions or abilities in the community. For our present purposes the most important aspect is the technology and material culture – tools, weapons, clothes, houses, boats, etc. Another important aspect of culture is language, which includes the way events are categorized and symbolized. Culture also embraces forms of social organization, rules and laws, ideas and beliefs, morals and religion. Within each society certain types of personality and certain forms of motivation are encouraged and become prevalent.

Culture is passed on and conserved in a number of ways. Children are socialized into the culture by parents and teachers. This teaches them the basic structure of the culture – its language, concepts and categories. Socialization also builds up motivational systems, such as aggression, achievement and power drives. Part of the socialization process prepares people for work. African peasants find industrial work very difficult because they have not been accustomed to working regular hours, under supervision, by set methods. In modern societies children are first prepared for work at school (p. 62), and are later given further training when they start work: they are taught working skills and how to behave in working groups and organizations. Many aspects of the culture are embodied in rules of various sorts; some are laws (e.g. against stealing) which are backed by official punishment for deviation; others are social norms (e.g. about what clothes to wear) which are backed by social disapproval and rejection of deviates.

The growth of science and technology introduced a new feature into the cultural scene – a regular and continuous source of change in the material conditions of life. The growth of social science is beginning to introduce a further source of social change, via research into the most effective forms of social organization, and perhaps of society as a whole (Beals and Hoijer, 1965).

Work in the Most Primitive Societies

In the rest of this chapter we shall try to outline the historical development of work in human societies, from the most primitive up to the present day. One of the main factors in the social organization of work is the particular technology, so we shall begin each section by referring to relevant features of the technology of the period for three main areas of work – agriculture, manufacturing and building. We shall then describe the main forms of incentive and motivation, and the subjective meaning of work; the nature of working groups; leadership and management; the division of labour; and relations with the wider society.

During the Stone Age, down to about 8000 BC, there were communities of 'hunters and gatherers'. There are still some very primitive tribes in remote areas little touched by civilization which are probably very similar to Stone-Age societies – the Aborigines in Australia, pygmies and bushmen in Africa, and tribes in New Guinea. These tribes were nomadic, following seasonal fruits and herds of wild animals. They did not keep domestic animals or cultivate crops, but hunted and fished, and gathered wild fruit and vegetables. Various tools were used for the production of food – axes, pestles and mortars, clubs, spears and missiles for hunting and fishing, baskets and pottery containers for holding and preparing food. Clothes were manufactured from skins and by weaving rushes and bark. There was some manufacture of tools from wood, bone and stone. These primitive people made simple dwellings such as tents from skins, huts from branches, or lived in caves. The incentive to work was the satisfaction of the immediate biological needs of the family – for food and shelter; there was no money and no barter. Work was not thought of as a separate category of behaviour; there was no word for it. Work was a pervasive and constant part of life, necessary for existence. There were no special groups to do it, and it was combined with purely social activity, and with ritual. Everybody worked, including children and leaders, and they had to work nearly all the time.

The working group was for many purposes the family, which was much more permanent than for most species of apes and monkeys. Families moved about in rather fluid groups, related by kinship. There was a second form of grouping when they engaged in hunting or fishing – groups of men. Tiger (1969) has suggested that the formation of close bonds between males has evolutionary advantages for hunting and fighting and is part of man's instinctive equipment.

Families were usually led by the father, the oldest and strongest male. There was division of labour between the sexes, women doing most of the gathering and preparing of food, while men did the hunting and building. Children were taught the patterns of work behaviour in their families. This was partly by imitation, since they could constantly see adults working; instead of playing, children were given scaled-down weapons and tools to use (Hobhouse *et al.*, 1915).

Pre-civilized Village Communities

From about 8000 BC onwards there were developments in agriculture – the cultivation of crops, such as barley and wheat, and the keeping of domestic animals, such as sheep and goats. These developments took place at different dates in different parts of the world, and occurred first in the fertile areas surrounding rivers in the Middle East, China, India and North Africa, where the climate was very favourable for agriculture.

These changes in food production were of crucial importance since they led to more permanent dwelling-places, and to the growth of villages of increasing size. At first these communities engaged in both pastoral and agricultural work, but later they specialized into pastoral and cultivating societies. These were the main kinds of human society until the rise of the ancient civilizations from 2500 BC onwards, although these village communities survived until much later in Britain and elsewhere. This way of life can still be seen in many contemporary primitive societies. Cultivation of the soil mainly consisted in the clearing, digging, planting and reaping of cereals; this involved the use of new tools, such as metal hoes and ploughs. Animals were kept for pulling, and there were herds of cattle. The manufacture of clothes became more elaborate and included spinning and weaving. Metal objects were made from bronze and iron; pottery and wooden canoes were made; and more substantial houses were constructed from wood or stone.

The incentive to work was still the satisfaction of fairly immediate needs, but on a more long-term basis than for the hunters and gatherers. Goods were also exchanged between families or villages, on the basis of either reciprocity or barter. At a later stage primitive forms of money developed, e.g. shells, and goods were sold in the market. In some societies there was a kind of primitive communism in which all goods belonged to the community, while in others individual families owned their own houses, land and animals (Weber, 1923). Work was less closely related to immediate needs than in more primitive communities; where barter or money were involved, work was still part of a traditional way of life, but led to material prosperity for the family. Work was motivated in other ways too: it was part of a collective task, performed as a duty to others, there was pride in craftsmanship, and it was accompanied by religious ritual, music and story-telling, and the enjoyment of social relationships. Work was an integral part of life and was not distinguished from leisure (K. Thomas, 1964).

Work was done in groups, for example groups of kinsfolk, but these were not organized specially for work. The whole village might work together on large projects such as building a house or gathering in the harvest. The leadership structure for work was the same as that for the tribe or village, with two or more levels of leadership, the leaders usually being male. When a hierarchical structure of leadership developed, subordinates were paid, work became specialized and rewards were proportional to the work done (Udy, 1959). Division of labour proceeded further in these societies; there were farmers and people who looked after the herds, craftworkers and traders, and some who did no manual work at all – priests, magicians and chiefs. Some forms of work conveyed higher status than others – dealing with animals was often prestigious, though owning land was important in some societies. Work created links with the wider society outside the village, through the exchange and marketing of goods, which both supplied complementary needs, and created social bonds between different communities. Men hunted, fished and did metal-work and boat-building, while women carried water, did most of the farming, prepared food, and made clothes and pottery.

The Ancient Civilizations

In Ancient Greece about half the population were slaves; many households had at least one. There were small factories making shields, for example, with up to 120 slaves who worked alongside emancipated slaves. In some places like the silver mines slaves worked in unpleasant conditions.

Aristotle accepted that a householder should provide for the needs of the household, but he disapproved of further 'money making'. He thought that ideally work was incompatible with the proper pursuits of a citizen – learning, the arts and politics – and that it was only fit for slaves. In fact many other people worked too, and craftworkers such as sculptors and potters were held in high regard. However, working for wages for another was rather looked down upon: to be acceptable and worthwhile it was thought that work should be done freely, for one's own needs (Murray, 1986).

In the Roman Empire, slaves, the prisoners from many wars, were much more extensively employed or were exchanged for goods. Many were looked after in a paternalistic way in households and on estates, while others were harshly treated and laboured unwillingly in chains. A few were in skilled trades such as teaching.

During this time there was considerable development of various industries, especially those which produced woollen clothes, and pots and ironwork; there were mines, mills and shipping. Some of this work, such as the making of clothes, was done by women and slaves, but most metalwork, pottery, leatherwork, glassblowing, brickmaking and textile work was done in 'ergasterions' (workshops) where up to a hundred men worked under a foreman. The workshops were owned by wealthy men, successful craftworkers, or by temples, and the goods were marketed, often abroad. Several kinds of incentives were operative. The slaves were compelled by law to work and were severely punished if they did not; in exchange they were given lifelong board and keep, but were not usually paid. In the workshops there were also free men who were paid for doing identical work to that of the slaves. There were prospects of promotion to the position of foreman for slaves and others who were good at their work. Independent craftworkers set up specialized workshops in the cities, where they sold their goods directly to the public. There were also wealthy owners of farms and workshops who delegated all management to promoted slaves and who did not work themselves.

Manual work, in field or workshop, was no longer accompanied by the intrinsic rewards and satisfactions of an earlier age. Such work was generally regarded as servile and degrading, and was passed on to slaves. It was more noble to do nothing or to engage in intellectual or administrative work (Neff, 1985).

The working group was still small in many households and small estates, but included perhaps six slaves. There were also larger groups in workshops and large farms, with up to a hundred slaves and freedmen under foremen.

In the large workshops and farms working groups were found very difficult to handle, both because of the unwillingness of the workers and the large numbers involved. Some of the supervisors were themselves slaves, others monks or soldiers. In any case they found it very difficult to extract efficient work from slaves, punitive discipline being the only incentive available, including lashing, chains and execution, even crucifixion. The position of slaves deteriorated, and eventually the whole institution collapsed. This was partly due to the teachings of Stoics and Christians which focused on the quality of the human race, and partly because of the competition from workshops of freedmen, the shortage of prisoners of war, and the expense of upkeep (Weber, 1923). Division of labour developed particularly in the metal and pottery industries, otherwise there was only division by crafts. Women no longer worked in the fields, but confined themselves to household crafts. The organization of work reflected the structure of the wider society – large-scale organization by authoritarian military rule, a subservient slave class, and large export markets in the Empire (Ingram, 1926).

A new form of motivation appeared with, and was partly responsible for, the great ancient civilizations – the need for achievement. McClelland (1961) has found evidence that this motivation was highest during the period of greatest economic growth in Greece, between 900 and 475 BC, and declined as trade levelled off and diminished. He measured achievement motivation by counting the number of achievement themes in samples of Greek literature from different periods; the measure of economic activity used was Heichelheim's listing of the areas in which Greek vases (for exporting olive oil and wine) were found. The degree of achievement motivation was consistent with two further measures – the proportion of passages of literature oriented towards the future, and vase designs which are similar to designs drawn by high achievers now – more diagonals and S-shapes and less unused space. The need to achieve motivated men to seek fortunes, expand empires, construct huge and often useless buildings, and drove them to be associated with great enterprises of all kinds.

Feudalism

Slavery collapsed in the West during the later years of the Roman Empire, and was replaced by serfdom under the feudal system, which was at its height in the Middle Ages before 1066. Feudalism was a system of economic and social stratification in which all land was owned by the king. Land was held (and eventually owned) by barons who gave military service in exchange; in turn, smaller areas were held by knights who were usually lords of the manor. Serfs held much smaller strips of land, and also received protection; in exchange they had to provide a certain number of days' work, military service and a proportion of their produce. The serfs, or yeomen, were free to hold land, whereas slaves and personal servants of the lord of the manor were not. The inequalities were accepted – each person had his or her place in society.

The teachings of the Church assisted in changing the way in which people looked at work. In the sixth century St Benedict founded the first of many monastic orders, with rules condemning idleness in order to avoid sin, and requiring manual work to discipline the soul; in addition it enabled workers to give to the poor and to the church. Work was not seen to be degrading, but as ennobling, a way of serving God (Neff, 1985). However, monks taught later that intellectual and religious work was superior to manual work, a view the upper classes were happy to accept.

There were no technological advances of note during this period. Farming was conducted on the three-field system; buildings were made of stone in the towns, but of wood, wattle and thatch in the country; manufacture of cloth and household goods was carried out on the estates, as well as by craftworkers in the town. Power was provided by water, wind and animals.

There were two main incentives to work – direct provision for the family, and sworn obligation. The bond of loyalty to and dependence on the landowner was the central and essential feature of feudalism, and people would work and fight for their superiors in the system with no direct economic reward beyond permission to farm a small area of land. Work was regarded as a moral and religious duty, and necessary for salvation; it was also enforced by law. Agricultural work and handicrafts were thought of as necessities of life, and were accompanied by many of the satisfactions of more primitive village life – it was closely linked with social life, church festivals and sport (K. Thomas, 1964).

There were small working groups composed of individual families, and larger groups based on the manor-house, including those serfs who were temporarily or permanently engaged in agricultural and craftwork around the manorial estate. This was a social network in which everyone had his or her place, and was looked after by the others.

The style of leadership within the feudal system was personal and paternalistic, and was based on a high degree of acceptance of authority, as well as the dependence of subordinates on landowners. There was a hierarchy of management: the bailiff was assisted by a reeve, who was sometimes a representative of the peasants. There was little division of labour on farms, but there was specialization in different crafts within the manorial system. The manorial village was the basic social and economic unit; it provided cohesive protection against the wider society outside, and created a system of political and military organization. The produce of the manor was sold to people in other villages and in the towns, different manors specializing in different kinds of manufacture.

By 1200, while 90 per cent of the population still lived in the country, most were on wages, and half were technically free of the demands of landlords, although the latter could still control their pay. The feudal system collapsed, partly as a result of the Black Death (1347–54), which created a shortage of labour and a rise in wages, and partly as a result of the Peasants' Revolt (1381) against feudal restrictions and the enclosure of land for sheep. The growth of the towns and a market economy led to peasants running away to better jobs, while landowners found they could do better by paying wages and charging rents for land (Prawer and Eisenstadt, 1968; Anthony, 1977).

Early Industry

During and after the feudal period craftworkers with small work-shops in the towns operated on a very different basis. There were no technological advances of note until the fifteenth century, when new ways of making woollen cloth were devised.

The main incentive was now payment, either by the day as in the building industry, or by results as in the wool trade. Rates of pay and other conditions of service were regulated by the craft guilds. Work was regarded not only as natural and necessary, but as serving God and society; people should work hard but not seek to enjoy the profits made. The working group was small, consist-ing of the master craftsman, journeymen and apprentices, usually working in the master craftsman's house; often the master had only one or two assistants. Leadership fell to the more experienced master craftsman, who also owned the premises and tools, but he worked alongside his assistants. There was no division of labour within workshops, only between them.

A second stage in industrial growth was the 'domestic system' of 'merchant capitalism' from about 1600 in England. Some master craftsmen became prosperous, ceased to do the manual work themselves, and became employers. They put out work to individual families in town and country on a piecework basis, providing the materials and sometimes the tools, and selling the produce. Some employees subcontracted the work to others. Under the domestic system the family, working in the home, was the main form of working group. Incentives were now entirely financial in contrast with feudalism, workers being paid by piece-work when the work was completed, or sometimes when it was sold. Payment was irregular and workers were often in debt to their employers. Some were retained on a permanent basis, which usually meant that they were legally tied to their employer and unable to move to another. There was virtually no supervision of workers – they often embezzled the materials supplied, there was no check on the quality of work, and the rate at which they worked was irregular. The domestic system made considerable specialization possible, as different family groups developed particular skills. This system survived until the technological advances of the Industrial Revolution made it necessary to bring larger numbers of workers to one place (Pollard, 1965).

The craft guilds were social and professional societies containing all the members of a craft in a town. They maintained standards, looked after the economic interests of their members, and cared for those in need, as well as arranging social and religious functions. They also set prices and wages, as well as providing accident and sickness benefits. They were jealous of their skills and acted as a kind of closed shop. There were grades of craftworkers – apprentices, journeymen and master craftsmen – and workers could work their way up. There was far more social mobility than under the feudal social structure of the countryside. While this system engendered a great respect for craftworkers during the Renaissance, at a later date these artisans simply became wage earners, and a social gap opened between them and the entrepreneurs (Shostak, 1982).

At this time there was also a growth in industry, especially in mining for iron, coal and salt, while sea fishing and the manufacture of glass and cloth prospered as well. However, all of this was on a small scale, given that technology was primitive and that it was directed by small entrepreneurs. The Church, and especially monasteries, did much to sustain early industry by organizing workshops, reviving trade, keeping crafts and technology going.

It is generally believed by historians that the ideas of the Protestant reformers, Calvin, Luther and Zwingli, influenced the development of capitalism. Max Weber (1904) observed that the rise of Protestantism and the rise of capitalism coincided in England and in several European countries; he thought that Protestant working girls worked harder and saved their money, and that Protestant entrepreneurs did better than Catholic ones. Weber's explanation was that certain Protestant ideas encouraged capitalistic activities. The reformers taught that people would be judged individually, and would be judged on the basis of their whole life's work, of which their 'calling' was the most important part; on the other hand money should not be spent on oneself. This led to a life of hard work, self-discipline, asceticism and concern with achievement; it also led to the accumulation of money which could not be spent on luxury, but which could be put into one's own business. Calvin taught predestination, and here the link with capitalism is more obscure: it was thought that the elect could be recognized by certain outward signs, which included self-denial and devotion to duty, and it was also believed that God caused the elect to prosper (R. Brown, 1965). A rather different interpretation was given to these events by Tawney (1926) who maintained that the spirit of individualism, rather than any specific Protestant doctrines, was the cause of capitalism. In fact, a number of early entrepreneurs in France and Italy were Catholics, while in Britain some were not Nonconformists but members of the Church of England. In any case, although entrepreneurs may have been influenced by these ideas, or felt that their money-making was legitimized, it is doubtful whether there was much impact on the workers, who were motivated more by hunger (Shostak, 1982).

When Catholic and Protestant countries are compared today, there is no doubt that the Protestant countries are more prosperous. McClelland (1961) reported the per capita electricity consumption in 1950 for twenty-five countries: for the Protestant countries the average was 1,893 kilowatt hours per capita, for the Catholic countries, 474. There were some exceptions however – Belgium, Austria and France were higher than Denmark and Holland.

McClelland offered a social psychological explanation for the link between Protestantism and capitalism. This is shown in Fig. 1. The theory is that Protestant ideas and values produce (1) a certain way of bringing up children, which (2) leads to the children acquiring strong achievement motivation, and (3) high achievers become entrepreneurs and create an expansion of business. McClelland found that in England during the period 1500–1800 achievement motivation as measured from the content analysis of samples of literature rose and fell with the level of coal imports, except that the achievement changes were about fifty years ahead of the coal import changes. There was a similar relation between achievement imagery in children's reading books and the number of patents issued in the USA between 1800 and 1950, as is shown in Fig. 2.

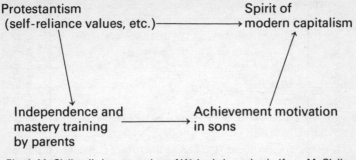

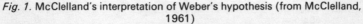

Fig. 1. McClelland's interpretation of Weber's hypothesis (from McClelland, 1961)

In a study of forty nations there was found to be a correlation of 0·53 between motivation in 1925 (assessed by content analysis of children's reading books) and growth in the electricity supply between 1925 and 1950. One way in which McClelland has modified Weber's hypothesis is in suggesting that capitalist activity is not produced simply by affiliation with a Protestant church but by a feeling that the individual is in touch with God, without need of priest or ritual, and a belief that salvation depends on one's life's work. Meanwhile McClelland's ideas have stimulated a great deal of research though the issues involved are by no means settled (Brown, 1965).

The Industrial Revolution

The conditions under which an industrial revolution occurs are not fully understood. The first industrial revolution took place in England between 1769 and 1850, the discovery of steam-power – and various inventions in the textile industry – playing an important role. In addition, for such an event to take place it is probably necessary to have banking and a supply of capital, and a sufficient number of skilled workers who are able to adjust to the new conditions of work. There must also be a number of innovators, entrepreneurs who want to build up industrial concerns, either in order to make money themselves or, as in communist countries,

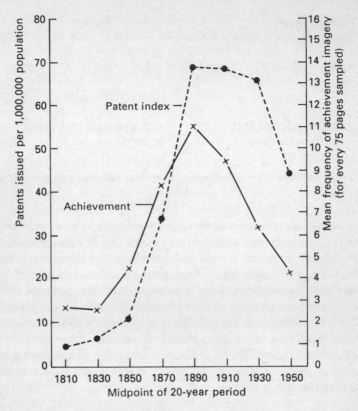

Fig. 2. Mean frequency of achievement imagery in children's readers and the patent index in the USA, 1800–1950 (from McClelland, 1961).

for other motives. In England the first important technological changes came in the cotton industry, such as Arkwright's spinning-jenny of 1769, giving cotton the lead over wool for a time. In the same year Watt patented his first steam-engine; these engines were rapidly to become the source of power, especially for the textile industry and for pumping in mines. Iron and coal were brought together for smelting iron ore, hence the use of iron in engineering at Ironbridge and elsewhere; demand was kept high as other industries needed machinery made of iron. Mass production was started in the pottery industry by Wedgwood. Canals and railways were built for the needs of industry. Larger numbers of workers were brought together in the same work place, partly because of the need for expensive capital equipment, partly because small-scale production was not economic, and partly to improve supervision.

The Industrial Revolution was preceded by a revolution in agriculture; less dramatic than that in industry, it was none the less essential to it as the increased productivity of farming supplied the towns with capital as well as food. In the year 1200 90 per cent of the population of England worked on the land; in 1688 this figure had dropped to 76 per cent; in 1800 it was 35 per cent; in the 1960s it was down to 4 per cent (Edholm, 1967); and in 1987 under 3 per cent. The main changes were improved machinery (such as ploughs and threshing machines), new crops and breeds (for example, turnips for feeding sheep), better drainage, fertilizers, specialization in different areas, and larger estates. During the Industrial Revolution the results of scientific and technological research were for the first time applied systematically to improve the techniques of production.

The entrepreneurs played a very important role in the Industrial Revolution. In the coal and steel industry, in particular, capital was essential; the early entrepreneurs in England were mostly middle-class merchants with some capital, while a minority were ex-craftworkers or self-made. They were not well educated, but they knew their own trade. They shared a faith in progress and an enthusiasm for technical inventions. They were a rising prosperous class, despised by the landed aristocracy; many lived austerely, reinvesting rather than spending their profits, and few sought to infiltrate the upper classes (Bendix, 1956). They fit perfectly the description of the high-need achiever. In addition, they must have had unusual originality to have had the vision of building up a totally new kind of working organization. While some were unscrupulous and many were authoritarian, others like Robert Owen had a Utopian vision of the ideal working community, in which there was cooperation, a happy and healthy environment and character training. The factories were administered by the owners, assisted by a new class of managers, some of whom were trained as accountants or lawyers. They had the skills of organizing supplies, managing the whole production process, controlling an ill-disciplined workforce, and marketing the product (Mathias, 1983). They were not professional managers so much as experts in their particular industry.

The engineers of the period, some of whom were formerly skilled craftworkers, while others were trained at mechanics institutes, were perhaps even more important and included the inventors of textile machinery and steam-power: Darby and Bessemer, who made iron and steel; and Stephenson, Telford and Brunel, who developed railways, canals and steamships.

However, there was little positive desire to go to work in the new factories. Small craftworkers were driven out of business and many peasants left the land through losing their tenure and because of population growth; while they were offered better wages, many preferred poverty at home to work in the factories.

The process of converting craftworkers and peasants into industrial workers was a difficult one. They had previously worked at home and were not accustomed to the conditions of industrial work, in particular having to keep regular hours. In their efforts to control workers, employers used fines for lateness and absenteeism, low wages (so that hunger would keep them at work), long hours (to keep them out of the public houses), corporal punishment (especially for children), dismissal or relegation to worse jobs – and resultant starvation and prison. The discipline enforced was tyrannical and brutal, and many children died in mines and factories. Only a few firms used wage incentives or gave a share in the profits. 'Factory discipline must have seemed as irrational, as irrelevant to one's interests, as unfree, as army discipline today. Self-respecting men would not send their children into factories which looked like workhouses. Women and pauper children filled the factories, plus Welsh and Irish immigrants who lacked the English tradition of freedom' (C. Hill, in Thomas, 1964). Despite these disincentives workers were frequently absent, late, idle or drunk, fought each other, produced poor quality work, and as a result had no ambition to become prosperous or respectable.

The unpleasant and boring nature of the work produced a sharper division between work and leisure, and forms of leisure which were mainly reactions to the stresses of work.

The organizations which employers built up were hierarchical structures, with maximum division of labour, where workers were controlled by money and the threat of the sack. Employers had considerable power over employees, since joint action by workers was forbidden, travel to other places dangerous, and many workers were legally tied to their employers. In addition, fluctuating unemployment meant that workers experienced extreme insecurity. In the new factories much larger groups were gathered together than before, many of them women and children, under supervisors. Bargains were often made with the male head of the family who brought the whole family to work (Mathias, 1983). The relationship between the supervisors and the workers was a curious one. On the one hand, the supervisors knew the workers personally, and exercised some degree of paternalistic benevolence; on the other hand, workers were clearly treated very badly. The traditional feudal relationship was used as a means of controlling workers by eliciting obedience and deference – but without the duties of the master being taken very seriously (cf. Bendix, 1956). In addition, very little concern was paid to the welfare of the workers, who were regarded as part of the factory equipment. This set of practices was later embodied in the 'classical organization theory'.

However, the conditions of work in a few firms were a good deal better than those mentioned above, notably in those run by Quakers, such as Cadbury and Fry. Similarly, workers were treated better in small village factories where there was a more personal relationship with the owners. On the whole, conditions in factories improved partly as a result of humanitarian influences and partly because it was realized that workers would work better if looked after better.

The Industrial Revolution transformed society, creating large towns and an urbanized working class which had no power and which was alienated and discontented with factory work. However, in time it also increased the prosperity of employers and, to some extent, workers, as they had been even worse off in agriculture and cottage industries, and led to the growth of trade unions (which first developed among skilled craftworkers and which took over from the guilds) and the Marxist ideology.

Other European countries followed a similar pattern of industrial development to that experienced by Britain. In the USA the process was somewhat different because of a shortage of labour and the availability of free land, resulting in an emphasis on mechanized methods of production. Countries whose technological take-off came later still were able to profit from the painful experiences of the first countries to undergo the process, and could make use of the latest technological and administrative methods.

Liberal Capitalism
1850–1939

During this period, the conditions of work changed in a number of ways in the West. There was continuous technological innovation, resulting in larger and more efficient factories of all kinds. Iron was succeeded by steel, steam by electricity, and new industries – such as those making cars and aircraft – appeared. In Britain there was a rapid growth in the membership and power of trade unions, considerable improvement in working conditions, shorter hours of work, and increased employment of women. However, many workers were still poor, there were periods of high unemployment, and there was no security of tenure (Ackrill, 1987).

Attitudes to work in other countries developed rather differently. In the USA wages were high and people worked in order to sustain a rising level of consumption; in post-Revolution Russia work was performed as part of a national effort in the face of a continual state of emergency (Fox, 1971); in Japan some workers were looked after for life in paternalistic firms, although to begin with their wages were very low.

Many firms in the UK and USA introduced systems of incentive payment. Due to new government regulations and the increasing power of trade unions, management was not able to use negative sanctions as much as before: there was still the fear of dismissal, but it was easier to move to other jobs. The conditions of work and the treatment of workers were greatly improved as a result of government regulations, e.g. against child labour, and the activities of the trade unions. Nevertheless many workers were extremely alienated and discontented with their work.

Working groups took various forms, including a new pattern characteristic of the period – assembly-line production groups. The style of supervision was usually authoritarian; workers were assumed to be inherently lazy and incapable of self-discipline and to be motivated solely by economic needs. Relationships were impersonal and rules were devised to define the rights and duties of employees. The introduction of Taylor's ideas (p. 31) led to an increased division of labour ('Taylorism'), so that each worker carried out a very simple task at which he or she could become expert. The invention of time-and-method study at the turn of the century made it possible to standardize every job in order that the simplest set of movements could be used and appropriate piece-work rates established. The invention of assembly lines led to efficient production at the cost of stress and boredom.

Recent Developments in Working Conditions
1950–87

One of the most striking changes in the Western world during the last few decades has been the decline of traditional industry (for example coal, iron, shipping), the introduction of automation and information technology, and the growth of white-collar work of many kinds. In addition, more women have joined the labour force. The result is that unemployment has increased in all industrialized countries, and the work that remains is of a different nature. It is clear that most people want to work, and are very frustrated when they cannot.

Use continues to be made of wage incentives for many workers, but there has been a search for forms of 'intrinsic', non-economic motivation, which are reliant on the fact that workers gain satisfaction from working. The greater education of much of the labour force has led to a demand for more interesting and satisfying work. This has been expressed by the Quality of Working Life movement in several countries.

While automation has often led to the breaking up of working groups there has also been a greater awareness of the importance of groups. Some organizations have constructed 'functional groups' to make the best use of group processes (p. 42ff); these are groups containing workers with a number of different skills who cooperate to complete a major task. The work of the Tavistock Institute of Human Relations in London has shown that the same technology can be handled by several kinds of sociotechnical systems; this point has been recognized in connection with the installation of automated equipment.

Styles of supervision have been much affected by the Human Relations movement (p. 206ff), via training courses and management consultants. There has also been something of a reaction against this movement, and a realization that concern for people and concern for productivity need to be combined in supervisory skills (p. 149ff). Consequently, new forms of social-skills training, designed to teach the most effective styles of behaviour, have been developed for supervisors and managers.

As a result of changing attitudes, the hierarchical structures of classical organization theory have been much criticized and there have been experiments with other kinds of organizational structure – decentralization, industrial democracy, and structures based on systems analysis (Chap. 8).

Much interest has been taken in the alternative kinds of management used in Japan and the USA, which are discussed in Chapter 8, and in the Appendix on Japanese industry.

3

TECHNOLOGY AND JOB DESIGN

Work consists of doing things to raw materials in order to change them into a more finished product. It is this finished product which is needed by others, and for which they will pay. The processing of the raw materials is done by workers, using tools or equipment of some kind, usually assisted by a source of power. The workers need skills, and they use a method of working, a way of using the tools.

Take the example of farming: the raw materials are seed, soil, fertilizers, weedkillers, etc. The finished products are grain, potatoes, milk, and other foods. Every industry produces characteristic transformations of materials. The car industry changes sheet and other metals into cars, the textile industry changes yarn into clothes. All work can be seen in this way, including medicine, research, transport, entertainment and writing.

The actual work done by the worker depends on the tools and the sources of power which are available. Farm workers may use spades, hoes and rakes – the tools used by gardeners. Or they may have the use of ploughs and so on which are pulled by horses or tractors. They may have much more sophisticated equipment, such as combine harvesters. This changes the nature of the work completely.

The growth of civilization has been accomplished and partly caused by the development of technology. One aspect of this has been a growth in the use of steam and other power: between 1850 and 1950 the percentage of industrial power derived from machines rather than from men or animals in the USA rose from

14 per cent to 80 per cent; the power controlled by each man was about fifty times more than in countries such as Turkey and Albania (Dubin, 1958). Other technological developments, for example automatic machine tools and textile machinery, have taken over the functions of individual craftworkers. Inventions such as television, aircraft and space travel create whole new industries for the manufacture and operation of new equipment.

The reason that new equipment is introduced is mainly economic – the same goods can be produced more cheaply, mainly because fewer workers are needed. The increase in industrial output in Japan of 217 per cent between 1953 and 1961 was not achieved by Japanese workers rushing round 3·17 times as fast: it was achieved by the installation of a massive amount of new equipment, so that there was an enormous increase of productivity per worker. The greater productivity of American firms compared with those in Britain is largely, perhaps wholly, due to the greater amount of capital equipment per worker in the USA. A second advantage of improved technology is that a higher quality of product can be achieved, for example very precise machining of engineered parts, higher quality of fabrics, better control of chemical products. Another goal is the development of new products or services, or the solution of military, medical or social problems. Carrying passengers from London to New York in under four hours was not achieved by getting crews to work harder or by training them better: it was accomplished by jet aircraft.

When new equipment is designed, thought has to be given to the people who will operate it and to the skills which they will need. However, we shall see that two aspects have been greatly neglected by the designers of equipment – the extent to which the job provides satisfaction, and the implications for relationships between workers.

Job Design

Modern industrial practice started with the idea of the division of labour, first expounded by Babbage (1835). Jobs were divided into smaller components so that they could be performed by less skilled, and less highly paid people who needed less training. This led to very short, repeated work-cycles, often shorter than one minute (Kelly, 1982); Friedmann (1961) reported a slaughterhouse in which one man did nothing but remove pigs' testicles, while another linked a sausage every three seconds.

A very influential set of ideas was put forward by Taylor (1911, 1947) in his *Scientific Management*. To the idea of division of labour he added time-and-motion study and wage incentives. By observing and timing each part of a manual task it was possible to find the best method of doing it; workers were then to be paid a good wage for achieving high rates of work. Gilbreth (1909) was also influential in studying methods of working. In one of his early studies he found that bricklaying could be reduced from eighteen movements to five, with the result that men could lay 350 bricks in an hour instead of 120. Even today it is sometimes possible to increase productivity by up to 200 per cent by these methods – using both hands, cutting out unnecessary movements, etc. However, everyone has to do the job in exactly the same way, whether they like it or not.

The next technological development was the invention in 1913 of the moving assembly line by Henry Ford; he produced 15 million Model T Fords between 1908 and 1928. The speed of work was controlled by machinery instead of by wage incentives. This kind of work, however, produced very low levels of job satisfaction, and high rates of absenteeism and labour turnover.

Workers do not respond like passive machines to the working conditions imposed upon them; they react constructively and creatively to satisfy any of their needs which are not being met. Assembly-line workers create interest and variety in their work by playing practical jokes, such as fixing cars so that stepping on the accelerator blows the horn and starts the wipers, or they may engage in various kinds of horseplay such as glueing each other's toolboxes to the floor. Together with these and other games workers may also attempt to gain control of their rate of work by saving it up, and by not handing in completed work during a busy period so that they can take it easy later. They may modify parts of the job, change with other workers, make a game out of it, set goals for themselves, let the machinery break down or deliberately sabotage it (Sayles and Strauss, 1966).

Walker and Guest (1952) found particularly low levels of satisfaction on the assembly line; 92 per cent of the workers studied preferred to be off the line, and labour turnover was twice that of other workers. Two of the main complaints were the lack of autonomy under machine-pacing, and the endless repetition of a small unit of work. Dissatisfaction led to attempts at job enlargement and enrichment, and a very large number of schemes of this nature were introduced, especially during the period 1964–76. Surveys of the reasons for introducing them found that personnel problems, such as absenteeism, turnover or low morale, were the main reason in just under half of the cases, but that productivity, costs or quality problems were cited more often (Kelly, 1982).

(1) *Improvement in job design.* Three main kinds of improvement in job design have been made in different areas of industry.

(a) *Reorganization of assembly lines* ('job enlargement'). The division of labour was reversed so that the work-cycle was increased, and each person did several different tasks, which often added up to a more satisfying unit of work. Some assembly lines were replaced by individual work stations. These changes were made mainly in the electrical consumer goods industry, where market competition led to batch production and constant design changes, making assembly lines uneconomic. This was made possible by advances in electronics which meant that the equipment could be reprogrammed quite easily.

(b) *Flexible work groups*, with collective responsibility for the final product, were introduced mainly in continuous-process industry, such as the chemical and textile industries. They will be discussed further below (p. 43ff).

(c) *Vertical integration* ('job enrichment'). In clerical work this took the form of adding new tasks such as signing and deciding upon the layout of letters, or operating computers. For manual workers it resulted in adding maintenance, inspection, and the setting up of machines to simply operating them (Kelly, 1982).

What is the effect of job enlargement on productivity? Hackman and Oldham (1980) proposed that jobs created intrinsic motivation and satisfaction if they possessed the following five properties: variety, autonomy, task identity (completing a satisfying and recognizable whole), feedback and impact on others (task significance). A further part of the theory was that job satisfaction should lead to less absenteeism and labour turnover. We shall see later that this has been confirmed, although the effects are rather weak (p. 255ff).

Kelly (1982) analysed a number of cases of job enlargement, and found increases in productivity per man hour of the order of 20 per cent. However, this was not necessarily caused by increased job satisfaction and motivation, but by removing delays due to workers waiting for each other to pass on materials, and by improving methods of working, e.g. using both hands, and better-designed work stations. If there was an increase in pay, then additional increases in productivity of the order of a further 35 per cent or so were found. In most cases job satisfaction increased, but in some cases productivity improved while job satisfaction did not, and vice versa.

Does job enrichment, or vertical integration, fare any better? According to Kelly's analysis, it does not for manual workers: any increases in productivity were due to bargains of more pay for doing more things, with a resultant reduction in labour costs. However, for white-collar workers the findings are more positive. For example, Janson (1971) studied the effect of the enrichment of the work of typists who were asked to change their own computer tapes and to correct their own mistakes. The results are shown in Table 1. A number of other studies have obtained similar increases in productivity without pay increases, associated with increased job satisfaction or other job attitudes.

It is noteworthy that complaints about boring work became most vocal in the USA, in particular, in the 1950s and 1960s, while many job improvement schemes were brought in from

	Before enrichment	After enrichment	Control Group	
			Before	After
Blocks typed per hour	70	85	68	68
Errors per week	15–20	<5	15–20	15–20
Herzberg job motivation scale	50	60	50	47

Table 1. Enrichment of the work of typists (from Janson, 1971).

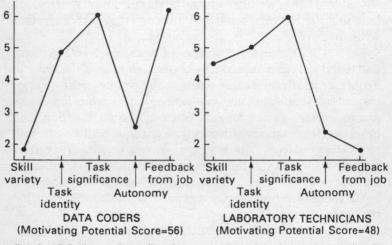

DATA CODERS
(Motivating Potential Score=56)

LABORATORY TECHNICIANS
(Motivating Potential Score=48)

Fig. 3. JDS diagnostic profiles for two problem jobs in a corporate head-quarters (from Hackman and Oldham, 1980).

1964–76. This was a period of relatively full employment, and perhaps a period when many American workers had satisfied their material needs, described by Maslow as 'lower-order needs' (see Chapter 5). It was found by Turner and Lawrence (1966) that those workers from small towns rather than from big cities were made more satisfied by interesting and demanding jobs. Hackman and Oldham proposed that such jobs were more motivating for those with stronger 'growth needs' (p. 55ff). They devised a 'Job Diagnostic Survey' (JDS), a method of rating jobs on five desirable characteristics by those doing them. Examples of the profiles of two jobs are shown in Fig. 3. This figure shows, for example, that the work of data coders was found to be high on task identity, task significance and feedback, but low on skill variety and autonomy. While it has not been shown convincingly that these five properties motivate performance (p. 100ff), we shall see later that they are strongly correlated with job satisfaction (p. 235ff).

(2) *Quality of Working Life movement.* During the 1960s, concern with these issues in a number of countries led to the appearance of the Quality of Working Life movement, with centres in different parts of the world (Davis and Cherns, 1975). This movement publicized a number of principles of good job design, especially the following.

(a) *The principle of closure.* The scope of the job should include all the tasks necessary to complete a product or process. Theoretically, the predicted result is that work acquires an intrinsic meaning and people can feel a sense of achievement.

(b) *Incorporation of control and monitoring tasks.* Jobs should be designed so that a large number of inspectors are not required. The individual worker, or the work team assumes responsibility for quality and reliability.

(c) *Task variety*, i.e. an increase in the range of tasks. This implies a principle of comprehensiveness, which means that workers should understand the general principles of a range of tasks so that job rotation is possible.

(d) *Self-regulation* of the speed of work and some choice over work methods and work sequence.

(e) *Job structure* that permits some social interaction and perhaps cooperation among workers.

The leaders of this movement were industrial consultants and academics. The trade unions had been more concerned with the consequences for unemployment of new machinery, but in Scandinavia they were active in the field of job design. Agreements were worked out in Norway, Sweden and Denmark requiring full consultation with employees before the introduction of new technology. Since then, this has been accompanied by the education of trade unions in technological matters, and a high degree of co-operation between management and unions (Gill, 1985).

Man-machine Systems

We saw that the Industrial Revolution occurred mainly because of the availability of steam-power and the invention of new machinery, as in the textile industry. New equipment is introduced because it helps workers to do a job better, or faster, or to do a completely new job. The present approach is to design 'man-machine systems', where both people and machines combine to do what they can do best. A person riding a motorcycle, a secretary typing, or a person operating twenty-two automatic looms, are examples. In each case the machine is introduced so that the operator can do something better or more cheaply than he or she could without it. In each case the person is there because the machine cannot do it all by itself. At any stage of the available technology there are some things the operator can do better, some things the machine can do better. A motorcycle can go faster and further than a bicycle by using machine power, but it still needs someone to steer it.

There are many things that machines can do better than people. They (1) provide power and physical force, (2) engage in repetitive activity without tiring, (3) make calculations and analyse large amounts of data, (4) are capable of long-term monitoring, and (5) can detect small sensory or other signals. On the other hand, people are better than machines in other ways, although the situation is changing constantly as new technology produces ever more sophisticated ways of computerizing human functions. At present humans are better than machines at (1) dealing with other people in supervision, selection, training, etc., (2) designing new work systems and machines, programming computers, planning new products, (3) making use of a wide range of past experiences in making decisions, as in the case of doctors and research workers, and of being able to learn by experience, (4) being able to deal with a wide range of stimuli or information, as in driving a car or flying a plane, and (5) being able to deal with emergencies, new situations, and problems which have not been met before (see Schultz, 1982).

A man-machine system combines some of the capacities of humans with some of those of machines. Equipment has to be designed with regard for those who will operate it. To date, designers have paid attention primarily to the physiological properties of the operator – for example, what he or she is able to see, hear or reach – but have had little regard for what the operator will find interesting or satisfying, or for the social relationships created by technology. The operator has three main functions to perform, and in each of these the machinery can be adapted to his or her physiological capacities.

(1) *Receiving information*, from visual displays, the environment or other people. Much research has been done in order to establish the kinds of dials which can be read most easily, and the conditions under which information should be visual or auditory.

(2) *Processing information in decision-taking.* A worker often has to take account of several kinds of information, and then make decisions on the basis of his or her knowledge and skills, e.g. the pilot of an aircraft.

(3) *Motor responses* – made by manipulating objects or controls in some way. Much research has been done into the design of these controls for maximum ease of use (Chapanis, 1965). Machines can not only 'think' now, they can read, talk, play games, plan ahead, control other machines, and be given 'personalities' (Minsky *et al.*, 1968).

The choice of how much of the task, and which part of it, is given to the operator is decided by management and is done so mainly on the advice of engineers and accountants. If labour is very expensive or troublesome, there is a case for making less use of operators. If the task is constantly changing, with many new or different designs, there is a case for choosing people over machines. In this chapter we shall develop some further considerations which should also be taken into account.

Socio-technical Systems
I Relations between a pair of workers

Most technological systems need more than one person to operate them. A bicycle can be ridden by one person, but operating a spacecraft requires a large number of people who do different jobs and who are closely coordinated with one another. Some technical systems impose certain social arrangements; others can be operated by alternative social arrangements which are each compatible with the technology. The combination of technology and social arrangements is called the socio-technical system (Rice, 1958). Until recently almost no attention was paid to the effects of technology on the social relations between workers. The main relationship envisaged was between the supervisor and the supervised. In fact the matter is far more complex than that.

When a worker has to deal with a job, and with other workers, he or she is combining a technical skill and a social skill. Although socio-technical systems have been studied as a whole as sociological units, little research has yet been done on the actual performance of the socio-technical skills involved. Three main kinds may be distinguished, with subdivisions.

(1) *Cooperation over a task*

(a) Parallel performance, e.g. independent assembly work, typing, research. There may be mutual help but this is unofficial.

(b) Sequential performance of different tasks, e.g. the workers on an assembly line. This needs coordination, and time is wasted while one worker waits for another.

(c) Cooperative performance of similar tasks, e.g. two-handed sawing, handling sheet steel in a press-shop.

(d) Cooperative and simultaneous performance of different but complementary tasks, e.g. pilot and navigator of an aeroplane.

In all of these cases the worker receives input information

from both the work of other persons and from task displays, such as dials; events can be controlled either by influencing the other workers or by manipulating the controls of the task. The different feedbacks have to be considered together; for example, it may be necessary for different jobs to be synchronized.

(2) *Supervisory relationships*

(e) Supervision, e.g. by a supervisor.
(f) Inspection.
(g) One person is an assistant to others, e.g. nurse–doctor, technician–research worker.

In these cases one person does not actually do the work but has to make sure that someone else does it properly. Exactly what a supervisor has to do, and how he or she does it, depends greatly on the technology. If there is machine-pacing, as on an assembly line, the supervisor does not need to motivate subordinates to work harder. There may be inspection, but this, too, may be automatic as the supervisor may have equipment which gives clear information about the performance of the workers. The usual situation, however, is that a supervisor takes account of feedback both from task-display indicators *and* from observation of the subordinates' behaviour. The action which he or she takes is usually to try to influence the individual, although it may also involve changes to equipment.

(3) *Other social relationships.* Other kinds of social skills are commonly found in socio-technical systems.

(h) Conveying objects or information.
(i) Discussion, by members of a cooperative problem-solving group.
(j) Negotiation, where there is some conflict of interest.
(k) Providing expert advice, without authority.

These situations are all examples of social skills, for which the model is shown in Fig. 4.

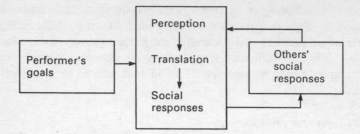

Fig. 4. Performance of a social skill.

The performer is *motivated* to influence *others' social responses* and emits a stream of *social responses* which are corrected continuously as the result of *feedback*, which is *perceived* and *translated* into appropriate corrective action (Argyle, 1969, 1983).

Several of these different socio-technical skills can be seen in the socio-technical system of a large restaurant, as described by Whyte (1948), although the 'technology' here is very simple.

(*a*) Parallel behaviour – waitress.
(*b*) Cooperative performance – cooks.
(*c*) Cooperative and complementary performance – waitresses and bartenders.
(*d*) Sequential performances – cooks and dishwashers.
(*e*) Supervision – at several points.
(*f*) Inspection – e.g. checkers and waitresses.
(*g*) Assistance – probably in the kitchen, but not shown.
(*h*) Conveying objects and information – e.g. runners take food from kitchen to pantry, and orders from pantry to kitchen.
(*i*) Discussion – between supervisors.
(*j*) Negotiation – between waitress and customer.
(*k*) Providing expert advice – no example here.

There may be difficulties in any of these relationships which could result in the system not working well. Some of these difficulties can be solved by better social skills on the part of performers, others by organizational changes, while others may require changes in the technology, such as new equipment or means of communication. For example, Whyte discovered that some waitresses

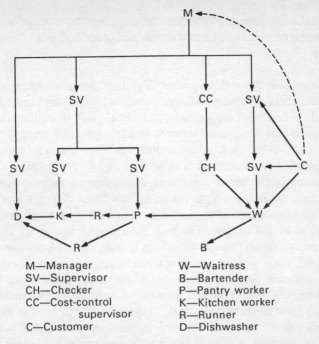

M—Manager
SV—Supervisor
CH—Checker
CC—Cost-control
       supervisor
C—Customer

W—Waitress
B—Bartender
P—Pantry worker
K—Kitchen worker
R—Runner
D—Dishwasher

Fig. 5. The social system of a restaurant (from Whyte, 1948).

found their jobs full of stress and strain, and as a result cried a great deal. One reason for this was that they were under constant pressure from customers, who wanted food that the cooks were not able to produce rapidly, this being worse at busy periods. Some waitresses, however, managed to deal with the situation by influencing the customers – they persuaded them to have the food that was readily available.

Socio-technical Systems
II Arrangements in working groups

The term 'socio-technical systems' simply means the combination of technical and social systems. The theory, developed by members of the Tavistock Institute of Human Relations, was that the two should fit together and produce optimum results; motivation was said to be derived both from the task structure and from the work group.

Better division of working groups. The first demonstration of the importance of matching social and technical structures came from a study of Longwall coal-mining (Trist *et al.*, 1963). In this system, groups of forty-one men under a single supervisor were divided into three shifts, each doing a different job – cutting, filling or stonework – although each shift was highly dependent on the others. Since the teams never met, it was impossible for cohesiveness and cooperation to develop, especially as different levels of prestige were attached to each job. One shift would not clear up properly, or fail to leave the roof safe for the next shift. It was extremely difficult to supervise shifts working at different times; in addition, these working groups were larger than those in earlier arrangements, and were more spread out in the mine, so that the cohesiveness, which served formerly to reduce the anxieties of mining, was never experienced. There was a high level of absenteeism and discontent. This arrangement was compared with a modified version, in which the men were divided into composite groups, so that all three tasks were carried out on each shift. The result was an output of 5·3 tons per man-shift compared with 3·5 in the conventional Longwall design, and absenteeism was 40 per cent lower than in the other groups. The reasons for this were probably that (1) better relations were established between those doing the three different jobs, and tensions between shifts were removed, (2) there was less division of labour and more variety of work, and (3) status differences between those in different shifts and those using different skills were abolished (Trist *et al.*, 1963). This study shows that the same technology can be combined with quite different kinds of social organization. Indeed, this is one of the most important implications of research on this topic.

Conflict or lack of cooperation between different groups is a common problem at work. This is particularly likely to happen if there are differences of pay or status, and if there is little social contact between groups. This problem is taken up again later 140ff).

Introduction of flexible working groups. In another Tavistock study Rice (1958) designed a new system of working groups in the Ahmedabad textile mills in India. Automatic looms had been introduced but production had not increased. Twenty-nine men, divided into twelve different jobs, and with a very confused pattern of relations between them, looked after 224 looms. Rice's solution was to create four groups of seven, three on weaving and one on maintenance, which were formed by the men themselves, plus one man on 'humidification'. Each group was collectively responsible for sixty-four looms, each performing its own ancillary services. The result was an increase of 21 per cent in productivity and a drop of 59 per cent in damaged cloth; the new organization was rapidly applied to other weaving sheds. The reasons for the success of this arrangement were probably that (1) workers belonged to small, cohesive groups working on a cooperative task, and that (2) the task was more varied and added up to a satisfying total performance.

The idea of autonomous and flexible work groups has led to many applications in a variety of industries. A famous instance occurred at a Swedish Volvo factory, where a production line was replaced by flexible work groups. In the assembly plant at Kalmar, each work group now has its own entrance, coffee area and small workshop. Car bodies are placed on carriers whose speed, while computer controlled, can be altered manually, making variation possible. Each group does its part of the assembly together, working in pairs, and is responsible for quality control. The cycle of operations is about twenty minutes (Francis, 1986).

Another instance is cited by Wall *et al.* (1986) who reported a field experiment in which autonomous groups were introduced in a large confectionery factory. In the experimental groups job satisfaction and commitment were increased, but there was no change in motivation, work performance or mental health. There were, however, some gains in productivity per worker since there were fewer supervisors. Kelly (1982) analysed the success of thirty-five cases in which flexible work groups were introduced, and reported a different result. He found that although there were productivity increases in many cases, improved figures were always accompanied by pay increases, and could have been due to these rather than to increased motivation based on the new working arrangements. In contrast, Pasmore *et al.* (1984) analysed fifty-three cases, all of which showed improvements in the sphere of attitudes, safety and quality of work. In addition, at least 81 per cent of cases reported an increase in productivity and a drop in costs, absenteeism and turnover.

The last word has not been said on the effects of flexible work groups. There is quite a lot of evidence to show that they improve job satisfaction and related variables, but the effect on productivity is less clear.

In the last section we considered how socio-technical problems can be solved by reorganizing jobs and relationships in working groups. In the previous section an example was given of how the use of better social skills can solve a socio-technical problem. In other cases there may be no solution with the existing technology: for example, very long assembly lines or automated plants which make social contact very difficult. It is extremely important that designers of equipment should take advice on the social relationships that their equipment will create, and how far these will produce effective cooperation and job satisfaction.

Sometimes groups find better ways of working with the technology, just as individuals do not react passively to the conditions of work imposed by technology. In laboratory studies of the effects of communication structures it has been found that the group is often able to set up its own structure within the limits set by the framework of the task. Experiments in Holland showed that the groups which arrived at a centralized communication structure did better at simple tasks, and this happened more often when such a structure was physically imposed (Mulder, 1960). Experiments in France found that groups of four tended to develop a centralized structure for problems which could be solved by simple elimination and a decentralized structure for problems requiring some creativity (Faucheux and Moscovici, 1960).

Kelly (1982) analysed the results of a large number of cases of work redesign of different kinds. The overall effects were as follows:

(1) 24·7 per cent of jobs studied were eliminated, the rest redesigned. This was most common in the USA (34·3 per cent), least in the UK (3·4 per cent).
(2) There were wage increases in 65 per cent of cases.
(3) There was 'intensification' of labour, i.e. more of the working day was spent working.
(4) There was increased quality of work through increased accountability.

Technology and Social Organization

Technology influences the kind of organization needed to supervise and coordinate different working groups, and to control and direct all aspects of work. We have seen examples of the social organization of restaurants, and of weaving sheds.

Woodward (1965), Blauner (1964) and others have studied the kinds of social organization linked with different kinds of technology. Woodward, for example, studied the production systems and social organization of a hundred English firms and found that at each level of technological development there was a characteristic kind of social structure, and that this did not vary much with the size of organization or the kind of work done.

One-off and small-batch production. Craftworkers, and those producing single units to customers' orders, either work by themselves or with a few helpers: working groups are small and cohesive, although work is carried out fairly independently. There is little need for supervision (in fact craftworkers may be difficult to supervise) and there is no pressure from supervisors or conflict with them. There is a simple management hierarchy, with no specialization between managers; it is a 'flat' hierarchy, with twenty-five to thirty workers per manager. Any specialists work in research and development departments.

Large batches, assembly-line work, mass production. Employees work in large groups, though social contact between them on the job is limited and there may be no real social groups. There is more use of incentives and machine-pacing, and less close contact with supervisors. There is, typically, a more hierarchical structure, divided into four levels with fourteen to eighteen workers per manager. Managers are more likely to be specialists in particular areas, and more use is made of professional and technical people.

Continuous-process technology. In oil refineries and similar plants there is a return to smaller working groups, less close supervision, and better relations in the hierarchy, with about eight workers per manager.

Reeves and Woodward (1970) developed this analysis further by looking at the different control systems used with different kinds of technology. In unit and small-batch production 75 per cent of the firms studied used personal control by the owner-manager, where different aspects (e.g. quality, cost) were highly integrated (by him or her). In continuous-process technology there was integrated control in 95 per cent of the firms, now by electronic rather than personal methods. But in mass-production factories controls were fragmented, looked after by different departments (for cost, quality etc.), sometimes by personal control, or sometimes mechanically or electronically. The similarity found before between small-batch and process technologies may be because both use integrated control systems, one personal, the other automated, whereas in mass production the fragmented controls lead to constant managerial problems (Dawson, 1986). While the technology seems to determine the managerial control system for continuous-process technology, this is less true for batch production, and much less true of mass production, where there is a choice between automated and personal methods of control.

We shall see later that organizational size is as important as technology, or more so, as a determinant of the structure of the firm (p. 210ff).

There are a number of other ways in which technology can influence the structure of working organizations. The Industrial Revolution brought large numbers of workers together in the same place in order to take advantage of various 'economies of scale' connected with steam-power and heavy machinery. Assembly-line work in the past has led to very large factories. However, there is now a trend towards greater decentralization as a result of improved means of information transfer which enables people to work at a distance, such as at home.

Burns and Stalker (1961) found that the organizational structure varied with the rate of change of the technology. In large manufacturing firms with a slowly changing market and technology there is a 'mechanistic structure', such as assembly-line work in large factories. However, in industries undergoing rapid change, such as some of the Scottish electronic firms they studied, a more 'organic structure' had developed, with a more flexible and less hierarchical framework, and less role specialization. Individuals had more general responsibilities to the whole organization, instead of carrying out a single defined role.

The nature of the raw materials handled can affect the organization. Perrow (1970) argued that a formal, mechanistic hierarchy is appropriate when there is little variation of inputs, but that a more informal system is needed when inputs vary and diverse searches or tests are required – as in medicine or research, for example. However the effects of technology on social structure are most marked for those parts of the organization most concerned with production, and much less for indirect specialist departments (Hickson et al., 1969).

Organizations, like individuals and groups, adjust to different technological systems. In a later chapter we shall describe the various kinds of 'informal organization', such as new communication channels, that may develop in this way (p. 129ff). It is also possible to redesign whole organizations to provide more effective structures, just as groups can be reorganized. Chapple and Sayles (1961) described the reorganization of the sales department of a company, where there had been a lot of conflict between the credit manager and the sales manager. Conflict occurred because orders were handled first by the sales department, and later by the credit department which sometimes had to cancel orders at a late stage in the proceedings. The solution was (1) to reverse the sequence in which orders went to the sales and credit departments, (2) to put all the work connected with a single order under one supervisor, who saw that everything was done on one day, and (3) to ask sales *and* credit representatives to write letters to customers when higher-level attention was needed.

At one time working organizations were designed like quasi-military hierarchies, in which all the people doing similar work were placed together under a supervisor. More recent thinking about organization favours designing them for the particular technology and work to be done, with appropriate structures for control and decision-taking further up.

The Effects of New Technology

Since about 1950 the group of technical innovations known as automation have been making great changes to the industrial scene in advanced countries. The effects have been so great, in fact, that this has been called a 'second industrial revolution'. Since about 1970 this revolution has taken another leap forward with the development of microchips, and the enormous expansion of information technology. The extent of these technical changes can be illustrated by the fact that a 5 mm chip can now contain up to 100,000 components, computers have increased in power (i.e. the speed of processing) by 10,000 in fifteen years, while the cost per unit of performance (i.e. the cost of processing data) has decreased by 100,000 (Gill, 1985).

We have discussed one kind of automation already – continuous-process technology, as found in chemical works and electric power stations, manned by a few people who mostly watch dials. The entire process, however, can be under computerized control – keeping the chemical composition of the product right, ensuring furnace temperatures are correct, and so on. This is in fact a model which many other kinds of work are increasingly coming to resemble. The main impact on manufacturing industry is that jobs formerly done by people are being taken over by machines. In the car industry increasing use is being made of 'robots', or automatic machine tools, and of 'transfer machines' which move materials from one robot to the next. While the early applications were only introduced for very large-scale production, micro-electronics now make similar automation possible for batch production – the equipment is simply reprogrammed (Gill, 1985). However, it is not possible to have completely unmanned factories, since computers cannot deal with disturbances or other unforeseen events; in addition, people are needed for flexibility, maintenance and further development of equipment (Wilson and Rutherford, 1987).

The new technology has also had a great effect on offices, for example banking and insurance, and for white-collar work generally. Typewriters are being replaced by word processors which will eventually be voice-operated; information can be relayed from one computer to another across the world; electronic information storage is already in existence; while teleconferencing with video links, and personal computers housing expert systems of various kinds will become the norm one day. In banking, the introduction of computers has taken over much of the traditional work, and is threatening to take over the work of branch managers in connection with taking decisions about loans (Child, 1986).

There are four reasons for introducing the new technology. (1) The most important is probably to reduce costs of production by reducing the work-force, and also to make it possible for workers to work at home at their own terminals. Cutting labour costs enables firms to compete with those in Third World countries employing much cheaper labour. (2) Efficiency can be increased by better production scheduling, diagnosis of faults and stock-keeping. (3) Improved quality can be achieved by automated inspection. (4) There can be better managerial control through improved information about performance (Child, 1984).

Like other technological innovations automation can only be introduced when the conditions are right: when the relevant equipment has been invented, when there is enough capital to pay for it, when it will save money to use it, when there is a sufficiently standard product, and when skilled workers are available to install and operate it. These conditions exist far less in India and Africa, where labour is so cheap that there would be little economic gain from automation. Automation has gone ahead most rapidly in Japan, because of the electronic developments there, and in the USA, because of the high costs of labour, with Britain and the rest of the developed world not far behind.

The effect on working groups. In assembly work the jolly working groups which sometimes existed before are likely to be replaced by isolated operatives who are tied to remote work stations, although they may be free to walk about. (Maintenance staff, on the other hand, work in small, autonomous teams.) The social side of office work is important for the job satisfaction of clerical workers. It is reported that automation often damages this side of office life by creating typing pools where there is less scope for conversation, and by reducing personal contact with management. In addition, the introduction of computer systems often leads to more isolation, since people do not need to move about to collect information, although the computer itself can become a common interest (Frese, 1987).

Siegel *et al.* (1986) carried out an experiment in which groups of three decided about the level of risk to be recommended in a series of decisions. If they interacted via a computer rather than face-to-face the following differences were found:

(1) The task took longer.
(2) Fewer remarks were made.
(3) There was greater equality.
(4) The operator felt less inhibited, and expressed views more strongly.
(5) There was more shift from the original position.

This may be compared with the effects of communicating by

telephone compared with face-to-face, where Short *et al.* (1976) found:

(1) Most communication was equally effective.
(2) The participants came to know and trust each other less.
(3) There was less concern for the other's approval and the person with the stronger case won negotiations.

Home-working (see Chapter 12), the 'electronic cottage', linked by computer, VDU or telephone to head office will produce isolation, unless neighbourhood centres are set up (Clutterbuck and Hill, 1981).

The effect on supervision. Following the introduction of new technology the power of supervisors can be increased if, for example, they have automatic information about the performance levels of their subordinates, or if they are responsible for programming the equipment. Supervisors and middle managers, on the other hand, can become almost redundant if additional skills are taken over by subordinates, such as responsibility for quality, and programming the machines. Which way this goes depends on bargaining and managerial decisions, and the skills of those involved. In any case the technical skills of supervisors will become more important. However, there is no need to fear, as Gill (1985) forecasts, that the human relations skills of supervisors will become less important. Handling and looking after subordinates cannot be automated, and it will become increasingly necessary for supervisors to ensure that their workers are given satisfying jobs and do not suffer from isolation.

Further effects of automation. We shall discuss recent and predicted effects on the level of unemployment and de-skilling in Chapter 12.

4

PERSONALITY AND WORK

Dimensions of Personality

There are great individual differences between people at work: in how well they can do different jobs, how hard they work, and how much they enjoy different kinds of work. They differ in *abilities*, which determine how well they will be able to do a particular job, and for which job each person is best suited. They differ in *interests* and *motivation*, which determine what kinds of work each person most wants to do, and how hard he or she will work at it. They differ in patterns of *social performance*; this is partly a matter of temperament – differences of mood, energy, reactions to stress – but is also a question of styles of social performance in different social situations. From the point of view of personnel selection these aspects of personality are important, since they enable predictions to be made about which people will be most *effective* in a particular job. From the point of view of vocational guidance these factors are vital since they enable predictions to be made about which job will give a particular person the greatest *job satisfaction*. From the point of view of social psychology these elements are interesting since they help us to understand why people behave differently at work.

In this chapter we shall consider how people choose occupations, and how organizations select people to work for them. In later chapters we shall go into more detail on individual differences in the motivation to work, and how different kinds of personality react to stress and other aspects of working conditions.

Not all aspects of personality are relevant to behaviour at work, and we have picked out those areas of personality which have been found to be most relevant, for purposes of selection or guidance. The traditional approach to this problem has been to look for correlations between personality traits and measures of work performance. Recent research has shown that the relation between personality and work behaviour is more complicated than this. In the first place, behaviour may depend in a complex way on a number of traits in combination. Secondly, the model of general traits which has worked so well in the field of abilities does not work so well in the fields of motivation or social behaviour, where the same person may behave quite differently in different situations.

(1) *Intelligence and other abilities*. Jobs vary in the intellectual and other abilities they require. To select the best person for a job it is obviously important to choose someone who has the necessary abilities; it may also be necessary to exclude those whose abilities are too great, since they will be discontented. For the most effective use of the personnel available, the most talented of those available should be given the most difficult jobs; where different jobs call for different abilities the problem is more complicated (p. 74). From the point of view of the individual, he or she should do the work which makes the best use of his or her abilities. In fact people are found to choose the jobs which require the abilities they have (p. 66), and in vocational guidance this is one of the main considerations.

(a) *Intelligence* is the capacity to solve problems, apply principles, make inferences and perceive relationships. General intelligence consists of a number of abilities which enable a person to succeed at a wide variety of intellectual tasks; it can be measured by intelligence tests with abstract, verbal, mathematical and problem-solving items. There are other more specific mental ab- ilities, which are correlated with general intelligence, but which are also partly independent of it – verbal fluency, numerical ab- ility, spatial ability and mechanical aptitudes.

There are three other dimensions of mental ability which are widely held to be important for predicting occupational success but for which tests are less well established.

(b) *Judgement* is the capacity to make realistic assessments of practical situations, and produce workable solutions to particular problems where it is more a matter of weighing different factors and guessing probabilities than of applying logical principles. Judgement can be assessed by interviews, by asking candidates their views about a number of complex practical situations with which they are familiar.

(c) *Creativity* is the ability to see situations from a new point of view and to propose original solutions. There are a number of tests for creativity, such as the test in which people are asked to think of unusual uses for common objects.

(d) *Motor skills* form a further and largely independent set of abilities; there is no single dimension here – there appear to be eleven separate dimensions (Fleishman, 1965).

(e) *Social skills* are now recognized to be of crucial importance for managers, supervisors, and all those who deal with people. It is not yet known whether there is a general factor, or how many dimensions there are. It probably includes rewardingness and the capacity to persuade, the expressive use of non-verbal signals, sensitivity to others, the ability to carry out various kinds of conversation effectively, and the ability to sustain relationships with others. In practice, ratings are made of performance at interviews, in leaderless group discussions, or other exercises, although not all of the abilities listed above can be assessed in this way.

(2) *Motivation*. It is not enough for a person to have the necessary abilities for a job, there must also be sufficient interest and motivation to want to do it, or he or she will not work very effectively and will not find it satisfying. Effective performance is a joint product of abilities and motivation. French (1958) found that the ability to solve problems was a function of *both* intelligence and achievement, the effect of intelligence being greater for more highly motivated subjects, which shows that the relationship is

multiplicative, i.e. performance = (ability × motivation). The strength of motivation in turn depends both on an individual's enduring drive strength and on the incentive conditions. Both the choice of occupation and the choice to work hard are products of incentives and drive strength. The amount of satisfaction is a product of the motivation and rewards obtained.

(a) *Achievement motivation.* This is the motive to achieve success in exams, in organizations, by making money, or in other ways (McClelland, 1961). We have already encountered it in connection with industrial revolutions and the growth of capitalism (p. 20ff). We shall meet it later in connection with intrinsic incentives to work hard (p. 102ff). Achievement motivation has been found to affect the performance of scientists and some kinds of managers. Individual differences in achievement motivation are important in predicting and understanding vocational choice (p. 67).

There is some evidence that entrepreneurs, people who start their own businesses, are high in need for achievement (Perry *et al.*, 1986). However, it has been found that they have other characteristics – they are high on internal control (p. 59), and have somewhat deviant personalities, making it difficult for them to fit into large organizations. Case studies have found that some entrepreneurs at least are non-conformist, rebellious, distrust authority, are unwilling to work with others, and come from families where they were not appreciated, or from marginal minority groups, giving them a great drive to succeed and establish a new identity (Kets de Vries, 1977; Chell, 1986).

(b) *Need for power.* Managerial success, for non-technical managers, has been found to be predicted by the need for power, combined with a low need for affiliation, and high self-control (McClelland and Boyatzis, 1982).

(c) *Growth need strength.* Rather similar to achievement motivation is 'growth need strength', put forward by Hackman and Oldham (1980) to explain why some workers are motivated and satisfied by complex and demanding jobs, while others are not. The former want to accomplish something, learn and develop themselves. Similar thinking lies behind hierarchical schemes of motivation, put forward by Maslow (1954) and Alderfer (1972). There is some disagreement about the percentage of workers for whom this is important, but it probably includes most managers and technical staff. There are other workers, paid less, and doing more boring work, for whom it is not important, and who work mostly for the pay (Goldthorpe *et al.*, 1968), though perhaps too for the social life.

(*d*) *Type A personality.* This kind of person is aggressively competitive and hard working, has a great sense of urgency, feels that time is passing quickly, and is highly involved with the job. The original interest in Type A personalities was in their proneness to heart attacks. However, they also tend to be very successful, since they work harder without external pressure, feel less tired, and seek challenges – they are workaholics (Ortega and Pipal, 1984). On the other hand, there is evidence that top managers are more often Type Bs, perhaps because Type As do not last the course, or because they make too many enemies, or because calmer decision-making is needed (Baron, 1986). We shall discuss these types further in connection with stress (p. 271).

(3) *Personality traits.* The traits most relevant to work are those governing social behaviour. At one time it was believed that traits such as 'dominance' functioned like 'intelligence' in that each person would display the trait consistently in different situations. However, it has now been recognized that this is not the case and that individuals behave very differently in different situations. The same person may behave quite differently when at home or at work, with superiors or subordinates, with males or females, and so on. The traditional approach, in terms of universal personality traits, does not do justice to these variations. It has been realized for some time that 'leadership' is not a personality trait: whether or not a person will be leader in a particular group and in a particular situation depends primarily on whether he has more of the abilities needed to deal with that situation than the others present. The following kinds of social behaviour in which

individual differences appear *cannot* be accounted for primarily in terms of personality traits: dominance, dependence, leadership, conformity, persuasiveness, honesty, likeability (Mischel, 1969; Argyle, 1969).

(*a*) *Extroversion* is one of the most pervasive dimensions of personality, and is correlated with many aspects of behaviour, although often these correlations are quite small. Extroversion contains two components which are correlated but which are also partly independent. These are behavioural extroversion, which consists of impulsiveness and a preference for action as opposed to thinking about action, and social extroversion, which consists of a liking for social situations, especially large and noisy ones.

Extroverts choose occupations such as management, sales and teaching. They talk a lot, are persuasive, become chosen as leaders, and emit more non-verbal signals such as smiling and looking. They are happier than introverts, and their job satisfaction is high. However, they are easily bored if they have to stick at the same job (Morris, 1979).

(*b*) *Neuroticism* consists of an inability to tolerate stress, a tendency to be anxious, to work ineffectively, to suffer from minor ailments such as headaches, sleeplessness and pains, and to find people difficult to deal with. Neuroticism is a matter of degree; about 5–10 per cent of the population would be classified as neurotic by psychiatrists, and could benefit from treatment. Neuroticism can be measured by questionnaire (e.g. the Eysenck Personality Inventory), interview, or from performance at laboratory tasks. Although neuroticism has often been regarded as a consistent feature of personality, it is much less so than intelligence and a person is often neurotic only in some areas of behaviour. For example he or she may have a quite isolated phobia for heights, animals or travel. However, those high in neuroticism are more upset by stress at work, and their job satisfaction tends to be low.

Social anxiety is a partly independent aspect of neurosis: some people are anxious in social situations, are shy and self-conscious, tense, embarrassed and generally unable to cope. They may possess social skills, but if they are too anxious will be unable to use them.

(c) *Authoritarianism*. After the Second World War, ex-army officers caused trouble in British industry and had to be sent on T-group courses (p. 192ff). The trouble was that they were too authoritarian: they gave orders without explanation, demanding obedience, but were deferential to their own superiors.

Pronounced authoritarian personalities are in favour of authority and tradition, are often hostile to members of ethnic and other minorities; they have a narrow, moralistic and prejudiced outlook, and are opposed to change. At the other extreme are rebellious people who reject tradition and authority; in between are different degrees of acceptance and rejection of authority. It is probably necessary for members of working organizations to have some balance between the two extremes – enough acceptance of authority to carry out orders, enough rebelliousness to appreciate that what the boss says is not always right, and that what was done last year may be out of date. Authoritarianism can be measured by questionnaire, or by interview, asking about relationships with superiors and subordinates, and attitudes towards respectable and less respectable social groups or institutions.

(d) *The self.* Self-image is the way an individual consciously thinks of him- or herself. It exercises a controlling effect on behaviour by restraining that which is inconsistent with it, and seeking to elicit appropriate reactions from others. For each class of social situation a different part of the self-image is emphasized (e.g., father, research worker), corresponding to social performance in those situations. One way of describing an individual's social behaviour is to list the main roles played in the groups to which he or she belongs; each role is linked to part of their self-image. The self-image also includes self-perceptions such as being 'intelligent' or 'lively', which may extend across all these roles, and lead to their being played in a characteristic way. The occupational role, and the way it is played, is a core feature of identity; the crystallization of identity and choice of an occupation proceed side by side during late adolescence.

Self-esteem refers to how favourably people think of themselves, absolutely or in comparison with others. Those high in self-esteem will tackle tasks and social situations with confidence, and have good social skills. Their job satisfaction, motivation and productivity are high (Tharenou, 1979). Those low in self-esteem are subject to depression, and fail to search effectively for a suitable job (Ellis and Taylor, 1983). Another aspect of the self is the degree to which an integrated identity has been achieved; this is described below (p. 60ff).

(e) *Internal–external control.* Some people ('internals') believe that their rewards and satisfactions are mainly due to their personal ability and efforts, while others ('externals') think that these outcomes arc mainly due to other people or to luck. The usual measure is Rotter's Locus of Control scale (1966). It has often been found that internals work harder than externals, but only in situations where there is opportunity for initiative and the use of skills, and where there is some degree of autonomy. The explanation may be that internals make more effort because they believe that this will lead to reward, i.e. that they can control the outcome (O'Brien, 1986). While internal control is at least in part a personality trait, it may also reflect the degree to which individuals actually do have control over their work and the rewards they receive for it – which is greater for those in better jobs and for middle-class people generally (Kohn and Schooler, 1982). Internal controllers do better in their careers in terms of promotion and pay (Andrisani and Nestel, 1976). They are happier and higher in job satisfaction, and they deal better with stress by using a variety of coping strategies, and are 'hardier', i.e. less likely to be made ill by stress (Argyle, 1987).

Learning How to Work: Occupational Choice

Stages of development. In primitive societies children learn how to work at an early age. The work their parents do is simple and clearly visible, children are provided with scaled-down implements, are taught the basic work skills and help their parents. In more advanced societies there is much more division of labour, children do not see their parents at work, often have no clear idea of what their work consists, and are allowed to spend a lot of their time at 'play'. The work they are expected to do is schoolwork. Children may play at being the teacher, doctor, vicar, or other work roles which are visible to them. Many children later go into occupations similar to those of their parents; it is interesting that doctors' children very often become doctors – surgeries are often at home and the work can be seen clearly by the children. Childhood experiences affect later occupational choice and work behaviour in a number of ways. It has been found that those who become social scientists or social workers had more strained relations with their parents than engineers, physical scientists or biologists (Roe, 1964).

After the fantasy stage of wanting to be an engine-driver or a film-star there is a period of tentative choice (between the ages of eleven and sixteen) when preferences are based first on interests, but later on awareness of capabilities, and values. From the age of seventeen onwards there is a more realistic stage, during which actual career decisions have to be made, such as which exams to take and which courses of training to choose; this stage may last for some years (Ginzberg et al., 1951).

The process of deciding on an occupation goes on at the same time as the development of an identity, or a stable self-image. Children play at roles, adolescents experiment with them. During student life it is possible to try out a number of roles and identities without commitment, such as being an actor, journalist or revolutionary. However, pressures to commit oneself build up, and somewhere between the ages of sixteen and twenty-four there is often an identity crisis, when a person is forced to make up his or her mind about which of all these bits and pieces of identity to hang on to and which to suppress (Erikson, 1956). The basis of this is partly the need to choose one job rather than another, to choose a marital partner, a political and religious outlook, and a lifestyle.

Marcia (1966) found four main types of identity development among students in North America, based on how far they were committed in two main spheres – occupation and ideology. These are (1) identity achievement – a decision has been made after a period of uncertainty or crisis; (2) moratorium – a state of indecision or crisis; (3) foreclosure – a decision has been made, based on parental guidance without a period of indecision; (4) identity diffusion – no decision has been made, and there has been no attempt to make one. Occupation is a central part of identity: occupational choice and identity formation take place together.

During the moratorium period, in particular, adolescents try out various kinds of work, first at home, then at school, in part-time jobs, and sometimes by a period of floundering in the labour market with a succession of jobs. During this period they become aware of their own capacities and for what they are best suited, and of the possibilities available (Ginzberg *et al.*, 1951; Super, 1957). A number of studies have shown that adolescents are attracted to occupations which they see as similar to their self-image, or as requiring skills which they believe they possess. Their degree of realism here can be checked by measuring the actual properties of jobs and of the qualities needed to perform them. It has been found that as adolescents grow older they develop greater understanding of different jobs and their own abilities. They are helped in choosing an occupation by parents, teachers and other adults, and the process is accelerated by offers of jobs and the need to fill in application forms for courses. Ginzberg (1951) maintains that the choices made at any stage are irreversible, in that early decisions make some later choices impossible. However, it has been found that only 17 per cent of 15-year-old boys and 26 per cent of girls of the same age had the same occupational plans a year after leaving school (Super and Overstreet, 1960). Final choices were more predictable from aptitude tests than from vocational plans in adolescence.

Socialization for work. As we have seen, in primitive societies children perform a scaled-down version of the work carried out by parents. In contrast, there are a number of difficulties in socialization for work in modern societies which are absent in more primitive societies – the need to choose between about twenty thousand different occupations, the difficulty of knowing what these jobs are like, the difficulty of seeing how these jobs contribute to society, and the lack of continuity between schoolwork and later work.

In modern societies, children from six to twelve years of age have no serious ideas about choosing a job, but they are expected to carry out schoolwork. As McClelland and his colleagues (1953) have shown, the need for achievement is established during this period. As a result of exhortations from parents and teachers, imitation of successful models, and rewards for successful achievement, the child acquires a drive to carry out school tasks with persistence, and to do well at them. Neff (1985) maintains that it is at school that the child learns the difference between work and play, and acquires a 'work personality'.

Certain basic components of the work personality appear to be laid down in the early school years – the ability to concentrate on a task for extended periods of time, the development of emotional response-patterns to supervisory authority, the limits of co-operation and competition with peers, the meanings and values associated with work, the rewards and sanctions for achievement and non-achievement, the affects (both positive and negative) which become associated with being productive.

This preparation for work plays a more important part in modern society than is often realized. The Industrial Revolution was traumatic for many workers and produced a great deal of conflict between workers and employers because people were quite unused to the conditions of industrial work. Industrialization in Africa has proceeded slowly because Africans are not accustomed to working regular hours, under supervision, at a regular speed with standard methods.

There are several ways in which adolescents may fail to learn how to work or choose a suitable job (Erikson, 1956; Elder, 1968). Some decide too early on a career, before they have fully explored the possibilities, and before they have achieved an independent identity. They may decide to work in, for example, their father's firm, in which they would still be in a dependent relationship to adults, and for which they may not have the right interests or aptitudes. They may fail to develop an integrated identity, fail to make any occupational choice, and thus be unable to work. In contrast, some people may deliberately seek an alternative kind of identity and may opt not to work or to work irregular hours. They may also decide to delay the decision about what to do. University life and graduate work may provide such a period of 'moratorium', and this may be followed by one or more years spent in remote countries overseas, wandering about looking for an identity.

Neff (1985) describes various kinds of people who are unable to adjust to work. Some of those studied lacked work motivation and regarded work as something unpleasant; others were anxious in response to the demand to be productive; some were aggressive; others dependent; others still were socially naïve, unfamiliar with work and work standards. These groups of people are not usually found at work, but in treatment centres which are trying to adjust them to work.

Once a person has started a job he or she is usually exposed to further socialization. An initial period may be experienced which has some of the characteristics of an initiation: trainees may be isolated, exposed to stressful experiences, issued with a uniform, and helped through these experiences by senior members of the organization. This happens in the military, the medical profession, the clergy and some other professions; it has the effect of enhancing the feeling of belonging to a special élite group, and of inculcating a powerful attachment to the organization. In a study of medical students it was found that 31 per cent thought of themselves as doctors at the end of their first year, 83 per cent at the end of the fourth year. However, even in the first year 75 per cent thought of themselves as doctors in relation to patients if they were given some patients to look after (Merton et al., 1957).

After the trainee period, when the person starts doing the job, further kinds of socialization take place. The new member of an organization is likely to imitate the behaviour of prominent existing members. He or she is expected to conform to a particular role, and the complementary behaviour of performers of interlocking roles will elicit standard role behaviour from the new member (p. 200ff). The effects of training on the job, and other forms of training, are discussed in Chapter 7.

There may be a period of 'reality shock' when the work or the organization do not live up to expectations; for example the boss is difficult to deal with, the job is ill-defined, or people show resistance to change. Eventually a 'psychological contract' is worked out in which individual and organization come to accept one another, 'secrets' of the organization are revealed and the newcomer is given a regular job to do. This may be assisted by some kind of ceremony, a rite of passage. A little later the worker becomes interested in the prospects of promotion (Hall, 1976; Schein, 1978).

Perception of occupations. Adolescents are familiar with the main range of occupations chosen by others from their school, family or social circle, and they have some idea what these jobs are like. However, this includes a good deal of mythology derived from books and television. Hudson (1968) found that British school-boys thought that the typical male arts graduate would probably wear fashionable clothes, flirt with his secretary, like expensive restaurants, and get into debt; the novelist was seen as 'imaginative, warm, exciting and smooth'; the psychologist as similar to the novelist, but intelligent and lazy. Physicists were seen as dependable, hard-working, manly and valuable; engineers as similar to physicists but less intelligent, colder and duller. Of course stereotypes may be partly correct – though there is a far wider range of personalities in an occupation than the stereotype suggests. Engineers (supposedly dependable, dull, etc.) are actually found to be interested in things rather than people or ideas, to be stable, orderly and tough-minded, and like working out of doors and with their hands (Morrison and McIntyre, 1971). In addition to responding to stereotypes, school-leavers know what their chances are of getting a job; Furnham (1984a) found that they thought science subjects were more useful for this purpose.

Among those who leave school at fifteen or sixteen, some go straight into jobs, others to further training or education. Veness (1962) surveyed 1,300 British school-leavers and classified their reasons for choosing jobs into the three categories established by Riesman *et al.* (1950). About 11 per cent made 'traditional' choices, following family and local patterns; about 53 per cent were 'inner-directed' and tried to suit their own abilities and interests; while about 36 per cent were 'other-directed' and responded to recent social influences.

For those who go to college the beginning of work proper is postponed, although they do realize that work is likely to start at the end of college and that they will have to reach a decision about what to do by then. Some do vocational courses, but others do courses which are not very relevant to any job apart from teaching the same subjects to others. In a study of 500 student mental patients at Oxford it was found that the breakdown rate was lowest in the more vocational courses, such as Law and Natural Science, and the highest in the least vocational courses, such as English and Greats (Davidson and Hutt, 1964). A lot of students change their ideas about their career while at college. In an American survey it was found that the students most likely to change were those whose values (i.e. self-expression, interest in people, money and status) were in conflict with the values of their initial occupational choice, and that they shifted to an occupation with more similar values. However, those who had started specialized training were less likely to change (Rosenberg, 1957). Future problems can be averted if students find out more about possible jobs, for example by talking to careers teachers, by studying literature and by visiting places of work. The more they do so, the more likely they are to find something that suits them.

Vroom's expectancy theory (1964) is directly relevant to the process of occupational choice. It notes that *preference* for occupations depends on the sum of the valences of all the outcomes involved, i.e. pay, promotion prospects, etc. However, occupational *choice* depends on the perceived probability of obtaining each of these outcomes. This model was confirmed by Janman (1985) in a study of 168 British school-leavers who were asked to rate preference for jobs and the likelihood of getting them, as well as rating the various predictors.

The influence of personality on occupational choice. Psychologists have tended to emphasize the importance of personality variables in determining occupational choice, while sociologists have emphasized environmental factors, such as the jobs available. In reality, both factors are important, but their relative weights are different for different sections of the population. For working-class people there is a rather narrow choice of occupations, so that personality factors are relatively unimportant, while in the middle class there is a wider range of possibilities so that people are more able to choose what best suits their personality (Elder, 1968).

Intelligence and other abilities are the most important factors. There is an approximate correspondence between the distribution of intelligence in people doing different jobs, and the intelligence needed to do them. Himmelweit and Whitfield (1944) analysed the intelligence test scores of 5,000 British army recruits; the average scores for different occupations varied from 40·7 for schoolmaster to 12 for carter, but there were wide variations within each occupational group. There is also a characteristic profile of more specific abilities for different jobs. Thorndike and Hagen (1959) studied the abilities of over 10,000 American air-force recruits, and found that different occupations varied not only in general intelligence, but also in mechanical ability, numerical fluency, visual perception and psychomotor ability. For example, manual workers tended to score low in general intelligence but high in mechanical tests.

As stated earlier, young people have a fairly good idea of their own abilities. A study was carried out in which students gave themselves scores for fifteen attributes such as creativity, leadership and intelligence and the extent to which various occupations required them. There was an average correlation of ·54 between the two sortings for the occupation that they had chosen themselves, and lower correlations for other occupations (Vroom, 1964). They developed this perception through experiences of success (or failure) in career-relevant activities (Hall, 1976). In contrast, however, young people may be over-optimistic about their prospects: a survey of 1,725 high-school pupils in Alabama found that 40 per cent aspired to professional or managerial jobs, although only 20 per cent of jobs are like this; about 37 per cent were judged to be making unrealistic choices in relation to their academic records (Fottler and Bain, 1984).

Individual differences in other aspects of personality are less closely related to occupational choice – there is a very wide range of personalities in most occupations. For those people who fall in the middle range of the population on personality traits occupational choice is not much affected by personality. In fact for many jobs there are no special personality requirements. On the other hand, there are families of jobs which only fit certain kinds of people. Some jobs are very stressful, and therefore require individuals who are stable enough to stand up to them. Some jobs involve a great deal of contact with other people, and call for extroversion and social skills. In a survey of 1,500 managers it was found that they were somewhat more extroverted and less neurotic than the population norms; those in sales and personnel were the most extroverted, research and development people and consultants the least (Eysenck, 1967).

Values also affect our choice of jobs. Rosenberg (1957) found that students high on his people-oriented scale chose social work, medicine, teaching and social science; students scoring high on his self-expression scale chose architecture, journalism and art; students scoring high on extrinsic-reward orientation chose sales, hotel management, estate agency and finance.

Differences in motivation also affect occupational choice. Those high in achievement motivation choose high-status and risky occupations; in the USA, at least, they choose finance and business in preference to other professions. They want to take risks in the hope of making a lot of money; they want to build up large enterprises and make their mark in the world (Atkinson et al., 1958). There is also evidence that they play a crucial role in initiating economic growth (p. 20ff). A different pattern of motivation is found among successful male physical scientists, who in addition to working extremely hard are often from Protestant backgrounds, avoid interpersonal aggression and complex human emotions, and are intensely masculine (McClelland, 1962).

People tend to gravitate towards jobs which 'fit' their personalities; in fact, one of the main causes of work stress is lack of fit between the two (p. 273ff). In vocational guidance the most widely used method of finding out which job would suit someone

(1) *Realistic.* Involves aggressive behaviour, physical activities requiring skill, strength, and co-ordination. (Examples: forestry, farming, architecture.)

(2) *Investigative.* Involves cognitive (thinking, organizing, understanding) rather than affective (feeling, acting, or interpersonal and emotional) activities. (Examples: biology, mathematics, oceanography.)

(3) *Social.* Involves interpersonal rather than intellectual or physical activities. (Examples: clinical psychology, foreign service, social work.)

(4) *Conventional.* Involves structural, rule-regulated activities and subordination of personal needs to an organization or person of power and status. (Examples: accounting, finance.)

(5) *Enterprising.* Involves verbal activities to influence others, to attain power and status. (Examples: management, law, public relations.)

(6) *Artistic.* Involves self-expression, artistic creation, expression of emotions, and individualistic activities. (Examples: art, music, education.)

Table 2. Six types of personality and their corresponding environments (Holland, 1966).

best is the Strong Vocational Interest Blank, now revised as the Strong-Campbell Inventory (Campbell, 1971). This measures vocational interests in six areas: realistic, investigative, artistic, social, enterprising and conventional. A later system was devised by Holland (1966) which matched these six categories (now types of personality) with corresponding environments (see Table 2).

Women and occupational choice. Men and women tend to seek different things in their work. Men want to have a job that is well paid, secure, and gives prestige; they are quite happy working with things rather than people, and do not mind risk. Women are more concerned with self-expression and creativity, want to work with people rather than things, and to be helpful to others (e.g. Goldsen *et al.*, 1960). As a result men and women tend to choose different occupations. Women often become nurses, teachers, social workers, secretaries, shop assistants and hairdressers; men become engineers, managers, builders, farmers, scientists and lawyers. It has been found that taking both sex *and* patterns of interest into account enabled a good prediction of occupational choice: 70 per cent of women with 'service' interests chose teaching, compared with 5 per cent of men who were oriented towards money (Davis, 1963). For some women work is a short-term affair before getting married, perhaps to be resumed later, although women are moving increasingly into senior positions, for example in management. American studies of career-oriented girls show that they are high in educational ambitions, and in concern with self-expression, but this particular group are somewhat lower on interest in people. These sex differences can partly be accounted for by the traditional roles played by mothers and fathers in families: the mother has a nurturant, socio-emotional, people-oriented role, while the father is more concerned with the economic support of the family, and looking after physical aspects of the home – a thing-oriented role (Argyle and Henderson, 1985). Sex differences in occupations are partly due to historical and cultural factors – women in Russia, India and Israel do heavy manual work and may occupy senior management positions.

It was believed for some time that the reason most women fail to achieve as much as men was a female 'fear of success'. However, it has now been found that what women fear is not success, but success in male-oriented professions and the supposed resultant loss of femininity. Even going to college, compared for example with nursing, is seen to involve this 'danger' (Janman, 1985).

An increasing number of women are now working, and many of them are married. The dual-career family produces a more satisfied wife, and therefore a happier family member, and a larger income. On the other hand, the woman often experiences conflict and guilt over 'neglecting' the children, and domestic life can be frantically busy with little time for joint leisure. And usually it is not really egalitarian – more often than not it is the husband whose job takes priority, and the wife who does most of the housework (Argyle and Henderson, 1985). Career women have problems: by the age of 30, married women with children attain lower occupational achievement and lower positions in hierarchies; career women also often withdraw from work between the ages of 25 and 45 to have a family, while some marry later, or not at all, and have fewer children (Dion, 1985).

Environmental factors in occupational choice. The social class of a child's family may affect his aspirations and final occupational choice in a number of ways. Working-class adolescents are much affected by local employment opportunities, while those from middle-class homes become aware of a wider range of possibilities. They are also likely to get a better education, may be able to go into a family business or be helped by family contacts or capital. In an American survey it was found that 71 per cent of students whose fathers earned over $30,000 planned to enter law, medicine or business, compared with 38 per cent of those whose fathers earned less than $7,500 (Rosenberg, 1957).

Children have been found to choose the same occupations as their fathers more than would be expected by chance. This is well known in the case of doctors' children; in an American study Werts (1968) found that 35 per cent of the sons of physical scientists chose scientific careers. If they do not enter the same occupation children are likely to enter one with similar values or patterns of activity, e.g. being concerned with people rather than things. There is some evidence that boys who identify strongly with their fathers choose the same occupation, though this may not be true of their final choice. Those with high achievement motivation aim higher than their fathers if the latter are in low status jobs, and are less likely to move downwards if their fathers are in high status jobs (Vroom, 1964). Schools influence occupational choice in a number of ways – preferences for school subjects are extrapolated to occupations, courses taken may limit later choices, information about abilities is received from teachers and about occupations from careers advisers. In any school there are about three or four jobs or further courses of training which are common, though many of the children have almost no idea what the jobs entail, apart from their names, e.g. 'scientist' or 'manager' (Morrison and McIntyre, 1971).

The development of careers. It is only in the stable work period that commitment to a career develops. The extent to which a job is seen as part of a career varies between occupations. There are class differences here; middle-class adolescents think in terms of careers, working-class adolescents are more likely to think of jobs – perhaps offering good pay and job satisfaction, but not promotion. Careers can be thought of more generally as a sequence of jobs, or as 'stages or steps in a progression toward culturally defined higher rewards' (Schein, 1978).

A study of the careers of forty-four male management graduates led to the development of the concept of 'career anchors'. These men had consistent careers in the sense that they gave the same reasons at different times for their job changes. They discovered their basic abilities, motives and values, and these aspects of self-image anchored their careers. For some this was technical competence, for others it was managerial competence (analytical and interpersonal competence, and the ability to cope with crises), creativity or autonomy (Schein, 1978).

It used to be thought that careers involved upward mobility through fixed stages, like the ranks in the army; this can still happen for some. However, during the course of a lifetime there are extensive historical changes which affect the rise and fall of organizations and types of work. Furthermore, to some extent the individual contributes to the changes in the organizations in which he or she works – both are developing together.

As they get older some people become more committed to their work, which becomes more central to their personality, while others become less committed, and spend more time with family and on interests (Runyon, 1978). This second strategy is one way of coping with failure to realize ambitions – and evidently not a very successful way (Pearlin and Schooler, 1978). In mid-career, around the age of forty, managers have been found to be preoccupied with promotion prospects (Sofer, 1970), or to be in a period of crisis, in which they have to come to terms with their limited prospects.

Personnel Selection

How can the best people be found to fill jobs? This can be extremely important, especially for senior posts, and those needing a high level of expertise, such as positions in research. The traditional model is as follows.

(1) Analyse the skills or other capacities needed for the job.
(2) Find tests or other measures of these capacities.
(3) Find measures of success on the job.
(4) Validate the selection tests on a sample of applicants.
(5) Retain the measures or combination of measures which best predict success in the job.

Job analysis. In order to fill a job it is necessary to know what qualities are needed for success at the job. There are three main ways of discovering these. First, an analysis of the detailed activities of which the job consists can be carried out, by observation or interview. This may lead, via statistical analysis, to establishing the dimensions along which jobs differ. One widely used method is the Position Analysis Questionnaire (PAQ), which consists of 187 job elements in six areas. Factor analysis of the scores for 2,200 jobs produced thirteen factors (McCormick and Ilgen, 1985):

(1) Having decision, communicating, and general responsibilities
(2) Operating machines and/or equipment
(3) Performing clerical and/or related activities
(4) Performing technical and/or related activities
(5) Performing service and/or related activities
(6) Working regular day versus other work schedules
(7) Performing routine and/or repetitive activities
(8) Being aware of work environment
(9) Engaging in physical activities
(10) Supervising and/or coordinating other personnel
(11) Public and/or customer and/or related service
(12) Working in an unpleasant/hazardous/demanding environment
(13) Having a nontypical schedule

Once an analysis has been effected judgements can be made of the personal qualities required to carry out the main components of the job. Secondly, 'critical incidents' can be recorded by supervisors or others who are familiar with the job. These are occasions when the employee's performance has led to clear success or failure. Kirchner and Dunnette (1957) asked a large number of sales managers to describe critical incidents in selling, and grouped the incidents into thirteen categories of behaviour which delineated a difference between successful and unsuccessful selling. Third, groups of successful and unsuccessful performers in a job can be compared, in terms of observed behaviour, education, age or other demographic data, or in terms of test scores. Examples of this approach are given later in connection with the study of supervisory skills (p. 155ff).

Measuring job success. It is usually possible to obtain a number of different measures of success, but they may not correlate very well. Seashore *et al.* (1960) found very low, sometimes negative correlations between productivity, rated effectiveness, accidents, absence and errors. Part of the problem is that most jobs involve more than one activity and set of skills. University teachers for example are expected to teach, carry out research, and do administration – three totally different activities. The only solution is to measure competence in each area separately, and give it some weighting. In a study by Albrecht *et al.* (1964), district marketing managers were ranked separately on forecasting, sales, interpersonal relationships, and overall effectiveness. In addition, even apparently objective measures can be very unsatisfactory since it is difficult to compare the effectiveness of people working under somewhat different conditions, such as sales personnel working in quite different areas. Compared with performance ratings, promotion or training success, higher follow-up validities are found when objective measures are used, such as work samples (Hunter and Hirsch, 1987).

Assessing validity. Where there are a number of candidates (Cs) for one job, the procedure is to select the C with the combination of qualities making him or her most likely to do it well. However, if there are a number of rather different jobs to be filled, and there are a number of Cs with various combinations of attributes, selection is more complex. What is now needed is *differential* selection, i.e. finding the best way of allocating available Cs to the vacant jobs, so that the most important jobs get the Cs best suited to them. Selecting for a number of jobs at once has several advantages – it enables Cs to be placed more accurately, to the advantage both of the organization and themselves, and it is more economical. From the C's point of view the problem is choosing the most suitable job for him or her; this must be taken into account by the selectors, otherwise the C may become discontented, or may leave. A psychologist giving vocational guidance would of course consider the problem solely from this point of view. The overall policy of selection therefore should be one of differential selection, in which due account is taken of the preferences of the Cs (cf. Dunnette, 1966).

The correlation between a selection test (or combinations of tests) and a measure of job success is known as the *validity* of the test. Fig. 6 shows diagrams corresponding to correlations of ·25 and ·75. Individual scores on the test are measured on the y-axis, scores of later success on the x-axis. The distribution of scores is plotted, and the envelopes containing most of the sample are shown here. If the correlation was perfect ($r = 1 \cdot 00$) the distribution would take the form of a straight line at 45 degrees; if there was no correlation ($r = 0$) there would be a completely random scatter of points. The envelopes corresponding to correlations of ·25 and ·75 are shown together with the percentages of individuals falling above and below the average on each axis.

Let us suppose that the top half of the Cs on the test (the y-axis) were selected; we can see the proportions that fall in the top half in terms of effectiveness on the job (x-axis). With the correlations shown, the proportions correctly accepted and rejected are as shown. There are two rather different kinds of error: those wrongly accepted might be disastrous in positions of seniority, while it is socially undesirable for people to be wrongly rejected in educational selection.

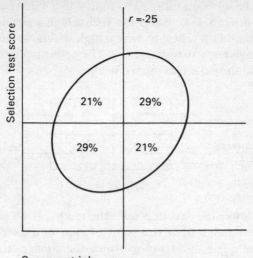

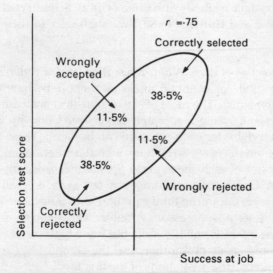

Fig. 6. The validity of selection (from Vernon, 1964).

Usually the selection ratio is less than 1 in 2 (shown above), for example 1 in 10. Selection is easier with a high selection ratio. To get the best intake it is best to have a high selection ratio, e.g. 1 in 10, *and* a high test validity, e.g. ·75. The percentages who will be successful at the job are as shown below.

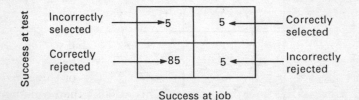

In fact the lower the selection ratio the more difficult selection is. On the other hand, from the point of view of a good C a high selection ratio is a disadvantage since the chances that a good person will be selected are reduced.

Many follow-up studies of the main methods of selection have now been published, and several meta-analyses have been carried out, for example by Reilly and Chao (1982), Schmitt *et al.* (1984), and Hunter and Hunter (1984); we shall refer to their findings later.

The combination of data. When more than one selection measure has been used, for example interviews *and* tests, how best can they be combined? The most effective statistical procedure is *multiple regression*: from a moderately large-scale follow-up study the optimum weights for each measure can be found. These are quite different from the raw correlations with the criterion, and depend on the power of each measure to predict independently of other measures. Under some conditions a test with a small positive validity comes out in the final equation with a negative sign; it is functioning as a 'suppressor' variable. This happens when the second test has little validity itself, but has a high correlation with invalid components of another test; the second test can best be used to improve the predictions of the first test.

Recent developments in selection statistics have produced other procedures which can produce higher validity from the same data than can multiple correlation. In sequential selection procedures, scores are obtained on *moderator* variables, which have no predictive power themselves, but can be used to allocate Cs to different test procedures. It has been found that some tests give good predictions for some Cs but not for others. In attempting to predict success among engineering students ability tests were found to be quite successful for stable extroverts but not at all for neurotic introverts (Furneaux, 1962). Thus extroversion and stability can be used as 'moderator variables' to decide whether or not to use other tests. Using moderator variables, two- or three-stage schemes of this kind can lead to higher validity than equations combining different test scores for all Cs where the same test data is used. A validity of ·66 was obtained with a regression equation and ·73 with moderator variables when identifying successful managers among 443 oil company managers (Hobert, 1965).

Statistical procedures are clearly very useful, but they cannot be used in small organizations, and they cannot be used until a large-scale follow-up study has been completed. A recent development has been to ask a sample of experienced psychologists to estimate the validities of a number of predictors. These estimates have been found to correlate very well with empirical validities – and to be much more economical: thirty judges can do as well as a proper follow-up of 1,164 candidates (Schmidt *et al.*, 1983).

Problems with the Classical Model of Selection

The upper limit of validity. The most effective selection measures have failed to produce an overall validity greater than ·6 in meta-analysis (de Wolff and van den Bosch, 1984). In other words, only 36 per cent of the variance in later success is accounted for, and a high proportion of the two kinds of error shown in Fig. 6 must occur. Admittedly half of the published studies covered by meta-analysis would have done better, so that there are conditions under which validities could be higher.

Follow-up validities are certainly reduced in light of the limited range of people studied, i.e. only those people selected, who may, in fact, be quite homogeneous. Part of the trouble must also lie with problems of criteria, when little agreement between different indices of success exists. Part of the difficulty is that future careers are only partly predictable, as a result of the organization constantly changing.

Selection takes too little account of the candidates' interests. The criteria of job success are always based on productivity or other variables from the organization's point of view. The expected job satisfaction of Cs is not taken into account – although this will affect how long those appointed will stay with the firm. There is, then, a case for employing vocational guidance, at least for the most desirable candidates. In fact, selection procedures give lower validity in terms of tenure than to any other criterion: the best predictors are references ($\cdot 27$), followed by biographical data ($\cdot 21$, $\cdot 26$) and the Strong-Campbell Interest Inventory ($\cdot 22$).

Traditionally it was assumed that the newly appointed employees would have to adapt to the organization. Again, for the most desirable Cs it might be considered how far the organization might adapt to them (de Wolff and van den Bosch, 1984). These considerations might lead to more importance being given to interviewing, since it is in the interview that the C's point of view can be explored.

Problems of fairness. In the USA in particular employers have been under attack from lawyers who have argued that selection procedures are unfair to blacks, women, and others. Interview and rating methods are most open to attack, unless evidence of validity can be produced. Objective measures have been criticized too – intelligence test items have been said to be biased against blacks. A partial solution to these problems is to calculate separate weights for prediction variables for each ethnic or gender group. However, this still leaves open the question of the different cut-off points to be used, i.e. whether or not some degree of affirmative action is to be practised (Schmitt and Noe, 1986). Least open to these attacks are work samples, and some of the role-played pro-

cedures used in assessment centres, which clearly resemble the
actual job.

Costs and utility. Some of the most valid selection methods are also
the most expensive. For example, assessment centres need special
premises, and a team of selectors for two to three days to assess
five or six Cs. The cost of this would only be justified for appoint-
ments to fairly important positions. A formula has been devised to
estimate the economic gains of a given selection procedure. The
gain over chance selection is proportional to the validity coef-
ficient, and to the standard deviation of the criterion in money
value (also to the number of Cs, and the number of years they
stay). Schmidt *et al.* (1979) calculated that $US36,800 per annum
would be saved per computer programmer if a selection procedure
of ·5 validity replaced one with ·3 validity.

Selecting the Measures to be Used

A wide range of selection procedures are in common use. We will
discuss their usefulness in terms of their follow-up validity, as
shown by recent meta-analyses, their fairness and their utility.

Interview. An interview is nearly always used in selection, despite
scepticism about it on the part of psychologists. It is generally
used as a means of improving on other sources of data; the interviewer (I) has the C's dossier in front of him or her, explores
points which are not clear, and bases questions on the C's record.
  Meta-analyses of follow-up studies have produced rather low
validities of ·09 and ·19, although a recent meta-analysis obtained
·29. However, there is high variability in the success of the
interview and some studies have found much better results. The
highest validities are found for structured, job-related interviews
involving several such interviews. It has been found that interviews partly measure intelligence, but that their incremental validity is about ·14 (Hunter and Hirsch, 1987).
  However, another way of looking at this problem is to find
how much an interview increases the validity based on dossier

material alone. It has been found that validity rises typically from about ·3 to ·4, using the dossier alone, to ·5 to ·6 when the interview is added (Ulrich and Trumbo, 1965). The validity of the interview varies greatly according to the I and is greater when the I is of a similar age and comes from a similar background to the C, and has been trained in interviewing.

It is usual to have more than one I, for example one to explore technical competence and a personnel person or psychologist to deal with personality. There is something to be said for one-to-one interviews, and a lot to be said against large and terrifying panels of Is. Is often disagree about Cs; accuracy of selection can be increased if they discuss their judgements and try to arrive at an agreed set of ratings.

Interviews are more successful if Is know exactly what the job requires, and ask questions which are relevant to it. For example if the job requires a high level of social skills, or the capacity to stand up to stress, the C can be asked questions about his or her experience which might reveal the required information. It is also desirable for Is to record their impressions on five-point or seven-point rating scales.

The reason interviews are so popular is probably that employers want to meet potential employees. It is also a very useful occasion for the C to assess the firm, and may turn into an interview in reverse. The interview is useful for interesting Cs in the job, and for assessing their compatibility with other employees. It is one of the few ways of assessing motivation, stability and other aspects of personality.

It has often been suspected that interviews may not be fair; for example the I may form judgements based on the social class, race, religion or sex of the C. These doubts have not been entirely dispelled by recent studies (Schmitt and Noe, 1986; Muchinsky, 1986). In addition, interviews are stressful, and may not show Cs as they normally behave, and there are a number of common errors made by Is (p. 171).

Testimonials, or references, are widely used, and are particularly important for senior jobs and in the educational and academic world; in both cases there is a network of known and trusted referees. Referees should know about the C's recent performance at work. The main difficulty is that each C is reported on by different referees with somewhat different standards, styles of reporting, etc. In addition, referees often give a biased case in favour of their C. Validity, in turn, has been found to be quite low (for example ·14 and ·23 in two meta-analyses reported in 1986 by Muchinsky). Testimonials can be more helpful if a questionnaire is devised, and standard rating scales provided.

Psychological tests. These carry the promise of objectivity, accuracy and fairness. How well do they do? Several different kinds must be distinguished.

(a) *Intelligence tests* have been used for all kinds of jobs, and hundreds of follow-up studies have been carried out. The average validity is ·54 (for training success), and ·45 (for job proficiency). Validity is highest for management and other complex jobs. However, intelligence may predict negatively to persistence at low-level repetitive jobs, since intelligent people are bored by them. There is a possible fairness issue: blacks achieve lower scores than whites on average, perhaps because the items favour whites in some way (Schmitt and Noe, 1986).

Intelligence can also be inferred from the academic record, although this has a lower validity of ·14 or ·2 in meta-analyses (Muchinsky, 1986).

(b) *Aptitude and special ability tests* include perceptual (e.g. visual acuity), cognitive (e.g. spatial ability, mechanical comprehension) and psychometric (e.g. motor coordination, mechanical ability, arm strength) tests. The overall validity is ·27 although much higher figures have also been reported (Muchinsky, 1986). These tests are suitable for a wide range of skilled manual jobs, and are fair to all Cs. Better results are obtained with *work samples*, where the test is very similar to the job, as in typing and driving tests. These have produced high validities (·54 and ·38) in meta-analyses (Muchinsky, 1986). They are highly acceptable to minority group job applicants, because of their obvious face validity.

(c) *Personality tests*, such as the Minnesota Multiphasic Personality Inventory (MMPI) and the Bernreuter Personality Inventory (both lengthy, self-report questionnaires), have been widely used for management selection in the USA: in 1957 44 per cent of firms were using tests such as these (Hale, 1982). However, they were attacked by Whyte (1957) and others, who pointed out how easy it is to cheat and to give the 'right' impression, while others objected to the invasion of privacy incurred when asking personal questions with no obvious connection to the job. The use of personality tests declined in the USA, and they have never been used much in Britain. It is not surprising that the validity of this kind of test for selection purposes is very low (·15 and ·18 in meta-analyses).

Another way of assessing personality is by projective tests. The most widely used is part of the Thematic Apperception Test (TAT) used to measure achievement and power motivation (p. 55). This has had modest success, with validities in the ·2s (Schmitt and Noe, 1986). Many psychological tests were designed to assess mental disturbance, e.g. the MMPI, and are not really suitable for selection. Recent developments of tests designed to discriminate within the normal population have shown signs of better success (Muchinsky, 1986). While personality tests are seen to be fair, they usually need a psychologist to administer and score them, and they are often quite expensive. The main alternative way of assessing personality characteristics is by interview.

(d) *Interest inventories*, such as the Strong-Campbell Inventory and the Kuder Preference Record, are used for vocational guidance and are not normally used for selection. When the Strong-Campbell has been used for selection it has given rather low validities but as high as ·22 to tenure and ·25 to promotion (Hunter and Hunter, 1984).

Biographical inventories. Up to 800 items bearing on the C's past history, interests and other topics are used in these tests. The items are then validated against promotion, productivity, or other indices of success, and the most predictive are chosen. This method really needs a sample of 400 Cs or more, and should be repeated every three years, since the validity of items decays (Hunter and Hunter, 1984). In one follow-up study 484 items were used which were then found to fall into five statistical factors. Comparison with the criterion of patents submitted by 418 research scientists showed that two of the factors predicted to success in this job: these were 'inquisitive, professional orientation', and 'tolerance for ambiguity' (Morrison *et al.*, 1962).

The follow-up validity of this procedure is quite good: ·3 or more in meta-analyses, although it has often been over ·5 (Muchinsky, 1986). One problem is the low face validity of some items; however blind empiricism here is more successful than 'rational' selection of items with face validity (Mitchell and Klimoski, 1982). Another problem is that items about class, race, gender, etc. can add to validity but may be objectionable on grounds of fairness. A third problem is the possible invasion of privacy – some people do not like being asked about finances, social background, interests and values. However, the method is applicable to all jobs and is cheap to employ.

Peer assessment. Employees are asked to rate, rank or nominate each other. This can be used for promotion, although not for initial entry (unless a group of Cs are being assessed together). The follow-up validity is very high: ·41, ·43 and ·49 in meta-analyses (Muchinsky, 1986). However, the method is not widely used, partly because it is felt ratings will be affected too much by friendship biases, and because it can lead to a kind of popularity contest. In addition, individual prejudices might disadvantage some employees.

Situational exercises. These are only used for the selection of managers and other administrators and may take the form of a leaderless group discussion between five or six Cs, role-played committee work as chairperson and as member, or in-basket exercises for one C at a time. The behaviour of Cs is rated for social skills such

as persuasiveness and the ability to get on with others, for cognitive abilities such as judgement, and for the attitudes expressed.
This method has quite good validity, in the range ·25 to ·35
(Muchinsky, 1986). In Britain this was first used together with
other measures by the army for officer selection, and has been
used for many years with success for selecting civil servants,
diplomats and managers. However, there are some doubts about
the fairness of the method to blacks in the USA and working-
class Cs in Britain – they feel disadvantaged, and the ratings may
be biased against them (Schmitt and Noe, 1986).

Assessment centres. A group of five or more Cs are put through a
series of tests and selection exercises for one or two days by a
team of selectors. The Civil Service Selection Board in Britain, for
example, uses three interviews (one conducted by a psychologist),
leaderless group discussion, role-played committee exercises, a 3-
hour administrative exercise, and shorter tasks modelling the
work of civil servants (Vernon, 1950). The follow-up validity of
these methods is good: ·41, ·43 and ·49 in meta-analyses averag-
ing across different criteria of success. They are, however, better
predictions of promotion rate than of objective measures of performance, so that it is possible that the promotions are influenced by
knowledge of the selection scores, or that the selectors know the
kind of person who 'fits' and is likely to be promoted.

The method is expensive and needs special premises. On the
other hand it has been calculated that these costs are outweighed
by the economic gains of selecting good people. The method is
only justified for senior jobs, i.e. for senior civil servants, diplomats,
managers and officers in the armed forces. It has been said, however, that this group of methods puts too much emphasis on
social skills, and that it benefits Cs from the social and educational
backgrounds which impart such skills and the self-confidence to
use them. However, selectors are usually well aware of this problem, and do their best to overcome it.

The best predictors are different for Cs entering an organization
and for those being promoted. At entry the best predictors are
ability tests, performance at job try-out, biographical inventory

and references. For employees being promoted the best predictors are work samples, ability measures, supervisor or peer ratings, assessment centres and biographical data, in that order. The validities in the second case are considerably higher than in the first (Hunter and Hunter, 1984; Schmitt *et al.*, 1984). In Britain interviews and testimonials are nearly always used for selecting managers, while tests and assessment centres are only used by a minority of firms (Robertson and Makin, 1986).

5

THE MOTIVATION TO WORK

Not so long ago it was widely believed that people disliked work, and only did it because it led to rewards. For animals and primitive people the rewards were food and shelter, for modern workers, it was thought, the main reward was money. Many psychologists believed that activity was motivated by 'deficits', like those of hunger and thirst, to reduce 'tensions', and that rest and satiation were the goals of activity.

These views have had to be considerably revised. Surveys have asked workers if they would carry on working if it were not financially necessary: one survey found that 31 per cent of men and 34 per cent of women would stay in their present job, while 35 per cent of men and 29 per cent of women would work but try to change their jobs (Warr, 1982). A number of surveys in different countries have found that having interesting or challenging work, and a good work environment, are more important than pay (Baron, 1986). We shall show later that satisfaction with pay depends on how far it is seen to be fair (p. 94ff).

Incentives are rewards which are seen to depend on some aspect of performance. Therefore paying workers more is not an incentive to work harder, though it is an incentive to stay with the firm, i.e. labour turnover should be less. Expectancy theory has taken this further and predicts that effort depends on (1) the desirability of rewards, (2) the perceived probability that effort will lead to successful performance, and (3) the perceived probability that performance will lead to rewards (Vroom, 1964).

There has been a lot of research on this model. The overall

success has been modest, with correlations of ·3 with effort – 9 per cent of the variance (Schwab *et al.*, 1979). The third factor, 'instrumentality', the belief that performance will lead to rewards, has been extensively studied, and is the most strongly confirmed part of the theory, both in correlational field studies and in laboratory experiments. We shall see that people work a lot faster under wage incentives, or if they believe that their rate of work will affect their promotion prospects. Field studies have found correlations as high as ·4 or ·5 between instrumentality and productivity (Campbell and Pritchard, 1976). However, the limited success of the model overall shows that workers are not simply seeking rewards in a rational way (McCormick and Ilgen, 1985).

Maslow (1954) suggested that there is a hierarchy of needs, beyond the physiological ones, where the higher needs start to operate only when lower ones have been fulfilled.

(1) Self-fulfilment, or self-actualization
(2) Self-esteem
(3) Social needs (acceptance)
(4) Safety needs
(5) Physiological needs (hunger and thirst)

The main supporting evidence for this theory comes from the lowest needs in the hierarchy – when people are very hungry, thirsty, cold or afraid, they are not much concerned about higher needs, as a number of studies have shown (Cofer and Appley, 1964). There is not such clear evidence about the upper part of the hierarchy. However, as we shall see, managers attach a lot of importance to the higher level needs. And 'growth need strength' has been found to be important – the need to grow in skills and competence.

However, the motives which have been found to affect work do not all fit the Maslow scheme. Money is the most obvious one, and we shall deal with the various kinds of economic incentive in the next section. One of the main limitations to economic incentives is the concern for fairness or equity, which is itself a source of motivation. Then it has been found that many people find work intrinsically enjoyable. There are people who enjoy flying planes, driving cars, operating computers, writing books, making furniture or working in the garden. After all, a lot of them do these things in their spare time, without payment. This is a major source of motivation, and needs to be understood.

Managers in particular are much concerned with achievement and promotion (which comes into the Maslow list), and with power (which does not). Most people at work feel a sense of commitment and responsibility to the organization, or a commitment to work as such.

Economic Motivation

Classical organization theorists assumed that workers had to be driven to work by the carrot and the stick, which may often have been true during the Industrial Revolution. A similar view has been taken by most economists, with their concept of 'economic man'. Occupational psychologists reacted very strongly to these views, and in some books failed to discuss economic incentives at all. This second point of view appeared to receive some support from surveys in which workers were asked which factors were most important in making a good job or bad – 'pay' commonly came sixth or seventh after 'security', 'co-workers', 'interesting work', 'welfare arrangements', etc. (Viteles, 1954). This has been confirmed in more recent surveys which have found that pensions and other benefits are valued more (McCormick and Ilgen, 1985). These results may, however, be misleading since people do not have accurate or objective insight into their motivations, and in addition may want to give socially desirable answers. Which side is correct?

(1) *Does money motivate people?* The basic psychology of incentives is that behaviour can be influenced if it is linked to some desired reward. Speed of work is an example. There is little doubt that people work harder when paid by results than when paid by the time they put in. There have been numerous studies of the effects of wage incentives. An American survey of the introduction of

514 incentive schemes found an average increase in output of 39 per cent, a decrease in labour costs of 11·6 per cent, and a wage increase of 17·6 per cent (*Modern Industry*, 1946). A careful British study of six factories where no other changes had been introduced found an increase in output of 60 per cent, and an increase in earnings of 20 per cent (Davison *et al.*, 1958). A recent American meta-analysis of 330 intervention programmes found that a change of financial incentives had the greatest impact, of up to 2·12 times the standard deviation in thirteen studies (Guzzo *et al.*, 1985). However, all these figures are probably exaggerated since whenever an incentive scheme is introduced other improvements are made as well, for example improvements in methods of working, or delivery of supplies.

Another study showed the effects of an incentive plan for reducing absenteeism, which fell at once as soon as the plan was introduced, and which rose again when it was discontinued (Scheflen *et al.*, 1971). Other evidence shows that money can act as an incentive for people to stay with their organization. It was found that labour turnover at one factory fell from 370 per cent to 16 per cent after an increase in wages (Scott *et al.*, 1960). This does not mean that people will do anything for money, and many people choose a lower paid job rather than a higher paid one because the lower paid job is more interesting, is thought to be more worthwhile, carries higher status, is in a nicer place, or because their friends work there.

There are a number of different ways, which are suitable for different kinds of workers or conditions, of linking pay to performance.

(*a*) *Piecework* is payment based on the number of units of work completed, and is really only suitable for repetitive work, with a single kind of job, or a small number of jobs. Each job has to be timed, and pay depends on these timings. A common problem with piecework is that there may be restriction of output, enforced by group norms and social pressures, because the workers believe that if they work too fast the jobs will be re-timed less generously, or that they will run out of work, or even become unemployed.

Roy (1955) took a job as a machine tool operative and found that when jobs were being timed workers would run cutting tools at a slower speed, but when the rate had been fixed they speeded up the tools and 'streamlined' the jobs in order to earn maximum piecework rates. In another field study it was found that members of a sales group worked out a quota system so that each member earned the same amount, thus defeating the management's incentive scheme (Babchuk and Goode, 1951). In addition workers tend to resist changes in working arrangements; they do their jobs faster, so that they are making good money, in addition to devising the informal arrangements referred to above. This makes it difficult for management to introduce changes and results in considerable clerical and accountancy costs.

Lupton (1968) concluded that payment by results is suitable under certain conditions only – for repetitive work, for introducing slow changes, with a good time-study department, when industrial relations are good, and when a tradition of incentive payments exists, as occurs in the car factories etc. in the west Midlands.

(b) *Group piecework.* One alternative is group piecework, which avoids friction inside groups and encourages cooperation and help. As an incentive, however, it is usually less effective than individual payment by results, and it has been found that the larger the group the weaker the effect (Marriott, 1968). However, there are situations in which group piecework produces better results than individual piecework. Individual incentives in department stores, for example, lead to salesmen grabbing the best customers, hiding the goods, and neglecting stock and display work. Group piecework is appropriate for small, cohesive work groups, where workers are closely interdependent, such as the coalmining and textile groups described on p. 42ff. In large groups of independent workers it simply acts as a weak incentive and results in hostility towards slower workers.

(c) *Measured day work.* Here there is a regular wage for each job together with a bonus which is paid so long as a certain rate or standard of work is maintained. If it is not, through no fault of management, the bonus is withdrawn until the standard is met (Shaw and Pirie, 1982). Jobs are graded in terms of the skill, training and effort required, and pay differentials are established. The whole scheme depends on a bargain over what is felt to be a fair relationship between reward and effort. This method is often used when mechanization is introduced and payment by results is no longer possible. While there are no systematic studies of its effectiveness, it is said to result in better relations between management and workers, to increase workers' feeling of responsibility (making them feel more like members of the staff), to provide more security and a stable wage, and to reduce administrative costs (Marriott, 1968; Lupton, 1968).

(d) *Performance appraisal and merit ratings.* Piecework and measured day work are appropriate for repetitive jobs, but not for more complex or varied work. However, it is possible to reward anyone, for any aspect of their performance, by means of merit ratings which are reflected in pay. Over 85 per cent of firms use it for some of their personnel. It is not applied much to shop-floor workers, but it is used for clerical staff, and it is widely used for managers. Even professors (in the USA) have salary increments based on the chairman's assessment of their publications, teaching and other contributions. It is a central part of Management by Objectives (p. 220ff), and it requires a system of rating on scales and of appraisal interviews, at which the ratings (and the consequent salary adjustments) are discussed (p. 172ff). On the other hand there is such a widespread expectation of salary increases with age that there is often a tendency to give automatic increments. A great advantage of the scheme is its flexibility; increments can be linked to ratings for stress tolerance, delegation, initiative, oral expression, or anything else. It is also useful in building up information about personnel, which is very helpful for making promotion decisions (Cameron, 1982).

There are other incentives for managers, where payment of a bonus, in cash or shares, is dependent on the performance of the manager's division, e.g. the profits made. If the bonus is spread between several managers it is similar to group piecework.

However, a study over time of twenty managers found that the introduction of such a scheme had no effect on eleven out of twelve measures of the effectiveness of their divisions (Pearce *et al.*, 1985).

(e) *Monthly productivity bonus.* In addition to a guaranteed weekly wage, a monthly bonus is paid, based on the output or sales of the whole firm or individual department. This bonus may be arrived at by comparison with a target figure. From studies of the incentive effects of group piecework one would think that the whole firm would constitute far too large a group for there to be any effect on productivity. However, one version of this appears to have been quite successful. In the Scanlon Plan up to 75 per cent of savings in labour costs are paid as bonuses. In the very first application of the method profits increased two and a half times and wages by 54 per cent. In other case studies productivity increased by about 25 per cent after the introduction of monthly bonuses (Lesieur, 1958). The plan seems to work best in small firms with a few hundred workers. However, since it requires a joint consultative committee to administer it, there are other gains for commitment and job satisfaction (p. 229ff). It has also been found that labour turnover is reduced, and cooperation increases where there is a productivity bonus (Marriott, 1968). There can, on the other hand, be some resentment towards those who do not pull their weight on the part of the more effective workers, though this may take the form of constructive social pressure.

(f) *Profit-sharing and co-partnership.* Here there is a guaranteed weekly wage, and an annual (or twice-yearly) bonus based on the firm's profits. This is very widely used in British and American industry, although the actual amount distributed may be small, and many firms have abandoned it. No very precise data are available but it is generally agreed that there is no effect on productivity as the group is too large, and the time-lag too great. Firms have often introduced profit-sharing more in the hope of creating a sense of belonging, and promoting industrial peace and teamwork, but there is no evidence that industrial relations have improved. The advantages may lie in reduced labour turnover and increased job satisfaction, but this too remains to be demonstrated. Part of the trouble is that profits are partly outside workers' control, and depend on other factors besides production, such as the economic position of the firm; profits are small during times of economic depression and workers become dissatisfied with the scheme.

There are certain conditions which must be fulfilled if schemes based on collective output or profits are to be effective: the group on which the incentive is based must not be too large; the time unit on which the bonus is based must not be too long; and there should be full worker participation in management.

(2) *The limits of economic motivation.* We have seen that the effect of piecework payment is often limited by output restriction norms – people would rather earn less than be unpopular. The amount of money people want to earn depends on how much their friends and neighbours have, how large their family is, whether they are trying to buy a house or car, the availability of hire purchase, etc. (Porter and Lawler, 1968). However, most people seem to want more money than they have already. They may change their level of aspiration and want more or bigger houses and cars, and this will depend on their social reference group. Or they may want money as an index of success. Or they may find new ways of spending money. In a very interesting social survey in the USA it was found that the most poorly paid workers said they would be satisfied with an increase in income of 162 per cent, those in the middle ranges wanted about 60 per cent, and the most highly paid 100 per cent more, the overall average being 86 per cent (Centers and Cantril, 1946). There is evidently no point at which people do not want more money.

On the other hand there are individual differences in attitudes towards money. There are a number of people who have to choose between better and less well-paid jobs, and choose the latter – for example as clergymen, research workers, hospital orderlies, or those who just want to live a simple life. Furnham (1984a) carried out a factor analysis of attitudes to money, and found six factors:

(a) *Obsession.*
    'I put money ahead of pleasure.'
    'I worry about my finances much of the time.'
(b) *Power.*
    'I sometimes "buy" friendship by being very generous to those I
    want to like me.'
(c) *Retention.*
    'I prefer to save money because I am never sure when things
    will collapse and I'll need the cash.'
(d) *Security.*
    'I always know how much I have in my savings account.'
(e) *Inadequacy.*
    'Most of my friends have more money than I do.'
(f) *Effort/ability.*
    'I believe that my present income is far less than I deserve
    given the job I do.'

Furnham found several interesting correlates of these factors.
Obsession with money was greater for women, people with high
incomes, and those who believed strongly in the Protestant
Work Ethic; they also believed that money was acquired through
ability or effort. Poor and alienated people were much less obses-
sed, and did not believe that money comes through effort or
ability. Older, better-educated females were more conservative
and retentive about money, and felt inadequate about how much
they had.

However, money is not the only source of motivation, and the
other limits of pay arise out of the other sources, which will
occupy the rest of the chapter.

Equity

One of the main limits on the effects of pay is whether or not the
amount is seen as fair. But what, exactly, will people regard as
fair? One interpretation of fairness is that everyone should be paid
equally, but in almost all cultures it is accepted as just that some
people should be paid more than others. The only exception to

this is in the Israeli kibbutzim, though the differentials in Japanese factories are also small; in communist countries there are quite large wage differentials. Although there are variations between cultures in the jobs which are paid most, it does seem to be generally assumed that those who are skilled and those in higher levels in the supervisory hierarchy should be paid more. Total egalitarianism would work only if people were carefully socialized and indoctrinated to believe in it as in the kibbutzim.

Another interpretation of fairness is that people should receive rewards in proportion to what they have put in, or 'invested'. Equity theory proposes that people compare the ratios of their inputs and outcomes with those of other workers. The main outcome is income, but there is also status, and other benefits from the job. Inputs include time and effort, qualifications, or whatever is generally believed to be relevant.

There have been many experiments, most of them in laboratories, where equity theory has been applied to wages. One of the more realistic was by Pritchard et al. (1972) who paid students to work for seven half days, some being paid more, others less than the advertised rate for the second part of the period. The results are complex, but generally supportive of equity theory. As Fig. 7 shows, the more subjects were paid the harder they worked, i.e. to restore equity, while job satisfaction was greatest for the equity condition. A number of studies have found that men are more concerned than women with the effects of inequity (Brockner and Adsit, 1986).

Greenberg and Ornstein (1983) found that if subjects were asked to do additional, unpaid work, their level of performance fell, unless they were compensated by another outcome, for example a high-status job title. Whether or not payment arrangements are perceived as fair depends partly on the actual amounts paid ('distributive justice'), but much more on the methods used for deciding on pay ('procedural justice') (Greenberg, 1987).

Rae (1981) found that black baseball players thought that they were not paid enough in relation to white players, although they were, in fact, paid a lot more. However, the black players were

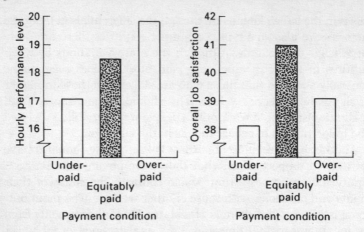

Fig. 7. Inequity: its effects on performance and job satisfaction (Baron, 1983; based on data from Pritchard *et al.*, 1972).

also better; at the same level of scoring it was the white players who were paid more.

In experiments on equity, the manipulation of overpayment is achieved by paying subjects more than the advertised rate or more than they were paid earlier, or by suggesting that they are underqualified for the job. Some of the main results of these experiments are as follows:

(1) *Overpaid, piecework.* Prediction: reduced quantity, increased quality; confirmed only for subjects high in moral development or if the performance is central to the self-concept (Vecchio, 1981).

(2) *Overpaid, hourly pay.* Prediction: increased quantity or quality; confirmed in some studies (e.g. Fig. 7), but not all.

(3) *Underpaid, piecework.* Prediction: increased quantity, reduced quality; generally confirmed.

(4) *Underpaid, hourly pay.* Prediction: reduced quantity or quality; generally confirmed (Mowday, 1979.)

However, equity research has been much criticized, in particular the fact that it has mostly been laboratory-based or conducted over a short time-scale. And there are other ways of restoring

	$US	$US	$US
Years of education	Single female	Single male	Married male
7	7,125	8,471	9,217
16	14,040	16,059	18,447

Table 3. Fair incomes in the USA, 1974 (from Jasso and Rossi, 1977).

equity, especially for the overpaid, who can easily persuade themselves that they are worth their pay. If overpayment is created by telling subjects that they are underqualified, they may work hard to show how good they are; when over-benefiting is produced by paying subjects more, there is less effect on the amount of work (Mowday, 1979).

Job satisfaction is much less for those who are underpaid, and they are likely to leave. Is job satisfaction also less for those who are overpaid? Laboratory experiments find that overpaid subjects think their overpayment is unfair, but they are nevertheless satisfied (Austin et al., 1980). Or they may say they feel unhappy and guilty, but with the 'bogus pipeline' (where they think that a physiological measure of their true feelings is being taken) they are quite happy and not at all guilty (Rivera and Tedeschi, 1976).

Jasso and Rossi (1977) presented a large number of vignettes describing hypothetical individuals with different jobs, years of education and other variables, and asked a sample of 200 respondents to rate the fairness of the income in each case on a scale from underpaid to overpaid. The results (in Table 3) show how a sample of Americans in 1974 thought pay should vary between different kinds of jobs. Years of education were linked to grade of job in the vignettes. The intervening steps were given intermediate incomes. These results suggest that a top-bottom salary of ratio of about 2:1 was seen as fair, rather less than actually applied at the time.

Emler and Dickinson (1985) asked British children how much they thought various occupations should be paid. Middle-class children of eleven thought that doctors should be paid 2·64 times as much as road sweepers, while working-class children of the same age thought they should be paid 1·61 times as much. The authors concluded that these class differences reflected the social representations and prejudices of their cultural milieux.

In fact there are considerable wage differentials in nearly every country, including Russia, China and Cuba; an exception is the Israeli kibbutz. For the main salaried jobs there is a ratio of about 4:1 from the top of the scale to the bottom. Doctors are paid about three times the average wage, professors about two times. Administrators and professionals are paid more than manual workers, while those with skills are paid more than those without. Economists explain these differences in terms of the operation of the market forces of supply and demand. Sociologists argue that wages reflect social status, the value society traditionally places on different jobs. Trade unions have managed to raise the wages of manual workers above those of many white-collar workers. The most highly paid are some of the self-employed – successful pop singers, sportsmen and women, actors and entrepreneurs – because the public values their product (Phelps Brown, 1977).

Systematic attempts to evaluate different jobs have been fuelled by pressure to remove sex discrimination; the problem is that women often do different jobs. The most widely used is the job component method: a committee awards points for different aspects of jobs, e.g. the skills required, the effort, responsibility and the job conditions. The total points are found to correlate well with actual salaries. The points for a range of jobs are plotted against salaries to give the best-fitting line, and salaries of particular jobs can then be deduced (McCormick and Ilgen, 1985). This has had important consequences for wage settlements in some American states and in Canada (Greenberg, 1986). It was estimated, using this method, that the correct 'salary' for housewives in the USA in 1968–9 was $8,800 per annum, about the same amount received at the time by electricity supervisors, firemen and repairmen (Arvey and Begalla, 1975).

Rawls (1972) proposed that inequalities are acceptable if everyone is better off as a result of them. For example doctors have to undertake long training and do hard and stressful work; unless

they were paid enough, perhaps there would not be enough recruits. This is probably why length of training is regarded as a
relevant input.

Another solution to the problem of pay differentials is the 'time-
span of responsibility', i.e. the period of time which may elapse
before a worker's supervisor can know whether he or she is working efficiently (Jaques, 1961). In practice this is the length of the
longest jobs performed. These predictions were tested on 141
managers in an American firm. It was found that the correlations
between pay and time-span were positive but were extremely
small, in the range of ·1 to ·2, thus providing very weak support for
the theory as stated (Goodman, 1967).

In fact satisfaction with wages is more dependent on relative
than on absolute pay, on comparisons with others, and perceptions of fairness. We show later that equity is an important source
of satisfaction (p. 238ff).

Therefore, there is a managerial problem in deciding on the
differentials between different grades of skilled workers, and, for
that matter, grades of managers. The differences which will be
regarded as fair can only be found out from those concerned, a
clear case for consultation and participation. The trouble is that
the higher- and lower-paid will probably have different ideas on
the subject.

Intrinsic Motivation

It seems very likely that work, for some, is a source of intrinsic
satisfaction. Even rats engage spontaneously in behaviour, such
as running in activity wheels, for no reward other than the enjoyment of the actual activity. Other experiments show that rats like
to explore interesting mazes, while monkeys like to solve puzzles
and manipulate equipment. Experiments with humans in conditions of sensory deprivation show that the absence of stimulation
and activity is very disturbing. It seems that exploration, manipulation, the receiving of novel and interesting stimuli and, possibly,
sheer activity are rewarding.

While interesting work provides its own reward, those engaged in boring work do their best to make it more interesting: the games and practical jokes often engaged in by manual workers were described in Chapter 3. There are individual differences in tolerance for boring work; intelligent people are most discontented with it (Vroom, 1964) and, if Eysenck (1967) is correct, introverts should be able to tolerate it more than extroverts.

It follows from all of this that people should want to do interesting work to satisfy their needs for exploration, stimulation and manipulation. Herzberg *et al.* (1959) found that when people are asked to report times when they were particularly satisfied with their jobs they often speak of occasions during which the work itself was very interesting or went well. Some of this satisfaction derives from a sense of completing an important or difficult task, and it sometimes includes elements of achievement motivation. We shall show elsewhere that 'the work itself' is rated along with 'recognition' and 'achievement', and higher than 'promotion' as a source of positive satisfaction (p. 235ff).

Deci (1980) proposed that intrinsic motivation is based on the desire for competence and self-determination, and can be measured by the amount of time a person spends on a task during a free time period. It can be increased by giving more free choice, and by enhancing an individual's sense of competence and expertise by giving positive feedback. Fisher (1978) found that the combination of those two factors did increase motivation. The more controversial part of the theory is the expectation that external rewards, such as pay, will *decrease* intrinsic motivation. However, there is no evidence that when money is withdrawn people will work harder, in fact the opposite is the case. Nevertheless, some jobs are clearly more interesting than others; 'intrinsic satisfaction' is one of the main components of job satisfaction.

What are the characteristics of jobs which make them intrinsically interesting and enjoyable? Hackman and Oldham (1980) proposed that five job characteristics motivate work performance. The effects of these job characteristics on work performance were expected to be greater for those with strong needs for growth. While some studies have found the predicted effects of job characteristics, and interaction with growth needs, others have not

Job characteristic	Psychological states	Outcomes
(1) Skill variety		
(2) Task variety	*Meaningfulness of work*	
(3) Task significance		High internal motivation, quality of work, satisfaction, reduced absenteeism and turnover
(4) Autonomy	Responsibility for work outcomes	
(5) Feedback	Knowledge of results	

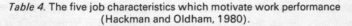

Table 4. The five job characteristics which motivate work performance (Hackman and Oldham, 1980).

(Locke and Henne, 1986). Graen *et al.* (1986) argued that growth need strength should come into operation when there is a chance to respond to opportunities for enriched work. They confirmed this interpretation in a setting where vertical collaboration and more independent work were on offer. However, the effects on job satisfaction are very strong, as we shall see later (p. 235).

Knowledge of results (see Table 4) has often been found to be a source of increased motivation. It works for individuals and for groups, in a great variety of jobs (Luthans and Martinko, 1987), and in the meta-analysis by Guzzo *et al.* (1985) it produced an increase of ·41 of the standard deviation. One way in which it works is through generating competition, but achievement motivation may operate without competition.

It is obvious that many people enjoy their work, that many do voluntary, i.e. unpaid work, and that many people put a lot of effort into serious, work-like leisure activities. It follows that intrinsic motivation in some form affects work behaviour. On the other hand there is little evidence that it affects the speed or quality of work.

Achievement and Promotion

There is no doubt that what motivates many people at work is the need to achieve something, or the hope of promotion. These usually entail more money, but that is only part of the story.

Some individuals are more ambitious and hard-working than others. If they value success in relation to standards of excellence they are said to be high in need for achievement (n.Ach), but this is not a 'need' like hunger since there is no bodily deficit. The measure most often used is a projective test derived from the TAT (Thematic Apperception Test) in which subjects answer questions about what they imagine might be happening in a number of vaguely drawn pictures, and their answers are scored for the number of achievement topics mentioned. It is also possible to measure n.Ach, and more easily, by questionnaire. Unfortunately the two kinds of measure have a very poor correlation. High-need achievers are found to be over-achievers at academic work (i.e. they do better than their IQs would predict), they work hard at laboratory tasks, set high but realistic targets, and are optimistic about the future (McClelland et al., 1953).

Does n.Ach affect work performance? The main application originally envisaged was to managers and entrepreneurs, although it has also been applied to scientists and other academics. A number of studies, although not all, have found substantial correlations with measures of effort or success, e.g. number of scientific publications. For managers it has been found to predict the rate of promotion, or seniority, although the questionnaire measure predicts this better (Locke and Henne, 1986).

More recently McClelland and Boyatzis (1982) decided that n.Ach is relevant only to the success and promotion of entrepreneurs, managers in small firms, and those in sales – all of whom can achieve success through their personal performance, rather than influencing others – for whom, the authors maintained, a different kind of personality is relevant (see below). We have seen, however, that n.Ach affects occupational choice; a preference for risky, entrepreneurial professions is displayed (p. 67). High n.Ach individuals respond more positively to enriched, more interesting and demanding jobs; this goes a long way beyond entrepreneurs.

There is a problem applying the n.Ach theory to women as n.Ach measures do not predict achievement very well in women. Achievement motivation has been conceptualized in male, instrumental terms, while achievement for most women may be more a matter of expressiveness or communion (Buck, 1988). However, women too can be ambitious and keen to succeed. Spence and Helmreich (1983) found, for example, that men scored higher on competitiveness and preference for challenging jobs, while women scored higher on the desire to work hard. An interesting application of this approach has been made to the explanation of cultural differences in economic growth, and also to the emergence of industrial revolutions (p. 20ff).

These results encouraged McClelland and Winter (1969) to carry out experiments on stimulating achievement motivation in underdeveloped countries. They reported the results of a short course for managers and businessmen in India, in which trainees played management games and were taught the behaviour of high achievers. A before-and-after comparison showed that compared with a control group who did not go on the course, the course members made considerable efforts to increase the productivity of their industrial concerns. An interesting feature of this study is that 'achievement motivation' is not mentioned as such. The results could indeed be due to the learning of new management techniques rather than to any increase in motivational state. A similar experiment in Indonesia is reported to have been much less successful.

It has now been proposed that managerial motivation is better predicted from a combination of high power motivation and *low* affiliative motivation (i.e. the need to form close relationships), and there is evidence that this predicts managerial success for non-technical managers at least (McClelland and Boyatzis, 1982). For senior management and for managers in large firms, it is argued, success and promotion depend not on individual achievement, but on the capacity to influence others.

Although achievement motivation has been thought to apply mainly to managers and entrepreneurs, many others can achieve success at work – salespeople, engineers, research workers, craftworkers, indeed anyone in skilled work, and anyone whose rate or quality of work can be assessed and recognized. Vroom (1964) suggested that people are motivated to make use of their abilities.

Several experiments show that if subjects are led to believe that a task requires abilities which they think they possess they will work harder at it.

Miner devised a test of managerial motivation, and it has been found that the test and most of its sub-scales give higher scores for top managers in organizations, especially those in marketing, compared with lower managers, and entrepreneurs. The test includes positive attitudes to authority, desire for power, competitiveness, wanting to stand out from the group, and being prepared to do routine administration (Berman and Miner, 1985).

The desire for promotion is probably linked to achievement motivation: promotion is an index of success, especially for managers. Promotion also brings more power and more pay. Many studies have shown the great desire on the part of managers for promotion, their preoccupation with this topic and their great dissatisfaction when they do not get it, or when they think it is being done unfairly (Vroom, 1964). Herzberg et al. (1959) found that recognition was often mentioned as the reason for occasions of high job satisfaction. Among salesmen and women, competition based on number of sales has always been the custom. Among manual workers, on the other hand, there has been a long tradition in Britain of group solidarity: individuals do not want to be promoted over and separated from their workmates – they would prefer the whole group to be upgraded or better paid. In an American study, however, Georgopoulos et al. (1957) found more productive workers among those who thought that high productivity would lead to promotion.

Promotion is a very unsatisfactory incentive, however, since it can only be made when there is a vacancy, and criteria other than hard work have to be taken into account, such as qualifications, age, personality, and even social connections. In fact, a number of American studies have reported a decline in aspirations for managerial success since 1960 (Miner and Smith, 1982).

In modern society the work a person does is a major component of his or her identity. In the Twenty Statements Test subjects are asked to give twenty answers to the question 'Who am I?' Occupation is one of the most frequent kinds of answer, and it usually appears early in the list (Mulford and Salisbury, 1964). Self-esteem is greatly dependent on success at work, as shown by money earned, promotion, status symbols, or other kinds of recognition of success. In this way several kinds of motivation become incorporated into an autonomous drive for success at work which can become a central feature of the personality (Neff, 1985). This does not happen to everyone: those employed in low-status jobs are often not deeply committed to their work, and do it mainly for the pay and the social contacts.

It has been found that various 'higher' needs, for fulfilment, growth need etc., are strong for managers, and that this is particularly true of senior managers. Lower-level managers on the other hand are more dissatisfied in this respect. Porter (1964) used a slightly different set of needs from Maslow (p. 87), adding a need for autonomy (see Figs. 8 and 9). The need for *esteem* is satisfied by achievement and respect from others.

Self-actualization is described as 'a desire for self-fulfilment, namely to become actualized in what one is potentially . . . the desire to become more and more what one is, to become everything that one is capable of becoming' (Maslow, 1954). These ideas 'comprise almost a programme of what life should be' (Cofer and Appley, 1964). This concept of self-actualization is popular with existential psychologists, but is regarded as mysterious and unmeasurable by their more scientific colleagues. Nevertheless, there is evidence that managers at least find this an important area of satisfaction and these ideas have attracted a lot of interest.

Goal-setting

Locke (1968) proposed that conscious goals or intentions affect task performance. It is necessary for a goal to be understood and accepted. This can be seen as an example of the arousal of motivation, or as making salient the link between performance

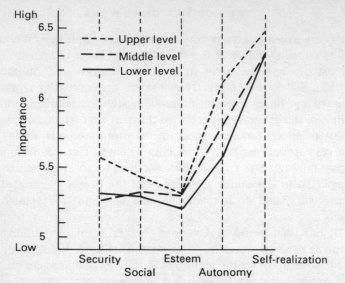

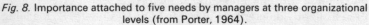

Fig. 8. Importance attached to five needs by managers at three organizational levels (from Porter, 1964).

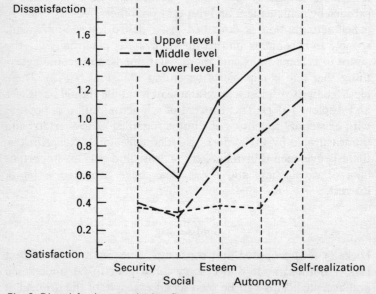

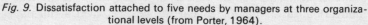

Fig. 9. Dissatisfaction attached to five needs by managers at three organizational levels (from Porter, 1964).

and rewards; for example goal attainment often leads to more pay.

There have been many studies of the effects of goal-setting on performance, and the effects have been impressively and consistently positive for a wide variety of jobs, from logging crews to managers and professors. Tubbs (1986) carried out a meta-analysis of eighty-seven studies and found that it has less effect on job satisfaction but is most effective under the following conditions.

(1) *Specific goals*. Goal-setting has more effect on performance if specific production targets are set as opposed to encouraging people to do their best, although this may involve close supervision. Goal-setting is part of the Management by Objectives (p. 220ff) plan for supervisors, and has usually been found to be effective. It is also part of the Scanlon Plan, and of the use by supervisors of group decisions (p. 225ff).

(2) *Difficult goals*. There is more effect on performance when difficult goals are set, as opposed to easy ones. Target goals may correlate with performance ·45 or more, although the goal should be acceptable, i.e. not too difficult, or it will be rejected.

(3) *Feedback*, or 'knowledge of results', increases the level of performance if people find they are lagging behind. The combination of goal-setting and feedback is more effective than either alone or neither, as is shown in Fig. 10. Here the results of appraisal interviews, conducted by trained managers using the various combinations and with three criteria of effectiveness are shown.

However, knowledge of results alone can improve performance in three ways. (a) If this information is given before the action is completed it enables the performer to correct his or her performance to make it more accurate. (b) If the performer is not highly skilled at the task and if knowledge of results is given after each performance, it helps him or her to learn to perform better. (c) Feedback can also arouse achievement motivation at work. A number of laboratory studies have shown that when the first two

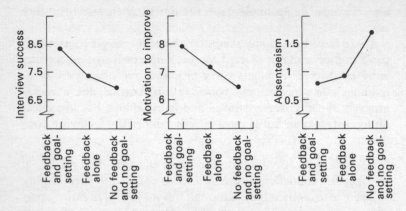

Fig. 10. The benefits of combining feedback and goal-setting (based on data from Nemeroff and Cosentino, 1979).

processes are eliminated knowledge of results increases work motivation. A field experiment was carried out in an American electric power station: instruments were installed which showed each man how efficiently his boiler was working, and daily and weekly records were announced; the result was a saving of $330,000 per year in coal consumption, as well as a drop in labour turnover. However, this was partly due to rivalry between men and between shifts, and to the men being given a new title of 'stoker operator' which increased their status (Bingham, 1932). Knowledge of results has also been found to improve the performance of *groups*. In a laboratory experiment it was found that feedback about task performance had most effect when group members were high in achievement motivation; when they were low in achievement motivation, feedback on the social interaction of the group had more effect (French, 1958).

(4) *Participation in goal-setting.* How can workers, at any level, be persuaded to accept goals? A number of field studies in working organizations have proved the effectiveness of participation by groups of subordinates. However, the overall results of seventeen such studies showed that participation had very little effect. This

may be because participation results in higher goals being set; with goals held constant six studies *did* find an effect of participation (Tubbs, 1986). If workers are properly consulted, and take the decision as a group, they become committed to a new group norm (p. 230ff).

Earley and Kanfer (1985) found that students accepted higher goals for their academic work and performed better if they could choose the specific goals, and choose their strategy, and if there was a role model. Wage incentives make people more likely to accept goals; there has to be some reward for trying harder and this is the most obvious one. On the other hand, incentives, if they are large enough, will increase performance if goal-setting is held constant (Pritchard and Curtis, 1973).

Organizational Commitment

Several kinds of commitment have been measured and studied, and five kinds have been distinguished (Morrow, 1983).

(1) Valuing work as an end in itself, e.g. the Protestant Work Ethic
(2) Commitment to a career
(3) Absorption and involvement in the job
(4) Loyalty to the organization
(5) Loyalty to the union

We shall discuss the 'Protestant Work Ethic' and 'commitment to a career' later, while 'absorption in the job' is much the same as intrinsic motivation.

Commitment or loyalty to the organization has attracted the most research interest, partly because of the power of this variable to predict work behaviour. It has been thought of in two ways: (a) calculative commitment based on rewards, and (b) affective commitment, based on non-instrumental attachment, through internalizing the values of the organization. Calculative commitment corresponds to Etzioni's utilitarian involvement (p. 199), to exchange theory and to investment theories. Affective involvement corresponds to Etzioni's moral involvement and to theories of emotional attachment. The most widely used measure of this is the Organizational Commitment Questionnaire (OCQ) (Porter *et al.*, 1974). Another way of measuring commitment is to ask about intentions to stay with the organization (Rusbult and Farrell, 1983).

Does organizational commitment affect work performance? There have been a number of studies of this, and generally the effects have been positive but rather weak. On the other hand, there is a very clear relationship with (low) labour turnover, which has been shown in longitudinal studies. The same has been found for absenteeism and lateness (Mowday *et al.*, 1982). In addition, organizational commitment predicts these aspects of performance rather better than job satisfaction does (p. 251ff).

In decentralized organizations commitment is greater for people who have a financial interest in the organization, when there is participation in decision making and experience of responsibility. Those factors have been emphasized as sources of work motivation by the Quality of Working Life movement (Mohrman *et al.*, 1986). It was shown above that participation in goal-setting decisions can result in somewhat higher performance. The participatory style of leadership works under certain conditions (p. 163ff); these effects are fairly modest compared with the more striking effects of industrial democracy (p. 222ff).

Commitment tends to be higher among those who are older, who have been with the organization longer, and who are strong in achievement motivation and other higher order needs and professional values. Commitment is greater if there are 'investments' in the job which would be lost on leaving – retirement and pension plans, provision of housing, skills or knowledge which could not be used elsewhere etc. The commitment of some Japanese workers to their firms is especially high, probably because of lifetime employment and other benefits (p. 330).

Commitment is greater when a person has made a free choice, is aware of what he or she has given up, when his or her decisions are made public, and if there are joining ceremonies or initiation rites (Salancik, 1977; Griffin and Bateman, 1986).

The Protestant Work Ethic

The Protestant Work Ethic (PWE) and its suggested role in the Industrial Revolution was discussed earlier. How important is it as a form of work motivation today? A number of questionnaire measures have been constructed which correlate quite well with one another. The best known is the nineteen-item scale by Mirels and Garrett (1971), although this and other scales have been criticized as sexist, as not displaying different dimensions, and as suffering from acquiescence response bias. The PWE is part of a wider syndrome of beliefs, attitudes and motivations: it is consistently found to correlate with achievement motivation, conservatism and internal locus of control. Individuals who are high on PWE value ambition and achievement, rather than pleasure and relaxation (Furnham, 1984c).

Does the PWE produce harder work? There is not a great deal of research here, but what there is has found that PWE correlates with such work behaviour as the rate of performance at laboratory tasks, and the improvement of performance following negative evaluation – especially if the subjects received unearned rewards (Greenberg, 1977), more constant attendance at work, and greater commitment to the organization (Furnham, 1984c).

'Workaholics' are probably extreme products of the PWE, although their intrinsic motivation is probably also very high. They work very long hours, spend little time with their families, have almost no leisure time, no holidays, and are clearly addicted to work. It is found that they enjoy their work very much, and are happy with their lives (Macholowitz, 1980).

Is the PWE declining in society? American surveys carried out since the early 1960s have found some decline in work values, for example the belief that hard work pays off and that work is central to life, although this decline has levelled off since the mid 1970s (Baron, 1983). Unemployment has become a more familiar and normal feature of life, and increasing numbers of people are living without work (p. 285ff). However, there are still many people for whom work is very important. We have seen that the majority of people say that they would work if it were not financially necessary. In addition, those not at work in fact do a lot of unpaid work of various kinds (p. 286ff). Employed men and women experience a great deal of value fulfilment through work, more than through leisure (Veroff *et al.*, 1981).

We shall see that most people do not like being unemployed, although they are quite happy being retired (p. 300). We shall also see that the most satisfying kinds of leisure are those that have some of the properties of work, such as doing things in a group, and engaging in constructive, goal-directed activity (p. 315ff). Furnham (1984c) argues that since the PWE is part of a general, conservative outlook, and is the product of certain styles of child-rearing, both of which show little sign of decline, it is here to stay.

Product value. Other values affect work motivation, such as the value of the product. In very primitive societies men and women work to provide food, shelter, clothes and household goods for themselves and their families, and this work is obviously important and necessary. In more advanced societies work is more specialized and the products are bartered or sold. Under modern conditions most people are paid for their work, but they are still interested in the social value of their goods or services, and will work harder if they think that the work they are doing is useful. For example, it was found that an experimental incentive scheme had no effect on girls engaged in a clearly useless task (unwrapping chocolates), but when they were given the task of wrapping they worked at three times the speed after the incentive was introduced (Wyatt, 1934). During the Second World War workers in British and American armament factories were shown the aircraft and tanks they were making, or were visited by aircrews, and this dramatization of the importance of the product is believed to have affected their motivation. Job satisfaction and motivation is related to a belief that the work done is important or useful. One of the Hackman job characteristics was 'task significance', the belief that the product would have a useful impact on others, one of the main factors producing 'meaningfulness' of the job.

Some working organizations are more obviously concerned with socially desirable purposes than others, for example hospitals, churches, voluntary organizations and universities. Etzioni (1961) called these 'moral' organizations, and suggested that they are different from others as members can be motivated by appealing to their commitment to the goals of the organization (p. 199).

6

WORKING GROUPS AND RELATIONSHIPS

The Importance of Working Groups

One of the central features of work is that it is nearly always done in groups. Groups are increasingly regarded as the building blocks of working organizations – the groups of workers under supervisors, autonomous work groups, teams, and groups of managers. A variety of social relationships are formed between supervisors and co-workers, and others. We shall see that these relationships have a special quality, making them different from relationships outside the work group.

Group behaviour in animals is presumably the result of natural selection, since operating in groups has biological advantages. This has led to the development of social needs in order to restrain aggression within the group and to encourage cooperation.

Groups can cooperate over large tasks, such as nest-building among animals, or mud-hut building in primitive societies. Some tasks simply require the combined efforts of a number of individuals; the division of labour allows the development of specialized skills which can then be combined to good effect. Special skills or knowledge may complement those of another member and may help achieve things which would otherwise have been beyond the powers of any one individual. The solutions found may become embodied in the practices of the group.

Groups are often under attack or have to deal with competition from other groups. Animals cling together when danger threatens, and humans seek the company of the group, for example soldiers bunch up under fire. Group members may also collaborate to protect their interests against action by management, the public or other groups.

The importance of groups and relationships was overlooked by traditional industrial psychology and is still being ignored in many current ways of observing working organizations. Work has always been done in groups and today continues to be done so even in highly automated plants. Sometimes, however, working groups have been disrupted through a failure to realize their importance in getting work done more effectively, as well as making it more enjoyable.

The working group is one of the main types of social group, and social interaction at work is one of the main forms of social interaction. A working group differs from other groups – friends, families, etc. – in that people are brought together in order to collaborate over work, and the pattern of relationships in the group is primarily determined by the task to be done. The interaction which takes place in a working group can be divided into 'work proper' and 'sociable'. It consists mainly of cooperation, help and information (work proper), and jokes, fooling about and gossip (sociable). By these various kinds of interaction the group members cooperate over the group task, and sustain a pattern of relationships between them. Social behaviour in the group can also be analysed in terms of the social system – its friendship structure, informal hierarchy, different roles and norms. One of the most important aspects of the social system is the *cohesiveness* of the group, i.e. the extent to which the group members are attracted towards the group and are prepared to cooperate with one another. Behaviour within groups is produced by two main kinds of motivation, and generates two kinds of satisfaction – one is to achieve task goals, the other to enjoy social interaction.

The impact of the internal dynamics of working groups on productivity was first suggested in the Relay Assembly Test Room at the Hawthorne works (Roethlisberger and Dickson, 1939). Five girls were moved into a test room and subjected to various changes in rest periods and refreshments; it was found that output increased by about 30 per cent, this being unrelated to any

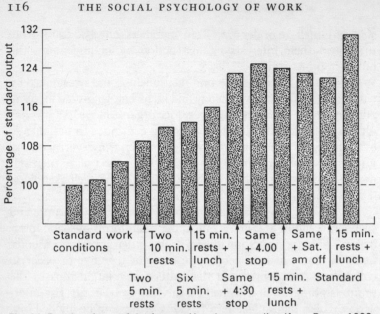

Fig. 11. Results of one of the famous Hawthorne studies (from Baron, 1986; based on data from Roethlisberger and Dickson, 1939).

ticular experimental conditions (see Fig. 11). It was concluded that the increase was in some way due to social factors, although there are other explanations (Argyle, 1953).

Different Kinds of Working Group

Most people work in groups, but the grouping can take a number of forms. In addition, working groups do not always have clearcut boundaries. We must distinguish between the groups that appear on organization charts, and the actual groupings of people who interact with one another with some frequency, like one another, or feel that they have something in common. There are people who interact who are not supposed to, and people who do not interact who *are* supposed to.

Formal and technological 'groups'. A number of workers under the same supervisor, on the same assembly line, or working in the

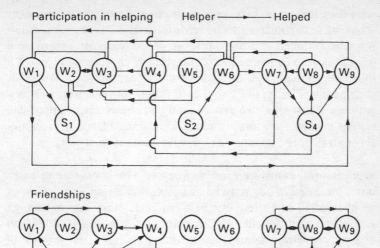

Fig. 12. Bank Wiring Observation Room, Hawthorne plant (from Roethlisberger and Dickson, 1939).

same room can be regarded as a group, even if there is little interaction between them.

Informal groups and networks. One way of discovering the real groups is to observe the frequency and type of interaction between individuals in a place of work. In the study of the Bank Wiring Observation Room at the Hawthorne plant it was found that there were two informal groups in this sense which engaged in friendly interaction, such as helping and playing games (Roethlisberger and Dickson, 1939). Of the twelve workmen (comprising the official work group), five made up a socially superior group A, four were in group B, and three did not interact much with either (see Fig. 12).

Another way of identifying informal groups is to ask people

who they talk to, or help, etc., most often. From this information it is possible to construct sociometric diagrams, or networks, showing who is linked to whom. If seven people work in a team on a joint project in the same room, they clearly comprise a group. If a manager knows people in several different departments, and deals with people who do not know each other, this is better seen as a network. Networks, like groups, can be cohesive and supportive; unlike groups they may include long lines of communication through the organization (Argyle and Henderson, 1985).

Work teams. Teams are groups of people who cooperate to carry out a joint task. They may be assigned to different work roles, or be allowed to sort these out between each other and to change jobs when they feel like it, for example the crews of ships and aircraft, research teams, maintenance gangs and groups of miners. Other kinds of teams may carry out specialist services, or may be engaged in negotiation (Payne and Cooper, 1981).

Decision-taking and managerial groups. Managers, administrators, planners and research workers spend a lot of time on committees or in working parties where the main activity is talking, with the aim of taking decisions or solving problems. The same person may belong to a number of such groups which come to life intermittently. In addition groups of managers constitute permanent groups, linked by proximity of offices, frequent interaction, and pursuit of the same goals.

The Productivity of Groups

Is it an advantage to work in groups as opposed to working alone? It depends on the nature of the task.

A group of workers may be doing independent work, for example craftworkers, or may cooperate to produce a joint product, such as those on an assembly line. With independent work, the presence of others may provide a motivating effect: this comes about partly from the sheer stimulating effect of other people, and partly through self-presentation, the desire to show the others how good you are, which may take the form of competition (Zajonc, 1965).

However, the very opposite effect, commonly known as 'social loafing', has been found in groups of workers cooperating within large groups, where individual effort cannot be clearly identified. In experimental tug-of-war teams it has been found that for each new person added, the others pulled 10 per cent less hard (Latané et al., 1979).

In teamwork it is not possible to compare individuals and groups, since usually one person would not be able to perform the task alone. Conversely, decision-taking and problem-solving groups are very interesting because the work of the group could be done by *any* member. We shall discuss below whether or not a group does the job any better.

However, the performance of work groups of all kinds is affected by the basic properties of groups in a number of similar ways.

Cohesiveness, the attraction of members to the group (p. 132ff). The most important effect of cohesiveness for work groups is that their members cooperate more; this has been found for many different kinds of work. This means that people help one another more, assistance is reciprocated, and there is more division of labour. A meta-analysis of 120 studies found that cooperation leads to greater productivity than either competition or individual motivation (Johnson et al., 1980). For example Van Zelst (1952) put together cohesive teams of bricklayers on the basis of a sociometric survey and found that over an eleven-month period the cohesive groups achieved 12 per cent more output, with a 16·5 per cent reduction in costs for materials, and a reduced labour turnover. Keller (1986) found that cohesiveness was the best predictor of the rated success of project groups. However, in some studies a *curvilinear* relationship has been found between cohesiveness and productivity, with a fall in output under very high cohesiveness – probably because too much time and effort is devoted to social activities. The productivity of cohesive groups may also depend on whether the work *entails* social interaction and cooperation is necessary (as in bricklaying), *prevents* it (as in weaving sheds), or is *irrelevant* to it (as in side-by-side assembly work). Cohesiveness increases output when the work requires interaction because it is socially motivated and a source of social satisfaction. Cohesiveness probably affects output most when helping is important. It was found, for example, that the foremen of 60 per cent of high-output sections in a heavy engineering factory said that their men were good at helping each other, compared with 41 per cent of foremen in low-output sections (Katz and Kahn, 1952). If individuals are working quite independently, and little help is needed, cohesiveness produces little advantage. Cohesiveness also affects the amount of conformity to group standards of output, and may result in output being restricted or kept to a high level, as was found by Seashore (1954) in a company manufacturing heavy machinery.

Labour turnover and absenteeism are lower in cohesive groups. A ratio of 3:1 in absence rates has been found between groups of different cohesiveness (Mann and Baumgartel, 1953). Which members are most likely to leave can be predicted from inspection of the sociogram – those who are isolated or rejected.

Group norms. There are norms about the best and easiest methods of working. They represent collective solutions to problems connected with the job, and usually go beyond the instructions of supervisors. There are norms about how fast people should work, how hard and how long, what standard of workmanship should be attained, what safety regulations should be enforced, etc. These may all be kept down to a reasonable level to make life comfortable without management penalizing any individual. Roy (1955) describes the elaborate set of dodges and fiddles invented in a machine shop to outwit the time-study man, keep up earnings and keep them steady (p. 90). Goffman (1961) maintains that in all 'total institutions' – and many workplaces are rather similar to these – the inmates resort to a variety of 'secondary adjustments', most of them infringing the regulations, in order to make life tolerable. Group norms include such secondary adjustments – the permissible limits of time-wasting, scrounging, cheating on

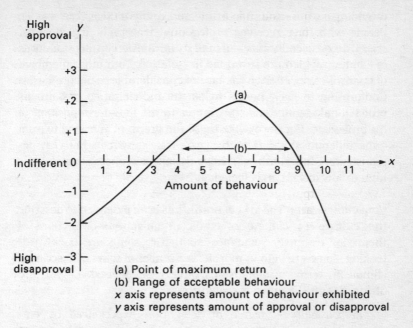

(a) Point of maximum return
(b) Range of acceptable behaviour
x axis represents amount of behaviour exhibited
y axis represents amount of approval or disapproval

Fig. 13. Jackson's return potential model (based on data from Jackson, 1965).

incentive schemes, etc.; management is compelled to go along with these practices, condoning them and attempting to manage them. For norms like these there is group approval of behaviour, e.g. a certain rate of work, within a certain range, but disapproval for those who do too little or too much. Jackson (1965) showed how this can be expressed in quantitative terms (Fig. 13).

On the other hand, the group norms may sustain a high level of output. Military units are sometimes based on a cadre of experienced men who have worked together before and who will pass on both working methods and standards of work. Groups of research workers have norms of high productivity in terms of number of publications, visits abroad, and so on. It has been found that productivity norms were set high in industrial working groups which were both cohesive and saw the company as providing a secure and supporting environment (Seashore, 1954). People who have received professional training – e.g. doctors, scientists or accountants – usually internalize certain standards of conduct, which are sustained in isolation from other members of the profession, often in the face of considerable social pressures. Conforming to such norms helps the individual to sustain his professional identity and contributes to the long-term position of his profession. For norms like these the graph of approval takes a quite different shape (March, 1954), as shown in Fig. 14, demonstrating that norms can have the effect of encouraging either high or low output and efficiency.

Corporate climates. The idea of norms has been extended to describe the 'culture' or 'climate' of whole organizations or sections of them; for example, some are apathetic, some are backward-looking, some are high in morale. A number of ways of describing climate in terms of dimensions have been devised. Litwin and Stringer (1968) found five dimensions:

(1) *Responsibility* – degree of delegation experienced by employees
(2) *Standards* – expectations about the quality of one's work
(3) *Reward* – recognition and reward for good work versus disapproval for poor performance
(4) *Organizational clarity* – orderliness (versus disorderliness)
(5) *Friendly, team spirit* – good fellowship, trust

Corporate climates can be looked at as anthropologists look at primitive tribes – in terms of particular beliefs and ideology, language symbols, ritual and myth (Pettigrew, 1979), although these are difficult to quantify.

It may be desirable to change a corporate climate, for example to make it more flexible and less rigid, to increase cooperation between groups, or to make employees more friendly. Kilmann (1985) devised twenty-eight items, and surveyed organizations to find the 'culture-gap' between what employees think the culture is and what it should be. Feeding back the survey results helps to change undesirable norms.

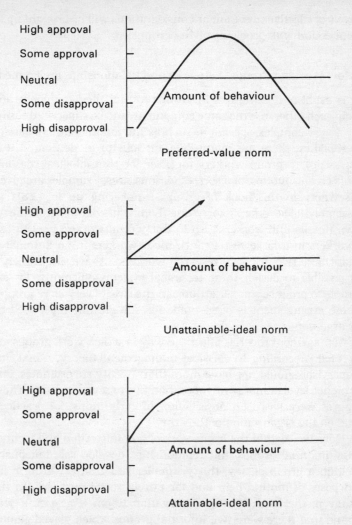

Fig. 14. Types of group norms (from March, 1954).

Organization of groups. The composition of groups is important. Tziner and Eden (1985) found that in three-man task crews the combination of individuals of high ability produced very high levels of effectiveness. Similar considerations will be brought up in connection with problem-solving groups.

How Working Groups, Networks and Relationships are Formed

It is usual to put workers in groups so that they can cooperate, help each other, use the same equipment, and be supervised easily. In a very complex operation, such as the manufacture of cars or aeroplanes, there are many different jobs to be done, and it is necessary to group workers together for technological reasons. This creates groups, of a sort, of various sizes. Examples are given elsewhere in this book of groups numbering up to 128 (car assembly-line workers), forty-one (Longwall coal-miners), thirty-two (textile mill workers), up to thirty (craftworkers), seventeen (workers in a large restaurant), nine (workers in an automated plant) and two or more (research workers). As we saw earlier, it is possible to design these technical systems differently, for example to produce smaller groups. In the case of very large groups, some arrangement is often made for sub-groups, supervised by charge-hands.

Management theories affect the way in which work groups are created. According to classical management theory, a first line supervisor should not have more than twenty subordinates, and a higher level manager no more than five to seven (p. 205). These figures were based on observation of early industrial practices, and on the organization of the army.

However, within the framework of administration and technology informal groups and relationships develop spontaneously. Within a group of, say, thirty, smaller sub-groups will form for purposes of mutual help and for purely social purposes. In the study of the Bank Wiring Observation Room (Fig. 12), it was found that there were two informal groups which played games, and that the people who played games also helped one another. Homans (1951) generalized this finding to form a theory about working groups. He argued that people come to work in order to get the work done and to be paid for it; they have to cooperate with other people, then discover that they like some of them, and start engaging in extra social activity with them. Working relationships are first brought about by the formal system of work, but are elaborated in several ways by informal contacts of different kinds. It is essential for social relationships to develop if cooperation at work is to succeed. This informal system then affects the pattern of work itself, through the formation of norms about how much work to do, the division into sub-groups, and the emergence of a status hierarchy not recognized by management.

Working Relationships

Relationships between people at work have a special quality. They differ from relationships outside, between friends and kin for example, in that they arise out of the work setting – the proximity of people at work, how they are brought together in the work-flow system, and their respective roles, as supervisor–supervised, co-worker, etc. The interaction is primarily to do with work, although there are purely social activities as well, and people value each other at work for their work competence, whereas this is not important for friends or kin. In particular person B is valued if he is helpful or instrumental to A's work goals, e.g. promotion prospects, or gives support in promoting some scheme (Gabarro, 1986).

Different views have been expressed about how important social interaction and relationships at work are. Goldthorpe *et al.* (1968) found that among car workers a majority were not bothered about being moved away from their present workmates, and many did not have friends at work (see Table 5). This is a very interesting set of data, but car assembly lines have about the worst possible conditions for the development of group cohesiveness (see below). A number of other studies have reported weak relationships at work (e.g. Wish *et al.*, 1976), but such studies have used students as subjects, and they may not have had much personal experience of long-term working relationships.

It is useful to distinguish between four main kinds of

Frequency of talking to workmates (%)

A good deal	Now and then	Hardly at all	Don't know and other
47	39	12	4

Feelings about being moved away from present workmates (%)

Very upset	Fairly upset	Not much bothered	Not bothered at all	Don't know and other
4	23	32	36	5

Number of workmates regarded as 'close friends' (%)

None	1 or 2	More than 2
45	25	31

Meetings with workmates regarded as close friends outside the plant (%)

Visiting at home	Arranged meetings	Semi-casual meetings	Purely casual meetings or none at all	No workmates regarded as close friends
16	11	11	17	45

Table 5. Social interaction between industrial workers (from Goldthorpe *et al.*, 1968).

relationships at work, at different levels of closeness (Argyle and Henderson, 1985).

(1) *Friends outside work.* People who become friends in the usual sense, i.e. are seen outside work; many friendships are formed at work. Managers and professional people make friends at work rather easily as a result of leisurely lunches and events which spouses can attend.

(2) *Friends at work.* Others who are seen regularly for lunch, or coffee breaks, but who are not seen outside the work place. Goldthorpe *et al.* (1968) found that while 55 per cent of car workers had one or more close friends at work, only 27 per cent saw them outside, and only 16 per cent invited them home.

(3) *Friendly working relationship.* Others who are seen quite often at work, and with whom social contacts are on the whole rewarding, but who are not seen regularly for lunch or coffee.

(4) *Work relationship only.* A minority whose company is not enjoyed, and who are only seen at all because of the work.

Activities	Modal rating of each work category*			
	Person 1	Person 2	Person 3	Person 4
(1) Helping each other with work	4·5	3	2	1
(2) Discussing work	5	4	2	1
(3) Chatting casually	5	4	3	1
(4) Having an argument or disagreement	1	1	1	1
(5) Teaching or showing the other person something about work	2	2	1	1
(6) Joking with the other person	5	4	2	1
(7) Teasing him/her	5	3	2	1
(8) Discussing your personal life	4·5	1	1	1
(9) Discussing your feelings or emotions	2	1	1	1
(10) Asking or giving personal advice	4·5	1	1	1
(11) Having coffee, drinks, or meals together	5	3	3	1
(12) Committee work, or similar discussion at work	1	1	1	1

*1 = never or very rarely; 5 = nearly all the time; 4·5 = collapsed rating of 4 + 5

Table 6. Frequency of activity according to type of work colleague (from Argyle and Henderson, 1985).

Social Interaction in Work Groups

There is a great deal of social activity at work, some of it necessary for the work itself, much of it purely sociable, especially among members of the immediate group. However, this varies with the strength of the social relationships formed.

Workers in a large fish-processing factory were surveyed and asked about the social activities which were shared with workers in the four categories described above, with the results shown in Table 6 (Argyle and Henderson, 1985). It can be seen that friends engaged more in both work-related activities and in purely social ones.

Work-related interaction. There is a great deal of talk at work, especially for managers. Rosemary Stewart (1967) asked 160 managers in British firms to keep diaries, and she found that they spent between 30 and 90 per cent of their time talking to other people, mainly, it can be assumed, about work.

One of the most important work-related activities is helping other people, often by giving information, instructions or advice. Indeed, this is the main advantage of group over solitary work. Another advantage is that workers can develop a sense of belonging or of comradeship by gossiping about what is happening in the organization.

Some work-related interaction is non-verbal – some kinds of help and instruction, coordinated activities such as lifting a load together, and rewards and punishments, approval and disapproval for working in the right or wrong way or too fast or too slow, for example.

Sociable interaction. Both during work breaks and during the work itself there is a great deal of irrelevant gossip, talk about personal life or problems, joking, games and general fooling. A delightful example is 'banana time', one of several diversions invented by a group of bored workers studied by Roy (1959). At a certain time each day one man would steal and eat another's banana; at another time someone would open a window, thus creating a draught and a row. They said, 'If it weren't for the joking and fooling, you'd go nuts.'

Again, some important forms of sociable interaction are non-verbal. It has been widely established that making friends, and expressing attitudes such as approval and disapproval are primarily done by facial expressions, mutual gaze, body language etc. (Argyle, 1988).

We saw above the extent of such important social activities as asking for personal advice and helping with work. We shall see below that social support at work is a major source of job satisfaction, and of both mental and physical health (p. 241, 274ff).

However, there is also conflict and friction within groups, and

(1) Accept one's fair share of the work load
(2) Respect other's privacy
(3) Be co-operative with regard to the shared physical working conditions (e.g. light, temperature, noise)
(4) Be willing to help when requested
(5) Keep confidences
(6) Work co-operatively despite feelings of dislike
(7) Do not denigrate to superiors
(8) Address the co-worker by first name
(9) Ask for help and advice when necessary
(10) Look the co-worker in the eye during conversations
(11) Do not be over-inquisitive about each other's private lives
(12) Repay debts, favours and compliments no matter how small
(13) Do not engage in sexual activity with the co-worker
(14) Stand up for the co-worker in his/her absence
(15) Do not criticize the co-worker publicly

Table 7. Rules for co-workers (from Argyle and Henderson, 1985).

there is more in working groups than among friends outside work since it is not so easy to leave, and because there are special sources of friction in the work place. In a study of the informal rules applicable in a number of different relationships it was found that the rules listed in Table 7 were relevant for co-workers and provided a key to the sources of friction at work. The existence of these rules indicates that friction may occur when fairness, co-operation, help, mutual support and privacy are brought into question (Argyle and Henderson, 1985).

Informal Communication Outside the Immediate Group

We have already described social behaviour in working groups; now we shall deal with interpersonal behaviour in the wider organization. Some communication goes through the formally approved channels; some does not. While it is essential to limit communication to definite routes, these are often inadequate, and extra 'informal' channels have to be created, for example between opposite numbers in different sections of an organization whose official channels are through a shared superior.

Lateral communication is to other members of the organization of about the same status, often in different sections or departments; such social contacts may be allowed for in the organization chart, but generally they are not. Inside working groups there is, of course, a lot of lateral communication, such as help and information about the job.

It is found in American firms that 41 per cent of messages sent or received by line production managers are with other managers at the same level (Landsberger, 1961). These contacts with other departments are needed to get the work done, and may be quicker than using official channels, but they involve conflicts of interest and outlook. The following social techniques are commonly used here: appealing to rules or a common authority; evading the rules, e.g. ignoring requests; relying on friendships, past or future favours, or using political allies; persuasion or showing the other the nature of the problem; trying to change the work-flow or other aspects of the organizational arrangements in an advantageous way (Sayles and Strauss, 1966).

. The working of organizations is often helped by lateral friendships, which create additional channels for cooperation and the flow of information. Another kind of lateral communication is the spread of information and rumours through the 'grapevine'. Such information travels surprisingly fast, and is sometimes quite accurate. It plays a useful function in satisfying curiosity and providing topics for enjoyable gossip, as well as keeping people informed about what is going on.

Downward communications are the main kind envisaged by classical organization theory and shown on organization charts. In fact such communications usually involve two-way interaction – questions lead to answers, and it is important to know whether instructions have been understood. We shall deal here with interactions which are *initiated* from above. First, instructions about the job: how this is done depends on the style of leadership used and the amount of delegation of responsibility practised in the organization, and can vary from orders to advice or guidance. This is discussed in more detail in Chapter 7. Second, information may be given about a subordinate's performance, as in an appraisal interview. Other information may be passed on about organizational matters or impending changes. Third, communications from experts need not be 'downwards' in terms of the organizational hierarchy, since the most expert person on a given matter is not always the most senior. Special lines of communication may be built up, in which people consult 'opinion leaders' on certain matters, who in turn consult even better informed experts. Fourth, two-step and indirect communication: a manager often wants to communicate with people two or more levels below him in the hierarchy; he has two main ways of doing so, neither of them very satisfactory. He can go through the 'usual channels' of speaking first to his subordinates, but at least four separate messages are needed before any feedback is received. There are also likely to be various delays and distortions; for example, the intermediate supervisor may re-interpret or play down the instructions; or when these arrive they may be so mysterious that 'research' has to be done to find out what they are really about. The senior manager can otherwise use letters, notices or the public address system, which is faster and avoids distortion; however, there is no way of verifying that the information has been received or understood. Such methods can be improved by asking supervisors to reinforce them, or encouraging subordinates to discuss any problems with their immediate superiors.

Upward communication. Seeking help: it might be expected that workers would often seek help from the most knowledgeable and experienced person available – their immediate supervisor. It has been found, however, that it is more common for help to be sought from equals (and for it to be reciprocated), apparently because this avoids loss of reputation (Blau, 1955).

Reporting progress: while it is essential for senior staff to have fast and accurate information about how the work is going, difficulties encountered, etc., it is often very difficult for them to find out what is going on. Bad news is likely to be ill received and may reflect on the competence of the person who brings it;

consequently such information is delayed and distorted – supervisors and managers are told what they want to hear, and when they are thought to be in a good enough mood to hear it. Upward communications are less accurate when the senders are keen to be promoted, and when they do not trust their supervisor or feel insecure (Jablin, 1979).

Suggestions and complaints: although people at lower levels may be reluctant to report difficulties or lack of progress, they like to be consulted, to air their grievances and to have their ideas heard at higher levels. There is a considerable gap in knowledge and understanding between superiors and subordinates which is often underestimated by the latter (Jablin, 1979).

Cohesiveness in Work Groups

Working groups, unlike groups studied in the laboratory, last a considerable period of time. During this time the social system of the group develops slowly. One of the most important aspects of this system is the *cohesiveness* of the group – the extent to which the group members are attracted towards the group.

With the passage of time a group is likely to become more cohesive, though some groups become more so than others, and the process can take place quite quickly. It is sometimes measured by the percentage of pair-bonds taken up within the group, e.g. sociometric choices; however, this measure does not include other sources of attraction to the job, e.g. to the task itself, or to the rewards obtained from belonging to the group. Other measures of cohesiveness sometimes used are feelings of loyalty or pride, the relative frequency of the words 'we' and 'I', or the amount of helping which occurs.

The causes of cohesiveness

(a) *Physical proximity* results in more social interaction, and in people seeing themselves as a group. Physical enclosure does more than this – there is a symbolic boundary, less effort is required for interaction, and there is some privacy. Sundstrom (1986) describes a number of cases in which cohesive groups were formed among clerical workers sharing the same offices. There were more friendship choices in small, enclosed offices than in large, open-plan offices (67 per cent versus 38 per cent of choices). In one case a group of clerical workers was installed inside a steel mesh cage; they worked hard and had time for a lot of fooling about, such as 'sniping' with elastic bands. The cage was altered so that the group came under improved surveillance from managers, who imposed better discipline but with the result that the group no longer kept up with work schedules. Some new developments in the organization of work are leading to the weakening of working groups – not only open-plan offices, but even more automation and home-working (pp. 50, 313).

(b) *Same or similar work.* Under traditional working arrangements a number of workers sit side-by-side doing identical or similar work, as in the Relay Assembly Test Room. This is a source of group formation since workers are faced by the same problems and can help each other in many ways. Other conditions of work may stimulate group formation, such as sharing the same supervisor.

(c) *Homogeneity.* Cohesiveness is greater in groups that are homogeneous in such things as race, age, social status, and in attitudes relevant to the work situation. If members are of unequal status, cohesiveness will be greatest when there is 'status congruence', i.e. those with high status in one respect (e.g. education or length of training) have high status in others (e.g. pay). Groups containing both skilled and less skilled members can be cohesive if their skills are complementary, although there will usually be two sub-groups. Informal bonds may depend more on similarity of status (directors talk to directors), or on common interest (e.g. between people of different status inside research groups, but with similar research concerns).

(d) *The work-flow system.* Cohesiveness is increased if the work-flow brings members together in a mutually rewarding or cooperative manner, rather than when it creates friction, frustration or competition. Some of the technological arrangements which make for good and bad relationships in groups were described earlier (p. 41ff). Cohesiveness will be greater if members can communicate easily with one another, less if distance or noise makes communication difficult. Goldthorpe *et al.* (1968) found rather low cohesion among car assembly workers (p. 126), but they recognized that stronger groups form where there is teamwork, as among miners, steel workers, dockers, railway workers, trawlermen, textile workers or printers.

(e) *The task or incentive system* may be so organized as to generate *cooperative* behaviour in the group, which in turn results in cohesiveness. Individual incentive schemes can create bad relations between group members if they are constantly competing to get the best jobs. A group bonus system, on the other hand, creates a shared group goal, so that the efforts of each member of the group will promote the interests of other members. However, there may be very strong pressures on slow workers to keep up, if they are holding back the whole team, as in assembly-line working. Small assembly lines have been found to work faster than larger ones, partly for this reason and partly because slow workers are forced out of the group. Another example of cooperation based on common tasks and incentives is the small research team, whose members all receive recognition and professional advancement from successful research results.

Cohesiveness develops if belonging to the group is *rewarding* in any of a variety of ways. A number of laboratory experiments have shown that members are more attracted to a group when it has been successful at a task in competition with other groups. In the work situation members are attracted to groups that are highly paid or enjoy high prestige for some reason.

(f) *Leadership.* The way in which the *leader* handles a group affects its cohesiveness. Democratic styles of leadership, encouraging group participation in decisions, increases it. Also useful are leaders who improve synchronizing by integrating newcomers and isolated people, who resolve conflicts, maximize interpersonal satisfactions, and skilfully handle disruptive group members.

(*g*) *Size.* If a group is too large it will divide into two or more sub-groups, usually based on differences of status, work, etc. Absenteeism is far higher in larger groups: in a British car factory it was found that the *rate* of voluntary absenteeism was four times as high in groups of 128 as in groups of four (Hewitt and Parfit, 1953).

(*h*) *Team development* has mainly been carried out with management groups. At first T-group methods (p. 192ff) were used, but these have given way to task-oriented, problem-solving and goal-oriented methods. A number of studies have reported positive results, but these have mainly been changes of attitudes rather than changes in behaviour (Woodman and Sherwood, 1980).

Group Norms

One feature of all small social groups is that they develop *norms*, i.e. shared ways of behaving, shared attitudes and beliefs, and shared ways of feeling and perceiving, particularly in relation to their central task or activity. For a group to function effectively and smoothly there has to be a certain amount of agreement on how to do things; on the other hand, it is important for the group to adapt to changing conditions, and change is brought about by individuals deviating from the norms.

Norms about work. There are norms about work – how fast or slow, how carefully done, etc. (p. 120ff).

Attitudes and beliefs. Group members come to hold the same attitudes towards management and unions, and about how difficult or satisfying their work is. They hold the same beliefs about what management policy is, and about economic or technical matters. Shared attitudes to other people or groups are of course neither true nor false; they simply represent shared feelings.

Allen and Stephenson (1983a) studied some of the attitudes

to other groups in industry. They found that on a scale measuring favourable attitudes to management versus favourable attitudes to unions, the attitudes of the four groups were as follows:

Shop stewards	− 19·6
Shop-floor workers	− 3·8
Supervisors	10·2
Managers	12·9

Beliefs, on the other hand, are often quite mistaken – they are myths about matters for which information is lacking, on matters too complex to understand. Workers may have theories about how managers become managers, while managers may have theories about why workers are so idle, and how things were better in former years. These myths are mainly incorrect theories about the social behaviour of other people.

Interpersonal behaviour. Social behaviour connected with work has to be regulated; work becomes easier and also more effective if group members agree to proceed in a standard way. There are shared codes of non-verbal signalling, norms about helping and cooperating, about sharing tips or bonuses, and so on. There are also norms about social activities not directly connected with work – what is talked about at coffee time, where to go for lunch, the shared games and jokes that make work more enjoyable and knit the group together. Norms about interpersonal behaviour make the behaviour of others predictable, and shared routines can be enjoyed. They also resolve interpersonal problems and avoid conflicts over such matters as helping, division of rewards, and allocation of work. There are norms about such matters as clothes and language, such as the use of private slang and technical vocabulary.

How norms are formed. Norms develop by a process of convergence, a kind of informal group problem-solving, in order to find the most satisfactory way to tackle work and social problems. The dominant members of the group have the most influence over these solutions. In addition there will be some carry-over from the practice of other groups to which members have belonged before. Sometimes deliberate decisions are made by the group. Sometimes, by showing the need for concerted action of some kind, particular incidents are important (Feldman and Arnold, 1983).

Why do members conform to norms? If the norm involves a topic important to the group it will be enforced by arguments, threats and punishment. For example, a 'rate-buster', the other workers believe, may provoke a retiming of jobs so that everyone has to work harder to earn the same amount as before. Rate-busters in the Bank Wiring Observation Room were 'binged', i.e. given a sharp blow on the arm, symbolizing group disapproval (Roethlisberger and Dickson, 1939). Deviants are often rejected, being 'sent to Coventry' in extreme cases. They receive no help when in difficulties, and may find that they get landed with the worst jobs, or that their work is interfered with, sometimes in ingenious ways. Group members may also conform because they think the majority view must be correct. This is likely when the other members are more expert or experienced, or have been found to be right before.

Acceptance of group norms commonly goes through two stages – compliance and internalization. In compliance a deviant conforms simply in order to avoid rejection by the group, but may behave quite differently when away from the group, or privately may think the group is mistaken. After being part of the group for some time, however, a slow change often comes about – the member starts conforming whether the group is looking or not, believes the group is right, and starts bringing pressure to bear on deviants. The member has now internalized the group norm.

The existence of group norms makes groups rather conservative; they create resistance to change and prevent their members from changing their behaviour or ideas. This is not the whole story however – groups also act as channels of communication through which new ideas can flow. If a member of the group has a new idea though, this will only be acceptable to the group under certain special conditions. Firstly, the originator has to be an informal leader, or regarded as expert on the topic in question (a case of role-differentiation). In either case the member's ideas have probably been found to work in the past, so that his or her behaviour is seen not as a failure to conform, but as a potentially valuable innovation. Hollander (1958) described this as 'idiosyncrasy credit' – the good group members build up 'permission' to deviate, and hence to introduce new ideas. Secondly, the new idea must seem to be to the advantage of group members, such as making life easier or being financially advantageous: a skilled innovator can persuade other members of the group that this is so.

Another important source of change is the influence of a minority of two or more (p. 146ff).

The Internal Structure of Working Groups

Work groups have a formal structure. This is partly based on the technical work-flow system, and partly on the different jobs, such as supervisor and inspector. However, this does not describe well the actual pattern of interaction inside the group. One way of tracing the internal structure is to find out which people help one another, or which people engage in other interactions, as shown in Fig. 12. The working bonds develop in the course of episodes, for example A manages to obtain technical help from B, this favour is later reciprocated, and A and B help and talk to each other on further matters (Farris, 1981).

The sum of pair-links adds up to a whole structure or network. This may contain *sub-groups*; two cliques can be seen in Fig. 12. Burns (1955) found two different kinds of sub-groups in a factory: one consisted of 'cabals' of ambitious young men who helped each other in their careers by providing information and social contacts; the other was comprised of 'cliques' of older men with no hope of promotion but who provided social support and formed a kind of alternative organization.

There are *popular people* with many links to others; several of these can be seen in Fig. 12. Members of work groups become popular mainly because of their ability and willingness to help others, but also through being centrally placed in some way, and through being socially rewarding – friendly, cheerful and so on (Argyle, 1983).

There is also a hierarchical structure inside groups. Leadership hierarchies form in purely informal groups, especially in large ones; the groups are more effective at task performance when this happens (Argyle *et al.*, 1981). Of course working groups usually have supervisors, and sometimes charge-hands looking after smaller units. Even so, some workers become more influential than others and an informal hierarchy develops. An individual becomes powerful in this way if he or she can help a lot of others, as described above. For example, in a committee the members with the greatest knowledge and whose ideas seem most useful will become informal leaders.

In a working group the informal leader will have most say in decisions about matters such as the rate of work, methods of working, allocation of work between group members, and so on. There may be more than one informal leader, different people dealing with different spheres of activity, as will be described below. In groups whose main activity is talking the more influential members talk more; when they talk they address the group as a whole whereas less important members address individuals, and when an influential person speaks the other members take more notice. In other kinds of groups the leadership hierarchy can be seen in the frequency of attempts to influence other group members, by the success of such attempts, and by which member is turned to when difficulties have to be dealt with.

In some studies it has been found that two informal leaders of rather different types have appeared; one is a *powerful* person who exercises influence over matters connected with the group task, the other is a *popular* person who is more concerned with problems internal to the group – the welfare of members and relationships within the group (Argyle, 1969). The work proper requires different skills, motivation and activities from the internal management of the group, and some studies suggest that it is impossible for an *informal* leader to perform both; however, it is essential that a *formal* leader should do both, and we discuss later how this can be done (p. 159ff).

There may be other kinds of role-differentiation in a working group as well as differences of power, status and popularity. This often exists already as a result of division of labour, but there are further unofficial kinds of role-differentiation as well. Informal task leadership may be divided between different experts in the group – one who knows about trade-union matters, another who knows about time-study procedures, and so on. Working groups may contain informal leaders who help the formal leader, and others who oppose him or her – leaders of the opposition. Unfortunately there is little systematic evidence about role-differentiation in groups; research on other kinds of groups and on industrial case-studies suggests the following as possibly common roles: (1) assistant task-leader, (2) socio-emotional leader, most popular, (3) leader of the opposition, e.g. shop steward, (4) isolate and (5) deviant, e.g. rate-buster (Argyle, 1969).

So far we have been describing the informal hierarchy which is based on differences of power or leadership. A related dimension is that of *status* – the extent to which a person is esteemed or admired by other members of the group. Differences of status in working groups are mainly based on level of skill, or past achievement in relation to the work of the group. It was found in a government employment office that there were clear differences of status and that officials approached others of similar status to themselves when needing help; to have gone to someone of higher status would have involved loss of esteem, although better advice could have been obtained (Blau, 1955).

Inter-group Conflict

The different groups at work have a lot to do with each other, as there are numerous contacts across group boundaries. Usually there is some degree of interdependence with other groups, for example a group may provide essential information, technical help, or may pass on a partly completed product. Sometimes membership of two groups overlaps, and often there are personal links in the informal network (Friedlander, 1986).

However, there is often friction or conflict between different groups. The most obvious case is management versus unions, but there is also conflict between line and staff, and between different

departments, such as production, sales and personnel, and between groups with different skills, or different levels of pay. When
a member of one group meets a member of another, they often
treat each other as group members rather than as individuals.
Batstone *et al.* (1977) found this happening in negotiations between managers and shop stewards; conflict occurred not between
individuals but between groups.

(1) *Negative attitudes to other groups.* There are several causes of
negative attitudes to other groups.

(a) *Difficulties of coordination.* The output of one group is the
input or raw material for another, e.g. architects' plans have to be
finished before construction can start. Or there are reciprocal
links, as between production and sales – the goods cannot be sold
until they have been produced, and production does not know
what or how much to produce until there are sales orders. Or it
may be unclear exactly which group is responsible for part of the
task, or which has final authority (Feldman and Arnold, 1983).

(b) *Competition for resources or rewards.* Two groups may be
competing for things such as space, equipment, funds or people,
and management may encourage this as a form of motivation.
Differences of pay can produce friction, especially when these are
seen as illegitimate. Brown (1978) studied the attitudes towards
other groups in an engineering factory in which there were three
departments with somewhat different skills, and different rates of
pay, which were regarded as wrong by the two lower-paid groups.
The higher groups thought that they were more skilled than the
lower ones, and that the pay differential should be greater. The
lower groups thought they were just as skilled as the higher ones
and that the pay differentials should be less. In a later study
Brown *et al.* (1986) found that groups made more favourable
judgements of their own group, especially when members saw
realistic conflict between their group and other groups.

(c) *Differences without competition.* It has been found in a number of laboratory and field studies that in the absence of any actual

competition group members will make preferential evaluations of in-group members, and preferential treatment in the allocation of rewards will occur. What seems to happen is that group members exaggerate the differences between their own group and other groups, using dimensions which they regard as valuable. They also exaggerate the similarity within groups. The motivation for all this is believed to be enhancing self-esteem (Tajfel, 1978). Low-status groups discover dimensions on which they are better than higher status groups; for example in one study East African Hindus believed that they were superior in spiritual, social and practical fields to whites (Mann, 1963). However, Brown *et al.* (1986) found that such group identity processes were a very minor source of inter-group differentiation for industrial groups.

(*d*) *Lack of social contact.* Negative attitudes between groups are more likely to build up if the groups have little social contact. An example is the three groups of workers observed in the Longwall coal-mining study (p. 42).

(*e*) *Cohesiveness.* It has sometimes been found that in-group favouritism is associated with greater rejection of the out-group, and both of these with greater cohesiveness. More recent research has established that cohesive groups do make biased and favourable evaluations of the in-group. However, they do *not* have negative attitudes to out-groups unless there is also conflict or competition (Stephan, 1985).

Allen and Stephenson (1983a) devised a measure of Inter-group Understanding (IGU), based on the inaccuracy with which one group, e.g. shop stewards, perceived the attitudes of other groups, e.g. managers or workers. They found that IGU was greater in larger firms and correlated (0·37) with the amount of friction, for example disciplinary dismissals, written warnings, etc. (Allen and Stephenson, 1983b).

(2) *Minimizing inter-group friction.* What can be done to minimize inter-group friction?

(*a*) *Increase interaction between members of the groups.* A good example of how this can be achieved is shown in the Longwall coal-mining study in which members of three groups were reorganized so that they worked on each shift.

(b) *Sources of friction* can be removed by avoiding competition, unfair salary differentials, and better management of task coordination.

(c) *Shared goals.* Both sides can be made aware of shared goals, e.g. the prosperity of the firm, the welfare of workers.

Decision-taking, Problem-solving and Creative Groups

Committees and working parties of various kinds do their work by talking; this makes them different from other kinds of groups in a number of ways, although all groups do some talking and take some decisions. These groups are primarily concerned with coming to agreement on issues over which individuals or groups may disagree. Committees also have to solve problems and think of new ideas, indeed the latter course is often taken in order to find a solution to a problem which is acceptable to most members. In addition, particular aspects of problem-solving are often delegated to sub-committees. *Problem-solving groups*, such as sub-committees and working parties, have some resemblance to other work groups in that intellectual work is performed: they may have to collect information, study reports, and consider alternative solutions. *Creative groups* include research workers, advertising men, film producers, etc. These groups do other things besides talking, but there are usually meetings at which it is hoped new ideas will arise. The same is true of problem-solving groups and, to a much lesser extent, committees.

One of the most striking differences between all these and other kinds of working groups is that the work of talking groups could be done by an individual.

(1) *What is gained by using groups?*

(a) *Quality of decisions.* Laboratory experiments find that solutions arrived at by groups are usually better than those of the average individual, but not as good as those of the best group members (Shaw, 1981). In a study of groups of managers tackling management problems, Webber (1974) obtained this pattern of results, although the groups took longer. However, he found that the benefits of working in groups were greater for the younger managers, and that for these the group solutions were better than those of the best individual member (see Table 8).

(b) *Creativity*. In some groups, like those in research and advertising, the emphasis is on creativity. Osborne (1957) introduced the practice of 'brainstorming' in which critical judgement is suspended and members are encouraged to throw out ideas and develop one another's suggestions, leaving evaluation until later. When the results of brainstorming groups have been compared with those of individuals, however, they have usually been found to be inferior (e.g. Taylor *et al.* 1958). The trouble is that brainstorming groups often get into a rut and pursue the same line of thought; in the absence of disagreement, ideas do not get properly assessed, and fear of covert criticism inhibits the production of new ideas (Feldman and Arnold, 1983). It seems that individuals are usually better at thinking up new ideas, and that group meetings are needed to evaluate them.

(c) *Riskiness*. Early experiments showed that when subjects make individual decisions and later reconsider their decisions in groups there is often a so-called 'risky shift' to a less safe decision. However, later studies found that on some issues cautious action was favoured. The more general phenomenon is one of 'polarization'; knowledge of the views of other group members, or discussion with them, can result in a shift towards any original norm held by the group. For some topics this means that the shift will be in a risky direction. These shifts take place partly since more of the arguments come from one side, partly from a desire to conform to or to exceed this norm (Moscovici, 1985).

An historically famous risky decision was taken in 1961 by John F. Kennedy and his advisors when they decided to back the

Subjects	Mean score (no. correct)	Mean time (min.)	Mean group effectiveness (group score minus mean of individuals in group)	Mean group excellence (group score minus best individual score in group)
Executives (mean age 47)				
40 indiv.	13·4	4·0		
8 groups	15·8	9·0	+ 1·8	− 1·4
Middle managers (mean age 40)				
55 indiv.	13·3	4·2		
11 groups	15·1	6·2	+ 1·7	− 2·9
Young managers (mean age 32)				
90 indiv.	13·2	4·2		
18 groups	15·3	5·3	+ 2·3	− 3·1
MBA students (mean age 25)				
90 indiv.	14·3	4·7		
18 groups	16·3	6·0	+ 3·7	0
BS students (mean age 20)				
40 indiv.	11·5	5·5		
8 groups	17·5	6·0	+ 3·5	+ 1·5

Table 8. How age/position level is related to individual and group performance (from Webber, 1974).

Bay of Pigs invasion of Cuba. Janis and Mann (1977) suggest that the explanation for this was that an inner decision-making group developed too much cohesiveness and conformity, and as a result engaged in what the authors called 'groupthink'. A group comes to see itself as invulnerable; there is rationalization of blind spots; it ignores ethical issues; stereotyped out-groups are seen as evil, weak or stupid; a lot of pressure is put on dissenters, who are regarded as disloyal; any doubts are not voiced, and there is an illusion of unanimity. The result can be 'irrational and dehumanizing actions directed against out-groups'.

There are a number of industrial examples of groupthink, e.g. the introduction of very unsuccessful models of cars (Feldman and Arnold, 1983). These problems can be avoided by restyling the way committees are chaired (see p. 177ff).

(d) *Acceptance of decisions.* An important advantage of group decision-taking is that those who took part understand why the decision was taken and why alternative solutions were rejected; they are therefore more likely to accept the decision, and are more prepared to implement it. It is no use taking good decisions if others are unwilling to carry them out. Lawler and Hackman (1969) carried out a field study in which a bonus scheme was introduced to reduce absenteeism among janitors. The same scheme was developed with the participation of janitors in one part of the company and imposed on others in another part. With participation there was a much more positive response to the scheme; without participation it was regarded with anxiety and suspicion.

The participatory style of supervision, sometimes including group decision techniques, has been found to be effective, under certain conditions (p 163ff).

(e) *Do minority views have any impact?* One difficulty with taking decisions in groups is that norms may persist after they have become outdated, and minority views may be suppressed. Groupthink is an example of the unwise suppression of criticism and alternative solutions. However, recent research on the effect of minorities in groups has shown that they are often very influential. If a problem is new, and there are as yet no established norms, a consistent and determined minority may succeed in crystallizing the new norm around their views. If there is a majority view a consistent minority who give the impression of confidence and certainty, and who refuse to compromise, can affect the views of the majority. While the majority may produce public compliance, the minority can produce conversion, a change in the way the others think about the problem, by consistently presenting an alternative view. This effect is greater if there is a minority of two or three rather than one, if they are flexible, and if their views appear to be objective, rather than based on self-interest (Moscovici, 1985; Maas and Clark, 1984). In addition, it is up to the person chairing the group to make sure that minority views are properly aired.

(*f*) *Composition of decision-taking groups.* Talking groups should not be too large; five is the size people prefer, and three to six is found to work well, although groups are often larger (Thomas and Fink, 1963). With six members there is enough variety of knowledge or expertise for most purposes. Problem-solving groups should be composed of members with varied skills, but should be homogeneous in other respects, so that cohesiveness can develop easily. Creative groups, however, produce better ideas if there is initial disagreement, despite the difficulties of interacting. But if there are large differences in age, seniority or status a steep informal hierarchy will be formed, which generally inhibits discussion.

7

SOCIAL SKILLS AND WORK

The Importance of Social Skills

Elton Mayo, one of the founders of the Human Relations movement, maintained that all that was needed to improve the
effectiveness and happiness of working organizations was to
improve the social skills of those who ran them, particularly supervisory skills. The same assumption may be found in the writings
of later workers in this tradition. Likert (1961), for example,
describes how organizational structures can be changed by
changing the social relationships in the hierarchy. While fully
accepting the importance of social skills at work, we would argue
for a broader approach that includes the possibility of other kinds
of organizational change, for example of the span of control and
the number of levels in the hierarchy, of changes in technology
and the work-flow system, and of changes in incentives.

For many years industrial psychologists concentrated their attention on the performance of manual skills, and devised improved
methods of working and training. No interest was taken in the
more responsible and highly paid supervisors and managers, who
had to learn *their* skills as best they could while on the job. It is
not only supervisors and managers who have to deal with people
as part of their work: everyone has to. Research is carried out by
teams, while manual workers work in groups; however, both
have to deal with co-workers, and have to collaborate with a
variety of other people such as their immediate superiors, shop
stewards, the personnel department, inspectors, and others. For

everyone work involves both dealing with people and dealing with physical objects, papers or ideas.

But how important are social skills? No one disputes that they have some effect, but the question is how much. There is little doubt that, for example, a supervisor with the worst conceivable style of supervision will have a negative effect on output, job satisfaction, etc.; in fact exceptionally bad social skills constitute a special problem, which will be discussed later (p. 195ff). It is more useful, however, to consider variations within the normal range of social performance which is commonly found in working organizations.

The best way of finding out the effects of different social skills is to compare the effectiveness of people whose styles of social behaviour differ.

(1) *The effects of supervisory skills on work groups*

(a) *Output.* The effect of supervision on output varies greatly under different conditions. Likert (1961) reports a number of studies showing large differences in the productivity of similar departments whose supervisors used different styles of supervision, e.g. democratic versus autocratic techniques. In one of these studies the rates of output of different clusters of departments were 6, 40, 46 and 71 respectively. However, the first cluster consisted of two departments which were very hostile towards their supervisors; none the less, the ratio of 40:71, or a 78 per cent increase, is still rather greater than has been found in most studies. The effects of supervision are much less than this where work is machine-paced (Argyle *et al.*, 1958).

(b) *Job satisfaction.* Fleishman and Harris (1962) found a ratio of about 8:1 in the number of complaints made under different kinds of supervision. If 'initiating structure' (p. 160) was too high, or 'consideration' (p. 161) too low the grievance rate rose.

(c) *Labour turnover.* A similar pattern, which rose sharply at very low levels of supervisory consideration, was obtained for labour turnover. However, the effect became marked only for the very worst supervisors – things have to get pretty bad before people go as far as leaving (Figs. 15 and 16).

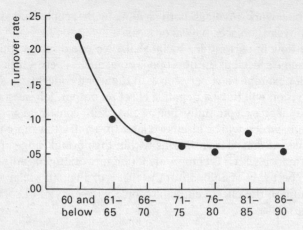

Fig. 15. Consideration (from Fleishman and Harris, 1962).

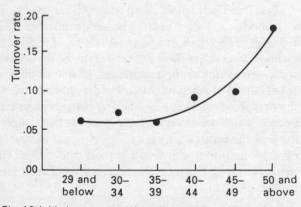

Fig. 16. Initiating structure (from Fleishman and Harris, 1962).

(*d*) *Absenteeism.* Similar findings have been obtained for absenteeism. In the famous Relay Assembly Room at the Western Electric Company, absenteeism dropped to one-fifth of what it was before the girls were moved into the test room (one-third the rate for the rest of the factory), as did the amount of illness and lateness (Roethlisberger and Dickson, 1939). Other studies have obtained similar results.

(2) *The effects of other social skills.* There is a very wide variety of social skills to be found in work situations but it is difficult to measure the effectiveness of most of them.

(a) *Selling.* Argyle, Lalljee and Lydall (in Argyle, 1983) studied the amounts sold by the best and worst sales personnel behind the same counters in department stores. Averaged over a period it was quite common for there to be a ratio of 4:1 in the amounts sold.

(b) *Selection interviewing.* (This involves the skill of controlling the candidate and asking the right questions, and also the skill of assessing him or her correctly.) The best index of the effectiveness of an interviewer is how much the accuracy of prediction over that made on the basis of application form, tests, etc. can be increased (p. 79ff). While some can raise it from about 0·4 to 0·7, others *reduce* it to below that of the dossiers. They also vary in their power to attract people to the organization; it is commonly reported that the number of candidates accepting invitations to second interviews in the same organization varies from 25 to 75 per cent for different interviewers.

(c) *Working abroad.* There is a very high 'failure rate' for people working abroad. As many as 60 per cent of managers posted to parts of the Middle East or Far East return home before their one- or two-year term is completed, because either they or their families cannot cope with the other culture.

The Nature of Social Skills

Social competence is an individual's ability to produce the desired effects on others in social situations. We have just seen that supervisors vary greatly in their capacity to affect productivity and job satisfaction. Similarly sales people vary in how much they can sell, and negotiators vary in the bargains they can attain. How are these results achieved? The basic way to find out which type of behaviour makes a difference is to compare the performance of those who are successful with that of those who are less successful. In order to do this we need to know what to look for, and to understand the basic processes of social interaction.

Social skills are, in certain respects, similar to motor skills, such as cycling or driving a car. In each case the performer is trying to influence events in the outside world, either a machine or other people. In order to do so he or she performs a continuous sequence of motor responses so that if earlier responses are not wholly effective they are modified to get better results, for example steering a car in the right direction (Fig. 4, p.40).

An example of such corrective action for a social skill is dealing with a person who talks too little: the structure of utterances can be changed towards easy, open-ended questions, and any replies can be rewarded by eye-contact, smiles, head-nods, or encouraging noises. Both motor and social skills have a hierarchical structure; the smaller units become integrated into habitual, automatic sequences, each with their own feedback loops – a cyclist does not have to think about each turn of the pedals. The larger units are less habitual, more under conscious control, and subject to deliberate plans of action and the rules governing behaviour. Any particular motor or social skill consists of a coordinated sequence of responses, the collection of feedback, and learned sequences of corrective action.

The moves made by social interactors are *verbal* and *non-verbal*.

(1) *Verbal skills*. Verbal moves made by social interactors include instructions, questions, information and informal chat. There are subtle differences between orders, suggestions and instructions. These can be given with differing degrees of persuasiveness, by explaining the reasons for the order, and the advantages to the recipient if it is carried out, or what will happen if it is not. The actual repertoire of moves is rather different for various social tasks, such as negotiating, selling and interviewing.

The social skill performer is trying to influence the other, partly by words. An interviewer is trying to obtain information: he or she may need to take corrective action, as described by the social skills model, for example to get the candidate to talk more (open-ended questions, reinforcement), or to give better answers (follow-up questions). The performer may follow a plan, for example an interviewer follows a sequence of topics; in a personnel interview it is a good idea to ask the subordinate for an explanation first, later shifting the conversation to a joint piece of problem-solving. Some situations have special sequences which are often followed, as for example in management–union negotiation (p. 179ff). However the sequence of utterances is governed by rules – each move should be relevant and responsive to what has gone before, and should provide enough information but not too much (Grice, 1975).

(2) *Non-verbal skills.* These components of social performance are less obvious, but are quite central to social performance. They play several important roles.

(a) *Interpersonal attitudes* such as friendly–hostile, inferior–superior and sexual attraction are mainly signalled non-verbally. In laboratory experiments at Oxford it was found that non-verbal signals for interpersonal attitudes had about five times as much effect as equivalent verbal signals; different verbal messages were delivered in different non-verbal styles by speakers who were seen on video and rated by viewers (Argyle *et al.*, 1970). However, it is important for supervisors, for example, to be both friendly and dominant; this combination is difficult for the face to express, but much easier for the voice (Argyle, 1988).

(b) *Emotional states* are similarly communicated by non-verbal cues, such as facial expression and the tone of voice used. However, 'display rules' control how far an emotional state is actually expressed. But the concealed state may be expressed via 'leaky' channels, such as the voice and body, which are much less well controlled than the face.

(c) *Self-presentation*, i.e. sending messages about the self, about how an interactor sees him- or herself, and how they would like to be treated, is mainly done non-verbally. The interactor might indicate that he or she is a manager or a research worker. The main signals used are clothes, tone of voice and general manner – there is a taboo in many parts of the world on direct verbal self-presentation.

(*d*) *Supporting speech*. A speaker adds vocal emphasis, pitch and gestures, and periodically looks at listeners to elicit feedback. Feedback is provided by head-nods, facial expressions of agreement, surprise, etc. and short vocalizations. The synchronizing of speech is managed partly non-verbally – at the end of an utterance a speaker makes a fall in pitch, ends gestures, and looks at the other – as well as giving a grammatical ending.

There is a general dimension of positive non-verbal behaviour – consisting of a high rate of smiling, looking, head-nods and other bodily gestures – together with more speech, and speech which is louder, faster and has more intonation. Those who are high on this dimension are more influential and socially skilled in other ways, those who are too low tend to be socially unskilled (Argyle, 1988).

Interactors have to deal with a range of social situations, some of which they may find difficult, or even avoid, such as disciplining a subordinate, reporting bad news to the boss, or presenting to audiences. Every situation has some specific goals for the various participants, and they use special repertoires of behaviour and may require special skills which need to be mastered. Every situation has special rules; it is widely agreed that certain things should or should not be done. Most of these rules represent solutions to common problems, just as the rule of the road prevents collisions. They are also like the rules of games – the game cannot be played unless people abide by the same rules.

To be effective at a social skill one should be aware of the elaborate set of rules governing it. For example, an interviewer should be aware of the conventions of the interview – that personal questions may be asked if they are relevant to the selection, that the interviewer can take notes, etc. Training courses on dealing with people from other cultures or social classes include information about the relevant customs and conventions, for example when buying from and selling to Arabs (Argyle *et al.*, 1981).

Most social behaviour takes place with people in certain relationships – e.g. with co-workers, subordinates, superiors, clients.

These relationships can be placed along dimensions such as friendly–hostile, and superior–subordinate (Wish *et al.*, 1976). However, this does not quite capture the distinctive properties which each relationship possesses. It requires effort and skill to build up and maintain any relationship; often this process fails and job performance suffers; complete breakdown can be very serious, and may result in the offender having to be replaced. Part of the key to establishing a relationship is that each participant must receive a sufficient balance of rewards minus costs. These rewards will be partly based on help with the job, and are partly purely social. The balance of rewards which is received must be seen to be fair in relation to what others receive and in relation to the efforts put in – as prescribed by equity theory (p. 94ff).

There is usually a certain amount of conflict in relationships, and this is particularly true of work relationships. In superior–subordinate links there is frustration for the subordinate over having too little power, and apparently poorer outcomes; the superior may be frustrated by the incompetence or lack of motivation of subordinates. Part of the solution to these relationship problems lies in keeping to the informal rules which develop. So tensions between work-mates can be controlled if rules about fairness and helping one another, and about behaviour with third parties, such as keeping confidences, are observed. We shall discuss the rules for superiors later (p. 157). The other general solution to relationship difficulties lies in using the most effective social skills available. These are not entirely covered by the rules, since they involve details of performance and of the conduct of social encounters (Argyle, 1983).

Supervision

A supervisor is the first-line leader, in charge of those who are doing most of the work. Classical organization theory recommended that he or she should not be in charge of more than twenty subordinates, but in production lines, for example, this number may be exceeded. Supervision of groups is one of the central social skills connected with work. We traced earlier the changing relationships between supervisors and working groups in different historical periods. The supervisor has two main tasks – (1) to see that the work is done properly, i.e. to keep up productivity, and (2) to look after the welfare of the group members, i.e. to keep up job satisfaction.

There is a lot of evidence that the relationship between supervisors and their subordinates is a difficult one. It is often felt, by subordinates, that it is a relationship which generates a lot of conflict, but very little satisfaction, and that it is hostile rather than friendly (Argyle and Furnham, 1983). The reason is not hard to find: a supervisor has power to reward and punish, which he or she may or may not use fairly. Subordinates may find it annoying that the supervisor is able to give orders and is paid more. On the other hand, supervisors *can* be a major source of job satisfaction and mental health. The way to achieve this is by using the optimum supervisory skills. Tjoswold (1985) carried out an experiment in which one subject supervised another. He found that supervisors who had been given a lot of power, under cooperative conditions, used their power constructively and helped their subordinate to improve his performance.

One problem about discussing supervision is that the actual job done by supervisors varies from one work setting to another (Thurley and Wirdenius, 1973). However, Child and Partridge (1982) did not find much variation with the technology, but a lot of informal variation in supervisors' jobs, as a result of different informal arrangements with managers, and supervisors' willingness to take on different parts of the job. Some had more technical knowledge than managers, which gave them more authority. However, a universal feature of the job is getting subordinates to work effectively, summarized under the dimension known as initiating structure (p. 160). Looking after subordinates is a second universal feature and is summarized under 'consideration' (p. 161). In addition supervisors have regular jobs to do, such as programming computers, ordering supplies and keeping records. And they are constantly having to deal with breakdowns and crises of a variety of kinds. In modern industry some of the work of traditional supervisors is done for them by impersonal mech-

(1) Plan and assign work efficiently
(2) Keep subordinates informed about decisions affecting him/her
(3) Respect the other's privacy
(4) Keep confidences
(5) Consult subordinates in matters that affect him/her
(6) Encourage the subordinate's advancement
(7) Advise and encourage subordinates
(8) Fight for subordinate's interests where necessary
(9) Do not be jealous of the subordinate's ability
(10) Do not give commands without explanation
(11) Be considerate regarding the subordinate's personal problems
(12) Look the subordinate in the eye during conversations
(13) Do not criticize the subordinate publicly
(14) Do not visit the subordinate socially, unannounced
(15) Do not supervise too closely
(16) Do not engage in sexual activity with the subordinate
(17) Repay debts, favours and compliments
(18) Do not discuss personal finances with the subordinate

Table 9. Rules for work superiors (from Argyle and Henderson, 1985).

anisms of control, such as automated and machine-paced equipment, and incentive schemes. However, supervisors are still needed because of unforeseen contingencies, changing environmental conditions, and the various problems of individuals that have to be dealt with.

An important part of a supervisor's job is taking decisions; some of these affect subordinates directly, and it takes some skill to carry them out. For example, the supervisor may have to decide whether a worker should receive some training, be allocated overtime, be upgraded, or disciplined, and may have to deal with wage queries, or adjust the times of jobs (Child and Partridge, 1982).

Lay people, who will have had some experience of supervising and being supervised, have clear and agreed ideas about the rules which supervisors should follow. In a study in the Oxford area it was found that the rules shown in Table 9 were endorsed for supervisors (Argyle and Henderson, 1985). This is a very useful guide to how supervisors should behave. However, these rules do not show exactly *how* it should be done, or the detailed pattern of social performance needed. And they do not say how the behaviour of supervisors should vary with the situation – which we shall discuss later as 'contingencies'.

One dimension of supervisory style. Employee-oriented versus task-oriented leadership. Early research used a single dimension when considering supervisory style. Some studies, although not all, found that task-oriented supervisors had more productive groups, but that employee-oriented ones had more satisfied groups (Bass, 1981).

This dimension was used by Fiedler (1967) who produced the first 'contingency' theory of supervision, i.e. that the best style varies with conditions. He devised the Least Preferred Co-worker (LP C) score, in which supervisors are asked to think of the worker with whom they are least able to work well, and rate him or her on scales such as 'cooperative–uncooperative'. A high score is taken to mean that the supervisor is person-oriented, rather than task-oriented. Fiedler's theory is that person-oriented supervisors are most effective when conditions are moderately favourable, while task-oriented leaders are more effective when conditions are clearly favourable or clearly unfavourable. Things are said to be favourable when the supervisor has a good relationship with group members, the task is structured, and when the leader has strong power. A great deal of research has been carried out on this model, often with results confirming it (Bass, 1981). It has also been much criticized: the findings have been very variable, sometimes negative; it has not been shown that these leadership styles cause productivity; and, rather than vice versa, the LP C score has been found to vary for the same leader when with different groups (Schriesheim and Hosking, 1978). It may be added that the theory has nothing to say about job satisfaction and related variables, and it confuses two dimensions of supervision which are quite independent, and both of which are important.

The scheme has led to a novel form of management training known as Leader Match. Trainees are presented with a series of cases, are trained to diagnose them in terms of the three dimensions, and are taught how to change situations to fit their own preferred style (Fiedler and Chemers, 1984).

Initiating structure and consideration. Two dimensions of supervisory behaviour have been identified in studies of industrial and military groups: *initiating structure*, i.e. concern with the group task, and *consideration*, i.e. looking after the group members (Halpin and Winer, 1952).

There are certain problems about undertaking research in this area. One method of studying these skills is to compare a number of supervisors in the same or similar organizations to see if there is any correlation between their style of supervision and their effectiveness. The difficulty with this method is that the direction of causation is not clear: if there is a correlation between output and consideration this might be because supervisors become more rewarding when their subordinates work hard, or it could be because some third factor affects both output and supervisory behaviour. Another research method avoids this problem: experimental changes are introduced, either by shifting supervisors round, or by retraining some of them. Now another problem arises: any changes that appear may be due to 'Hawthorne effects', i.e. are the result of there being an experiment and special attention being paid to those involved. The results of field experiments are only fully satisfactory if two or more different experimental conditions generate quite different effects in terms of productivity etc. Difficulties also arise in assessing the different styles of supervisory behaviour. It is rarely possible to observe this behaviour, while reports by subordinates are liable to be biased and may also produce spurious correlations with questionnaire measures of job satisfaction (for example, happy subordinates may ascribe supposedly good practices to their supervisors, but this is not a valid measure of supervisory behaviour as subordinates may give socially desirable answers). However, much of the research in this area has used a set of ratings known as the Leader Behavior Description Questionnaire (LBDQ) (Fleishman, 1953), which has undergone various improvements (Bass, 1981). The LBDQ allows less biased and more effective information to be collected, and as such is a relatively reliable way of measuring supervisory behaviour.

We shall now consider the effects of the two dimensions of

(1) Lets group members know what is expected of them
(2) Encourages the use of uniform procedures
(3) Tries out ideas on the group
(4) Makes attitude clear to the group
(5) Decides what will be done and how it shall be done
(6) Assigns group members to particular tasks
(7) Makes sure that role in the group is understood by the group members
(8) Schedules the work to be done
(9) Maintains definite standards of performance
(10) Asks that group members follow standard rules and regulations

Table 10. Items from the Leader Behaviour Description Questionnaire (Form XII) used to define 'initiating structure' (from Fleishman, 1953).

supervision on productivity and on job satisfaction, absenteeism and labour turnover.

(*a*) *Initiating structure.* There are a number of definite jobs which the supervisor should do which are directly related to the task; these aspects of behaviour have been found to correlate together and have been named 'initiating structure' (Table 10).

In a series of studies in different industrial settings undertaken by the Institute for Social Research at the University of Michigan it was found that productivity of work groups was higher when supervisors spent most of their time on the supervisory tasks in Table 10, as opposed to working with their subordinates, or doing routine jobs which could be delegated (Likert, 1961). On the other hand, output was higher under general rather than close supervision. Consequently, it looks as if too much initiating structure leads to a drop in output and job satisfaction, and an increase in labour turnover, i.e. people do not like too much bossing and interfering (see Fig. 16, p. 150). There is probably an optimum amount of guidance for any particular work group and type of task. The more highly skilled the subordinates, the less direction they need (as suggested by the Jaques time-span measure, p. 99). However, Komaki (1986) studied the most and least effective managers in a medical insurance firm, and rated them on their success in motivating others. The effective managers spent more time collecting information about the performance of subordin-

(1) Is friendly and approachable
(2) Does little things to make it pleasant to be a member of the group
(3) Puts suggestions made by the group into operation
(4) Treats all group members as equals
(5) Gives advance notice of changes
(6) Keeps to himself or herself (Reverse scored)
(7) Looks out for the personal welfare of group members
(8) Is willing to make changes
(9) Refuses to explain actions (Reverse scored)
(10) Acts without consulting the group (Reverse scored)

Table 11. Items from the Leader Behavior Description Questionnaire (Form XII) used to define 'consideration' (from Fleishman, 1953).

ates, which they did by watching them at work and by inspecting the product. Other research has shown that subordinate performance is best when supervisors give rewards which are contingent on performance, and this works in a range of situations (Podsakoff *et al.*, 1984).

(b) *Consideration*. The supervisor also has to look after the members of the group, as described by the items of the consideration scale (Table 11).

There have been many studies of the correlates of consideration: it has been found in a wide variety of organizations that it is associated with subordinates' satisfaction with their supervisor, and with low rates of absenteeism and labour turnover. The effect on the last two variables is of the order of 4:1 for supervisors at the upper and lower ends of consideration (Fig. 15, p. 150). However, it is not enough for a supervisor to have good intentions, he or she must be sufficiently powerful to deliver rewards. It has been found that there is a correlation between consideration and job satisfaction only for supervisors who are influential with their own superiors (Pelz, 1952).

The relationship with productivity has been more variable; the size and also the direction of this relationship have been quite different in different studies, and it is not clear under what conditions consideration affects output (Bass, 1981; Hollander, 1985). In fact, consideration is not the opposite of production-centred

	Productivity	Job satisfaction
Low on both dimensions	Usually low	Usually low
High on both dimensions	Usually high, but some exceptions	Usually low
Low on consideration, high on initiating structure	Often high	Usually low
High on consideration, low on initiating structure	Often low	Often high

Table 12. The combination of initiating structure and consideration and the effect on productivity and job satisfaction (from Baron, 1983).

behaviour, as was once supposed, but is independent of it (Halpin and Winer, 1952).

(c) *The combination of initiating structure and consideration*. These two dimensions do not operate independently, and the results of research on how they jointly affect productivity and job satisfaction can be seen in Table 12. A popular application of this approach has been the Management Grid (Blake and Mouton, 1964) which recommends high scores on both dimensions. However, this is a mistake, since the optimal style is contingent on the situation. More initiating structure is successful when the group is large, subordinates inexperienced, the leader has high power, and the task has low structure (Badin, 1974). Managers in banking were evaluated more favourably by subordinates if they spent more time consulting during crisis periods (Mulder *et al.*, 1986). The skills which should be used depend on whether a leader possesses them.

The path-goal theory (House, 1971) proposed that the main function of supervisors is to point out the path to successful performance and to see that this leads to rewards for subordinates. It was proposed that subordinates will work harder if the leader makes the satisfaction of needs contingent on effective performance. These ideas have been on the whole confirmed, and the theory also generates a number of contingencies, for example that more supportive supervision is needed with frustrating tasks,

(1) If a decision were accepted, would it make a difference which course of action was adopted?

(2) Do I have sufficient information to make a high-quality decision?

(3) Do subordinates have sufficient additional information to result in a high-quality decision?

(4) Do I know exactly what information is needed, who possesses it, and how to collect it?

(5) Is acceptance of decision by subordinates critical to effective implementation?

(6) If I were to make the decision by myself, is it certain that it would be accepted by my subordinates?

(7) Can subordinates be trusted to base solutions on organizational considerations?

(8) Is conflict among subordinates likely in preferred solutions?

Table 13. Problem attributes: criteria for participatory leadership (from Vroom and Yetton, 1973).

more direction when tasks lack structure (especially for authoritarian subordinates), and more participation for various combinations of tasks and persons. Subsequent research has given quite good support to this set of contingencies, especially for the effects on job satisfaction (Bass, 1981; Hollander, 1985).

Participatory leadership. Authoritarian and directive leaders give orders without explanation; democratic and persuasive leaders allow their subordinates to participate in decisions, sometimes by means of group decision-making. With participation there is usually greater acceptance of decisions and commitment to carry them out; without participation there can be resistance and hostility. Job satisfaction is usually greater under participatory supervision, and absenteeism is less, although this is not always found. However, there are no general findings for productivity or task performance; sometimes it is better under participation, sometimes worse. There appears to be an optimal level which varies with the situation (Bass, 1981). It was shown above, however, that goal-setting was more successful if combined with participation (p. 108ff).

Vroom and Yetton (1973) proposed a contingency theory

which specifies when participation should be used. They maintain that managers should go through the decision tree shown in Table 13, and that three main styles should be used – autocratic, consultative and group styles, which refer to three degrees of participation by subordinates. Greater participation should be encouraged when there are positive answers to these questions.

Vroom and Jago (1978) found that the behaviour of managers followed this model quite well, and that they were more effective when it matched the model. However, the managers did not vary their use of participation according to the situation as much as the model prescribed.

In addition, training courses based on this model have reported positive reactions from those trained, 72 per cent of whom thought that the model highlighted specific things they would do differently (Smith, n.d.). However, as noted above, leaders should be cautious about the use of participatory techniques if they do not have the necessary skills (Crouch and Yetton, 1987). Tjoswold *et al.* (1986) found that, rather than conformity to the Vroom–Yetton guidelines, the use of constructive controversy was a much better predictor of decisions rated as successful.

The role of intelligence. Early studies showed quite small correlations between intelligence and emergence as a leader and between intelligence and effectiveness as a leader. Fiedler and Garcia (1987) have found that intelligent leaders of a variety of kinds *are* more effective in that their groups have a higher rate of performance. However, this occurs only when the leader is directive and not under stress (especially interpersonal stress from his or her own boss), and the group members are supportive of the leader. This is a very interesting set of findings, and may be of general importance for the study of social skills. Intelligent people are more effective when conditions allow them to use their intelligence.

Handling different individuals. The path-goal theory specified that subordinates need to be handled differently, depending on their competence and their various needs. Graen *et al.* (1986) took this further, and proposed that leaders form separate vertical linkages with different subordinates. There is an inner circle of trusted assistants, who are given special consideration in exchange for extra help, support and hard work, and an outer circle of ordinary workers of whom less is expected, and who do not receive special benefits. Duchon *et al.* (1986) found that there was a clear distinction between the in-group and out-group, as seen by the leader and by the group. The in-group members tended to be more senior and to be female. Being in the out-group did not affect satisfaction with the leader, job satisfaction or sense of influence.

Another range of problems arises in connection with difficult group members. Sometimes such people are more amenable to group influence than to leaders, e.g. those who are hostile to authority should be left to the other group members to control. Another type is more responsive to people in authority and should be dealt with by the leader privately. When there is a persistent problem, e.g. lateness or absenteeism, it is common for a personnel interview to be given (p. 175ff).

Management

Above the first-line supervisors come second-line leaders, who can be called 'managers', although they are given different titles in educational, military, religious and other organizations. The manager's job is different from that of the first-line leader, and requires extra social skills

Stewart (1967) asked 160 industrial managers to keep diaries of how they spent their time. The results are summarized in Table 14. It can be seen that managers spend a great deal of their time (about two-thirds of it) with other people. For more senior managers even more time is spent with others. Mintzberg (1973) found that the chief executives of five large organizations spent 78 per cent of their time with others, 59 per cent of it in scheduled meetings of some kind, and 48 per cent with subordinates. These studies, made from diaries, found that managers have a very fragmented day, with many very short and unexpected social contacts.

There are different kinds of managers. Stewart (1976) found

	%
Alone	34
With one other person	32
With two or more people	34
With immediate subordinate	26
With boss	8
With colleague	12
With fellow specialists, elsewhere in the company	8
With other internal contacts	5
With customers	5
With other external contacts	6
Time spent on inspection	6
Time spent on informal discussions	43
Time spent on committees	7
Time spent telephoning	6
Time spent on social activities	4

Table 14. How managers spend their time (from Stewart, 1967).

that they could be distinguished on the basis of whether their contacts were mainly internal to the organization, whether they had some external contacts as well, or whether external contacts were essential to their work and took up 20 per cent or more of their time. They could also be differentiated on the basis of whether they had a wide variety of contacts in the organization, or whether these were mainly with peers, or with subordinates, or whether they mainly worked alone. A sales manager for example would have a variety of contacts, including essential ones outside the firm.

Most managers have some subordinates, who may be more junior managers, first-line supervisors, assistants or secretaries. It follows that what applies to supervisors also applies to managers. However, senior managers spend, on average, less time in actual supervision – 22 per cent of their time, compared with 36 per cent for middle managers, and 51 per cent for supervisors (Mahoney *et al.*, 1965). Participatory leadership is more important with more highly qualified and knowledgeable subordinates, and hence at more senior levels (Blankenship and Miles, 1968).

Managers are often unwilling to delegate responsibility, and they resist the introduction of democratic methods. Some may be afraid that if their subordinates participate freely in decisions they might turn out to be more knowledgeable and competent than they are themselves. Greater delegation of responsibility might also result in some managers becoming partly or wholly redundant, since there would be less work for them to do, and each manager could deal with a larger number of subordinates.

There have been a number of studies of the effects of the different supervisory styles of second-line leaders on productivity and job satisfaction. These show that they have a greater influence on productivity and satisfaction than first-line leaders (Nealey and Fiedler, 1968). A number of studies have shown that delegation and the use of participatory methods of leadership are effective at both levels. On the other hand, it was found that while first-line leaders in a nursing hierarchy should be *high* in initiating structure, second-line leaders should be *low* (Nealey and Blood, 1968). Styles of leadership are often passed down the hierarchy as each person copies his or her immediate superior, and may be rewarded by the superior for so doing. This 'falling dominoes' effect has been found for participatory leadership, closeness of supervision, charismatic leadership, and amount of interaction with subordinates (Bass, 1981).

'Management by objectives' is the name for a set of special techniques for handling subordinate leaders (although it can be applied lower in the hierarchy too). A company adviser helps managers to clarify the objectives of the units under their control; a *key results analysis* is prepared for each of their subordinates, listing their key tasks, the levels at which they should aim for each task, the criteria to be used for evaluating their success and any suggestions. Those concerned participate fully in the discussion of these analyses, and try to improve arrangements for each job; work proceeds for a period of time, perhaps three months, and performance is reviewed. The effectiveness of management by objectives is discussed on p. 220ff.

McGregor (1960) described a style of personnel management

in which an attempt is made to show workers how their own needs will be met by pursuing organizational goals. Supervisors discuss each person's work with them, find out what the worker's motivations are, and help set targets which will meet both the needs of the individual and the goals of the organization. Similar principles are applied in appraisal and personnel interviews, as described later. For the majority of workers the two sets of goals are fairly compatible, in that hard work may lead to promotion or higher pay, unless there are no prospects of promotion, or if the worker's main goal is increased pay and there is a fixed rate of pay.

Managers do not need technical expertise in the work of all the sections they handle, since they can depend to some extent on lower leaders and staff experts for guidance, although they should be familiar with the work of each section. They must, however, possess the skills of managing organizations: of designing the best work-flow systems, administrative hierarchies and committee structures. They must be sensitive to pressure from individuals or groups in their departments, and be able to keep them working together cooperatively. They must be sensitive to sources of job dissatisfaction. Managers also need to understand the total picture of how their department fits into the rest of the organization, and what area of freedom they have to operate in.

Looking after subordinates involves some set-piece occasions and social skills such as selection and appraisal interviewing, chairing committees etc. The other roles of the manager require some further skills, such as the ability to negotiate, to sell and to present to clients.

Some Specific Social Skills

(1) *The selection interview.* Millions of interviews for jobs take place each year, and the selection interview is a familiar social situation with established rules and conventions. It is usually expected that it should last between ten and forty minutes, that the interviewer (I) will ask most of the questions, and take notes, although the candidate (C) will be able to ask questions later, and that it is a

formal occasion where both will be properly dressed and behave politely. It is often expected that I and C will face each other across a desk, but this convention is changing in favour of a 90° orientation with a low coffee table or no table at all. If any of these rules is broken some explanation should be given to C, or permission asked, e.g. if a trainee interviewer is to be present to observe the interview.

Part of the skill consists in establishing the right relationship – one where C trusts I sufficiently to feel that they will be properly assessed, and is prepared to talk truthfully about past experience. I should convey interest in and sympathy with C by appropriate non-verbal signals and should try to understand C; however I should not take the role of C to the extent of trying to get C the job – because there are other Cs to be considered; I should remain somewhat detached while at the same time being genuinely sympathetic. While I's role is to carry out selection rather than vocational guidance, some vocational advice may be given if it is asked for. The interview should be a rewarding experience for C, who should feel that he or she has been properly and fairly assessed.

The selection interview has four main phases: (1) welcome, in which the procedure is explained, C is put at ease and encouraged to talk freely – I and C may chat briefly on safe topics of mutual interest; (2) gathering information, in which I goes over C's record, with the aid of the dossier, and tries to assess C on a number of traits; (3) supplying information, in which C is invited to ask any questions he or she may have; and (4) conclusion, in which it is explained what happens next. There may also be a phase of negotiation, in which C is offered the job, which requires further social skills.

There are special skills in asking questions. Each topic is usually introduced with an open-ended question, followed by a series of follow-up questions (e.g. 'What did you do for your third-year project?'). I's questions should be responsive to what C has just said, so that there is a proper dialogue, or flow of conversation. The questions on a given topic can be designed to obtain information about different aspects of C's abilities or personality. For example, leisure activities can be pursued to find out about social skills, creativity or emotional stability. Some areas need carefully phrased questions to elicit relevant answers; for example, judgement can be assessed from questions about C's opinions on complex and controversial social issues with which he or she is acquainted. Special care is needed when inquiring about areas such as physical disabilities, failure or other potentially embarrassing topics; questions on these areas should be asked in a friendly and objective manner, showing sympathy and avoiding loss of face by C.

I should try to assess a number of abilities and personality traits that are thought to be most relevant to the job. Some of the dimensions which are commonly assessed at selection interviews are intelligence, judgement, creativity, social skills, attitudes to authority, stability, self-image and achievement motivation.

Each of these dimensions can be assessed from the answers to suitable questions. For example, attitudes to authority can be assessed by asking questions about past relationships with others of higher or lower status, attitudes towards traditionally respected groups and institutions, and towards commonly despised social groups. In each area several different questions should be asked, in order to sample the dimension in question.

A strategy commonly adopted by interviews is one of looking for weak points in the C, i.e. looking for reasons to reject him or her. This is partly justified by the C's use of the complementary strategy, i.e. of covering up weak points. Nevertheless, it would be useful for Is to be on the look out for exceptionally strong points in Cs as well. It has been found that Is are often influenced by their early impressions of Cs based on their application forms, clothes, accents, etc.; these impressions should be checked carefully by collecting further detailed information in relevant areas (Webster, 1982).

The main problem with the selection interview is the proneness of Is to make a number of different kinds of error. These errors can be reduced by the use of five-point rating scales, where the dimensions are clearly understood by Is. An example of such a scale is:

Social skills

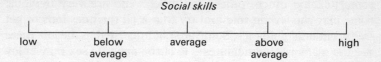

Five points are as many as an interviewer can use efficiently; he or she should distribute judgements on each scale so that about 10, 25, 30, 25 and 10 per cent of Cs fall at the different points; and it should be discovered through training, experience and comparing notes with other interviewers what the average level is for the Cs seen.

The main errors made by interviewers are:

(*a*) Assuming that C will behave in the same way in other situations, e.g. on the job.

(*b*) Being influenced too much by first impressions, especially by C's appearance and accent, and applying corresponding stereotypes.

(*c*) Trying too hard to construct a consistent picture of C; being unwilling to recognize that he or she may be intelligent *and* lazy, for example.

(*d*) Making positive evaluations, and giving favourable ratings to people from the same school, college, town, social class, etc.

(*e*) Being influenced too much by negative attributes, and not enough by positive ones.

(*f*) Giving too large or too small a scatter of ratings.

(*g*) Making constant errors, where for example all Cs are regarded as second rate or aggressive.

The behaviour of C during an interview cannot be regarded as a typical sample of his or her performance from which a prediction can be made; the interviewer should try to get Cs to talk about what they did in situations resembling the future work situation, from which predictions can be made. Thus an estimate of creativity can be obtained by asking Cs to describe situations in which they might have displayed originality.

Part of the skill of interviewing consists of being able to deal with awkward Cs. There are a number of types of awkward Cs:

some talk too much, others too little; some are very nervous; some play the wrong role and try to ask all the questions or get free vocational guidance. Some are not interested in the job; there are the glamorous candidates – Is of the opposite sex may enjoy interviewing them, but often fail to ask demanding questions or establish whether the C has the necessary abilities for the job; others are of a different class or culture from the I.

There are special ways of dealing with each of these problems. For example, the C who talks too little can be dealt with by asking easy, open-ended questions, by using reinforcement techniques (smiles, nods, eye-contact, and encouraging noises), and by I not talking too much. (Details about how to assess the traits mentioned and deal with the awkward Cs are given in Sidney and Argyle, 1969.)

The various errors of interviewing, and the accuracy of selection achieved, can be improved by training, to be described later (p. 187ff) and (Webster, 1982).

Meanwhile the social skills of Cs can help them a lot too. It is found that those who have a higher level of smiling, looking, head movements and gestures, and who speak more fluently and expressively, are more likely to get the job (Forbes and Jackson, 1980). Appearance, too, can alter a C's chances in an interview. If assessors read interview transcripts and are shown different photographs of Cs, the more attractive ones are assessed more favourably, regardless of whether attractiveness is relevant to the job (Gilmore *et al.*, 1986). Other studies have shown that selectors discriminate heavily against Cs who are fat, and in favour of men who are tall (Argyle, 1988).

(2) *The appraisal interview.* About 75 per cent of firms use appraisal interviews; these are usually conducted by the immediate superior, typically once a year, for all ranks including managers. This may be closely linked to other personnel practices – career structure, salaries and promotion, and job analysis. Where there is no formal scheme, supervisors still have to find out from time to time how their subordinates are getting on, give them feedback on progress and discuss their career prospects, and motivate them by

giving fresh targets. This kind of interview is an integral part of supervisory skill, and the way in which it is carried out is very important for the relationship with subordinates and the effectiveness of a working group (de Jong and Thierry, 1984).

The supervisor's manner in an appraisal interview should be warm, positive and sympathetic, indicating that he or she is on the subordinate's side in the sense that they belong to the same group and are pursuing the same goals, and that the supervisor has a personal concern for subordinates' welfare, and is trying to understand and sympathize with their problems. At the same time, the supervisor must remain detached in the sense that he or she is applying objective standards of assessment to the subordinate's performance, providing realistic information on his or her career prospects, and is concerned with the effectiveness of the group.

There are three main aims for appraisal interviews, which require somewhat different social techniques (Maier, 1958).

(a) *Evaluation.* This is needed for possible salary increases, promotions, transfers or dismissals, and as a criterion for the study of selection and training. The aim here is to obtain further information about someone's progress in addition to what is known already. This may be done as part of a general system of periodic appraisal by managers or personnel departments, or when a subordinate's work is not entirely visible to his or her immediate superior. Where possible, objective data should be obtained of quantity and quality of work, absenteeism, etc. Ratings should be made, not of personality traits, but of concrete behaviour on the job, such as dependability, need for supervision and cooperation. It is useful if more than one rater can be used.

(b) *Providing information on progress.* People want to know how they are getting on and like to be able to discuss their career prospects with someone in a position to know about them; on the other hand, they are often very defensive and resistant to this kind of information, are liable to quarrel and refuse to accept criticisms. It has been shown that appraisal interviews can result in lowered self-esteem and deterioration in work (Kay *et al.*,

1965). These authors found that the common use of a 'praise/blame/praise' sandwich led to positive remarks being ignored. Special skills are needed if criticism is to be accepted, such as giving specific examples of difficulties, evidence of performance from a valid source such as the supervisor, participation by subordinates, and more frequent meetings, so that fewer items are dealt with on each occasion (Landy and Farr, 1983). Sofer, in an unpublished study, has found that interviewers often say they discussed a particular topic with a subordinate, but that often the latter cannot remember this topic having been brought up, presumably because it was not emphasized enough. It is useful to start by asking for the subordinate's views about his or her standard of work, although these are not always very realistic, or both supervisor and subordinate can start by making separate assessments. The supervisor should then mention positive aspects of the subordinate's work, before going on to any specific criticisms; these should be given in an objective and constructive manner, avoiding conflict, avoiding damaging self-esteem, and discussing the matter on the assumption that the two of them are cooperating over a piece of joint problem-solving, to see how things could be improved. Careful attention should be paid to the subordinate's side of the story, as in the personnel interview.

(c) *Setting targets and arousing motivation.* This is an essential part of 'management by objectives', as prescribed by McGregor (1960), and stresses the importance of participation in target-setting, which was discussed above. The key technique here is aligning the individual's motivations with the needs of the organization. The supervisor should find out which kinds of motivation can be appealed to in a subordinate, and then demonstrate how these needs can be satisfied by pursuing organizational goals, e.g. if the subordinate works better he or she will be paid more or promoted. An appraisal interview can also show the subordinate how to improve him- or herself, by getting appropriate training, to prepare for a better job.

A follow-up study was carried out of fifty managers who were given thirty hours of training in the appraisal interview by means of role-playing exercises. It was found that 70 per cent of subordinates felt that their supervisors had a better understanding of how they performed their jobs, 67 per cent thought their supervisors understood them better as individuals and 65 per cent had a better idea of what was expected of them (Moon and Hariton, 1958).

(3) *The personnel interview.* This kind of interview is needed when an employee's behaviour has been unsatisfactory. The most common problems are absenteeism, lateness, smoking in the wrong places, carelessness, not using safety equipment, sleeping on the job, and being drunk. The personnel interview is the first stage in dealing with the problem; if it fails the next steps are an oral warning, a written warning, suspension and dismissal, the details depending on the labour laws operating at the time (Jackson and Keaveny, 1980). This is a very difficult kind of interview to conduct: it is feared and resented by the interviewees, and is often funked by those who ought to carry it out. Research on supervision has suggested a totally new approach to it, which can make it a pleasanter and more effective occasion. What is recommended is something like the strategy that follows.

(*a*) The supervisor (S) finds out as much as he or she can about the performance and relevant circumstances of the client (C). The S also decides on a strategy, what goals he or she will try to achieve, and what kinds of persuasion will be used. This strategy is provisional, as new facts may come to light during the interview.

(*b*) S establishes rapport with C, who may be very nervous about the interview. This will be easier if S maintains good day-to-day contacts with C. They might chat briefly about common interests, so that status barriers are reduced, and C is ready to talk freely. It can be enough for S to create an easy relationship by non-verbal signals.

(*c*) It may be necessary for S to explain that there is a problem – C has been persistently late so that production has fallen, C has been getting very low marks, etc. This should be done by stating objective facts, not by passing judgement, and should be done in a manner that is pleasant rather than cross.

(d) S now invites C to say what he or she thinks about the situation, and what the reason for it is. This may involve a certain amount of probing for fuller information, if C is reluctant to open up. S is sympathetic, and shows that he or she wants to understand C's position. S may ask C whether he or she thinks the situation is satisfactory; C can be asked to evaluate his or her own performance.

(e) There now follows a period of joint problem-solving, in which C and S try between them to work out a solution to the problem. This may involve action on S's side as well as on C's – such as giving C a different job, or making some other change in the situation. It may involve a trial period after which S and C will meet again to review the situation.

(f) If some change of behaviour on C's part is indicated, and if C proves uncooperative, further steps may be necessary. The first of these is persuasion. S may be able to point out that C will not reach his or her own goals by the present line of action – as with a student who will fail exams if he or she does not work harder. Such social influence is a subtle skill in itself, and depends on being able to appeal realistically to the right needs in a particular individual.

(g) If this fails, and if further interviews become necessary, sterner means of influence may have to be resorted to. Most Ss are in a position to control material sanctions, such as bonuses, promotions, and finally dismissal. S will not usually want to sack C – what S wants is to keep C but to get him or her to behave differently. The possible use of such sanctions should first be mentioned reluctantly as a rather remote possibility – for example by the quite objective statement 'there are several other people who would like this job', or 'I may have to tell the people who pay your grant about your progress'.

(h) The interview should end with a review of what has been agreed, the constructive steps that have been decided upon, when S and C will meet again to discuss progress, and so on. The meeting should end on as friendly a note as possible (Argyle, 1983).

(4) *Chairing a committee.* The task of committees and other discussion groups is to solve problems and take decisions in a way
that is acceptable to those present, and to those they represent. In
some cases the emphasis is on problem-solving and creativity, in
others the emphasis is on obtaining consensus. Such groups
usually have a chairperson, unless there are only three or four
people present. The chairperson has a generally accepted social
role of controlling discussion and helping the group make decisions. His or her position is often more temporary than that of
other group leaders, and the leadership of the group may be
rotated so that other committee members take it in turns. Being
chairperson carries a certain amount of power, but it has to be
used with skill. A chairperson should see that all members are
able to express their views, and that the decisions arrived at are
agreeable to as many of them as possible. He or she should be able
to keep control with a light touch, and keep people in order
without upsetting them.

At the beginning of the meeting the chairperson should create
the right atmosphere, by the use of appropriate non-verbal signals.
There are several phases to the discussion of each item on the
agenda. First, the chairperson introduces the item by outlining
the problem to be discussed, summarizing briefly the main background factors, the arguments on each side, and so on. Then the
committee is invited to discuss the problem; enough time should
be allowed for different views to be expressed, and the chairperson
should try to keep the discussion orderly, so that different points
are dealt with in turn. Now the chairperson can help the group to
come to a decision, by focusing on disagreements among them
and trying to arrive at a creative solution, evaluating different
solutions in relation to criteria if these can be agreed, considering
sub-problems in turn, or asking the committee to consider two
possible solutions. Finally an attempt is made to secure the group's
support for a particular solution. If this is impossible it may be
necessary to take a vote; this is unsatisfactory, since it means that
some members are not happy about the decision, and will not
support it very enthusiastically.

A certain amount of research has been done by Maier and

Solem (1952) and Hoffman (1965) into which skills of chairing a committee produce the best effects. They found, for example, that better and more widely accepted solutions are obtained if minority views can be expressed. The chairperson can help the group by focusing on disagreements and searching for a creative solution.

A chairperson should be aware of the main processes of behaviour in groups, and be able to prevent these processes interfering with the effective working of the committee. The formation of a status hierarchy will inhibit low-status members from contributing: they should be encouraged to speak. Conformity pressures may produce over-rapid acceptance of the first solution offered: this can be prevented by asking the group to consider a second solution; this is often preferred in the end. The 'risky-shift' phenomenon may lead committees to adopt risky solutions to problems, and the chairperson should be on the watch for this.

There are a number of subsidiary social skills involved in being a chairperson. The agenda should be studied carefully beforehand, and an introduction to the different items prepared. He or she should be able to anticipate the items which will cause difficulty of some kind. He or she should be familiar with the rules and procedure of the committee, and be able to explain what should happen when the voting is equal, what to do if there is no quorum, and so on. It is often useful to appoint a sub-committee or working party to deal with problems involving fact-finding or drafting. The composition of sub-committees is important: they should be small but contain the right combination of skills or experience. There may be problems about dealing with awkward members of a committee. The chairperson should avoid direct confrontation, or the use of naked power. It is better if he or she can apply impersonal rules, or leave it to the rest of the committee to deal with difficult individuals. People who want to talk too much can be gently discouraged by the use of non-verbal signals. Members who put forward preposterous ideas can be firmly out-voted (see Hoffman, 1965).

(5) *Negotiation.* Managers have to negotiate with trade unions,

firms other than their own and government bodies. Negotiation is a kind of joint decision-making between representatives of two sides which are in conflict, although there is joint interest in reaching a settlement. The goal of a negotiator (N) is to reach an agreement quickly which gives his or her side the best deal obtainable and will be accepted by all concerned. The success of N can be assessed by ratings from both sides concerning his or her effectiveness, N's record for reaching agreements and the extent to which those agreements stick.

The social situation of negotiation is a complex one. Both sides are representatives; it is easier for them if they are 'leaders' rather than 'delegates', since then they are in a better position to sell the agreement reached. There are usually several Ns on each side, and the two sides are in conflict with one another. On the other hand, they must cooperate over the process of negotiation and may know each other well. In the second phase of negotiation (see below) they shift away from their roles as representatives in conflict to one of more interpersonal cooperation.

The basic procedure is for each party to start by stating its case and its preferred solution. This is followed by exchange of information, for example about each side's problems and pay-offs, and a series of concessions, which are usually reciprocated until agreement is reached. Three phases of the negotiating process are often distinguished: (1) each side makes long speeches, emphasizing the strength of its case, Ns taking the representative role; (2) the range of possible solutions is explored and information is exchanged, Ns now assuming a more cooperative and problem-solving role; and (3) there is harder bargaining, and decision-taking, over the actual settlement point.

Sometimes a professional mediator or chairperson is appointed who may be able to steer Ns towards a problem-solving approach after a deadlock, to arrive at a solution which is face-saving for both sides. Sometimes informal discussion between junior representatives of the two sides can find a solution when their superiors have failed, since they are freer to explore possible concessions – although their solution may not be accepted in the end by their own sides. However, when it is known that an arbitrator will be appointed if negotiations fail, the amount of negotiation is reduced. 'Final offer negotiation' in the USA is a procedure to encourage constructive negotiation: if agreement is not reached an arbitrator will decide for one side or the other, but will not compromise.

There are variations in the skills of negotiation, and this is a source of power. Certain styles of negotiation have been found to be more successful than others in actual cases or in simulations:

(a) N should make a strong case, make strong demands and give small concessions.
(b) N should not be too tough, however, or there may be no agreement, and should not attack or irritate the other side.
(c) N should be open to a wide range of alternatives, and not plan a particular outcome in advance.
(d) N should adopt a rational, problem-solving approach, in which he or she explores all the options, finds out a lot about the other side and their problems as well as giving information him or herself, and communicates clearly and without ambiguity.
(e) N should create a reputation for honesty and firmness, and enhance the image of his or her party (Rackham and Carlisle, 1978, 1979).

The training of negotiators can also include encouraging them in the accurate assessment of the other side's position, and reducing over-confidence. Such training has led to greater compromises in role-played negotiations, especially for those with high scores on perspective-taking ability (Bazerman and Neale, 1982).

Negotiators do better when there is a close relationship with those on the other side – each side is more likely to get what it wants (Morley and Hosking, 1984). In what has been called 'integrative behaviour', both sides focus on possible concessions and alternatives, and attain the maximum joint profit (Pruitt, 1976). One strategy is to make concessions of low priority in exchange for more important concessions from the other side. Even better is to discover bargains which will increase the total benefits to be divided (Pruitt, 1983). The moves and strategies which are made in the course of negotiation indicate the complexity of this bargaining process – e.g. perceiving and exploiting power, standing firm but signalling flexibility (Morley, 1981). One famous strategy is Osgood's GRIT (1960) – Graduated Reciprocation in Tension Reduction – which is recommended for disarmament talks: N announces that he or she will make small concessions, and that if these are matched by the other side more will be made.

In addition a number of competitive, non-integrative, tactics are sometimes used, and have been studied. These include threats of sanctions and promises of rewards, withholding information and giving misleading information, imposing an agenda of negotiable issues, and causing delays or other kinds of annoyance in the tradition of gamesmanship (Greenhalgh, 1987).

(6) *Presenting material to an audience.* Managers often have to present schemes to colleagues or clients, or on other occasions address audiences, with the intention of conveying information, changing their attitudes or influencing their behaviour. This is often done very ineffectively, because the speaker is inaudible, boring, unconvincing, nervous, cannot handle an audience or presents the material badly. The manner of a speaker is very important. He or she will be more effective if seen to be an expert on the subject, and well intentioned towards the listeners; this can be indicated by the appropriate non-verbal signals of dress and general demeanour, especially perhaps tone of voice. The speaker should be seen as an expert, but also as a member of the group on equal terms with the audience. He or she should have a friendly, agreeable and lively manner, and should make the presentation interesting and enjoyable throughout. He or she should have 'poise', i.e. confidence and lack of anxiety, and 'presence', i.e. be in constant contact with and control of the audience.

A lecture or other presentation may have a number of phases. For a persuasive message, the following order is most effective (McGuire, 1969).

(a) *Opening.* The speaker makes contact with the audience,

secures their attention, puts them in the right mood, mentions his or her links with the audience or does other self-presenting, and explains what he or she is going to talk about and why. The speaker should arouse interest and create the expectation that he or she is going to solve important problems or show how to satisfy important needs.

(b) *Positive arguments.* The positive case is put forward with the support of sound and compelling arguments, clear evidence, good illustrations and clear visual aids. This should be clearly structured, and the materials used should be intrinsically interesting. When unfamiliar ideas are being put forward it is necessary to use striking examples to jolt the audience out of old ways of thinking.

(c) *Dealing with objections.* It is useful to deal with objections, especially when the audience is intelligent or would be expected to see them.

(d) *Drawing conclusions.* At the end the most important conclusions should be explicitly drawn, especially conclusions for action.

(7) *Keep audience's interest.* A number of subsidiary social skills are involved in presenting. The presentation should keep the audience's attention by a lively and enthusiastic delivery, the use of materials which are of special interest to them, are dramatic or funny, and by the effective use of visual aids.

(a) *Use of visual aids.* It is a convention of management presentations that visual aids of a high quality be used. These can be on the overhead projector, slides or charts, and should be clearly legible, comprehensible and in colour.

(b) *Spatial arrangements* are important, especially when visual aids are used: the best room available should be chosen and arranged to best advantage, so that everyone is comfortable and can see and hear.

(c) *Controlling the audience.* The presenter should study the audience's reactions carefully, and be on the look-out for people not able to hear, who are falling asleep, looking bored, puzzled or cross, or who are not taking it seriously enough. He or she should take rapid corrective action, for example, speaking louder, explaining points that are not clear, arousing more interest or quietening them down.

(d) *Voice quality*. A speaker should speak loudly and distinctly, 'project' his or her voice to all corners of the audience, keep his or her voice quality under control, and vary pace and tone enough to make it interesting. A presenter should not sound superior, nervous or boring, and the delivery should be appropriate to the size of the audience.

(e) *Dealing with discussion*. During the discussion the contributions of the audience should be taken seriously and sympathetically, and an effort made to see the points of view expressed. The speaker should not merely 'deal with' the points made, but should try to work out the best solutions with the audience's help. He or she should avoid any confrontation with the audience.

Methods of Social Skills Training

We have shown that social skills are extremely important at work. During recent years a bewildering variety of methods of social skills training (SST) have sprung up, some of them solidly based on interaction research, others of much more dubious value. We shall describe here the main varieties of training, and review the evidence of their success as shown by follow-up studies.

Because there is a widely practised method of training, and because those who experience it enjoy it and are enthusiastic about its benefits, it does not follow that the training does any good. It is necessary to show that there have been changes from before the training to after it, and that such changes are greater than those in a comparable untrained control group (to eliminate the effects of the passage of time and taking tests). The assessment

	First-level supervisors %	Middle managers %
Lecture/discussion	100	100
Films/videotape	92	90
Case study	74	78
Role-playing	69	70
Programmed instruction	54	44
Management games	45	60
Transactional analysis	23	23
Incident process	21	25
Behaviour modification	18	16
T-groups	4	6

Table 15. Training methods for in-house programmes (from Miner, 1977, in Yoder and Staudohar, 1982).

should not consist only of questionnaires, since the course may affect verbal responses but not other aspects of behaviour. When ratings by colleagues are used, these should be made 'blind', i.e. the raters should not know who has been trained, or their attitudes to the training may affect their ratings. The best criteria are objective measures of output, sales, etc., where these are available.

The extent of training. Most organizations provide training for managers, supervisors, and others, and this nearly always includes training in 'human relations', or social skills. An American survey of large firms carried out by Miner in 1977 found the extent to which different methods of training were being used (see Table 15). Since that date there has been a decline of behaviour modification, T-groups, and probably of transactional analysis, and an increase in role-playing in the USA. The British scene is different in a number of ways; the main difference is that there is a lot less management training of all kinds than in the USA, Japan or Germany; there are fewer graduates, accountants and MBAs, and only one day a year is spent in off-the-job training compared with five or more in the other countries (Handy, 1987; Constable and McCormick, 1987). There is much less SST. Table 15 does

	Subjective learning	Objective learning	Subjective behaviour	Objective results
Contents of training				
Overall	·34	·38	·49	·67
Human relations	·76*	·41	·44*	1·04*
General management	·14	·21	·4	·53*
Self-awareness	·86*		·65	·64
Problem-solving		·17		
Motivation/values		·85*		
Methods of training				
Lecture		·37	·46*	·82
Lecture/discussion		·23	·11*	
Sensitivity training (T-groups)	·86*		·73	
Behavioural modelling	·99*		·78*	
Lecture/discussion plus role-play or practice	·66*	·93*	·34*	
Multi-method (3 or more)	·76*	·81*	·51	·52*
Leader match			·4*	

Notes
(1) These are corrected effect sizes, i.e. E − C/σ.
(2) * means variance between studies was sufficiently low that 90 per cent of effects were > 0.

Table 16. Meta-analysis of seventy management training studies (from Burke and Day, 1986).

not mention an important method – training on the job – which we shall discuss below.

The success of SST. Many follow-up studies have been carried out, using before-and-after comparisons, with trained and control groups. A summary of the present state of knowledge is provided by a meta-analysis of seventy such studies of management training, which is shown in Table 16 (Burke and Day, 1986). In the top part of the table we are most interested in 'human relations' training. Of the columns, we are most interested in the third, which refers to ratings of social behaviour, and the fourth, which is about objective performance measures, such as costs and productivity. The first column refers to subjective judgements of trainees, the second to test scores. The figures here are the differences between any changes for experimental and control groups, as a proportion of the standard deviation. Account is also taken of the variability of results between studies. An asterisk shows that this variance was sufficiently low for 90 per cent of the results reported to be positive, i.e. the effect of training can be relied on under different conditions. It can be seen that human relations training has been quite successful, especially in terms of objective results, and that several other kinds of training have strong and consistent effects.

Baumgartel *et al.* (1984) studied the effects of a number of management courses, and found that they were more effective, in that the ideas were applied, for managers with a high need for achievement and internal control, in an organizational climate which is favourable to training and the use of new knowledge.

Before training can be planned it is necessary to identify where training is needed – who should be trained and what they should be taught. There are various ways of doing this – finding out how each person spends his time, collecting critical incidents to compare those that were effective with those that were ineffective, finding out which tasks the performers find difficult or which cause annoyance to others (Wexley and Latham, 1981). There may be quite specific needs for SST, such as dealing with a particular kind of encounter on the job, and special tasks, such as appraisal or selection interviews.

(1) *Role-playing and modelling.* This is now the most widely used method of training. It has long been used by clinical psychologists and for training teachers. It has replaced T-groups as the preferred method for industrial SST for supervisors, managers, and for specialized skills, such as selection interviewing.

It is first necessary to decide on the set of problems or topics where training is needed. Goldstein and Sorcher (1974) drew up a list of seventeen such topics for supervisors; Latham and Saari (1979) used nine of these in a successful training course:

Orienting a new employee
Giving recognition

Motivating a poor employee
Correcting poor work habits
Discussing potential disciplinary action
Reducing absenteeism
Handling a complaining employee
Reducing turnover
Overcoming resistance to change.

Having drawn up the list of topics it is then necessary to decide on the skills to be taught for each. Sometimes research of the kind described earlier, is available, sometimes it is not and the trainer has to fall back on the opinions of 'experts', which is much less satisfactory. The contents of the training may be distributed in the form of written or audio-taped instructions, and are explained by the trainer when coaching trainees prior to the role-playing (Goldstein, 1981). Supervisory training can also take the form of teaching people to use different styles of supervision, such as more use of participatory leadership.

The list of topics or skills to be trained will vary greatly with the job and the organization. Each topic will require one or more sessions of one to two hours and typically there will be a trainer and a group of six to ten trainees. There are three stages to this form of training. (1) A film or video is shown or a demonstration given, together with an explanation of the main points to be taught and some discussion. (2) A problem situation is defined, and stooges are produced for trainees to role-play with for seven to fifteen minutes each. The background to the situation may be filled in with written materials, such as the application forms of candidates for interview or background information about personnel problems. The stooges may be carefully trained beforehand to provide various problems, such as talking too much or having elaborate and plausible excuses. (3) There is a feedback session, as described below.

An example of an SST laboratory, set up for interviewer training, is shown in Figure 17. A laboratory such as this is ideal but SST can be conducted with just a video-camera and recorder. It is possible to set up role-playing exercises for a variety of

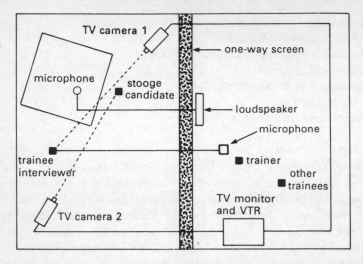

Fig. 17. Laboratory arrangements for interviewer training (from Argyle, 1983).

skills, including management–union bargaining, interviewing and teaching (Bazerman and Neale, 1982).

(*a*) *Feedback.* Feedback is a crucial part of the training. It can come from several sources. The trainer, who should be in a position to give expert guidance on the social techniques which are effective, and who may be able to increase sensitivity to the more subtle nuances of interaction, can provide feedback. He or she may correct errors, such as interrupting and looking or sounding unfriendly. The trainer can suggest alternative social techniques, such as ways of dealing with awkward clients or situations. This has to be done very carefully: the trainer's remarks should be gentle and kind enough not to upset, but firm and clear enough to have some effect.

Other trainees can provide feedback either in free discussion, discussion in smaller groups, or via questionnaires or behavioural check-lists. This must be done carefully, or it will be disturbing to the recipients of the feedback; on the other hand, it is probably a valuable part of the training process for those observing.

The performance of a trainee can be recorded on video and

then played back. This directs his or her attention to the behavioural (facial, bodily and gestural) aspects of the performance, as well as to the auditory. It may be useful to play back the soundtape separately to focus attention on what was said during the 'interview'.

(b) *Training for contingencies.* We have seen the strong evidence that optimum leadership style varies with the situation. Vroom and Yetton (1973) devised a way of training managers to adapt to different situations by first showing films of managers using different degrees of participation for the same problem, followed by training in the use of these techniques, and learning the conditions in which they should be used. Another example is the system of interviewer training described above (p. 172), which includes role-playing with a variety of difficult 'candidates'.

(c) *Generalization* from training centre to the work situation can be a problem. It is possible to enhance it by teaching general principles, overlearning and training in situations similar to the work setting.

Another solution is to give 'homework', widely used in clinical SST. Trainees are asked to try out a new skill several times between training sessions and to discuss their experiences with the trainer and group.

There is a problem with training for some social skills that the real situation cannot be reproduced at all realistically in the training lab. One solution is training on the job – see below.

(d) *Effectiveness.* Role-playing with modelling has been found quite effective in a variety of SST settings. Table 16 shows that, especially when combined with lectures, it is quite effective for managers, and it enhances productivity. The course by Latham and Saari (1979), in which nine topics were covered in nine two-hour sessions, is one of a series of successful supervisory courses.

(2) *Learning on the job.* Many people learn their social skills by doing the job, with or without the help of coaching from others, and this is the main way in which most manual skills are taught.

However, simply doing the job does not guarantee success. Fiedler (1970) actually found a small negative correlation ($-\cdot 12$) between the effectiveness of leaders and years of experience, i.e. the more experienced were slightly less effective. It has been found that some supervisors seem to have learned the wrong social skills through experience, e.g. they use close, punitive and authoritarian methods (Argyle *et al.*, 1958). Salesgirls *on average* slowly increased their volume of sales with time, but some stayed unchanged, while others become worse (Argyle, Lalljee and Lydall in Argyle, 1983). Experience with training interviewers has shown that after years of experience interviewers may not have acquired quite simple and basic social techniques – such as how to make a candidate talk more – which can be taught in a few minutes.

Coaching can make a great difference by providing detailed feedback and individualized instruction, and when the coach acts as a model, delegates jobs, and gives encouragement and recognition (Bass, 1981). The trainer should be an expert performer of the skill being taught, and sensitive to the elements and processes of social interaction. The success of such coaching depends on there being a good relationship between the trainee and the supervisor; they should ideally be of similar backgrounds, the trainer should know how to teach, and there should be some reward or recognition (Wexley and Latham, 1981).

Simply providing feedback from survey results can be very useful. Clear feedback must be given on what the trainee is doing wrong. Some 3,900 schoolchildren were asked to fill in rating scales to describe their ideal teacher and how their actual teachers behaved; the results were shown to half of the teachers, who subsequently improved on ten of the twelve scales (Gage *et al.*, 1960).

It is possible to make use of data about on-the-job behaviour of supervisors or managers for training. Maxwell and Pringle (1986) made observations of supervisors for an hour, and used diaries kept by trainees (as well as role-play videos) as the basis for coaching in better skills. In police training use has been made of videotaped vignettes and tutor-constables, who give feedback and coaching on the beat (Bull and Horncastle, 1983).

(3) *Educational methods.* Most education is carried out by means of lectures, discussion and reading. Can social skills be taught in this way?

(*a*) *Lectures* were at first very popular for human-relations courses, until early follow-up studies suggested that they were ineffective. As Table 15 shows, lectures with discussion are used universally, although much of this is for factual and technical instruction, rather than for the teaching of social skills. Lectures are good for conveying information and enhancing understanding. In SST there *is* a certain amount of information to be put across, for example when coaching people in the recommended skills. The transfer or generalization of training to diverse work situations is helped if general principles can be applied. It is now realized that there are important cognitive processes in social behaviour of the kind expounded earlier in this chapter. However, follow-up studies suggest that lectures do not have much impact on social performance unless they are accompanied by more active methods of training such as role-playing.

(*b*) *Films* are sometimes used for modelling in connection with role-playing. A number of suitable films are now available, mainly for management skills. Social skills trainers often make up their own videotapes of modelling behaviour for trainees. Films have been used for training *manual* skills for some time, and these are found to be successful under certain conditions – if the trainee has to try out part of the skill after each piece of film; if there is discussion before or after the film; if the film is shot from the trainee's point of view, e.g. over his or her shoulder; and if appropriate use is made of slow motion, animation and sequences of stills, showing the successive steps in the skill. Films are increasingly being used for the modelling component of role-playing, for example in demonstrating the degrees of participatory leadership distinguished by Vroom and Yetton (p. 163ff).

(*c*) *Discussion*, following lectures or other activities, is quite successful in changing attitudes, which is a common goal of training. This may also give useful experience of taking decisions in groups.

(d) *Case studies* can provide a good basis for discussion, and often do so in management training. They consist of problem situations to which the group has to find the best solution, and may be presented as a film or in written form. Case studies are used for general education in management problems, but can also be focused entirely on the human relations aspects. The main weakness associated with using case studies is that trainees do not acquire any general principles of social behaviour. It might be possible to design case studies in such a way that they illustrate and draw attention to basic principles; perhaps if a large enough number of cases were used trainees could be helped to make inductive generalizations from them. However, there is very little follow-up evidence to demonstrate the value of case studies, although they are widely used (Table 16).

(e) *Reading* is rarely discussed and perhaps little used in connection with industrial training, although presumably managers and supervisors can read. However, it is quite widely used elsewhere, for example in do-it-yourself assertiveness training (Bower and Bower, 1976). An area of social skills where reading has been successful is inter-cultural training, where 'cultural assimilators' are used. This is a sphere in which there is much factual information to learn. In addition, SST based on role-playing often makes use of written hand-outs which accompany the exercises (e.g. Goldstein, 1981).

(4) *T-groups*. T(training)-groups were first developed in the National Training Laboratories at Bethel, Maine, in 1947, and they became very popular in the 1960s and early 1970s as a form of management training. As Table 15 shows, by 1977 T-groups were used very little, and they are now used even less. However, the T-group is still a very interesting invention and should be described.

The members of a T-group spend their time studying the group and the processes of social interaction that take place in it. The trainer typically starts off by saying, 'My name is . . ., and I am the appointed staff training of this group, and am here to help you in the study of this group as best I can.' T-groups consist of about twelve trainees who meet weekly or during a residential course for a series of two-hour periods. The sessions are often combined with lectures, role-playing and other activities, but the T-group is regarded as central.

One of the main things that the trainer does is teach people how to give and receive feedback, so that members may become aware of the impact of their behaviour on others and find out how others see them. The trainer shows how to make non-evaluative comments on the behaviour of others, and tries to reduce the defensiveness of those whose behaviour is being commented upon. Feedback is provided in other ways; members may take turns to act as observers who later report back to the group, tape-recordings of previous sessions are studied, and analyses by professional observers may be presented.

T-groups are quite successful in increasing self-awareness, although this is a rather dubious variable based on ratings by self or others, and may bear no relation to effectiveness. A typical finding is that 30–40 per cent of trainees show some positive change, compared to 10–20 per cent of control group members, although these improvements are often very short-lived, the majority are unaffected, and up to 10 per cent are worse, sometimes to the extent of needing psychiatric help (Campbell and Dunnette, 1968). A number of studies have found increases in cohesiveness in intact working groups, but there is little evidence of increased productivity (Bass, 1981). However, it is the negative effects on some individuals, which have been widely noticed in Britain, which were mainly responsible for the decline in the use of T-groups. In addition, it has been felt in the USA that T-groups result in an invasion of privacy, and that they give too much control over the feelings and private lives of employees (Wexley, 1984).

(5) *Other group methods of training.* In Britain a number of alternatives to T-groups have been devised and have been widely used, although there is no follow-up evidence for their effectiveness. Three different varieties will be described briefly.

(a) *Experiences in groups.* First introduced by Ralph Coverdale, the aim in this case is for trainees to understand group processes better, and to understand their own behaviour in groups, especially their weaknesses. Groups are given miniature managerial tasks, such as deciding how to build towers of bricks, or make paper boats, or discuss a problem at work. Part of the group does the exercise, while the others act as observers, and provide comments afterwards; then these roles are reversed (Boot and Reynolds, 1984; Taylor, 1979).

(b) *Rackham's behavioural analysis.* Rackham and Morgan (1977) have developed a set of procedures for training in committee work, chairing meetings, selling and related skills. They use a set of categories dubbed the 'chairman list', which is modified for particular skills, containing items such as content proposals, procedural proposals, building, supporting, disagreeing, defending/attacking, testing understanding, summarizing, seeking information and giving information. Good and bad performers are nominated and their rates of using the categories compared. Trainees learn the use of categories and participate in role-play exercises while observers record how often they use the categories. The trainer then gives feedback, consisting of information about each trainee's scores in the categories, which are compared with the rates for the good performers. Follow-up studies have shown positive results, although these studies were not very carefully controlled.

(c) *Management self-development.* A group of managers meets with a trainer, and in the course of lengthy discussion (perhaps lasting two days), each member identifies the areas in which he or she would like to improve his or her performance. These may include some social skills, such as:

> Why do people see me as a miserable bastard?
> Help in motivating a subordinate bored with his or her job.
> Help in solving a problem concerning my relationship with my boss.
> Help in developing presentation skills.

The group then meets every five weeks for four to six hours, and sub-groups meet to discuss particular problems. Self-ratings are made on a range of skills, before and after a year of meetings. Positive shifts have been reported (Temporal, 1984).

(6) *New developments in SST.* There have been extensive developments in social psychology which are directly relevant to questions of social competence, and which have clear implications for training. This suggests a number of possible extensions to traditional role-playing and modelling, which have been taken up to some extent in clinical SST, but not much as yet for work skills. These methods are perhaps most suitable for those individuals at work who are suffering from some kind of social inadequacy. Several kinds of social inadequacy are familiar at work.

(a) *Authoritarians.* Authoritarianism used to be a serious problem in British industry, due to the presence of survivors from a more authoritarian era, and to the influx of a large number of ex-army officers after the Second World War. Indeed this was a problem for which T-groups were used.

(b) *Social anxiety.* Some people experience acute social anxiety either in all social situations or in specific ones, such as public speaking, taking the chair or seeing superiors. This leads to their avoiding these situations and makes them ineffective at their job.

(c) *Inadequate social skills.* There is another group of people who simply fail to cope with social situations at work. They may be always quarrelling instead of cooperating, they may be very unpopular and generally avoided, they may be unable to deal with certain categories of people – superiors, subordinates, other social classes, women, etc. – or they may be very ineffective on committees or other kinds of encounter at work. Such inabilities commonly stand in the way of promotion, and may lead to dismissal, but they can be modified by appropriate training.

(7) *Extending SST.* It is possible to extend and enhance SST by the use of new methods, both for socially inadequate individuals

and for training employees for particular jobs (Argyle, 1984).

(a) *Non-verbal communication.* Effective social performance requires the correct use of facial expression, tone of voice, gaze, gesture, and other non-verbal signals. This can be taught by the skilled use of mirrors, video and audio-tape, and modelling from photographs or other sources (Argyle, 1988).

(b) *Verbal communication.* All social behaviour involves the use of language and conversational sequences. Special skills, such as interviewing and negotiation, require specialized types of utterance and sequences of utterances. 'Bad conversationalists' make a variety of technical mistakes which need to be identified and corrected.

(c) *Perceptual sensitivity* to the emotions and attitudes expressed by others, especially non-verbal ones, can be trained by exercises with photographs, video and audiotapes. This is particularly important for interviewers and those in personnel work.

(d) *Self-presentation*, that is sending information about the self, by clothes, hair, accent, etc., can go wrong in several ways. This can be fairly easily corrected by advice and simple forms of training. This is most important for those in sales or other outside representatives of the firm.

(e) *Social relationships.* Some individuals have difficulty in establishing or in maintaining particular relationships; we have seen that the supervisor–subordinate relationship is a difficult one, for example. Training can include instruction in the nature of the relationship, teaching the rules, and learning the special skills needed (Argyle and Henderson, 1985).

8

WORKING IN ORGANIZATIONS

From early times people have worked not only in small social groups but also in organized social groups. For example, working groups with leaders based on kinship structures, the Roman 'ergasterions', the feudal system, the domestic system – these were all different kinds of work organization (Chapter 2). In an organized group the pattern of relationships is fixed, having been worked out by earlier members of similar groups. The behaviour of the present members is therefore to a considerable degree *programmed*. Each person occupies a position – such as slave, feudal lord of the manor, merchant capitalist, shop steward – and associated with each position is a standard pattern of behaviour, or *role*. These roles *interlock* – for example, there was a standard pattern of interaction between a feudal serf and his lord of the manor, which was quite different from that of subordinates and supervisors today.

The tendency to form social organizations is probably not innate, but rather the result of slow cultural growth, partly to deal with the increasing size of human groupings, partly in response to the development of more elaborate technology. All advanced civilizations have produced large-scale organizations for industrial, military, governmental, educational, religious and other purposes. The pattern of these structures has changed historically, and ideas have developed about how work should be organized, culminating in contemporary theories of management. However, we have now moved into a new historical phase, in which social scientists are able to examine social organizations, compare the efficiency of different designs, and see which ones work best. It is clear that working organizations as we know them today are far from satisfactory, and their shortcomings will be discussed below.

Organizations develop gradually out of small social groups. Informal leaders become formal leaders, role-differentiation becomes division of labour, and norms become rules.

Leadership and hierarchical structure

We saw in Chapter 6 how small social groups spontaneously develop a hierarchical structure. It has been found that when a group develops a clear leadership hierarchy it is better at problem-solving (Heinecke and Bales, 1953). In the most primitive communities work leadership was based on the status system of the community, itself usually a matter of kinship. It looks as though working groups usually develop a hierarchical structure, and this is useful for organizing the work.

When a group gets larger it tends to split into sub-groups, indeed this happens by the time a group reaches ten in size. Each sub-group then has a leader, and these leaders have to coordinate the activities of their sub-groups, so that with increasing size a second line of leadership may emerge of people whose job it is to coordinate and direct the first-line leaders. Very large organizations often become bureaucratic, with ten or more levels in the hierarchy – a source of great discontent for those at the lower levels, and also a cause of enormous communication difficulties (p. 131). In small groups the hierarchy is based on different degrees of expertise at the group task. In traditional organizations it is based on family relationships. In modern working organizations it is based largely on competence at the administrative tasks to be performed at higher levels – the managing director of an oil company is not necessarily better at drilling holes than the others, but must be an expert at administering large-scale organizations; those who want to be promoted must abandon their speciality.

These leaders have to control and coordinate the different individuals and groups in the organization; they also have to help the organization to cope with a changing environment, and to develop it so that it attains its goals better. In order to do this leaders must have some power, and this may take several forms.

One basis for the classification of organizations is in terms of the type of authority used and the main form of motivation appealed to in the members. Etzioni (1961) suggested the following types:

(1) *Coercive.* Authority rests in the power of punishment; the members do not enjoy being there at all, and are motivated primarily by fear of punishment. In the past a great deal of work was organized in this way, for example that carried out by Roman slaves, and workers in the Industrial Revolution. The latter were motivated both by fear of punishment and by fear of dismissal and consequent starvation.

(2) *Utilitarian.* Authority rests on the power to reward, and workers will work in exchange for rewards, usually money. This is the main system in modern industry, especially where wage incentives are used.

(3) *Moral.* In research establishments, hospitals, voluntary and professional organizations, the members work because they believe in the importance of the organization's goals, and are personally committed to them. Authority rests on a leader's ability to appeal to these motivations in the members. The feudal system was partly coercive and utilitarian, but tenants were also committed by sworn obligations, and believed in the right of their landlord to their work and obedience. In more recent times there has been a high degree of commitment among entrepreneurs and senior management, but very much less commitment among their subordinates, some of whom are completely alienated from the goals of their organization.

Role differentiation. This appears in small social groups, as division of labour appeared in the earliest human communities – different people specializing in farming, looking after animals, crafts, trade, etc. The larger the group and the more complex the technology the more division of labour there is. In a modern factory there may be hundreds of distinct jobs, each with its own special skills, for which selection and training are needed. In addition to a large number of different kinds of manual work there are also many kinds of non-manual work – accounting, computing, clerical, managerial and research work, inspection, time-study, and the work of supervisors, shop stewards, management services specialists, financial and legal experts, and many others: all are 'working' in the organization and contribute to its effectiveness.

Roles and Role Conflict

To understand how organizations function we have to study the patterns of social interaction between the members. Every member of an organization occupies a *position*, e.g. supervisor, shop steward, personnel manager. For every position there is a *role*, i.e. a pattern of behaviour typical of the people in that position, and behaviour which is expected of them. Work roles primarily include the requirements of the job – the task to be performed, the way it is done, the speed and quality of work. Roles include broader aspects of behaviour, such as ways of behaving towards people in other positions, styles of non-verbal performance, attitudes and beliefs, clothes or uniforms worn, and styles of life outside work, such as the kind of car to drive, and where to have lunch.

The pressures to conform to a role can be very strong. Zimbardo (1973) paid a number of normal, middle-class student volunteers to play the roles of prison guards and prisoners, assigned arbitrarily, with appropriate uniforms in an imitation prison. Many of the 'guards' became brutal, sadistic and tyrannical, and many of the 'prisoners' became servile, selfish and hostile, and suffered from hysterical crying and severe depression. The experiment had to be stopped after six days and nights.

Why do roles have such a powerful effect on how individuals behave? Why do all supervisors behave in a similar way that is different from the way personnel managers behave? The job requirements are made clear by immediate supervisors, by co-workers, and in the course of training. The social behaviour of employees is affected by the interlocking of roles; if a doctor plays the doctor role the patient has to play the patient role, and the same is true of other pairs of roles.

The way in which different roles interlock is at the heart of social structures. A supervisor has a relationship of interlocking roles with subordinates and with superiors. These relationships may vary in terms of amount of participation, consideration and initiating structure (p. 160ff). The work-flow system creates another set of interlocking roles, for example between workers and inspectors, or between successive workers on an assembly line (p. 38ff). Role relationships between sales staff and customers, managers and shop stewards are other examples. In each case those concerned meet and relate to one another partly as individual personalities, but more as occupants of positions and performers of roles.

There is selection for the job – only certain people can become managers. There is also self-selection – only certain people want to. There are various social learning processes which succeed in making new occupants behave like old ones – imitation and instruction, both on training courses and on the job. Goffman (1961) suggested that in order to perform a role effectively, the newcomer has to put on a mask to act the part; however, when he or she has acted the part for long enough and others have accepted the performance the 'mask' becomes a real part of their personality.

The extent to which an individual's behaviour is programmed varies according to status. People in less skilled jobs have little scope for variation from their standard roles; more senior people have considerable leeway to do their job as they like, although still within the broad limits defined by the role (Cyert and Mac-Crimmon, 1968). Behaviour also depends on personality, as well as role, and this becomes more important the more a role allows for variation. The extent to which a manager behaves in an authoritarian way, for example, depends both on the role *and* on his or her personality; personality has rather less effect on the behaviour of a skilled manual worker.

Members of organizations often experience *role conflict* when other people have different expectations and exercise different social pressures from one another about the role they should be performing. Kahn and his colleagues (1964) found that 48 per cent of a sample of American industrial employees experienced such conflict, for example between the demands of management and the unions, between those above and those below, or between company and clients. *Role ambiguity* occurs when people do not agree about what the role should be and they do not know what is expected of them. Kahn and his team, in their industrial survey, found that 35 per cent were disturbed by lack of clarity about the scope and responsibilities of their jobs. This was particularly found in new jobs where there was no established tradition.

Many studies have been carried out on role conflict and ambiguity; Jackson and Schuler (1985) report a meta-analysis of 200 such studies (see Table 17). The two variables are correlated, although also fairly independent ($r = \cdot 27$), but have a rather similar set of causes and effects. It can be seen that role ambiguity in particular is greater when the job has less feedback, task identity and autonomy, when the supervisor allows less participation, and displays less initiating structure and consideration, and when there is less formalization. The effects are very marked: both role ambiguity and conflict are associated with less job satisfaction, commitment, involvement, and more tension; there is a greater propensity to leave and a lower self-rated performance (ambiguity only). It appears that role ambiguity and conflict have little effect on absenteeism.

When a person experiences role conflict he or she tends to be tense and unhappy, is dissatisfied with the job, tends to withdraw from social contact with those exerting conflicting pressure, and becomes bad at his or her work. The worker may also attempt to resolve the conflict or ambiguity in various ways – by giving one demand priority over another, bargaining with those exerting pressure, seeking official clarification or guidance, or trying to make changes in the organizational structure. Organizations can avoid or reduce role conflict by introducing appropriate rules, e.g. preventing husband and wife from working in the same part of the organization, or protecting from sanctions people who might

	Role conflict	Role ambiguity
Causes		
Autonomy	− ·23	0
Feedback	− ·35	− ·18
Task identity	− ·27	− ·25
Leader – initiating structure	− ·28	− ·17
consideration	− ·3	− ·28
participation	− ·36	− ·24
Formalization	− ·21	− ·07
Effects		
Job satisfaction	− ·3	− ·31
with supervisor	− ·36	− ·36
work itself	− ·33	− ·3
Tension/anxiety	·3	·28
Commitment	− ·27	− ·24
Involvement	− ·28	− ·16
Propensity to leave	·18	·21
Absenteeism	·09	− ·01
Performance – self-rated	− ·24	− ·02
rated by others	− ·08	·07

Table 17. A meta-analysis of the causes and effects of role conflict and ambiguity (from Jackson and Schuler, 1985).

easily incur them, such as lawyers or trade-union organizers.

There can also be conflict between an individual's needs or personality and his or her role. For example, a professor may be more interested in research than administration, an authoritarian person may find him- or herself in a democratic organization, some workers may be primarily interested in the social life of their firm. This kind of conflict can be avoided by selecting people with the right abilities, needs, interests and personalities for the particular job. Existing selection procedures could be improved by putting more emphasis on the individual's needs and interests, so as to bring about more alignment of the goals of the individual and organization. During training and the early period in the job, a person's goals may change to fit the role better. This applies particularly to doctors, the clergy, marines, and others whose initial training period is long and emotionally arousing and who become very dependent on their trainers. If the individual becomes influential in the organization he or she may be able to modify the organizational goals to be more compatible with his or her own. If all these processes fail, the worker will simply leave: indeed most labour turnover can be ascribed to conflicts of this kind (Cyert and MacCrimmon, 1968).

Ideas about Organizations

In the nineteenth century in England there was a slow growth of management practices to deal with the increased size and techno-logical complexity of industrial concerns. At first each firm was dominated by one person, the entrepreneur owner-manager, who did all the different management jobs, and who exercised a highly personalized control over everyone; there were no regular methods of working or of dealing with personnel. With increased size the span of control became too great for one person to handle and a regular chain of command was established with salaried supervisors and managers. Sometimes different partners were re-sponsible for different spheres, production, finance, etc. Following the increased scale and the rise of professional managers came a carefully planned work layout, division of labour, organized mass-production methods, definition of duties, and regular person-nel practices. The majority of owners and managers regarded the labour force as a hostile group whose culture had to be destroyed and whose character had to be reformed by means of economic incentives and punitive discipline. The forms that organization took were partly a matter of trial and error and were also influ-enced by ideas about how organizations should be designed. The same is true today: the way organizations are designed depends, in part, on the beliefs of managers about the effects of size, for-mality, and so on (Ford and Hegarty, 1984).

(1) *Classical organization theory.* In 1911 Taylor put forward his 'scientific management', with its division of labour, time-and-motion study, and incentives. The story of this movement, and the reaction against it was told in Chapter 3.

A little earlier Weber (1904) had put forward ideas about how an efficient bureaucracy should be designed, with an impersonal hierarchy, formal rules, and a high degree of specialization. These ideas were introduced to England in what came to be known as 'classical organization theory' (Urwick, 1929). It was not based on research, but on the observations and experience of a number of early industrialists and soldiers. The principles were the methods of management which they had seen used and which seemed to work. They also contained a number of ideas and assumptions about the social psychology of workers. Some of the main ideas of classical organization theory are: (a) *span of control* – executives should have no more than five to seven subordinates reporting to them, and first-line supervisors no more than twenty; (b) *chain of command* – there should be a continuous chain of command, each person reporting to his or her immediate superior, in a pyramidal structure; (c) *written responsibilities* – there should be clear and written responsibilities for every job; (d) *division of labour* – the work should be divided up so that no one has duties which are too varied or unrelated; and (e) *handling procedure* – workers should be motivated by economic incentives, controlled by fair discipline and impersonal rules, and be promoted on the basis of technical competence.

These ideas have been criticized from several points of view. The first of the main ideas, the principle of span of control, is not universally true. In particular, the organization can be much flatter at higher levels than was recommended. A vice-president of Sears Roebuck can have 200 store managers reporting to him or her if he or she has access to adequate measures of performance (Bass, 1965). We have seen that span of control varies considerably with the technology (p. 45ff).

In regard to the second idea, a number of sociologists have criticized excessively hierarchical structures on the grounds that vertical communication is difficult (p. 131), and that those at the lower levels can exert very little influence on what happens and thus become alienated (e.g. Blau and Scott, 1963). We have already considered one solution to this problem – the introduction of democratic-persuasive supervisory skills. Another solution is to have formal arrangements for participation in decisions (see p. 222ff). A third solution is to change the structure of the organization by decentralization or by having fewer levels and a larger span of control.

The fourth idea, division of labour, has resulted in workers doing very boring, repetitive jobs, sometimes undertaken every minute or even more frequently. This has caused very low levels of job satisfaction (p. 235ff). As for the fifth idea, it assumed that workers are naturally lazy and uncooperative and need to be controlled by payment and punishment. No reference is made to eliciting their cooperation, to their participation in decisions, or to personal relationships between leaders and those led (Bass, 1965; Massie, 1965).

Sociologists have been very critical of bureaucratic organizations. One of the most frequent criticisms is the tendency of people to become too attached to 'red tape', i.e. to pursue administrative procedures at the expense of the real goals of the organization. Merton (1957) has suggested that this is because an effective organization depends on strict devotion to regulations, so that there are strong social pressures to conform, and as a result some people take the rules, regulations and administrative procedures as ends in themselves.

Parkinson (1957) pointed to a number of related kinds of organizational pathology. 'Parkinson's Law' is that 'work expands so as to fill the time available'. Parkinson also observed how people build empires regardless of the amount of work to be done, and showed that the number of officials in the British Navy expanded far more rapidly than the Navy as a whole, and the Colonial Office expanded while the actual colonies were contracting. Again, little is known about the precise conditions under which unnecessary officials are able to multiply.

(2) *The Human Relations movement.* The Human Relations movement began with the Hawthorne studies in the early 1930s and was widely approved of by social scientists (although not always by managers) in the 1950s. The Hawthorne investigations included a study of informal organization and output restriction in the Bank Wiring Room (p. 117), a survey of workers' complaints, and the famous experiment in the Relay Assembly Test Room at

the Western Electric Company (p. 116) (Roethlisberger and Dickson, 1939). The latter experiment appeared to show that output was more affected by social relations within the group and with the supervisors than by wage incentives and the physical conditions of work. In my opinion, these conclusions were unfounded. These experiments were initiated, and the general Human Relations outlook propagated by Elton Mayo (1933, 1945).

After the Second World War research in industrial social psychology, mainly in the USA, extended the Human Relations approach in three related directions. First, research at the University of Michigan and elsewhere showed that democratic styles of supervision led to more output and job satisfaction (e.g. Likert, 1961). Second, laboratory and field studies of small social groups showed that social relationships *within* groups affected productivity. Third, many surveys were made of job satisfaction and it was found that social factors, such as relations with peers and supervisors, were important in satisfaction with work; it was also widely believed that job satisfaction was correlated with, or was a cause of, high productivity.

The Human Relations outlook had a considerable impact on American and British industry, particularly on supervisory and management training courses, although personnel departments were usually more enthusiastic about it than production departments. The movement helped to reform industry and improve the way in which workers were treated. Other factors in this improvement were the influence of the trade unions and a shortage of labour during part of the period in question.

This movement has received criticism as well, the main points being:

(*a*) The Relay Assembly Test Room study itself was very unsound (Argyle, 1953) – a true but unimportant observation, as the five women nevertheless helped to change the shape of industry.

(*b*) The movement was thought by some to be promanagement, just another way of manipulating workers. In fact Mayo and his followers believed that management and workers had common interests and what was needed was better cooperation between them.

(c) On the other hand some critics felt that there was too much emphasis on job satisfaction, and not enough on making profits. Later research found that the correlation between performance and job satisfaction is quite low, although labour turnover is more strongly correlated with satisfaction (Chapter 9).

(d) The effects of the style of supervision and of working groups are not as great as expected, and the findings are a lot more complex (Chapter 6).

(e) Above all, the Human Relations movement was primarily about individual motivation, and no attention was paid to organizational structure, to technology or to job design.

(3) *The integration of employees and organizations.* Likert (1961) belongs, in part, to the Human Relations group, but he introduced some further ideas. He wanted structures to make the interactions of individuals supportive and to contribute to their sense of personal worth. This should be done partly by belonging to cohesive work groups, partly by a positive relationship with supervisors; reciprocal support would overcome conflicts of interest. Many people are 'linking pins', i.e. belong to one group as a leader, and to another group as subordinate; they have a loyalty to both. As leaders they try to establish effective work groups, with members participating in goal-setting, and open communication.

Argyris (1964) also emphasized the integration of individual and organization. He used a motivational model like that of Maslow with a hierarchy of needs, and assumed that needs high in the hierarchy are important at work, where earlier theories had assumed that only lower needs were relevant. He was critical of bureaucratic types of structure which do not allow any outlet for such higher needs, especially for individuals lower in the hierarchy. He linked personal growth in individuals to the growth of organizations. The recommended method for achieving both was the use of T-groups. This approach has also been criticized:

(a) Many believe that there are real conflicts between management and workers, making it impossible to integrate subordinate members with the organization (p. 216).

(b) While these theories have definite recommendations about participation, and about other aspects of organizations, it turns out that the most effective design is contingent on the technology and the environment.

(c) Argyris assumed a version of the hierarchical needs theory, which has not in fact received much empirical support (p. 87ff). It may be a mistake to emphasize 'higher' needs if most people are not much motivated by them at work (Veen, 1984b).

(4) *Contemporary views.* Current thinking about organizations has assimilated these earlier theories, and the criticisms which have been made of them. Several key developments can be identified.

(a) *Later Human Relations approaches.* The importance of working groups, leadership skills and job satisfaction are still recognized. It is now realized that different social skills need to be used in different situations and different specialized roles, and that there are better methods of training than T-groups.

(b) *Organizational design.* Classical organization theory laid down inflexible rules for organizations, while the Human Relations group was silent on this topic. It is now recognized that organizational design is of central importance, that the optimum designs can be discovered empirically, and that they are contingent on technology and environment.

(c) *Effects of technology.* We have already seen how organizations are affected by technology, and how they are being affected by automation and information technology. The design of sociotechnical systems includes design of the technology.

(d) *Contingency theory* emphasizes how organizational structure should vary with the environment in which the firm operates (p. 213).

(e) *Recognition of conflict.* The Human Relations theorists were right in emphasizing the common interests of management and labour. However, it is clear that there is a lot of conflict as well, and research in industrial relations has analysed the processes involved, and how conflicts can be handled (Gordon and Nurick, 1981).

(*f*) *Industrial democracy*. It is widely believed that a solution to these conflicts is increased participation, in various forms of industrial democracy (p. 222ff).

Different Kinds of Organization

Working organizations can take a variety of forms. This is particularly striking if one looks at different periods of history (Chapter 2), or at different countries today. Part of the difference is due to the nature of the work or the technology. On the other hand, quite different activities can be embodied in identical organizations – factories, churches and schools can be run with essentially the same structure, for example. Recent research has shown that under certain conditions some structures are better than others. In addition, new designs, not yet investigated by social scientists, have been invented by management. The main dimensions along which organizations vary are as follows.

Size. Since the Industrial Revolution there has been a continuous increase in the size of working organizations – for technological reasons, and to take advantage of other economies of scale. By size one usually means the number of people working at a particular location, although it may be necessary to take account of several plants together if there is centralized administration. For some purposes other aspects of size may be relevant, such as the number of beds in a hospital, the production capacity, or capital funds. While firms became large because of early technological developments, they may become smaller again, or may be broken up into smaller units, as a result of advances in information technology.

Size affects other aspects of organization. Larger concerns usually have more levels in the hierarchy, are more centralized, and more formalized (Child and Mansfield, 1972) – aspects which will be discussed below.

It has been found repeatedly that in smaller plants, and in smaller departments, job satisfaction is greater, while absenteeism, labour turnover, accidents and labour disputes are reduced, in

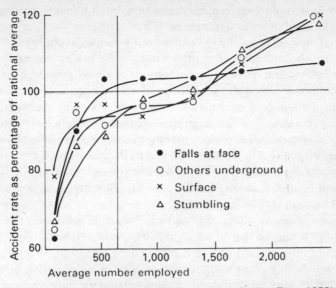

Fig. 18. Accidents and size of mine (from Acton Society Trust, 1953).

many cases by a large amount (Revans, 1958). For example, the
Acton Society Trust (1953) found that the rate of absenteeism
correlated ·67 with the size of coal mines and ·6 with supervisory
span of control; rather smaller correlations were found for shops
and factories. The accident rate in coal mines was nearly twice as
high in the larger mines as in the smaller ones (Fig. 18).

Size can be kept down by decentralization; this is easier when
sub-units are independent (e.g. shops), or can be given specific
programmes of work to do.

Performance, productivity per worker, is *less* in large departments; Gooding and Wagner (1985) found an average correlation
of − ·23 in a meta-analysis of thirty-one studies. There was no
variation of productivity with size of plant; there are no 'economies
of scale'.

Shape. Classical organization theory recommended a small span of
control – five to seven subordinates for managers, and up to
twenty for supervisors. This makes for a rather 'tall' shape. With

flatter structures there is more delegation, but it imposes a greater load on supervisors and managers (Child, 1984).

Pugh and Hickson (1976) carried out a statistical study of fifty-two British firms and other organizations. Each was assessed on sixty-four scales; principal components analysis produced four dimensions of which the percentage of subordinates was one. Tall versus flat can be measured by span of control or by percentage of subordinates. In a flat organization there are relatively more subordinates per supervisor or manager, and therefore fewer levels in the hierarchy. The number of levels in the hierarchy is typically six with 1,000 employees, rising to seven or eight at 10,000. The span of control is twenty or more for first-line supervisors, six to eight for managers (Child, 1984).

Shape is partly the result of technology. Woodward (1965) found that the number of levels in the supervisory hierarchy was typically three in unit or batch production, four in mass production and six in process work; the span of control also varies, being greatest for mass production. She reported that the most successful firms of each type were those that were near the typical structure for each type of work. However, Pugh *et al.* (1969) found that size was a more important prediction of organizational shape than technology. Marsh and Mannari (1981) in a study of seventy-eight Japanese factories found that span of control was equally affected by both, complexity was more affected by size, proportion of graduates by technology. We shall see later that Japanese firms usually have a tall, hierarchical structure (p. 332ff), although in the West this kind of structure is on the whole less successful.

Organic–mechanistic. Burns and Stalker (1961) studied twenty Scottish firms, and identified two contrasted types of organization. Some ('organic') had weak hierarchies, flexible division of labour, lateral as much as vertical communication, and decision-taking at all levels. Others ('mechanistic') were more hierarchical, more formal and with centralized control. This division corresponds to the rate of change of technology. In an uncertain and fast-changing situation, such as that associated with electronics, organic structures developed, while in a more static environment mechanistic ones prevailed.

In traditional industry large firms have mechanistic structures, i.e. strong hierarchy, centralized control, high division of labour, and a great deal of formality in the form of written rules and job specifications. On the whole these are sources of low job satisfaction, although they may be inevitable features of this kind of industry to some extent. However, Child (1976) found that in Britain large firms were more successful if they adopted bureaucratic structures.

There is an interesting contingency here: in a less static environment, such as that faced by high-tech firms, organic structures do better. The typical case is a small electronics firm, in a new market, staffed by a highly skilled work-force. An increasing amount of work in the future may be like this.

Contingency theories. Contingency theories recommend that the structure, like other working methods, should be adapted to the situation, and in particular to the technology and the outside environment. It is maintained that there is a sort of natural selection, whereby only firms with the shapes which are appropriate for their environment survive, or that they learn by experience and change towards the shapes which work best. In either case the firms whose structures are congruent with the environment tend to be more successful in meeting their goals (Hazewinkel, 1984).

Lawrence and Lorsch (1967) found evidence for this theory at the departmental level: those departments facing more uncertain environments adopted less formal structures, i.e. fewer written rules and job descriptions. Where departments differed in their environments, and hence adopted different structures, there was greater need for integration between them. We discussed above a number of other studies of contingencies based on environmental uncertainty, for example that by Burns and Stalker (1961).

Other examples of contingency are:

(a) *Leadership skills.* We have seen that the optimum skills vary with the situation, for example in the amount of participation allowed and the amount of initiating structure used (p. 160ff).

(b) *Span of control and technology*. We have seen that at different levels of complexity the span of control is quite different, and that there is evidence of greater effectiveness when the appropriate structure is adopted (p. 45ff).

While contingency theories appear to offer practical guidance on how to plan organizations, there are a number of problems. (1) There may be several different contingencies to apply in a particular case. (2) The benefits of congruence may be quite weak, so that there is considerable latitude of choice for choosing structures (Child, 1976). (3) While contingency seems to work best at the departmental level, adopting different structures in different departments causes serious problems for integration and employee commitment. (4) It may be true that organization and environment should be congruent, but organizations can change their environments, for example by choice of products or services offered, or by reducing uncertainty in other ways (Randolph and Dess, 1984). (5) The contingency approach overlooks the possibility that there may be universal principles of good organization after all (Dawson, 1986).

The detailed design of working organizations. The detailed organization has still to be constructed for dealing with problems of coordination between different departments, information flow, control of cycles of operation, and introducing innovation. In practice the chart is designed by managers in the light of their experience, and modifications are made if things do not work smoothly.

One basic design is to divide the organization by functions – research and development, manufacture, marketing, personnel, etc. – with a manager in charge of each. Another design is to divide in terms of products, with departments for research and development, manufacturing, etc. within each product division. The first design might be better if technically high standards of work are very important, the second if new markets are more important.

What if both considerations are very important? 'Matrix' structures are now popular, and originate from the NASA space programme. Specialists belong to their functional group, but are also responsible to the leader of a special project or product team, i.e. they have two bosses. Lateral links are strong, and there is an avoidance of formalization as in organic structures. The main advantages of matrix structures are the flexible use of people, the capacity to respond quickly, and improved communication between managers. The main drawback is that a lot of time is spent in meetings, and there is a danger of conflicts between the two bosses (Dawson, 1986).

Conflict in Organizations

Despite the developments in industrial democracy, and despite the efforts of social scientists and enlightened managers to create harmony, there is still a great deal of conflict in industry. The main conflict is between employers, or managers, and 'workers' represented by trade unions. This conflict is most visible in the form of strikes; there are also go-slows, working to rule, overtime bans, while absenteeism, lateness and labour turnover can be seen as further manifestations of conflict. Over a recent two-year period about one-third of British firms had a strike, and 46 per cent had strikes or other industrial action (Hartley, 1984).

Many social scientists think that all this is unnecessary, and point to the common interests of those involved – both sides want to keep the firm in business, and therefore to compete successfully with other firms; both sides want to keep efficient workers with the firm. For these reasons some social scientists think that it would be better if workers could participate more directly in decision-taking in the firm, in some form of 'industrial democracy'. It is hoped that by further application of participation, better social skills, more equitable incentives, and the rest, conflict will not occur. However, Karl Marx and others have pointed to an underlying conflict between employers and workers; for example, workers are paid less, and are laid off, when such action is economically advantageous to the firm.

The system of trade union representation and bargaining itself perpetuates the idea that there are 'two sides' in industry, despite the fact that managers are usually salaried employees themselves, and the fact that a large proportion of employees occupy intermediate positions.

Some industrial sociologists have argued that conflict is inevitable and proper because of the different goals and points of view of the two sides (Fox, 1973). It has also been maintained that conflict has some positive functions in defining the opposing groups and helping the organization adjust to change, although it does need to be 'regulated' (Dahrendorf, 1959).

(1) *The causes of conflict.* Strikes, stoppages and other manifestations of conflict have causes at different levels – the frustrations of individuals, the influence of leaders, the failures of management and the processes of inter-group behaviour. Strikes are usually triggered by an event – when management is thought to have broken an agreement, a new worker is employed in a situation where there is fear of redundancy, a possible hazard is created when equipment is not supplied, a worker or group is thought to have been treated unfairly, etc. But this will only lead to a strike if other processes, such as frustrations over pay, are also present.

(a) *Low pay.* Most strikes are about pay, so it must be an important factor. On the other hand, striking over pay may simply be a ritualized way of expressing a range of less obvious discontents. In fact there are more strikes during economic booms and high employment, when unions have most power (Knowles, 1952). In addition, the strike-bound industries are not the worst paid, for example coal, iron and steel, motor-vehicle manufacture, shipbuilding and docks. Strikes are much less frequent in retail and distribution, footwear and railways, which are less well paid (Hartley, 1984). However, if pay is felt to be inequitably low in comparison with other groups, this is a threat to identity and self-esteem, and may well evoke an aggressive response.

(b) *Low job satisfaction.* There is little correlation between union membership and job satisfaction, although there is between union membership and job commitment. And there are more strikes among skilled workers, whose job satisfaction is above average. It is quite possible, however, that frustration or very low job satisfaction is a factor in strikes, although it is clearly not the only or even the main factor, since most discontented workers do not strike.

(c) *Trade union leaders.* It is widely believed (by management) that trade union leaders are the main cause of strikes. In one study it was found that 14 per cent of union members and 54 per cent of managers thought that labour trouble was caused by outside union organizers (Bass, 1965). The two sides also differ in the extent to which they see managers and union officials as honest, fair, trustworthy, cooperative, etc. (Haire, 1955). However, research has shown that some shop stewards do indeed orchestrate strikes, often against the initial wishes of their followers, while others simply reflect the opinions of their members (Batstone *et al.*, 1978). On the other hand, even militant activists are unlikely to be successful unless there are widespread grievances. Batstone *et al.* found that stoppages and strikes were often initiated by a worker with a grievance; however, whether or not a strike developed any further depended on informal opinion leaders, shop stewards, and particularly on the 'convenors', i.e. senior shop stewards. The conduct of some unions is often far from satisfactory, although the gradual introduction of ballots before strikes is changing things. A very small proportion of members are actively interested in union business, and few attend meetings; they and the officials carry a great deal of power; votes are usually quite unrepresentative; since membership is voluntary the leaders must keep satisfying the needs of their members, which may lead to constant warfare with management; and the higher leaders are often quite out of touch with the ordinary member (Allen, 1954).

(d) *Management.* There are great differences in the frequency of strikes between plants in the same industry. From 1976–8 in Britain 4 per cent of manufacturing plants had 49 per cent of strikes (Brown, 1981). There are also more strikes in larger plants. At least some of this is probably due to failure of managers to communicate, inform, consult, persuade, and to meet the needs of employees. Different managerial interventions can produce a fall in the number of disruptions. A meta-analysis found reduced disruption rate of ·31 of a standard deviation for goal-setting, ·2 for appraisal and feedback, and ·39 for training (Guzzo *et al.*, 1985).

(*e*) *Inter-group conflict.* As we showed earlier there is often conflict between groups, not only because of real conflicts of interest, but also because of in-group versus out-group hostilities. Each side exaggerates the differences between them, especially in cohesive groups, and rejects the other group accordingly. This is worse when there is little communication between the two groups (p. 140ff).

(2) *The development of strikes.* How does frustration, or whatever is the underlying cause, become translated into a strike? There is usually a triggering event. Batstone *et al.* (1978) studied twenty-five stoppages or strikes in the vehicle manufacture industry. The shop stewards played the main role in organizing the strikes, which they did by building up minor frustrations into a coherent story, with justifications which the authors called 'vocabulary of action'. Managers also played a role, by deciding whether or not to regard a stoppage as a strike. The whole affair can be seen as a social process to which both sides contribute. Van de Vliert (1984) described the processes of escalation involved in a strike, such as attacking the other side, withdrawing from interaction, extending the issues involved and looking for allies.

(3) *Resolving and preventing conflicts.* From the radical point of view, the desired outcome is a change of ownership followed by workers' control. Management may make structural concessions short of this, such as changes in pay, hours or conditions of work. Conflicts may also be resolved by making 'psychological' changes, such as increased contact between management and workers, sharing information, and better social skills, all of which lead to changed perceptions by workers and increased trust. This kind of change is more acceptable if accompanied by structural changes (Hartley, 1984).

Conflict can be resolved by negotiation between management

and unions or at joint consultative committees. The skills required for doing this were described earlier. There are various strategies which are helpful in resolving conflicts, such as 'integrative bargaining', and sometimes a third party is brought in to mediate (p. 179ff).

Conflicts can be prevented from escalating into strikes by the existence of formal channels, such as joint consultative committees, and rules for using them. Spontaneous action can prevent things getting worse, such as calming people down, considering events to be of minor importance, generally perceiving an event and persuading others to perceive it as a less serious affair (Van de Vliert, 1984).

Producing Organizational Change

Organizations have to change constantly because of changing technology, economic conditions or government policies, or because of internal problems (Baron, 1986). There are several kinds of change – in products, technology, administrative procedures or organizational structure.

Changes in organizations cannot be brought about simply by telling people about the new arrangements. There is great resistance to change as people fear loss of income or status, or changed relationships with other people, while some may choose the even greater upheaval of leaving the organization entirely – in fact labour turnover is a common result of changes. Members need to be taught and persuaded to accept the new arrangements; there are several ways of doing this.

Organizational Development (OD) consists of trying to introduce planned changes, to enhance organizational effectiveness by making use of research findings. OD has become a kind of social movement in industry, reflecting growing confidence in the power of the behavioural sciences to solve organizational problems, and the importance attached to personal growth and the integration of individuals and organization; it often uses an outside consultant as a 'change agent' (Guest, 1984). There are several ways of bringing about change, as noted below.

Intervention	
Financial compensation	2·12
Training	·85
Decision making strategies	·7
Socio-technical changes	·66
Goal-setting	·65
Work redesign	·52
Supervisory methods	·51
Management by objectives	·45
Appraisal and feedback	·41
Work rescheduling	·3

Table 18. The average effect on output of various organizational interventions expressed as ratios of standard deviation as found in a meta-analysis by Guzzo *et al.* (1985).

A review by Kondrasuk (1981) of 185 follow-up studies of the effectiveness of OD found generally positive results: 5 : 1 positive for quasi-experimental designs, less than this for true experiments. In some of the better-controlled studies the effects were short-term – two or three years (e.g. Ivancevich, 1986). The first systematic meta-analysis of organizational intervention was carried out by Guzzo *et al.* (1985), who studied 330 intervention programmes with control groups. Their findings are given as ratios of the standard deviation and the effects on productivity can be seen in Table 18. We shall discuss some of these results later.

Management by objectives (MBO). First devised by Drucker (1954), MBO is now used by most American companies, and by many outside America as well. Those to be involved are 'oriented' to the system; supervisors and subordinates at all levels agree on specific goals which they think are most important (these are measurable, limited in time and there is a plan for attaining them); progress is reviewed regularly, and discussed typically at appraisal interviews (p. 172ff); and an overall review assesses progress and begins the next cycle of objectives and plans (Baron, 1986). Table 18 shows quite modest effects of MBO, but Rodgers and Hunter (1986)

found that when MBO had strong support from top management
there was a 42 per cent increase in productivity.

Survey feedback. A survey is carried out of part or all of the organization. The results are then presented and interpreted by a consultant in group discussion sessions, and plans for dealing with any
problems are discussed. Each group discusses the problem at its
own level and receives reports of the discussion of more detailed
problems at the next level below (Mann, 1957).

The management grid method. Blake and Mouton (1964) maintained that managers should have a high concern for people
and a high concern for productivity. As we saw earlier this view
is in conflict with evidence that leadership style should vary with
the situation (p. 160ff). Blake and Mouton devised a method for
moving managers in these two directions. There are six stages:
(1) group laboratory sessions are used to demonstrate interpersonal phenomena and skills, such as the use of power in
supervision and ways of dealing with conflicting ideas about how
work should be done; (2) trainees are helped to analyse the working of their own work teams; (3) lateral links between colleagues
are strengthened; (4) diagonal-slice groups (made up of workers
from different levels who are not in the direct line of command)
discuss new organizational goals; (5) help is given with the
detailed implementation of the changes; and (6) there is consideration of further areas where changes are needed. This approach
in a firm of 4,000 employees, including 800 managerial and
technical staff, over a five-month period produced increases in
productivity and profits, together with better ratings by subordinates of the performance of managers. There also appeared to be
improvements in supervisory skills and managers' relations with
subordinates.

Other methods of OD. We discuss several other methods elsewhere,
notably social skills training (p. 183ff), T-groups (p. 192ff), and
industrial democracy (below).

Appendix: Industrial Democracy

One of the main sources of discontent in traditional industry is the feeling, on the part of the majority of those at lower levels, that they are not consulted, and have no say in what happens. As we have seen, upward communication is often very difficult. This leads to a feeling of alienation in which many workers feel that they do not belong properly, and are not interested in productivity or other organizational goals. We have also seen from studies of decision-making groups that groups make better decisions than individuals (p. 143ff), and produce greater commitment to the decisions taken. Participatory, consultative supervision leads to greater satisfaction and commitment, and often to better performance (p. 163). A further, more political, motivation is the belief that in a democracy people have a right to have a say in decisions which affect such a central part of their lives, and is just as important as the right to vote at elections.

Industrial democracy consists of the creation of formal channels for participation or consultation by a system of committees and elected representatives. This can be a supplement to normal trade union negotiation, can be integrated with it, or can be a substitute for it. There are different degrees of participation in decision-making by workers, from being able to make suggestions, to being consulted (but their decisions not being binding on management), to the right of veto, the right of joint decision, to overall control (Blumberg, 1968). Employees may participate in decisions on very trivial issues, or in more important matters to do with the speed and method of working, pay and promotion, or wider matters. There are also several different ways of representing employees.

(1) *Trade union representation.* This is the main system of representation available to employees in Britain. Shop stewards are elected by trade union members to negotiate for better wages and working conditions. This takes place at different levels – individual departments, firms, and whole industries. The skills needed for negotiation were discussed earlier (p. 179ff).

(2) *Joint consultation.* This is also used in some British firms, although it is more extensively used in European countries (Andriessen and Coetsier, 1984). It involves setting up joint committees of representatives of management and of other groups in the organization to discuss a wide range of problems connected with running the enterprise. There may be a number of such committees at different levels of the organization – one dealing with the affairs of the whole concern, others dealing with divisions within it. These committees may have decision-making powers, but they are more often advisory. The members are elected and are expected to represent the interests of their group rather than act with delegated powers (National Institute of Industrial Psychology, 1952).

Joint consultation was set up in many industries in Britain during the Second World War, especially in armaments factories, to obtain greater cooperation from workers. After the war many firms abandoned it, but it was built into the organizational structure of the nationalized industries on the theory that joint consultation would produce a cooperative industrial society, while collective bargaining was appropriate to areas of conflict, e.g. wages. Since the war there has been a gradual decline in the use of joint consultation by private industry, and it has come to be seen as a minor tool of management.

(3) *Workers' councils.* This is the broadest form of industrial democracy, and is most widely used in Yugoslavia and in Dutch cooperatives. The factory is controlled by a workers' council, all of whose members are elected representatives. In Yugoslavian factories there are about twenty members, representing different sections and levels, who meet once a month, and who take major decisions as a group. There is also an administrative hierarchy, with a director and technical staff, who are employed by and answerable to the council, although their views are usually accepted on technical matters. In Yugoslavian factories there is also a management board, which consists of the director and between five and eleven members who are appointed by the workers' council and who are usually members of it. It carries out the policies

made by the council, and usually meets weekly. Workers' councils are formed at departmental level, especially in large or geographically dispersed firms. Where possible accounts are decentralized, so that departments are financially autonomous. There are more specialized committees dealing with finance, sales and other such areas. The members of these committees receive no extra pay, often meet after hours, and have no individual power, status or privileges. Turnover of membership is rapid, and members are often removed on the initiative of one group or another, for laxity or other minor offences. However, during the 1950s half to one-third of all workers in Yugoslavia served on committees, 75 per cent being manual workers. Those most in evidence were male skilled workers and members of the communist party (Blumberg, 1968).

Experience of committee work is regarded as a form of training and as a vehicle for promotion. The committees are also regarded as a channel of information for management to find out the views of workers, and, in addition, for workers to learn about the problems facing management. The committees work closely together with management and exercise considerable influence over matters of wages and working conditions, although less on more technical aspects of production (Kolaja, 1965).

(4) *Worker-directors.* 'Co-determination' in West Germany consists of the establishment of supervisory boards, which are rather like boards of directors and meet monthly; five of the eleven members are elected representatives of the workers in the coal and steel industries, one-third in the case of all other industries. Three of the labour representatives are nominated by the unions. These boards are different from the British joint consultative committees in that they take final decisions on all matters. There is also a labour director who is nominated by the union, although paid by the firm, who is one of the three members of the management board. This board consists of three directors who run the firm – the technical, commercial and labour directors. They meet weekly, and they carry out the policy decided by the supervisory board (Schuchman, 1957).

It might be expected that this system would undermine the unions. However, the unions have been strongly in favour of co-determination and believe that it is important for them to penetrate and participate in management. It was found that sixty-three out of 252 labour representatives on supervisory boards were union officials, that unions were mainly responsible for choosing labour directors, and that union independence had not been weakened (Blumberg, 1968).

(5) *The Scanlon Plan.* This is the best-known American version of industrial democracy (Scanlon, 1948) and has two main components. First, departmental production committees are set up consisting of elected worker representatives and a member appointed by management, usually the supervisor. There is also a company-wide committee with representatives from both sides. The committees meet at least once a month and discuss suggestions for improving working methods and increasing efficiency. They are given considerable power of decision-taking, although a limit is placed on their expenditure. Second, the committees work out a 'formula' according to which a proportion of the savings made in labour costs is paid to workers as a bonus, over and above the rates set by collective bargaining. Usually 75 per cent of savings is paid as bonus. The firm makes a small profit on labour costs and better use is made of the capital assets.

Again it is difficult to assess how successful this system has been. It is found that workers are given much more information about production costs, competition, etc. They also have more suggestions to make. It seems likely that workers become more concerned with efficiency, and internalize the goals of the firm. Katz and Kahn (1966) conclude that

the Scanlon Plan appears as a creative solution to many of the typical problems of large organizations. It adds strong positive factors to the usual army of 'motivators', and it adds no penalties. There is a formal enlistment of the peer group via the representative committee structure, and such groups are strengthened through the close linkage of reward to group and super-group contributions to system efficiency. The job of the individual worker is enlarged and enhanced by the recognition and encouragement of innovative contributions, and the model of leadership which is called for comes much closer to the values of democratic practice as they exist in our culture and institutions outside industry.

Most of the follow-up studies which have been reported show increases in productivity, especially in small companies that are doing badly, and which are not automated (Lesieur, 1958). In addition, Miller and Schuster (1987) studied the introduction of the Scanlon Plan in a large manufacturing company, and found over an eleven-year period that there was a small positive trend in productivity, an increase in the labour force, a very large number of suggestions, and improved harmony between shop stewards and supervisors.

(6) *Quality circles.* These are voluntary groups of employees who work together, or who share some responsibility, and who meet regularly to discuss work problems. They originated in Japan, where they are very widely used, spread to the USA, and are used by some firms in Britain.

Typically a group meets for one hour a week during working hours. The groups can be at any level in the organization, and in any department. They are usually led by the relevant supervisor or manager, but are set up by consultants who teach the necessary skills of conducting brainstorming and other group methods. The group looks for problems which are interfering with work effectiveness, collects and analyses data, and produces suggestions which are passed on to management. Later they try to evaluate the success of any changes that are made (Crocker *et al.*, 1984; Hutchins, 1985).

Quality circles have become very popular – there were one million in Japan in 1979 – but little systematic evidence is available about their effectiveness. Norris and Cox (1987) found that those who volunteered for them were likely to be better educated, but lower in performance and job satisfaction, and with a higher rate of absenteeism than other workers. Perhaps some participants see this as an alternative route to success.

How far has industrial democracy developed? The Industrial Democracy in Europe research group (IDE, 1981) carried out an extensive survey of 8,000 workers in 134 establishments in twelve European countries. In Britain 20 per cent of lower-level employees had been representatives, while 60 per cent were trade union members. However, the actual amount of influence was felt to be very small, and it was concluded that, 'In spite of the seemingly elaborate systems for employee representation in several of the twelve countries, the effects on the distribution of power and level of individual involvement are mild, and generally we conclude that industrial democracy is still in an embryonic state.' Comparing the different countries, workers felt that they had by far the greatest amount of democracy in Yugoslavia, followed by West Germany and Norway.

Research into industrial democracy has focused on three main issues – do workers want it, does it increase job satisfaction, and does it increase productivity?

Do workers want industrial democracy? Surveys in Britain and the USA have found consistently that most lower-level employees feel that they have very little influence, and that 50–60 per cent would like more participation in their immediate affairs, while few wanted to take part in more distant decisions affecting the company as a whole (Wall and Lischeron, 1977). However, a study by these authors found evidence for a greater desire for participation. Surveys were made of nurses, factory workers and local authority employees. They were asked about participation in decisions at three levels – 'local' (e.g. pace of work, bonus earnings), 'medium' (e.g. promotions, purchase of equipment), and 'distant' (e.g. capital expenditure). The main results are shown in Table 19.

It can be seen that both the factory workers and the local authority workers wanted a high level of participation. The most typical view was that influence should be shared equally between management and workers. The desire for participation was greater for medium and distant influences than in previous surveys, perhaps because the climate of ideas has been changing. As before, the more skilled workers had a greater desire to participate

Decision-making level	Response categories	Percentage of workers endorsing the given response categories		
		Skilled industrial workers	Unskilled industrial workers	Local authority workers
Desired local influence	None	6	16	4
	Slight	6	6	5
	Moderate	16	21	21
	Considerable	22	27	29
	Complete	50	31	41
Desired medium influence	None	17	27	15
	Hardly any	5	4	6
	Less than management	6	16	13
	Same as management	54	37	55
	More than management	18	17	11
Desired distant influence	None	30	40	14
	Hardly any	7	11	4
	Less than management	12	12	18
	Same as management	47	36	60
	More than management	4	1	4

Table 19. The desire for local, medium and distant influence among blue-collar workers (from Wall and Lischeron, 1977).

in decisions. The nurses had lower scores than the factory and local authority workers, perhaps because of the authoritarian hospital tradition.

What form of participation is preferred? In the Wall and Lischeron surveys all three groups preferred direct contact with managers or supervisors, informally or at regular meetings, rather than indirectly through representatives on works committees or through shop stewards. The only exception to this was that for distant problems 46 per cent of local authority workers favoured the works committee, and 28 per cent favoured shop stewards.

Does industrial democracy increase job satisfaction? Correlational studies find a positive relationship. Miller and Monge (1986) carried out a meta-analysis of forty-one studies, which had an average correlation of ·34 between job satisfaction and perceived participation, and ·16 with actual participation. One investigation found that this held only for employees low on authoritarianism and with a strong need for independence (Vroom, 1960), but others failed to replicate this. Pelz (1952) found that it worked if supervisors had enough power. Wall and Lischeron (1977) found a correlation between satisfaction and perceived influence on local, i.e. immediate, matters, less on more distant topics. However, as these authors point out, perceived participation and job satisfaction use the same subjects, and possibly overlapping items; and correlation does not show causation.

There have been a number of American field experiments in which the amount of participation was increased for some workers, and reduced or left unchanged for others. While most of these studies found positive effects on job satisfaction, none found negative effects. In one of the best of these studies Morse and Reimer (1956) used matched divisions in a large clerical organization, and over a six-month period trained supervisors to increase participation in two divisions, and to reduce it in another two. After eighteen months several aspects of satisfaction increased in the first two but declined in the other two.

On the other hand, Wall and Lischeron (1977) carried out a similar study in which 'Action Planning Groups' were established over five months for 150 outdoor local authority workers, who were compared with 200 controls. The manipulation was effective in that the experimental subjects thought that they had more influence, especially at the medium level. However, there was little effect on job satisfaction: out of eight scales of measurement there was increased satisfaction with the immediate manager, less with pay, while six scales were unchanged.

What can be concluded from the above? The bulk of the evidence shows a positive link between participation and job satisfaction. However, this was not found for Wall and Lischeron's unskilled local authority workers, or for American workers high in authoritarianism. Nurses had a relatively low desire to take part in decisions. This suggests that there are some groups of workers with a low need to participate, whose job satisfaction is not increased by participation. On the other hand Miller and Monge (1986) found no difference in this relationship for different kinds of employees, e.g. managers versus workers.

Does industrial democracy increase productivity? There are several reasons for expecting that it should. Participation could increase motivation by increasing commitment to goals, employees may spend less time trying to beat or sabotage the system; on the other hand, more time is spent in meetings. Miller and Monge (1986) did a meta-analysis of twenty-five studies of the correlation between individual performance and participation. They found an average correlation of ·11 for participation in goal-setting, and ·27 for other kinds of participation in field settings. In studies comparing departments under different supervisors a positive correlation is sometimes found, but more often it is not (Bass, 1981).

Some field experiments have shown positive effects. In a pyjama factory there was an increase of 14 per cent in output when participation was introduced in connection with production changes, compared with a drop of 17 per cent in control groups. There was also an increase of 18 per cent in a later replication. No workers left the experimental groups during the study, compared with 17 per cent from the control groups. Even better results were obtained with groups of workers who participated fully in decisions rather than through their representatives (Coch and French, 1948). In the Morse and Reimer study (1956) productivity increased in both conditions, but can probably be considered a 'Hawthorne effect'. No cases of negative effects have been reported.

In Yugoslavia productivity has been rising at about 7 per cent per year, while wages have been rising at 10 per cent per annum over several years (Blumberg, 1968). There has been very little resistance to change during this period of rapid technological development. Communications within firms have been greatly improved, barriers and hostilities between groups have largely disappeared, and there is evidence of increased loyalty and commitment to firms. We reported evidence for the success of the Scanlon Plan earlier (p. 225ff).

There have been studies of the effectiveness of British joint consultation, in particular a survey by the National Institute of Industrial Psychology (1952) of 545 firms which used it. This survey found that most firms had certain 'problems', for example absenteeism, and problems associated with promotion prospects, canteen, safety and accidents. Nearly all the firms surveyed discussed these matters during joint consultations; an index of the extent to which joint consultation had contributed to the solution of these problems was averaged at 50 per cent.

How industrial democracy actually functions. A number of problems have been encountered.

(1) Management should be in favour of the scheme, take it seriously, see that issues are properly discussed on the committees, and should not just rush through their carefully prepared plans.

(2) The committees are taken more seriously by management and workers if they have real power and are more than advisory bodies, as they have been in most of the British schemes. It is interesting that in two of the most successful schemes – the Yugoslav one and the Scanlon Plan mentioned earlier – the committees decide the level of bonus payment.

(3) All levels in the hierarchy should be represented, not just the top and the bottom (Emery and Thorsrud, 1969).

(4) Representatives should sit on committees which deal with matters that they are able and willing to discuss. A number of studies have found that employees are keener to participate in decisions about their own departments than about company affairs (Hespe and Little, 1971).

(5) Members of commmittees experience conflict – between being representatives of workers and running the affairs of the firm. There can be a real conflict of interest between workers' representatives and management over wages, for example. However, wider issues are discussed than those involved in usual trade union bargaining, especially in the personnel field. There is little discussion of production, finance and sales, although here there may be no conflict of interest and representatives may take a company point of view.

(6) Management have more information and expertise, so still have more power than lower-level employees (Mulder, 1971).

(7) Supervisors need to be of a higher calibre, since they are likely to be short-circuited by complaints to committees. Their formal power is slightly reduced, and they need additional skills of persuasion and consideration.

(8) The solution to these problems may lie in the introduction of rules which equalize the distribution of power (IDE, 1981).

9

JOB SATISFACTION, ABSENTEEISM AND LABOUR TURNOVER

How much do people enjoy their jobs? What are the kinds of work that they enjoy most? Do happy people work harder? Is it possible to increase the level of job satisfaction? These are some of the questions we shall tackle in this chapter.

Job satisfaction, like happiness, can be defined in terms of the extent of positive rather than negative emotions experienced, in this case at work, or as a reflective, cognitive state of satisfaction with the work, the pay, and other aspects of the job (Argyle, 1987). A third component of happiness, and therefore of job satisfaction, is the absence of anxiety, depression, or other signs of mental ill health. A related concept is 'organizational commitment', that is the extent to which a person is committed to work as such, his or her career, is attached to the job, loyal to the organization, or to the union (Morrow, 1983).

We shall see later that job satisfaction is a major component of overall satisfaction or happiness, that people at work are a lot happier than those who are out of work, and that work is, on the whole, good for mental health.

How can we measure job satisfaction? The most widely used measure is a very simple one. Overall job satisfaction can be assessed by simple questions such as 'choose one of the following statements which best tells how well you like your job: I hate it, I dislike it, I do not like it, I am indifferent to it, I like it, I am enthusiastic about it, I love it' (Hoppock, 1935). A number of similar general questions can be put together and the replies averaged. Using a four-point scale, fifteen national surveys in the

USA from 1972–8 found that 51·8 per cent of workers were very satisfied with their jobs, 36·1 per cent were somewhat satisfied, 9 per cent were a little dissatisfied, and 3·1 per cent were very dissatisfied (Weaver, 1980). A survey of values in a British sample found that 79 per cent of those surveyed took a great deal of pride in their own work, while 72 per cent looked forward to work and enjoyed both work and weekends. A recent survey in Britain, using different choices, found that for 3 per cent work was the most important part of their lives, 36 per cent found work interesting and rewarding, 45 per cent quite enjoyed their jobs, and 12 per cent disliked their jobs (Whitehorn, 1984).

Another way of finding out how much people really like their jobs is to ask them if they would work if it was financially unnecessary. A British national survey found that about 64 per cent said they would carry on working, although half of them would try to change their job (Warr, 1982). While 91 per cent of American mathematicians and 83 per cent of lawyers would choose the same work again, only 16 per cent of unskilled steel workers would do so (Blauner, 1960).

	%
Mathematicians	91
Lawyers	83
Journalists	82
Skilled printers	52
Skilled car workers	41
Skilled steel workers	41
Textile workers	31
Unskilled car workers	21
Unskilled steel workers	16

Table 20. Percentage of workers who would choose the same work again (from Blauner, 1960).

So far we have dealt with overall job satisfaction. Later measures have used a series of scales to measure different components of job satisfaction. Many scales have been devised for this purpose: one book reviews no less than 249 scales of various kinds (Cook *et al.*, 1981). However, the most widely used is the Job Description Index, which contains five scales, seventy-two items in all, which are answered 'yes', 'no' or 'uncertain' (Smith *et al.*, 1969). The five scales are designed to measure satisfaction in the following areas: (1) *work on present job*, e.g. fascinating; (2) *present pay*, e.g. income inadequate for normal expenses $(-)$; (3) *opportunities for promotion*, e.g. fairly good chance for promotion; (4) *supervision on present job*, e.g. lazy $(-)$; (5) *people on present job*, e.g. talk too much $(-)$. The minus signs show reversed items, i.e. those that show dissatisfaction.

There has been a great deal of research on these scales. They predict overall job satisfaction, especially the 'work on present job' scale. Additional scales have been devised for use with managers to measure satisfaction with subordinates and with the firm (Warr and Routledge, 1969).

Work may produce other forms of satisfaction of which people are unaware – until they lose their jobs. Research on the unemployed has found a number of 'hidden benefits' of work: it structures and organizes time, provides social contacts outside the family, links the individual to broader goals and purposes, gives status and a sense of identity, provides a raised level of activity etc. (Jahoda, 1982; Warr, 1983).

The Causes of Job Satisfaction

(1) *The work itself*. This is a major cause of job satisfaction as a whole, and particularly of the component of it known as *intrinsic* job satisfaction. Hackman (1980) suggested that five features of work produce such satisfaction. Many studies have investigated this issue, and the latest meta-analysis found the following average correlations with job satisfaction: (a) *task identity* (completing a clear and identifiable piece of work) ·32; (b) *task significance* (the degree to which the job has an impact on the lives of others) ·38; (c) *skill variety* ·41; (d) *autonomy* (the degree to which the job provides freedom, independence and discretion) ·46; (e) *feedback* (the extent to which information about effectiveness is available) ·41 (Loher

et al., 1985). The overall job characteristics score has been found to have a high correlation with job satisfaction, ·53 and ·88 in two meta-analyses (Loher *et al.*, 1985; Spector, 1985). This correlation is higher for those high in growth needs: ·68 versus ·38 for Loher *et al.* (1985). However, the job characteristics measures are often ratings by workers, and are almost another measure of job satisfaction (Hunter and Hirsch, 1987). On the other hand, subjective ratings of job characteristics are found to correlate both with ratings by supervisors and with objective job changes. Both types of measure are associated with job satisfaction.

These studies depend on subjective ratings or perceptions of the five job characteristics, and it is found that these are influenced by job satisfaction as well as vice versa. James and Tetrick (1986) tested different statistical models, and found that job perceptions and job satisfaction each influenced the other. However, Hackman *et al.* (1978) and others have found that experimental job enrichment, which modified the job characteristics, did result in greater intrinsic job satisfaction. Job characteristics have the predicted effect on absenteeism, and a modest effect on task motivation and performance; task identity has the most effect here (Fried and Ferris, 1987).

While most managers and professional people may enjoy jobs that are complex, challenging and autonomous, how far is this true for manual workers? One estimate is 15 per cent, although others have put it higher (Hulin and Blood, 1968; Hackman, 1977). It has been found that many car-assembly workers do it for the pay, and that the main satisfactions at work for many female workers are social (Locke, 1976). On the other hand, there is some relationship between satisfaction and the five job characteristics listed above, even for those low in growth strength need (Loher *et al.*, 1985; Spector, 1985).

Csikszentmihalyi (1975) studied several groups of people who were very involved in their work, such as surgeons, and others who had serious leisure activities, such as rock climbers. Argyle and Crossland (1987) studied the dimensions of positive emotions and found a dimension of 'depth', which included intensely satisfying experiences at work and elsewhere. The basis of such absorp-

	Very satisfied %	Satisfied %
Professional, technicians	42	41
Managers, proprietors	38	42
Clerical	22	39
Sales	24	44
Skilled	22	54
Semi-skilled	27	48
Unskilled	13	52
Farmers	22	58

Table 21. Some of the results of an American national survey of 2,460 people (from Gurin *et al.*, 1960).

tion is not known, but one process is probably the undertaking of tasks which provide challenges which are commensurate with the skills possessed. If the task is too challenging there is anxiety, if it is too easy people are bored. At a high level of skill people are creative and have 'peak' experiences.

Herzberg *et al.* (1959) found that the occasions when workers felt 'exceptionally good' about their work were mainly connected with achievement and recognition. A number of scales have items such as 'I feel a sense of personal satisfaction when I do this job well' (Warr *et al.*, 1979). There is a close link between this side of intrinsic satisfaction and the five job characteristics, which include the impact of the job on others. On the other hand, the Hackman job characteristics do not quite capture the sense of challenge and absorption described by Csikszentmihalyi, nor do they include most of the social aspects of work, to which we shall return later.

(2) *Different occupations*. There are very large differences between occupations and the job satisfaction they provide. Table 20 shows the percentage of workers who would choose the same work again, while Table 21 compares the level of satisfaction in broader groupings of occupations. (Similar tables showing the levels of stress in different occupations can be found on p. 263.)

In some surveys it has been found that the most satisfied workers are university teachers, scientists, the clergy and social workers (Sales and House, 1971). This is probably because their work has the right job characteristics, such as challenge, autonomy and skill variety. Some of the most discontented workers are those on assembly lines. They use a fairly low level of skill, have little skill variety, have very little autonomy, and do not complete an identifiable piece of work: they do badly on all the job characteristics needed for intrinsic satisfaction.

(3) *Pay.* In a number of studies people have been asked to rank various sources of job satisfaction, and pay has usually come out among the first three (Lawler, 1971). It is more a source of dissatisfaction than satisfaction: in some studies as many as 80 per cent of employees were discontented with their pay. In job satisfaction scales, contentment with pay is always one of the main components, and gives a reasonably good prediction of overall satisfaction.

Many people try so hard to increase their pay in one way or another that it would be surprising if pay was not an important source of satisfaction – some go on strike, some try to be promoted, others do a second job. However, across the population pay has a surprisingly small correlation with happiness or satisfaction, in the region of ·15 to ·2 (Argyle, 1987). But within organizations there *is* a correlation between job satisfaction and pay, after other variables have been held constant, although it is still small (e.g. Remitz, 1960).

Relative pay is a better predictor of job satisfaction than the absolute amount paid: in one American study supervisors earning over $12,000 a year were more satisfied than company presidents earning under $49,000. People at work have a clear idea of what they ought to be paid in comparison with others, and in relation to their skill, experience, etc. (Lawler and Porter, 1963). It is widely believed that performance, seniority, age, education, etc. should be recognized and rewarded by higher pay. If there is a discrepancy between what employees think they should be paid and what they are paid, they are dissatisfied. We discussed the levels of pay which are regarded as 'fair' when dealing with equity (p. 97). People compare their present pay with what they were paid in the past, although inflation makes accurate comparisons difficult, and probably increases satisfaction with current pay a little.

A recent American study was conducted of 248 employed men in Madison, Wisconsin (Berkowitz *et al.*, 1987). It was found that pay satisfaction was predicted by current inequity ($-\cdot49$), intrinsic job satisfaction ($\cdot41$), non-pay economic benefits ($\cdot34$), quality of life ($\cdot3$), and future equity ($\cdot28$). This is the clearest demonstration yet of the importance of equity for job satisfaction, and also of the effects of non-economic factors on satisfaction with pay.

(4) *Security*. Findings on the importance of security are contradictory. The results depend on the country and historical period in which studies have been carried out. Those done in Britain or the USA during the 1930s usually found that security was thought the most important feature of a job (Viteles, 1954). Although it has dropped from first place in more recent surveys, it still comes very high on the list. When people are worried about losing their jobs this is found to spread to discontent with all other aspects of their work (Grove and Kerr, 1951). The people who are most concerned about security are those in the lower income group, and whose parents were in unskilled or semi-skilled jobs – presumably because there is less security for less skilled workers. On the other hand, it is also found that more intelligent people are also very interested in long-term security (Wilkins, 1950–51). In Britain some of the elements of security are provided by the state – health and unemployment insurance, and pensions. What workers would really like is guaranteed employment; despite a greatly improved employment situation, memories of the depression of the 1930s linger on. So far no solution to the problem of providing guaranteed employment has been found within Western capitalism, although the problem has been solved in other countries such as Japan and Israel.

(5) *Status*. There is a strong correlation between status and job satisfaction, both in terms of status within an organization and of

the social class generally believed to be associated with different occupations. This can be seen from Tables 20 and 21. However, higher status jobs usually have favourable job characteristics and tend to be paid more. On the other hand, the most highly paid people – managers, administrators and doctors – are *less* satisfied and more stressed than university teachers, scientists and the others. In addition, some people in low-status jobs are very satisfied – if they enjoy the use of skills and the company of their co-workers, for example. The main negative feature of high-status jobs is that they can be more stressful (p. 263ff).

(6) *Promotion prospects.* American surveys show that opportunity for advancement is usually ranked first or second in importance. Herzberg *et al.* (1959) found that achievement, recognition and advancement were the main causes of *positive* satisfaction. Several studies found correlations between job satisfaction and estimates of the likelihood of promotion. On the other hand, if people expecting promotion do not get it, they will be discontented. For manual workers the actual chances of promotion are often quite small – the ratio of subordinates to superiors may be 100:1. In a survey of affluent manual workers none thought their chances of promotion were 'very good', although 45 per cent thought they were 'fairly good' (Goldthorpe *et al.*, 1968). In the same study the corresponding percentages for white-collar workers were 13 per cent and 53 per cent. The importance of promotion is quite different for people in different social classes and at different skill levels. For managerial and professional people work is part of a career, and promotion is of the highest importance. For unskilled and semi-skilled workers promotion is less likely and is less sought after.

(7) *Working groups.* Many studies have found that the working group is one of the most important components of job satisfaction. The Human Relations movement emphasized the importance of social factors at work, and while it underestimated the importance of other factors, such as pay and the work itself, the findings are

still valid. Co-workers can be a major source of help at work, there is often a great deal of joking, fun and gossip, and they can provide social support at times of stress (p. 274ff).

Co-workers produce job satisfaction under the following conditions:

(a) *Cohesiveness.* Satisfaction is greatest in cohesive groups. The conditions for cohesiveness are discussed elsewhere – frequent interaction, group members of similar background and values, democratic leadership skills, members brought together by the work-flow in a cooperative manner etc. (p. 132ff). A number of studies have shown that labour turnover is much less in cohesive groups (e.g. Van Zelst, 1952), as is absenteeism.

(b) *Popularity.* There is a close correlation between popularity and satisfaction – as high as ·82 in one study (Van Zelst, 1951) – and unpopular members usually leave.

(c) *Group size.* Smaller groups have higher satisfaction than larger ones; the reason is probably that in smaller groups each member can exert a lot of influence and talk as much as he or she likes, while in large groups the majority will be at the lower end of the dominance hierarchy.

(d) *Opportunities for interaction.* Satisfaction is high when there are opportunities for interaction, and reduced when noise or physical separation makes this difficult.

Relations in working groups can be rather weak. In a British car factory, for example, it was found that although workers talked to each other quite a lot, most said they would not be bothered about being moved away from their workmates. Forty-five per cent had no close friends at work, and only 16 per cent visited other workers at home. Some working groups may be closer than this. Members of certain kinds of teams – crews of ships and aircraft, and those engaged in dangerous work – become very dependent on one another. Whole working communities may have strong cultures of their own in which people meet after hours to talk shop, as happens with universities. And 'railroading, like music and thieving . . . is a world by itself' (Caplow, 1954).

(8) *Supervision*. Satisfaction with superiors is the second source of social satisfaction at work, and is ranked as less important than that with co-workers; typically the two fall third and seventh in order of importance. Supervision was mainly a source of periods of *dissatisfaction* in the Herzberg studies (Herzberg *et al.*, 1959), and another study found that there was a great deal of conflict with supervisors (Argyle and Furnham, 1983). Supervisors may make demands for more or better work, may be felt to treat different subordinates unfairly, may be seen as distant, hostile or unsympathetic. On the other hand supervisors can provide benefits that are partly material, partly social (Locke, 1976); they are a greater source of instrumental, tangible help than co-workers (Argyle and Furnham, 1983). They can help with promotion, pay rises and conditions of work; they can do more to solve difficulties at work than either co-workers or spouses. The social rewards which supervisors can provide include praise, encouragement and the creation of a pleasant social atmosphere. Support from supervisors can reduce the effects of stress on anxiety and depression (Caplan *et al.*, 1975). Most supervisors feel that helping people in this way is part of the job (Kaplan and Cowen, 1981). But the social side of the relationship is made difficult by the difference in power, status and salary (Argyle and Henderson, 1985).

'Consideration', the classical supervisory dimension, is a reliable source of job satisfaction, as is, although to a lesser extent, 'initiating structure'. A number of variables have been suggested which might moderate the effects of supervision on satisfaction.

(9) *Characteristics of organizations*. Several aspects of organizational structure affect job satisfaction.

(*a*) *Size*. Satisfaction is greater in smaller companies, and absenteeism is much less. Smaller size can be achieved by decentralization.

(b) *Levels.* Satisfaction is greater when there are fewer levels in the hierarchy, i.e. in organizations which are smaller, or have a larger span of control.

(c) *Participation* in decisions or administration produces higher job satisfaction. There may be participation in formal works committees, it may be used by supervisors, or it may be used by management when some change is being introduced.

(d) *Other aspects of the company* mentioned in surveys are managers – their training and skills, the nature of contacts with them; personnel policies – appraisal schemes; relations with trade unions – liberal or conservative attitudes; pride in company and product – based on public reputation, social importance, etc. (Evans and La Laseau, 1950).

(10) *Individual differences.* Extroverts are happier than introverts, and this is partly because they have more favourable experiences at work (Headey and Wearing, 1986); this in turn is partly because they get on better with people and enjoy social contacts more. Neuroticism is negatively correlated both with job satisfaction and with happiness in general, probably because neurotics find more things stressful and a cause of anxiety and distress. Individuals lacking in social skills, intelligence, physical attractiveness, or other aspects of competence and personal resources are also unhappier (Argyle, 1987).

Job satisfaction depends on the 'fit' between personality and job. If an individual's profile of needs matches the profile of rewards offered by the job he or she will be more satisfied (Furnham and Schaeffer, 1984). The most obvious fit which is needed is between an employee's knowledge and skills, and those required by the job. It does not matter from the organization's point of view if an employee is over-qualified but it does matter for the employee. Those high in achievement motivation prefer more challenging jobs, and show more correlation between performance and satisfaction (Steers, 1975). Those with strong social needs are happier as members of close-knit, cooperative groups.

More highly educated and more intelligent people are generally more satisfied because they usually do more interesting and challenging jobs. However, if they are not doing jobs of this nature they are *less* satisfied (Gruneberg, 1979).

(11) *Age and sex.* It is usually found that older people are more satisfied with their jobs (e.g. Kalleberg and Loscocco, 1983). The effect is greatest for intrinsic satisfaction (Rhodes, 1983). It is partly because older people have more rewarding and higher status jobs (Janson and Martin, 1982), but there is still a correlation with age when such rewards have been held constant (Rhodes, 1983). The most likely reason is that for older people aspirations and attainments come closer, so that they almost meet (Campbell *et al.*, 1976). In other words older people become more adjusted to their work situation. They may also be able to adjust the work situation to their needs, for example by changing jobs or by altering their conditions of work.

There is little overall difference in job satisfaction between the sexes, although most women's jobs tend to be less skilled and less well paid than those of men. Adelmann (1987) studied a representative sample of 618 male and 330 female workers. She found that the job satisfaction of men was affected by pay and feelings of control, while that of women was influenced by job complexity. Women enjoy the social aspects of work more, but they are now increasingly concerned with achievement too. On the whole women at work are happier and in better health than those who are not, but they can experience a lot of conflict when combining work with the demands of a family (Argyle, 1987).

The Effects of Job Satisfaction

Job performance and productivity. Do happy workers work harder? This question has been baffling industrial psychologists since the review by Brayfield and Crockett (1955) which found an average correlation of only +·15 from the studies published up until then. The latest meta-analysis of 217 separate correlations found an overall correlation of +·17 (Iaffaldano and Muchinsky, 1985). However, Petty *et al.* (1984) found an overall correlation of ·31

for supervisors and above, ·15 for those at lower levels. Some
recent studies have found correlations which are higher than this
under certain conditions. An overall correlation of ·35 was found
in one, but it was as high as ·6 when there was little pressure for
performance, i.e. when hard work was more voluntary (Bhagat,
1982).

Job satisfaction is also correlated with other kinds of desirable
behaviour at work – there is less sabotage, stealing, doing work
badly on purpose, and spreading rumours or gossip to cause
trouble (Mangoine and Quinn, 1975). This effect was stronger for
those over thirty-five years of age, probably because they would
only engage in such behaviour if they had a very strong sense of
grievance. Bateman and Organ (1983) found that non-academic
university staff who were satisfied engaged more in a wide variety
of 'good citizenship' behaviour at work – they were more punc-
tual, dependable, helpful, cooperative and tidy, and they created
less waste, made fewer complaints and were angry less
frequently.

However, the direction of causation is still not clear, and in the
Bateman and Organ study both directions of causation, between
performance and satisfaction, were found by cross-lagged correlations. It would be expected that high performance should lead
to satisfaction, if the performance is rewarded (Locke, 1976). It is
also likely that some factors, such as fair allocation of rewards,
increase both productivity and job satisfaction (Schermerhorn *et
al.*, 1985).

There are probably individual differences which confuse the
picture. There may well be workers who work hard when content-
ed, or who are happiest when they can take things easy, or who
work hard to forget their troubles.

Health and mental health. Low job satisfaction is correlated with
high rates of anxiety, depression, psychosomatic symptoms and
coronary heart disease. (Poor) mental health is more closely associated with (low) job satisfaction than it is with features of the
job, suggesting that job satisfaction is an intervening state in the
causal chain (Wall *et al.*, 1978). However, to some extent job

satisfaction and mental health are probably both affected by similar features of work: repetitive, machine-paced work, bad supervision, conflict with co-workers, and other forms of stress (Cooper and Marshall, 1976). In particular, the combination of low status and low-grade work is associated with dissatisfaction and with poor health, but there could be several reasons for this, including a tendency for those in poor health to gravitate to poor jobs. On the other hand, clerical workers also have rather poor health, as do those whose jobs are stressful, such as airfield controllers and workers in the television industry (see Kasl, 1978).

Social support from co-workers and supervisors is a major source both of job satisfaction and positive mental health. It can buffer the effects of stress at work more effectively than other sources of social support. People in stressful jobs are in particular need of support from cohesive working groups or socially skilled supervisors (cf. p. 274ff).

Another investigation found that job satisfaction was a predictor of length of life among workers. It correlated ·26, better than physical functioning (·21) (Palmore, 1969). There is a high correlation between job dissatisfaction and coronary heart disease ($r = ·83$), with other variables held constant (Sales and House, 1971) (p. 264).

It has been found that job dissatisfaction among nurses predicted tension on the job, particularly for dissatisfaction with the work and with the doctors. On the other hand, tension also predicted job dissatisfaction – it worked both ways – particularly dissatisfaction with supervision and pay. This is an interesting example of pay dissatisfaction being affected by non-economic variables (Bateman and Strassen, 1983). Another investigation used causal modelling on the relations between some of these variables, and concluded that job dissatisfaction and boredom caused anxiety and depression, which in turn led to bodily complaints (French et al., 1982).

Life satisfaction. Job satisfaction is one of the main factors in overall life satisfaction, although it is less important than marriage and family life (Campbell et al., 1976). Some attempts to clarify the direction of causation have found that both directions operate (Schmitt and Bedeian, 1982), others that it is job satisfaction which influences life satisfaction (Chacko, 1983). Another possibility is that areas of work and non-work have a lot in common, such as friendship, status, similar styles of behaviour, and that they jointly affect satisfaction with life as a whole (Near et al., 1980). Another study concluded that 'we suspect that how one effectively evaluates various life concerns relates to essentially *one* phenomenon at the global level . . . perceptions of general well-being' (Andrews and Withey, 1976). At least part of the link between the two kinds of satisfaction is a 'top-to-bottom' one, i.e. general well-being affects job satisfaction.

Shaffer (1987) found that a majority of his subjects were satisfied both in work and in non-work, hence the positive correlation. However, substantial minorities were satisfied in one but not in the other ('compensators'), or in neither.

Union activity. Satisfied workers are less likely to engage in union activities, such as turning up to vote. On the other hand, union activities are more strongly correlated with the sources of economic satisfaction, such as pay and benefits, and with attitudes towards the unions (Schriesheim, 1978).

Absenteeism and *Labour Turnover* are discussed below.

Theories of Job Satisfaction

It is important to have some theoretical basis for job satisfaction phenomena, since this is likely to affect our understanding of how the causes and effects of job satisfaction work, and how it might be enhanced. Unfortunately most of the research has been carried out without reference to theory.

Herzberg's two-factor theory stated that (positive) satisfaction is due to good experiences, and these are due to 'motivators' — achievement, recognition, the work itself, responsibility and advancement. Dissatisfaction is due to bad experiences caused by 'hygiene' factors – supervisors, fellow workers, company policy, working conditions and personal life (Herzberg *et al.*, 1959). This was supported by critical incident studies in which workers were asked to describe occasions when they had felt exceptionally good or exceptionally bad. However, Wall *et al.* (1971) found that if workers were asked similar questions in an informal and confidential interview, this pattern of results was not obtained. They concluded that the Herzbergian pattern of results was due to 'ego-defensive processes'; the results would now be described perhaps as 'defensive attribution' or as 'self-presentation'. Good events are said to be due to one's own achievements, bad events to the failings of others. As a result it is generally considered that this theory has failed (Griffin and Bateman, 1986). However, the theory did draw attention to the importance of achievement, and to the work itself, as opposed to the mainly social factors which had been emphasized in the Human Relations approach. The distinction between satisfaction and dissatisfaction has proved to be important in the study of happiness, since the two are partly independent of one another (Argyle, 1987), although it has not been pursued any further for job satisfaction.

Need–satisfaction theories have also been attacked, and rejected, by some on the grounds that there is no agreed list of needs, that it is hard to assess when they are satisfied, and that attempts to test the approach have not been very successful (Salancik and Pfeffer, 1977). However, a number of studies have found that congruence between needs and rewards gives quite a strong prediction of job satisfaction, much better than that from rewards alone (e.g. Tziner, 1983; Furnham and Schaeffer, 1984). One version is Hackman's job design theory; Hackman and Oldham (1976) found that there was a significant interaction between individual needs and job characteristics as sources of satisfaction. Not everyone enjoys jobs which are demanding and responsible.

Comparisons and aspirations. Satisfaction depends partly on whether employees feel that they are receiving the pay and other benefits which they think are right and fair. We have seen that

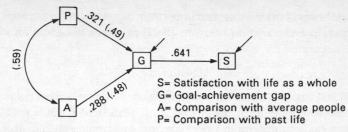

Fig. 19. Satisfaction with life as a whole: the goal-achievement gap model, showing regression coefficients with zero-order correlations in brackets (from Michalos, 1980).

equity is an important predictor, and that comparisons with others contribute to this.

Another source of satisfaction is one's own past experience. The Michigan model of life satisfaction proposes that comparisons with others and with past life are the main predictors of the 'goal-achievement gap' (the subjective distance between aspirations and achievements) which in turn predicts satisfaction. This model has been confirmed by Michalos (1980) (see Fig. 19). Similar findings have been obtained for job satisfaction, which is a product of the goal-achievement gaps for each component of work satisfaction, and the value of each area (Locke, 1976).

The social information processing model. Salancik and Pfeffer (1977) criticized need–satisfaction models on the grounds that tests of them have not given them very strong support, and in 1978 proposed a radically different view. They argued that job satisfaction is a socially constructed interpretation of the work situation, and not a direct consequence of an objective state of affairs. It is partly based on comparisons with other people, but also on observations of others' level of satisfaction, and there is much conformity to group norms and organizational climate in reporting job satisfaction. This theory was supported by Thomas and Griffin (1983) who reviewed ten studies, mostly laboratory experiments, which found that manipulation of social cues, e.g. comparisons with co-workers, affected the amount of satisfaction expressed with a job, as well as the perception of the job characteristics.

This theory is interesting and important, but it would be a mistake to overlook the real and proven effects of objective factors on job satisfaction.

Absenteeism

(1) *Meaning, measurement and distribution.* Absenteeism is a pervasive problem of working organizations. In England about 300 million working days are lost per year, 13·5 per employee, i.e. about 6 per cent. Things are better in the USA, with an absence rate of about 2·5 per cent, and worse in Italy with 14 per cent. The cost of absenteeism in the USA in 1983 was about $30 billion (Steers and Rhodes, 1984).

'Absenteeism' is usually taken to mean absence (for some period) from any planned work activity. It can include lateness, but not idleness. One problem with this definition is that it only applies in practice to manual or clerical workers who are paid by the hour, and not to managers, professionals or research workers. The latter have less definite hours of work, and are much more free to go shopping or to look after their family during working hours without being regarded as absent. Nothing actually stops, and there is no immediate loss of productivity if they are not there, as there is in the case of most manual workers. The distinction between work and non-work is much less clear for managers and professional workers, and they usually do a lot of work outside 'working hours', for example by taking work home.

A second problem is that it is necessary to distinguish between excused absence, usually for illness or – in the case of workers with families – the illness of others, and voluntary, unexcused absence. This is not a clear-cut distinction, as excused absence may reflect discontent rather than illness. The two kinds can be distinguished by whether permission to be absent or a doctor's certificate is obtained. It is also found that absenteeism is higher on Mondays than on Fridays; Behrend (1951) devised the 'Blue Monday Index' –the difference between Friday and Monday absences per 100 workers. She found that voluntary absenteeism accounts for about 33 per cent of total absenteeism. Neurotic or stress factors account for a further 20–25 per cent of absences (Fraser, 1947). It is sometimes assumed that one-day absences are voluntary, while those of two days or more are due to illness (Steers and Rhodes, 1984). This distinction is supported by studies of the distribution of absences between workers. A small number of hard-core individuals are prone to taking days off – half a day or one day at a time; studies of these individuals produce a J-shaped curve. However, there is no evidence for such proneness for absences of two days or more, which are therefore probably due to real illnesses (Landy *et al.*, 1984). The most common reasons for absence are:

> illness
> domestic reasons
> business (e.g. dentist, solicitor)
> feeling bored
> feeling tired
> wanting a break
> other reasons (e.g. shopping, football matches).

Something like half the single days taken off are regarded by those doing so as 'justified', the rest as 'unjustified' (Chadwick-Jones *et al.*, 1982).

On the positive side, the frequency and intensity of 'uplifts' – pleasant everyday events – known to increase happiness and reduce distress, also reduce absenteeism (Ivancevich, 1986).

(2) *Causes and predictors*

(*a*) *Job satisfaction*. It would be expected that happy workers would turn up more often to receive the benefits which they enjoy at work. In fact, the average correlation is quite low: $-·09$ in one meta-analysis (Hackett and Guion, 1985), and $-·22$ in another (McShane, 1983). However, there is a very skewed distribution of absenteeism – most people are not absent at all, which reduces the possible size of correlations (Hackett and Guion, 1985). In addition, Clegg (1983) found that job satisfaction is predictive of later absenteeism. The relationship is greatest with satisfaction for pay and promotion (Rosse and Miller, 1984), and for work commitment.

There is a clearer correlation with voluntary or unexcused absence which is not due to sickness. The relationship is stronger for women, manual workers, workers in larger firms and younger workers (Metzner and Mann, 1953). The explanation is probably that the commitment to work is less for these groups; they are less socialized into work, so that they respond to minor illnesses or problems by being absent more readily (Gruneberg, 1979).

(b) *Industry and job.* There is more absenteeism in certain industries – notably manufacturing, textiles, and transport, compared with finance and hospitals, The rate of absenteeism increases with the size of factory or other working unit, as does the incidence of accidents, while job satisfaction decreases (p. 210ff). There is more absence at lower levels in an organization, and among less skilled people, although, as noted earlier, absenteeism is rarely recorded at higher levels.

(c) *Culture and social norms.* There are often group norms about absenteeism. For example when workers are interdependent, norms will be against absence; if they work independently, at a low level of professionalism, and there is low job satisfaction or there are grievances, absence is tolerated more. Among academics and research workers there are sometimes norms of working all day and every day. The effect of group norms is greater in cohesive groups (Johns and Nicholson, 1982). There are absence 'cultures' in another sense, given that the causes given for absenteeism vary, i.e. members of different working groups discover the causes of absence which are regarded as acceptable. This partly depends on what is acceptable to employers and supervisors, and the organizational controls, if any, for absence (Chadwick-Jones *et al.*, 1982).

(d) *Economic factors.* Most workers who are paid by the hour will lose pay if they are absent, so those who need the money are likely to be absent less – unless they are so well paid that they are worried about income tax. If they are worried about losing their job and unemployment is high, they will be absent less. If they know they are going to be laid off anyway they are absent more (Steers and Rhodes, 1984). We shall discuss special incentives to reduce absenteeism later.

(e) *Individual differences.* We saw above that there is a core of workers who account for most of the voluntary absenteeism. Who are they? Voluntary absenteeism declines with age and among long-service workers, especially for men, although sickness absence is usually found to increase with age (Chadwick-Jones *et al.*, 1982). Women are absent more than men, especially women who are married or with larger families (Chadwick-Jones *et al.*, 1982). Sickness absence is, of course, more frequent for those in poor health. We showed above the relationship between absence, low work commitment and job satisfaction.

(f) *Non-work motivations.* When someone is 'absent' from work, he or she is 'present' elsewhere. Absenteeism is greater for women with families, as we have seen, and especially if there are no day-care facilities. Individuals may have leisure activities which are very important to them, for example competitive sports or other avenues for achievement. In these cases there is a balance between conflicting motivations. In addition, research workers and some professionals may be able to get more work done at home than at the office, or may want to discuss work with colleagues elsewhere.

(3) *Models to explain absenteeism*

(a) *The withdrawal model.* It has often been suggested that low job satisfaction is the cause of withdrawal, which may take the form of absence, lateness, labour turnover, and even sickness and accidents. One version is that these are alternative kinds of withdrawal; another theory is that they are hierarchically ordered, the minor forms of withdrawal being used first and leaving the organization last. While there are correlations between job satisfaction and the withdrawal variables, they are quite small, and the causal factors affecting each are rather different. Absenteeism has some correlation with turnover and lateness, especially voluntary absenteeism with voluntary turnover (Wolpin and Burke, 1985).

(b) *The adaptation model.* This model proposes that an individual is made dissatisfied by some event at work, e.g. not getting a pay rise. The worker is then motivated to take action to improve things; he or she considers a number of behavioural alternatives, and chooses between them on the basis of social norms, e.g. for absence, and the behaviour of role models, past experience, and the consequences of being late or absent. The alternatives include not only the various forms of withdrawal, but also aggressive behaviour, complaining and doing nothing (Rosse and Miller, 1984).

(c) *Exchange theory.* It was found by Patchen (1960) that absenteeism is greater among employees who feel that they have been treated unfairly. Chadwick-Jones *et al.* (1982) extended this to an application of exchange and equity theories: employees may be absent if they feel that the benefits they receive are too low in relation to their inputs, or if they feel the balance is inequitable. In this way absence is similar to the effects of underpayment found in equity research (p. 94ff).

(4) *Managing absenteeism.* Absenteeism is a source of a great deal of additional labour costs, as well as a lot of administrative trouble and loss of production. On the other hand, people may need absences in order to rest, and too many hours of work can result in decreased output as well as increased illness. But, as we have seen, about half of all absences are unjustified, and the absence rate is very high in some countries, in some industries (manufacturing, public transport), and among some kinds of employee (younger workers, women, those with low job commitment), and management may feel they should do something about it. What can they do?

(a) *Informal pressures from supervisors.* Permission to be absent is often easy, and many supervisors make no comment following absences. More vigorous reaction by supervisors is one obvious step.

(b) *Sanctions for absence.* Disciplinary rules can be announced, including definite sanctions. A sequence of oral and written warnings, suspension and finally dismissal may be used. However, these schemes have not been found to work, since employees obtain medical certificates and have longer periods of sickness absence instead, although it has been found that they have some effect on chronically absent workers (Goodman *et al.*, 1984).

(*c*) *Rewards for attendance* (and combined rewards and sanctions). The rewards can be small bonuses, badges, medals or other means of recognition, or choice of better jobs. Both rewards and combined reward and sanctions schemes have been found to be successful in reducing absence rates, especially if there is employee participation in introducing them (Steers and Rhodes, 1984).

(*d*) *Increase job satisfaction.* The improvements in jobs which are designed to increase job satisfaction are also found to reduce absenteeism – for example participation, job enrichment, team-building, setting own pace. The introduction of more flexible hours can also reduce absence among clerical and manual workers, since it makes it easy for them to go to the doctor, go shopping or get their car fixed, as managers and research workers can (Latham and Napier, 1984).

Labour Turnover

Labour turnover (LT) is the rate at which people leave a working organization. It can be measured by the number of members who left during a period as a percentage of the average number employed. The 'stability rate' is the percentage of those employed at the beginning of a period who remain at the end of it, which is a better measure if there are a lot of short-term members. Another measure is the average length of service of those currently employed. Typical levels of employees leaving in the course of a year are 20–25 per cent (Mowday *et al.*, 1982). LT would be good for the organization if the poor performers left; unfortunately it is the good ones who are more likely to leave (r = about ·5) (Hunter and Hirsch, 1987). In addition, LT involves the expense and trouble of selecting and training new personnel.

(1) *Causes and predictors*

(*a*) *Job satisfaction.* It is expected that job (dis)satisfaction is a cause of labour turnover. Many studies have been made of this relationship, and the correlation is typically ·2 to ·3 and rarely greater than ·4 (Mobley, 1982). Carsten and Spector (1987), in a meta-analysis of forty-seven studies, found an overall correlation of ·23 (but of ·51 under high unemployment, see below). In addition, job satisfaction does predict later turnover. LT correlates with different components of job satisfaction, but especially with satisfaction with job content (Mobley et al., 1979). Field experiments have shown that measures designed to increase satisfaction, e.g. job enrichment, reduce labour turnover (McEvoy and Cascio, 1985). Various causal models of LT have been put forward, in all of which low job satisfaction is proposed as one of the basic causes; tests of these models have on the whole confirmed the causative role of job satisfaction (e.g. Williams and Hazer, 1986). However, multivariate studies show that better predictions of LT can be made if a number of other predictor variables are used, showing that job satisfaction is not the only path generating turnover (Mobley et al., 1979).

(b) Job characteristics. The Hackman and Oldham model (1976) predicted that poor job content would produce low satisfaction and high LT. It has been consistently found that LT is greater when intrinsic satisfaction, motivation, or autonomy are low (Mobley, 1982). Studies of job enlargement and enrichment have found the most striking effects for job enrichment (vertical integration) with white-collar workers (Kelly, 1982).

LT varies between different jobs. It is higher for manual workers than for non-manual. It is greatest for entertainment, recreation, shop, construction and medical workers, lowest for railways, agriculture and postal workers (Mowday et al., 1982).

(c) Organizational commitment and attachment. Research has consistently found that organizational involvement, or commitment, and job attachment give strong predictions of LT, up to correlations of ·4 in some cases (Griffin and Bateman, 1986). Commitment gives a better prediction of LT than job satisfaction.

(d) Economic factors. Turnover is less for those who are paid more. It was found that LT at one factory fell from 370 per cent to 16 per cent after an increase in wages (Scott *et al.*, 1960). In fact level of pay is one of the strongest predictors of LT, and employees usually leave for better-paid jobs. This does not mean that people will do anything for money, and many people choose a lower-paid job rather than a higher-paid one for various reasons (p. 89). LT is less when other jobs are more difficult to find, for example when there is high unemployment. On the other hand, the link between turnover and job satisfaction is *greater* when there is high unemployment; under these conditions, when other jobs are hard to get, people leave mainly because they are dissatisfied. Under full employment some people drift in and out of jobs just for a change, not because they are dissatisfied (Shikiar and Freudenberg, 1982).

(*e*) *Social factors*. Mann and Baumgartel (1953) found that LT was much less in more cohesive groups, but a number of more recent studies found no effect at all (Mobley *et al.*, 1979).

Not all studies have found a relationship between supervision and LT; one of a number of studies showing that LT was greater under low consideration or high initiating structure on the part of supervisors was discussed earlier (p. 150).

(*f*) *Individual differences*. The longer an individual's tenure, the less likely he or she is to leave (·22 to ·25). Older workers have lower LT (·25 to ·3), as do women who are married or who have children (Mobley *et al.*, 1979). Those most likely to leave have *lower* intelligence, *higher* performance and interests which do not fit the job.

(*g*) *Organizational factors*. Although job satisfaction is greater in small organizations, LT is less in large ones. The reason is probably that in a large concern some internal mobility is possible, and personnel practices are more efficient, resulting in better selection and fitting of people to jobs (Mobley, 1982). There is also evidence that LT is greater in more highly centralized firms (Price, 1977). This is consistent with other findings about the benefits of small, cohesive and more autonomous groups (p. 241).

(2) *Models to explain labour turnover*

(a) *Mobley's intentions model.* Mobley (1977) proposed the following chain, with leaving work as the final stage:

> Evaluate present job
> Dissatisfaction
> Think of quitting
> Evaluate cost of quitting, chance of finding alternative
> Intention to search for alternative
> Search
> Evaluate alternative
> Comparison
> Intention to quit or stay
> Quit.

Several attempts have been made to confirm that this sequence actually occurs. It has generally been found that the sequence starts with low job satisfaction, and that intention to quit is a very good predictor (Mobley *et al.*, 1979). However, Hom *et al.* (1984) found that intention to quit led to a search for alternative jobs, and that some people quit without searching for alternatives.

(b) *The exit-voice model.* It has been argued that LT, absenteeism and lateness are among four general responses to job dissatisfaction: *exit*, i.e. leave, look for another job; *voice*, i.e. talk to supervisor, write letters; *loyalty*, i.e. stick it out, wait patiently; *neglect*, i.e. absenteeism and lateness (Farrell, 1983). Spencer (1986) found that turnover had a correlation of $-\cdot24$ with perceived availability of 'voice', e.g. formal grievance procedures, suggestion schemes, employee–management meetings. However, when there is high absenteeism, LT is also high – both forms of exit seem to go together.

(c) *Investment.* Rusbult and Farrell (1983) proposed that organizational commitment, and hence low LT, are determined mainly by 'investments'. These are what the employee has 'put in' to the job, and would lose or partly lose if he or she left. They include non-transferable pensions, job-specific training, friendships, and home-ownership. A twenty-item scale of such investments was found to be strongly correlated with intention to stay.

(d) *The balance between two utilities.* March and Simon (1958) proposed that turnover depends on the perceived desirability of leaving the organization, which in turn depends mainly on job satisfaction, and the perceived ease of movement from the organization, which depends on the availability of other jobs and the judgement of the likelihood of getting one. This model reflects the two main predictors of LT – low job satisfaction and low unemployment levels, as well as some other variables.

(3) *Managing turnover.* Turnover is extremely expensive when a long period of training is involved, or when careful selection is needed. On the other hand, there may be advantages in LT – for example if younger or better staff can be appointed instead.

There are a number of management strategies for reducing LT, most of them implicit in what has been said already. The intervention which has the most effect on LT, according to meta-analysis, is training (·63 of a standard deviation). Better matching of employees to jobs, by better recruitment and selection, can also reduce LT. Warnous (1980) recommends the realistic job preview (RJP), a method of giving newcomers accurate information, and increasing commitment. However, RJP has been found to have a modest effect on LT (r = − ·09) (Hunter and Hirsch, 1987). Redesigning jobs to improve job content (especially for workers with strong growth needs), and offering better pay (especially to maintain internal equity) or pay which is competitive with other employers can assist in a reduction in turnover.

Sufficiently rewarding and supportive styles of supervision can result in less LT, as can providing employees with possible career paths, and assessing and rewarding their progress along them (Mobley, 1982).

IO

STRESS, HEALTH AND MENTAL HEALTH
AT WORK

By stress we mean external conditions which produce feelings of discomfort and tension, since they are seen as threatening, frustrating, or they exceed the individual's capacities to deal with them (Baron, 1986). Stress produces a variety of negative effects, especially physical and mental ill health.

Surveys of ill health at work can create the impression that work is bad for us. However, we will see in the next chapter that school leavers who get jobs *improve* in mental health, while the mental health of those who do not get jobs becomes worse (p. 291). The health of the unemployed is worse than that of the employed; a study is reported later in which after losing their jobs the health of 27 per cent became worse although the health of 11 per cent got better – because there was no work stress (p. 294).

We can also compare the health of those at work with that of the retired. It is generally found that there is not much difference, although manual workers are in slightly better health, while others show a slight decline after retirement. Retirement has little effect on mental health (Kasl, 1980).

Another possible comparison is between women who go out to work and housewives. Brown and Harris (1978) found that women who had jobs were less likely to become depressed after stressful life events; other studies have confirmed that women with jobs are in better mental health than housewives. On the other hand, married women with jobs, especially those with young children, experience conflict between the demands of their two roles, and may feel guilty about 'neglecting' their families. In addition, women with jobs and who have young children at home have more coronaries (Haw, 1982). On the other hand, house-wives *without* jobs are likely to be isolated, bored and frustrated (Tavris and Offir, 1977). Women with jobs go to see the doctor less often; those in good jobs have fewer serious illnesses and live longer, but women in clerical jobs have a high rate of heart attacks (Haw, 1982). Women at work are more likely to have Type A personalities, although the rate is lower than for men.

There seems to be little evidence that the stresses of work overall are bad for people. On the contrary work seems to be good for us. Nevertheless some jobs are clearly more stressful than others. Karasek *et al.* (1987), in a study of 8,700 Swedish white-collar workers, studied the effect of demographic, work and family vari-ables on indices of health; work variables accounted for 60 per cent of the variance that could be explained. Parkes (1982) studied the effects of different kinds of work on 164 student nurses, who had been allocated to four different kinds of ward. As expected there was most distress for the nurses in medical rather than surgical wards, especially female medical wards.

The high illness rates for certain jobs are not only due to the stresses involved, they may be because certain kinds of people choose to enter those occupations. Perhaps some people become racing-car drivers, test pilots, television producers, politicians, or members of the SAS because they like the excitement and would find life in a museum or library too dull. We shall see that this is to some extent true of Type A personalities.

French *et al.* (1982) analysed responses to stress in terms of a number of sources of stress at work, some personality variables, and interaction between the two. All were important, especi-ally the last – distress is experienced if there is a mismatch between person and job demands: racing-car drivers may not experience much stress if they have the right personalities for the job.

A considerable number of measures have been used to study the effects of stress.

(1) *Subjective tension and distress* – low job satisfaction, work load dissatisfaction, tension.

(2) *Physiological measures* – blood-pressure, cholesterol, heart rate, adrenalin excretion.

(3) *Health* – mortality rate, incidence of heart attacks, ulcers and other stress-related illnesses.

(4) *Health-related behaviour* – consumption of cigarettes, alcohol, coffee.

(5) *Mental health* – general measures such as the General Health Questionnaire (GHQ) (Goldberg, 1978), anxiety, depression, burn-out, suicide rate, rates of treatment. This is not a unitary dimension; we shall see for example that anxiety is increased by paced work, while depression and job satisfaction are not affected (Broadbent, 1985).

(6) *Work behaviour*. It has been found that stress produces depression, anxiety and other stress responses, which in turn lead to lowered work performance (Motowidlo *et al.*, 1986).

Occupational Differences

There are considerable differences between occupations in the rates of the stress responses listed above, although these differences are partly due to the kinds of people in those occupations, and the degree of fit between them and their jobs.

One way to compare the stressfulness of different occupations is to carry out surveys. Cooper (1985) found that the most and least stressful occupations, rated on a nine-point scale, were thought to be mining and library work respectively (see Table 22).

Caplan *et al.* (1975) obtained measures of different aspects of stress for twenty-three occupations, for example the amount of unwanted overtime, job complexity, role conflict. These measures were found to be related to the effects of stress, such as anxiety, irritation and physiological measures (see Table 23). Karasek *et al.* (1987), in their study of 8,700 white-collar workers, found that the main sources of stress leading to ill health were work load, conflict and (low) job control.

	High		Low
Miner	8·3	Librarian	2
Police	7·7	Museum worker	2·8
Construction worker	7·5	Nursery nurse	3·3
Journalist	7·5	Astronomer	3·4
Pilot (civil)	7·5	Vicar	3·5
Advertising	7·3	Beauty therapist	3·5
Dentist	7·2		
Actor	7·2		
Politician	7·0		
Doctor	6·8		

Table 22. Survey of occupations rated on a nine-point scale for stressfulness (from Cooper, 1985).

Unwanted overtime	·39
Complexity	·47
Responsibility for others	·32
Underuse of skills	·59
Job future ambiguity	·39
Role conflict	·33

Table 23. The main sources of stress, with their loadings on subjective stress (from Caplan *et al.*, 1975).

	%
White-collar	65
Skilled and high semi-skilled	57
Ordinary semi-skilled	37
Repetitive semi-skilled	18

Table 24. Percentage of workers with high general mental health (from Kornhauser, 1965).

The Main Sources of Work Stress

Job status. We have seen that job satisfaction is greater in the better-paid, higher-status jobs (p. 235ff). General mental health is higher too, as Kornhauser (1965) found from interviewing 407 car workers and others (see Table 24).

	Per cent satisfied	Coronary rate	Social status
University teachers	93	71	84
Biologists	89	69	80
Physicists	89	69	80
Chemists	86	100	79
Farmers	84	66	14
Lawyers	80	124	93
Managers	69	116	79
Sales	52	126	50
Skilled printers	52	110	49
Clerical	42	103	44
Paper workers	42	73	19
Skilled car workers	41	68	21
Skilled steelworkers	41	85	15
Textile workers	31	120	3
Unskilled steelworkers	21	125	4
Unskilled car workers	16	176	13

Table 25. Occupational differences in job satisfaction, coronary heart disease and social status (from Sales and House, 1971).

Mortality rate among workers can be predicted from low job satisfaction (Palmore, 1969). Most of the better-paid, higher-status jobs have a lower death rate from heart disease, as well as higher job satisfaction, as Table 25 shows.

Warr (1987) regards having a valued position as a basic human need, and lack of it as a source of low self-esteem and stress. Jenner *et al.* (1980), in a biological survey of people in Otmoor, Oxfordshire, found that non-manual workers in senior positions demanding more mental effort excreted more adrenalin during the week. Some white-collar jobs are more stressful and have higher illness rates than others. Stress has the greatest toll on doctors, dentists, managers and administrators, and the least on university teachers, scientists, librarians and museum workers. Class differences in health are partly due to different life-styles in respect of exercise, diet and smoking (Argyle, 1987).

For jobs of intermediate status, police, air-traffic controllers, nurses and secretaries experience a lot of stress. Manual jobs demanding a lot of physical effort and boring repetition are the most stressful, for example jobs undertaken by unskilled and semi-skilled assembly-line workers, textile and restaurant workers. The least stressed are those in more skilled work which is not time-paced, such as toolmakers and other craftworkers (Caplan *et al.*, 1975; Cooper, 1985).

The self-employed, working alone or owning small businesses (apart from professionals), work very long hours and earn less money than employees but they are in *better* health (Curran *et al.*, 1987).

Job overload. A job may be too difficult, too physically demanding, allow insufficient time, or several things may be happening at once. French *et al.* (1982) found that mental ill health was most affected by difficulty and shortage of time, shown for example by the amount of unwanted overtime. However, some workers wanted an increased work-load, so that there is a curvilinear person–environment fit component (see p. 273) in addition to the main effect of overload. Time pressure is experienced by those on assembly lines, or other kinds of machine-paced work, and their health is found to be worse than for employees in general (Caplan *et al.*, 1975). Car workers doing paced work have higher levels of anxiety than those who are unpaced, although depression and job satisfaction are not affected. However, the effect is greater if workers are more concerned with satisfaction than money (Broadbent, 1985). Managers who work longer hours, have more telephone calls, visitors and meetings have been found to smoke and drink more and to have more coronaries (Cooper and Marshall, 1978). During periods of overload, cholesterol levels and blood-pressure rise, for example in accountants as tax deadlines approach, and in air-traffic controllers when there is a lot of traffic (Kasl, 1978).

The effects of overload are greater if there are rigid rule structures, a limited range of ways of dealing with the situation. Karasek (1979) found a factor of 'job decision latitude', with items such as 'have say on job', 'participate in decisions', 'make one's own decisions'. Stress was greatest for those under high job demands but with little decision latitude. Workers who had both high job demands and high decision latitude were very satisfied, and showed no signs of stress. Alfredsson *et al.* (1985) found that jobs which had a combination of high stress ('hectic') and little opportunity to learn new things had a high rate of heart attacks, especially for men under fifty-five years of age. For women the results were worse for work which was both hectic and monotonous. The high-status jobs were found to be most hectic and had the longest hours.

Lack of control. A lot of these findings may be due to a more fundamental source of stress – lack of control. We have seen in other chapters that job satisfaction is greater in jobs which give autonomy, and under the participatory style of supervision. We shall see below that those high on internal control can cope with stress better.

There is considerable evidence that lack of autonomy or control over the work is a cause of anxiety, depression, general mental ill health and heart disease; the effect becomes important at low levels of control (Warr, 1987). Meta-analysis of the effects of autonomy and participation on physical symptoms and emotional distress have found overall correlations of about $-\cdot35$ (Spector, 1986).

There is evidence from repeated surveys that job stress is increasing for many industrial workers. The introduction of new technology has led to loss of jobs, or fear of this, valued skills becoming obsolete, social isolation at work, heavier work-loads, tougher speed requirements and more mental effort (Ostberg and Nilsson, 1985). It has been found that VDU operators often find this work stressful because of the monotony, lack of control, constant pressure, breakdowns and physical strain (Mackay and Cooper, 1987).

Repetitive work. Walker and Guest (1952) found that workers on the assembly line greatly disliked the repetitive nature of their work. In this and other studies it has been found that assembly-line workers become bored and frustrated because their capacities are not realized. In a number of studies physiological effects of repetitive work have been found, such as raised adrenalin level and increased potassium in the blood (Cox, 1980). This has been interpreted as a process of adaptation to boring and unchallenging work – with lowered expectations, lowered needs, and the most being made of social interaction (Kasl, 1978). There may be changes in the self-image too in order to adapt to the performance of low-grade, low-status work, for example by keeping the identity of a previous job, or emphasizing leisure activities.

We have seen that opportunity to use skills is a source of job satisfaction (p. 235ff). There is also evidence that not being able to use skills is associated with anxiety, depression and psycho-somatic complaints (O'Brien, 1986).

Danger. The heart-rate of a parachutist goes up to 150 beats per minute, and that of a racing motorist to 200, compared with the usual sixty to seventy. Biological measures of blood contents are similarly affected (Carruthers, 1980). Perceived danger leads to lower levels of performance in most people, but training and experi-ence can prevent this (Poulton, 1978). Curiously, fighter pilots, air-traffic controllers and police all say that the most stressful parts of their jobs are administrative problems, contacts with the courts (for police), or housing and domestic problems; the dangerous aspects of the job are mentioned less often, or are actually liked (Kasl, 1978). There is probably a high degree of self-selection for these jobs, and those who like excitement and who are low in anxiety will be attracted. Nevertheless, prolonged exposure to danger in wartime produces high levels of 'war neurosis' among those involved.

Environmental stresses. Various aspects of the physical environ-ment are found stressful: poor visibility (too little or flickering light and glare), noise, vibration, heat, cold, wind, atmospheric pollution, increased or reduced pressure, shiftwork and loss of sleep (Poulton, 1978). These can become major sources of stress when the level becomes too high, for example when noise is intense or heat is intolerable (Warr, 1987). Commuting is another source of stress. Stokols *et al.* (1978) found that people who drove longer distances to work and who had done so for a longer time felt more tense, nervous and annoyed when they got there, and had higher blood-pressure.

Responsibility for others. It is found that supervisors report sick much more often than those in non-supervisory jobs of the same status. Managers have worse health than professional workers. University teachers have very low stress levels – unless they are in administration (French *et al.*, 1982). French and Caplan (1970) found that responsibility for people, compared with responsibility for things, was associated with smoking, high blood-pressure and high cholesterol levels. Responsibility for others means a lot of extra tension and worry and sustaining many sometimes difficult relationships, coping with pressure from above and below, making decisions about subordinates, dealing with frictions, taking the blame for others' failures, attending endless meetings and consultations (Baron, 1986). Nevertheless, some people would like *more* responsibility for others, and there is a curvilinear person–environment fit component here, in addition to the main effect (French *et al.*, 1982).

Role conflict. Kahn *et al.* (1964) found that reported role conflict or ambiguity correlated with work tension, especially if those sending conflicting messages were powerful. We saw earlier that role conflict results in low job satisfaction too. These results have been criticized as being at least partly due to content overlap between the different self-report measures. However, at least one study has shown a causal effect following a change in role ambiguity (Caplan and Jones, 1975). In addition, several studies have found physiological effects of role conflict – no question of overlapping measures here. Caplan *et al.* (1975) compared twenty-three occupations and found that role conflict and ambiguity correlated with anxiety, depression, irritation and somatic complaints. Shirom *et al.* (1973) studied 762 kibbutz members and found that role conflict and ambiguity were correlated with blood-pressure, cholesterol etc., but especially for those in managerial and professional positions. An important kind of role conflict is now common for women – conflict between work and domestic roles, especially for those with young children.

'Burn-out'. This is a special form of stress, a kind of emotional exhaustion and loss of concern for people, which is commonly found among those in the medical and helping professions and among administrators who have to deal a lot with people. Maslach devised a scale, the Maslach Burnout Inventory, with three subscales, which are partly independent: (1) emotional exhaustion, (2) depersonalization (callous towards clients), (3) personal accomplishment (lack of). She found, for example, that nurses experienced a lot of emotional exhaustion and reduced personal accomplishment, whereas doctors suffered high emotional exhaustion and depersonalization (Maslach and Jackson, 1982).

There are many studies of stress in the medical professions. It is found that doctors and dentists have high rates of heart disease, especially general practitioners. There is a high suicide rate (three times the average for some groups) for those in medicine, dentistry and pharmacy, especially among women, and for certain specialities such as psychiatry. On the other hand, the suicide rate is low for clergy, teachers and social workers, who also have to deal with a lot of clients. There is a high rate of alcoholism and drug abuse in the medical profession – perhaps because they have more access to drugs. Doctors often seek psychiatric help, especially for depression. In addition, many nurses drop out from the profession (Cartwright, 1979).

Maslach and Jackson (1982) argue that burn-out is the result of a special kind of stress which occurs when dealing with people, especially difficult clients. They found that burn-out scores were higher for doctors who spent a greater proportion of their time with patients. Patients can be stressful in a number of ways, and some of these problems are met by all administrators, supervisors and managers outside the medical world. Clients can be angry, rude, abusive, anxious, frightened or upset. They may have difficulty communicating their thoughts and fears, or may be demanding, sometimes over trivial matters. Doctors and nurses may find their patients disgusting, and may have to cope with blood, vomit, excreta and mutilation. Patients or their families may have to be given bad news, or be helped to make difficult decisions. Medical staff may experience stress when patients are dying, and nothing can be done about it.

Burn-out also affects people outside the medical professions. Gaines and Jermier (1983) studied 208 police, and found they had quite high scores on the emotional exhaustion scale – although lower than Maslach's doctors and nurses. Emotional exhaustion was higher for women, those in physical danger, with poor promotion prospects, and little social support. Outside the medical world, possible sources of burn-out include danger, difficult and unsatisfactory subordinates, and conflict with others. However, we are perhaps moving a little away from burn-out to simple job dissatisfaction and depression.

While social stresses may be the main cause of burn-out, there are other possible factors too.

(1) Feelings of failure, and resultant helplessness, may occur when patients do not recover. This may apply to social workers, or to medical workers, for example those dealing with cancer patients.
(2) Lack of control may be experienced, either over uncooperative patients, or over unhelpful colleagues or administrators.
(3) Contact with depressed people may lead to depression. It has been found in laboratory experiments that listening to other people's troubles is very depressing.

There are various ways in which people try to cope with burn-out. One method is by withdrawal, spending more time away from people, reduction of contact hours, absenteeism, or by psychological withdrawal, i.e. not thinking about the job. A second method is turning towards others, i.e. to supervisors, peers, or other sources of social support which can give a sense of shared responsibility and reduce isolation. Both of these styles of coping have been found to be effective for doctors and nurses (Maslach and Jackson, 1982).

Personality and Stress

Type A personality. We described this type of person earlier – how they strive for achievement, are competitive and aggressive, and have a sense of urgency (p. 56). The immediate point of interest is that they have twice the rate of heart attacks than the relaxed Type Bs, and also have a higher rate for other illnesses – for example respiratory and intestinal complaints, viruses and injuries. Is this due to stress at work, and if so how?

Type As are also in better jobs, are more successful and are promoted faster. In the study by Caplan *et al.* (1975) it was found that university teachers in administrative positions and doctors had the highest scores in mental ill health, while toolmakers had the lowest. Type As work for longer hours and travel more; in laboratory experiments they work harder and faster.

However, Type As do not report any more overload, anxiety or dissatisfaction; they seem to enjoy being challenged and rise to meet the competition; they may seek those jobs and situations which provide such challenge. Why, then, do they become ill? Laboratory experiments show that they become distressed in situations where they are exposed to uncontrollable stresses (Glass, 1977). Chesney and Rosenman (1980) found that Type A managers in externally controlled work environments scored high on anxiety, while Type Bs reported anxiety when there was too little external control. What seems to happen is that Type As, in the face of uncontrollable stress, become highly aroused. They smoke more, have higher blood-pressure and cholesterol levels, and are at risk to heart disease. It has also been found that Type As put less effort into spouse and family, friends and leisure activities, thus depriving themselves of major sources of social support (Burke and Greenglass, 1987).

Recent research has questioned the link between heart disease and Type A personalities. Some studies have found a stronger link between heart disease and hostility, or a cynical, mistrusting attitude to others, or self-involvement and a feeling of isolation and incompleteness (Fischman, 1987).

Neuroticism. We described this dimension of personality earlier (p. 57ff); one of its main components is that the neurotic is upset by stress and experiences greater anxiety than others under a given level of stress. An example comes from a study of role conflict; Kahn *et al.* (1964) found that neurotic people experienced high role conflict and were more intense, experienced more tension, and withdrew more from other people. Parkes (1986) found that up to a certain point nurses with low neuroticism used more active and adaptive coping behaviour as work demand increased; those with high neuroticism, however, did not increase their coping efforts as demand increased.

Hardiness is the term that has been given to a number of personality qualities which distinguish between those who are and those who are not made ill by stress. It has three components, which can be assessed by questionnaire (Kobasa, 1982).

(1) *Commitment* – 'the ability to believe in the truth, importance, and interest value of who one is and what one is doing, and thereby to involve oneself fully in the many situations of life, including work, family, interpersonal relations, and social institutions'.
(2) *Internal control* – 'the belief that one can control events; external controllers think that the outcome of events depends more on other people or on luck'.
(3) *Challenge* – 'the belief that change, rather than stability, is the normative mode of life . . . much of the disruption associated with the occurrence of a stressful life event can be anticipated as an opportunity and incentive for personal growth, rather than a simple threat to security'. The reason internal controllers do better may be that they use more active methods of coping with problems, and are more flexible in their ways of coping; these include seeking help and advice from others.

Of these, internal control has received good support, commitment some support, and challenge the least (Hall *et al.*, 1987). Internals

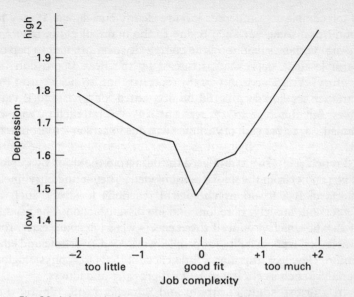

Fig. 20. Job complexity and depression (from Caplan *et al.*, 1975).

are more resistant to stress; one way in which they resist it is by making adaptive use of different coping strategies (Parkes, 1984).

Another factor behind hardiness may be the capacity to discharge work tensions, the 'tension discharge rate'. Matteson and Ivancevich (1983) devised a questionnaire measure of this which was found to relate to fewer health problems, less smoking and drinking, and less use of aspirins and tranquillizers.

Person–environment fit. We have seen that stress responses are affected by overload and other variables. However, some people are bored and frustrated if they have too little load. To some extent stress is due to lack of fit between person (P) and environment (E). It is likely to happen both for ability – work should be neither too easy nor too difficult, and also for motivation – the job should provide the kind of rewards which the individual wants. An example of the effects of P–E fit is given in Fig. 20. The effects of job complexity on depression are clearly curvilinear. It may be found that some variance is due to the main effects of environmental variables (e.g. too little complexity overall), and to person variables (e.g. depression, assessed by the Beck Depression Inventory). Van Harrison (1978) reported that 26 per cent of the variance for boredom could be accounted for by P and E variables, but this rose to 37 per cent if P × E interaction was included, i.e. 11 per cent of variance was due to person–environment fit.

French *et al.* (1982) analysed the data from the study by Caplan *et al.* (1975) from the above point of view. They found curvilinear effects of P–E fit on psychological reactions to stress, such as depression, anxiety, boredom and job dissatisfaction. The aspects of P–E fit which produced these effects were job complexity, role ambiguity, responsibility for people, work-load, overtime and education. However, there was little effect of P–E fit on physiological variables such as cholesterol, blood-pressure and illness.

In a British study Furnham and Schaeffer (1984) found that P–E fit on the job dimensions introduced in 1966 by Holland (p. 68) correlated with mental health (r = ·23), and with job satisfaction (r = ·37).

This line of research has important practical implications. To reduce stress, individuals need to be in the right jobs. This can partly be achieved by better selection in the first place, and later by good supervision and personnel management, sometimes leading to transfer and retraining. Individuals can change themselves, by training and following a career pattern, to fit the job better. The reason that older workers are more satisfied is probably that they have adjusted more to the job or have managed to alter the job to suit them (p. 244). Participation in decisions has been found to be one way to improve P–E fit (French *et al.*, 1982).

The Effects of Social Support

Stress produces tension, distress, ill health and mental disorder, but social support can prevent all this from happening. By social support we mean the existence of relationships with co-workers,

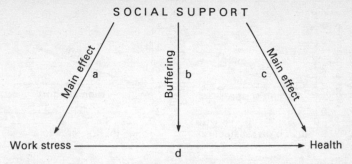

Fig. 21. Potential effects of social support on work stress and health (from House, 1981).

friends or others who can be relied upon to help when needed. Social support can offset the effects of stress in three possible ways, as shown in Fig. 21. (1) Social support may affect the perceived stressfulness of events. (2) Support may 'buffer' stress so that it comes into action only when stress is present. (3) Support may have direct beneficial effects on health.

The effect of social support on perceived stress was shown by House (1981) in a study undertaken in a tyre factory: perceived stresses of seven kinds were less when supervisor support was high, and to a lesser extent when co-worker support was high. This was confirmed by Caplan *et al.* (1975) in their larger study of twenty-three occupational groups. A wide range of dependent variables was shown to be affected in a wide range of occupations so this appears to be a very general, although not very strong, effect. The way in which it may work is that when there is social support the stressed individual knows that he or she can obtain help in dealing with the problem; helpful supervisors are in a good position to do this.

The 'buffering' of stress has been called the 'suntan lotion' model – it only works when it is needed. An example can be taken from Cobb's (1976) study of men who lost their jobs: of those who had a supportive wife 10 per cent became arthritic in two joints, compared with 41 per cent of those who did not. A number of studies have confirmed the effects of social support on health, and indeed on survival. Berkman and Syme (1979) found, for example,

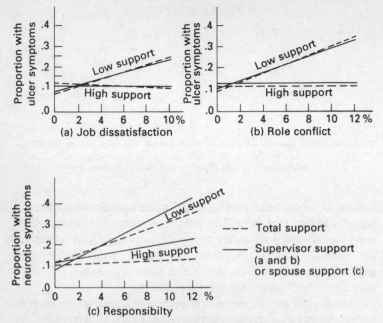

Fig. 22. Buffering effects of social support on relationships between stress and health among factory workers (from House, 1981).

that 9·6 per cent of men aged fifty to fifty-nine died over a nine-year period if they had a strong supportive network, compared with 30·8 per cent for those who did not. However, support from spouse and friends was more important than that from people at work. The probable mechanism is that this kind of social support can restore the immune system (Jemmott and Locke, 1984).

The buffering effects of social support are greater for mental health. The buffering model has been tested in a number of industrial studies, comparing the effects of stress for those with high and low social support. The results of the study by Caplan *et al.* (1975) showed that social support buffered the effect of stress on depression, somatic complaints and job satisfaction, but had no effect on anxiety. The effects of three stress variables on somatic complaints are shown in Fig. 22. It can be seen that for workers with high social support, increased stress has no effect at all. The process involved is probably different from the one for physical health. Stress produces negative emotions such as anxiety, depression and loss of self-esteem; these can all be removed by social support.

There may be a third effect of social support, route (c) in Fig. 21; a number of studies have found a main effect of social support on health, which is independent of buffering. This might operate via reduction of perceived stress or simply as a direct biological gain from social relationships.

There are three main sources of social support: supervisors, co-workers and family, especially partners. It is found that the first two are much more important sources of help at work, probably because they can help to deal directly with the source of stress. Henderson and Argyle (1985) found that feelings of job stress were less for workers who had at least one friend at work. However, partner support is very important when loss of job is threatened or actually happens. Social support is manifested in several different ways, of which the main ones are (1) tangible help, (2) informational help, (3) integration into a social group, (4) acceptance, providing confidence and esteem, and (5) close attachment to a confidant (Argyle and Henderson, 1985).

Co-workers can be a great source of social support, but they can also be a source of stress in several ways; there may be competition for promotion or other advantages, conflict of views, social rejection as a result of deviation, or social pressure to behave in a certain way. Problems experienced by shop-floor workers may be created by the pressure to get things done, lack of consultation, and others not pulling their weight. For managers, 'personality clashes' troubled 20 per cent of one small sample (Marshall and Cooper, 1979); loneliness, promotion over a colleague's head, and a 'bad atmosphere' can also cause stress for managers.

Supervisors, too, can be a major source of stress. They may make demands for more or better work, may be felt to treat different subordinates unfairly, may be seen as distant, hostile or unsympathetic. Supervisors can also provide benefits that are partly material, partly social (Locke, 1976); they are a greater source of instrumental, tangible help than co-workers (Argyle and Furnham, 1983). They can help with promotion, pay rises and conditions of work; they can do more to solve difficulties at work than either co-workers, or spouses. On the other hand, they can also create difficulties by not offering support. The social rewards which supervisors can provide include praise and encouragement, and the creation of a pleasant social atmosphere. Support from supervisors can reduce the effects of stress on anxiety and depression (Caplan *et al.*, 1975). Most supervisors feel that helping people is part of the job (Kaplan and Cowen, 1981).

The Prevention of the Effects of Stress

The extent of stress at work. We have seen that in Britain on average 13·5 working days are lost per head of population per year, of which about a third is voluntary; eight days are due to illness, and two to mental ill health (*Social Trends*, 1987). There is a great deal of minor illness which is partly due to stress. About one person in six is diagnosed by doctors as having anxiety, depression, or other mental symptoms, some of them due to stress at work; 31·5 per cent of men and 18·7 per cent of women die before the age of sixty-five, mostly of heart disease, strokes, cancer or hypertension, all of which are partly due to stress. Can some of these effects be alleviated?

For those stressed at work, the ideal solution would be to change jobs to less stressful occupations. This cannot always be done, and some jobs are stressful only part of the time, e.g. tax accountants experience more stress at the end of the tax year. We shall consider first ways of helping individuals. Of course, helping the individual helps the organization as a whole: American studies have found that for each dollar spent on treatment for job stress, the organization gains $5·52 in benefits from improved work performance (National Institute for Occupational Safety and Health, 1987).

Relaxation. One approach to the problem of stress is to train people how to relax. Peters and Benson (1978) trained volunteer office workers in a physiological relaxation technique which they practised during two fifteen-minute breaks each day. Over twelve weeks the members of the group showed a drop in blood-pressure, as well as increased health, overall performance and sense of well-being. These changes were greater than for another group who simply relaxed for the fifteen-minute period, or control groups who did not relax at all. Other courses have added biofeedback as a further relaxation method, as well as instruction on breathing (Ganster *et al.*, 1982). A number of follow-up studies of different relaxation courses have all shown positive results (Murphy, 1984).

There have been a number of studies of the effects of Transcendental Meditation (TM). This is a special technique of relaxation in which the eyes are closed, and the mind is emptied of thoughts and images by repeating a mantra for twenty minutes twice a day. Most of these studies have not been very well controlled, but as far as they go suggest that TM has certain physiological effects, such as brainwaves typical of a very relaxed state and reduced oxygen consumption. Meditators have been found to be more satisfied and productive, and less ambitious for promotion (Burke and Weir, 1980).

Leisure activities can reduce the effects of stress at work: leisure satisfaction has been found to buffer the effects of work stress (Broadbent, 1985). Leisure can provide relaxation (in front of the television), but exercise, social activities and serious leisure pursuits provide greater benefits (p. 315ff).

Other stress-management techniques. Workers can be taught better ways of coping with stress. Certain styles of coping are associated with low levels of symptoms and, therefore, are to be recommended – plenty of sleep, exercise, separating work from non-work, good health habits and talking problems through with work-mates. On the other hand, working harder or changing to a different work activity are associated with *more* symptoms. Some styles of coping work well in particular situations; for example overload can be coped with by analysing the situation and tackling it in a different way, and inability to influence a supervisor can be managed by talking to others (Burke and Weir, 1980).

A form of cognitive therapy has been used, in which employees are shown that a lot of their stress is due to the way in which they perceive and interpret situations, and taught that stressful situations can be seen in less threatening ways. For example, instead of reacting to overload by feeling incompetent, workers could blame the supervisor for mismanaging the work allocation. Individuals can also be trained in positive imagery, time-management and goal-setting (Bruning and Frew, 1987).

Several studies have investigated the effect of a stress-management package combining relaxation with stress-management training. Ganster *et al.* (1982) set up eight two-hour sessions for civil servants, most of them women. The first four sessions consisted of cognitive therapy which helped participants recognize self-defeating and other negative thoughts which contributed to stress; the last four sessions were devoted to muscular relaxation and biofeedback. After four months there was still a lower level of epinephrine anxiety and depression for the trained group.

Type A personalities are a particular cause for concern, since they are more likely to have heart attacks, and because they are found among the most hard-working and successful members of organizations. However, a recent meta-analysis has found that while heart attacks are predicted by overall Type A scores ($\cdot 21$ effect size for the interview measure), they are *not* predicted by the speed and job-involvement components. Heart attacks occur in individuals with negative emotions and low frustration tolerance, not in impatient workaholics (Booth-Kewley and Friedman, 1987). Suinn (1982) has shown that stress-management courses of the kind described can be successful in reducing scores on the Type A inventory, as well as on other measures.

Exercise and other health habits. There is extensive evidence that exercise is good for both physical and mental health, and exercises have been introduced to places of work with positive results. The most extensive follow-up to be reported was of two North American insurance companies, where a fitness programme was introduced to the 1,125 employees of one company but not to the employees of the other. Following the introduction of the programme absenteeism fell by 22 per cent after a year, and labour turnover decreased (Melhuish, 1981). Other similar studies have found that exercise schemes in firms can result in improved health, greater energy and stamina, improved work performance, weight-reduction, and less tension (Burke and Weir, 1980), as well as a reduction in anxiety and depression and other effects of stress, especially on exercise days (Falkenburg, 1987).

Alcoholism is a serious source of ill health and of impaired work performance. In one American firm 6 per cent of employees were found to have a serious drinking problem, while in Britain 35 per cent of young men can be regarded as heavy drinkers – defined as drinking seven drinks (e.g. half-pints of beer) once a week or more (*Social Trends*, 1987). The response rate for counselling services is rather poor, but one American firm managed to rehabilitate 414 of 990 people who asked for help (Melhuish, 1981).

Smoking adds greatly to the risk of heart disease, lung cancer, and other illnesses, and thus adds to the effects of stress on health. There is little relation between smoking and personality measures such as neuroticism. However, some people smoke in order to control stress; if they are not allowed to smoke at work, as in the case of nurses, their absenteeism rate goes up in the face of stress (Parkes, 1983).

Diet is very important for health. The effects of stress on health are magnified by poor diet. People who eat too much and become overweight and those who eat too much fat are at greater risk of heart attacks. Too much salt leads to hypertension and strokes. Parkes (1987) showed that the combination of excess weight (mainly due to bad diet) and smoking have profound effects on the health of and absenteeism in nurses. She fitted quadratic curves to data on mortality (from Lew and Garfinkel, 1979) showing the same pattern (see Fig. 23).

The considerable social class differences in health are probably largely due to differences in health habits. Middle-class people in Britain take far more exercise than working-class people, smoke a lot less, and are less likely to be overweight (Argyle, 1987).

How can workers be persuaded to take more exercise, drink and smoke less, and to improve their diet? The propaganda efforts

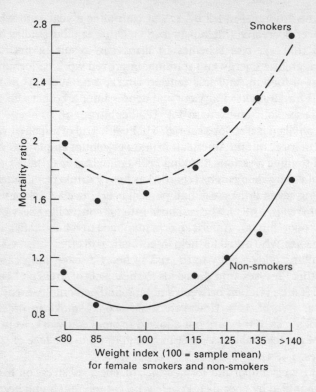

Fig. 23. Mortality and weight for female smokers and non-smokers (from Parkes, 1987).

of the Health Education Authority are a start. Some firms have annual health check-ups, which can spot the beginnings of trouble and which may result in employees being advised to mend their ways (Marshall and Cooper, 1981).

Increasing social support. We have seen that social support at work is able to eradicate the effects of stress. The most available source is the working group, individuals brought together for doing the work but also capable of providing job satisfaction and social support. This will happen if the working group is cohesive; we have seen the conditions required for this to occur – physical proximity, homogeneity and cooperative incentives (p. 132ff). We have also seen that co-workers are often *not* found to be very supportive. The Japanese have a way of enhancing supportiveness: new workers are taken on only once a year, and are formed into a strongly cohesive 'entering cohort' (Masumoto, 1970).

Some workers are physically isolated – the police, dentists and salespeople for example – but it may be possible to create groups or at least pairs to avoid isolation. The second main source of support is from the immediate supervisor, manager or shop steward. This is an important part of their job, and they often recognize this. However, they may need to be trained in listening skills and how to be emotionally supportive. They may need encouragement by seeing their own supervisor doing it, and by organization-wide commitment to the importance of this activity (House, 1981). It was found by Burke and Weir (1980) in a study of seventy managers that the individuals who were rated as most effective in providing support were often younger and of lower status than the person needing support, of the opposite sex (usually female), and outside the immediate work setting.

Organizational measures. It is useful to consider separately those jobs which are unavoidably stressful (e.g. police, firemen), and those where the stress could be reduced (e.g. assembly-line workers) (Van Dijkhuizen, 1981). Where stress cannot be avoided entirely, there are several steps which can be taken:

(1) *Better selection*, i.e. better matching of person and environment. For stressful jobs it is important to select people who can stand up to stress, or who even enjoy it. This can be done by personality tests, or by interviews which explore how candidates have coped with, and sought or avoided, similar stresses in the past.
(2) *Training* in stress management, as described above.
(3) *Job rotation*, giving periods of rest from the most stressful work.
(4) *Part-time work*, with only short periods of it, as is used for divers and radar plotters.

(5) *Regular medical checks*, and availability of counselling (Marshall and Cooper, 1981).

Where the work need not be stressful, more far-reaching organizational changes can be considered.

(1) *Improving the job*, for example by job enlargement or enrichment; reducing repetition, physical overload or time pressures; reducing travel and hours of work for managers; improving equipment or automating parts of the job which are boring or dangerous; reducing noise levels and making other environmental improvements.

(2) *Organizational changes*, such as flatter shape, decentralization, reduced role conflict and ambiguity, and better-designed socio-technical systems. Wall and Clegg (1981) studied a sweet factory where work identity, work group autonomy, and job complexity were increased, a lot of control being transferred from supervisors to the work group. This led to increased mental health and job satisfaction, and reduced labour turnover.

(3) *Increased social support*, by the creation of small work teams, encouraging and training supervisors and managers to be more supportive.

(4) *More participation in decisions* by industrial democracy structures, consultation by supervisors and managers, surveys of job satisfaction, suggestion schemes.

11

UNEMPLOYMENT AND RETIREMENT

Unemployment

Unemployment has become an extremely important practical problem in its own right. However, it is also interesting because of the light that it sheds on the nature of work, especially the benefits that work provides. In Britain a person counts as 'unemployed' if he or she is claiming unemployment or related benefits, that is if an individual does not have a paid job and is actively trying to obtain one. This does not include the retired, most married women without jobs, or students on vacation, who can all be regarded as 'non-employed'. The unemployed may be doing some 'work', depending on how this term is defined, such as housework, gardening, child care and study, but they are not paid for it, and there is no 'contracted relationship with a regulating institution' (Fryer and Payne, 1986).

The rate of unemployment in the Western world is now 7–15 per cent of the potential labour force. In Great Britain in 1986 the unemployed numbered 3·29 million or 13·1 per cent of the labour force; by the middle of 1988 this figure had fallen to 8·4 per cent, partly by changing the definition. The level of unemployment is much greater than this for certain groups in the population, such as among people living in areas like South Wales where traditional industry (e.g. coal-mining and steel production) has declined (*Social Trends*, 1986). Many unemployed people are between jobs – the median gap is 3·4 months. However, 40 per cent of them have been out of work for over a year; these tend to be the old, the young, the unskilled or disabled, ethnic minorities, or those who have been in prison (Smith, 1985–6). There is a growing 'hard core' who have been out of work for a long time, and some who have never had a job. A study of the predictors of individual unemployment found that young people were also more likely to be out of work if they had a smaller desire to be at work, if their father was out of work, and if they were of lower social class (Stafford *et al.*, 1980). Some young people accept periods of voluntary unemployment as part of life, and this gives them the opportunity to sample different kinds of work (Kelvin and Jarrett, 1985).

There has always been unemployment, especially in times of economic recession. It was during the Depression of the 1930s, when there was a very high level of despair and apathy, that unemployment was first studied by social scientists. Jahoda *et al.* (1933) described the devastating effects of unemployment in Marienthal, a small Austrian village. However, the current situation is quite different in several ways, especially the higher level of unemployment benefits and other sources of social welfare. Between the 1930s and 1980s unemployment was relatively low, usually under 3–4 per cent. The reasons for unemployment then were mainly individual. During the 1980s the rate has been much higher, and unemployment now reflects the decline of whole industries (Kelvin and Jarrett, 1985). One result is that unemployment has lost some of its stigma.

The Effects of Unemployment

(1) *How the unemployed spend their time.* A British survey asked a sample of 1,043 unemployed people what they had done the day before, a weekday; the results are shown in Table 26. It can be seen that the main activities were housework, shopping, job hunting, visiting friends and relatives, and gardening. 'Personal and household care, child care, the calls of family and public duty still continue' (Fryer and Payne, 1986).

Compared to those who are at work, the unemployed entertain less but smoke more than other people (Warr and Payne, 1982). Among unemployed males aged twenty-five to forty-four, 44 per

| | Morning | | Afternoon | | |
| | Men | Women | Men | Women | Total |
	%	%	%	%	%
Housework	19	49	7	21	19
Shopping	20	26	9	17	16
Job hunting	22	16	12	13	16
Visiting friends or relatives	6	10	12	17	10
Gardening	14	2	13	3	11
TV	4	2	14	12	8·5
Reading	9	5	8	10	8
Decorating	7	3	7	2	5·5
Walking	5	3	8	2	5·5
Nothing/sitting around	3	3	9	6	5·5
Staying in bed	8	8	1	0	4·5
Visiting town	5	7	3	4	4·5
Playing sport	4	1	4	0	3
Drinking	2	1	3	1	2

Table 26. How the unemployed spend their time (UK, 1982) (from *Social Trends*, 1984).

cent are heavy drinkers with 28 per cent for those at work (Smith, 1985–6). Middle-class unemployed read more than before, while working-class people show a reduction in forms of entertainment which have to be paid for (Warr and Payne, 1983). There is more 'unstructured' time – watching TV, chatting, reading the paper, 'hanging about' (Smith, 1985–6).

Some unemployed people keep up their skills, for example setting up an office or workshop at home; this is good for the self-image as well as for filling time. Some take part in the informal or 'black' economy, which both helps financially (although illegally) and maintains a social network. About 16 per cent of the unemployed do some unpaid work for good causes; this is less than for the employed, but the difference may be because the out-of-work include a lot of young and unskilled, who do less voluntary work (*Social Trends*, 1984).

(2) *Income.* Loss of job leads to loss of income for most people. In Britain 13 per cent of the unemployed say they have been very badly affected materially, and another 24 per cent fairly badly

affected. These percentages were higher for those who had been out of work for two years or more (*Social Trends*, 1984). It is true that some lower-paid workers become better off by being out of work if they have families and can claim both unemployment and supplementary benefits; however, in 1978 only 6 per cent received more, and in all cases only very little more (Davies *et al.*, 1982). The majority are worse off, especially after they have been out of work for a year. In 1982 the average family expenditure where the main income earner was unemployed was £129 per week, compared with £219 where the main income earner was employed (see p. 303) For some families the effects are smaller: a quarter receive as much as 80 per cent of their previous income. This is most common among middle-class men, whose wives can often find jobs (Warr, 1984).

Those out of work need more money for some purposes – more heating and lighting, the costs of job applications – although they save the cost of travel to work.

In addition to the material hardships of low income there is loss of self-esteem through ceasing to be the breadwinner and through becoming the recipient of unemployment benefits. Financial strain is likely to be greater when there are dependent children to feed, clothe and educate, and financial problems are a major source of emotional distress (Warr, 1984).

There is also less satisfaction with health and housing among the unemployed. The satisfactions and the stresses due to work are obviously not at issue, but those due to the family are greater (Campbell, 1981; Warr and Payne, 1983).

(3) *Happiness*. This has a number of separate components, all of which have been found to be affected by unemployment.

(a) *Positive affect*. Warr and Payne (1982) carried out a national survey of how pleased with things the respondents were on the previous day. The results are shown in Table 27. For men, the unemployed were significantly less pleased with things than those in jobs; the retired were a lot more satisfied. Women were most pleased if they were retired or in part-time work. Similar results have been found in other countries. In American surveys,

10–12 per cent of the unemployed describe themselves as 'very happy', compared with 30 per cent of the general population (Campbell, 1981).

Does unemployment cause unhappiness or vice versa? Unemployed people have on average lower qualifications, more psychological problems, poorer health, and, compared with those in constant employment, worse jobs before they lost them (Warr, 1978). However, longitudinal studies, for example of the closure of entire factories, show that unhappiness is at least partly, and probably mainly, the result of unemployment. In a study of 1,655 British steel workers, conducted six months after closure of their plant, the positive affect scores (self-ratings of positive emotions) on the 0–5 Bradburn scale were 3·05 for those who had found jobs, 2·3 for those who had not. A longitudinal study in Australia found that school-leavers who did not find jobs became less happy (Tiggemann and Winefield, 1984).

(b) *Life satisfaction* is a cognitive aspect of happiness. Campbell *et al.* (1976) found that this was lower for unemployed men, but not for women. Unemployment hits some domains of satisfaction more than others. One of the main areas is, of course, money and standard of living as described above. However, when income is held constant the unemployed are still less happy than those at work (Campbell *et al.*, 1976). The unemployed also, of course, lose their job satisfaction, and they become less satisfied with themselves, as described below.

(c) *Negative affect.* A British survey found that 19 per cent of an unemployed sample said that they had become miserable or unhappy since they became out of work, 17 per cent had become restless and bad tempered, while 13 per cent were easily upset or snappy (*Social Trends*, 1984). In the Australian study by Tiggemann and Winefield (1984), school-leavers who did not find jobs became more bored, angry with society, lonely and helpless. Table 27 shows that those in full-time jobs had the lowest levels of emotional strain, less than the retired, for women as well as men. Many research workers have described the states of shock, apathy and hopelessness produced by job loss.

	Full-time employment %	Part-time employment %	Unemployed – looking for work %	Unemployed – not looking for work %	Retired %
'Felt very pleased with things yesterday (all of the time).'					
Men	23	24	21	20	36
Women	17	28	19	24	35
'Unpleasant emotional strain yesterday (all or most of the time).'					
Men	6	16	16	17	12
Women	9	11	21	13	14

Table 27. The emotional state of the employed, unemployed and retired (from Warr and Payne, 1982).

(d) *Apathy*. The unemployed become bored and apathetic, especially if they find they cannot organize their time, and just sit around doing nothing (Feather and Bond, 1983). They have even been found to walk more slowly, to show a lowering of physical and psychological alertness; sitting about aimlessly can lead to physical deterioration.

(e) *Self-esteem*. Many studies have found that the unemployed have lower self-esteem than those in employment. Warr and Jackson (cited in Warr, 1984) found that only negative self-esteem was affected, with items such as 'I haven't got much to be proud of', and found a difference of ·6 on a five-point scale. Longitudinal analysis found a shift in negative self-esteem for those who moved in and out of employment, but no change for positive self-esteem; the two aspects of self-esteem are almost independent in this unemployed sample, and the authors suggest that positive and negative self-esteem have become 'uncoupled', so that positive self-esteem can be maintained in the face of adversity (Warr, 1984).

(4) *Mental Health*. The unemployed have higher rates of mental ill health and distress of several kinds.

(a) *General emotional disturbance* is lower for those at work than for all categories of unemployed, including the retired, as Table 27 shows. A good measure of psychological distress is the General Health Questionnaire (GHQ), devised by Goldberg in 1978. Banks and Jackson (1982) used this to find out whether unemployment caused mental ill health or vice versa. They surveyed more than two thousand school-leavers in Leeds and obtained their GHQ scores before they left school, and again one to two years afterwards. Table 28 shows that the GHQ scores (using the thirty-item version) of those who did not find jobs *increased*, while for those who did find jobs it *decreased*. Those who found jobs also had lower GHQ scores in the first place. This kind of longitudinal design shows that unemployment affects mental health. It

	Before leaving school	6–15 months after leaving school	16–23 months after leaving school
Unemployed			
Boys	11·4	13·6	
Girls	11·2		13·4
Employed			
Boys	10·6	8·4	
Girls	10·5		7·7

Table 28. Unemployment and mental health; self-reported mental health using the 30-item G H Q (from Banks and Jackson, 1982).

suggests in addition, however, that poor mental health has a small effect in making unemployment more likely.

It usually takes some time for the effects of unemployment on mental health to appear. An Australian study of 400 unemployed young people found that 56 per cent of them were clinically disturbed, and that in most cases this occurred after unemployment started, typically five months later (Finlay-Jones and Eckhardt, 1981). A British study found that mental and physical health were worst at about six months (Warr and Jackson, 1984). An American study found that many wives became depressed, anxious and sensitive about their social relationships two to three months after their husbands lost their jobs (Liem and Atkinson, 1982, cited in Furnham and Lewis, 1986).

(b) *Depression* is usually found to be higher among the unemployed. The level of depression increases with the period of unemployment (Warr, 1984). A series of studies in Australia found clear effects of unemployment on the Beck Depression Inventory – a well-known scale which consists of twenty-one items on different aspects of mental and physical depression. Feather (1982) found scores of about 11 for the unemployed compared with 5·5 for those at work. It was found that after a long period of unemployment people increasingly blamed themselves, were in a state of 'learned helplessness', in which they felt that the main cause of their unemployment, i.e. aspects of themselves, was uncontrollable (Feather and Davenport, 1983). However, Catalano *et al.* (1981) argue that economic changes really uncover existing cases of mental disorder, whose symptoms were previously regarded as trivial; families can no longer afford to support a marginal member.

(*c*) *Alcoholism*. While some studies have found that the total consumption is the same as for the employed, it has been found that the unemployed drink faster, and drink more at a single session, and are therefore more likely to get drunk (Warr, 1987). There are more 'heavy drinkers' (who drink seven glasses once a week or more) among the unemployed – 44 per cent v. 28 per cent (Smith, 1985–6).

(*d*) *Suicide* is more common among the unemployed. Attempted suicides in Edinburgh are eight times more common among the unemployed; the rate is highest during the first month of unemployment and after twelve months (Platt, 1986). How does unemployment lead to suicide attempts? One route is depression, or other aspects of poor mental health. Another route is via poverty, reduced social support and alcoholism (Platt, 1984; Smith, 1985–6). There is evidence that the yearly fluctuations in national suicide rates are correlated with the level of unemployment. The evidence for this is discussed below.

(5) *Health*. There is no question that the unemployed are in poorer health than the employed. The question is, why are they? Some people have to give up work *because* of bad health. Cook *et al.* (1981) found that men between forty and fifty-nine in Britain who said that their unemployment was due to ill health had higher rates of bronchitis, heart and lung disease. However, a British investigation of 2,300 men who lost their jobs in 1978 found that most of them were healthy at the time, and remained so (Moylan *et al.*, 1984).

Several studies have found evidence that unemployment causes illness. A small-scale American study of workers who had lost their jobs as a result of factory closure found that they had 'anticipatory' ill health before becoming unemployed, e.g. increased blood-pressure which fell to normal if they found another job (Cobb and Kasl, 1977). These workers also suffered increased cholesterol levels – which increase the danger of heart disease and strokes – and were likely to contract arthritis, especially if they lacked strong social support at home. In a British study 954 unemployed men were asked about their health after becoming unemployed; 27 per cent said it had become worse, but 11 per cent that it had improved because of less work strain, more relaxation and exercise (Warr, 1984).

The mortality rate is greater for those out of work. A careful ten-year census study of British men who lost their jobs in 1971 found that their death rate over that period was 36 per cent greater than for the whole population of males aged between fifteen and sixty-four, and 21 per cent greater if age and class were equated. The figure for their wives was 20 per cent, and the effect was greater in the second half of the decade, both results suggesting stress rather than previous illness as the cause (Moser *et al.*, 1984). It has been claimed by Brenner (1976) that the total death rate, the suicide rate, and other indices are correlated with fluctuating national levels of unemployment. He calculated that a 1 per cent increase in unemployment in the USA, if sustained for five years, would result in a 4·1 per cent increase in suicides, a 3·3 per cent increase in mental hospital first admissions, a 4 per cent increase in prison admissions, a 5·7 per cent increase in murders, a 1·9 per cent increase in death from alcoholism, and a 1·9 per cent increase in the total death rate. However, this is not found for all historical periods, and it has been claimed that the correlation in Britain was due to a decrease in unemployment from 1940–42, when there was also an improvement in diet and medical treatment (Warr, 1984).

Evidently unemployment does have some effect on health. What is the explanation for this effect?

(a) Poverty, resulting in poor diet, heating, clothes and housing. This was more important in earlier historical periods (Kelvin and Jarrett, 1985) but is still true today.

(b) Poor health habits, e.g. more drinking and smoking, especially for working-class men (Smith, 1985–6; Warr and Payne, 1983).

(c) Higher levels of stress, which in turn can produce higher levels of heart disease, and lowered activity of the immune system (Argyle, 1987).

When Does Unemployment Cause Distress?

Length of unemployment. According to some studies there are a series of regular reactions to loss of a job (Kelvin and Jarrett, 1985). (1) When people are first unemployed, they experience *shock*, anger and incomprehension. They then experience (2) *optimism*, a feeling of being between jobs, a kind of holiday with active job searching. (3) *Pessimism* follows and, as job searching is unsuccessful, people see themselves as unemployed, become worried about money and the future. (4) *Fatalism* results, hopelessness and apathy are experienced, and the individual ceases to look for a job.

While there is a certain amount of evidence for this sequence, it has not been demonstrated rigorously, and there are certainly many exceptions to it. There have been a few longitudinal studies; Warr and Jackson (1984) followed up working-class men for a year after they lost their jobs; scores on the GHQ fell during the first six months and then became stable. Other studies found that GHQ scores levelled off after three months, and that later some scores improved (Fryer and Payne, 1986). Measures of work involvement have been found to fall with time if unemployment continues, perhaps a form of adaptation (Warr and Jackson, 1985). However, low scorers on the GHQ have been found to look harder for jobs, such as making more job applications.

Commitment to work. Those who are most attached to their jobs are more distressed by losing them. A measure of work involvement is a six-item scale devised by Jackson *et al.* (1983). They found that people with high scores on this scale were more distressed by unemployment; their distress scores changed most when they lost or gained jobs. This is probably why unemployment is more distressing for middle-aged men than for young people or married women (Warr, 1987). Other studies have found that work involvement correlates with reduced positive affect, reduced self-esteem and greater negative affect (Warr, 1984). Feather and Davenport (1983) in Australia found that need for a job correlated with depression at ·5; however, there was no effect on physical health.

Social support from the family. Many studies have shown that social support, especially from the family, 'buffers' (i.e. reduces) the effects of stress. Cobb and Kasl (1977) found that among men who lost their jobs as a result of factory closure 12 per cent became arthritic, while others had raised cholesterol. However, for those with good support from their spouse only 4 per cent became arthritic, while for those with low social support it was 41 per cent. Brown and Harris (1978) found that many women became depressed if they experienced stressful life events, especially if they did not have jobs. However, the rate of depression was much lower if they had supportive spouses. Kasl (1982) found that social support became an effective buffer only when it had become clear that unemployment was likely to continue.

Does the family usually provide social support during unemployment, or does it fall to pieces? Families are certainly put under great strain, mainly because of financial hardships, but also because of the loss of status of the breadwinner. Some children do less well at school, their health may deteriorate, and a few are abused. Overall, however, most families hold up and do provide some support, although the relationships are changed – families sustain but also control (Fryer and Payne, 1986).

Family support is important since unemployment results in a serious loss of social relationships. There is a loss of all relationships at work, i.e. loss of a cooperative network and of friendships. At work people are part of a complex set of complementary relationships which convey identity and status: a teacher feels he or she is a teacher as a result of the interaction with pupils. All this is lost in unemployment.

There is usually some withdrawal from friendships during unemployment, partly because the unemployed often cannot afford to pay for drinks, entertainment or to go on outings. They may feel inferior and stigmatized, and may withdraw from the company of employed people, thinking rightly or wrongly that they are being ostracized. The bonds between unemployed people are weak: it is a group to which they do not want to belong.

Level of activity. We have seen that a minority of unemployed people undertake unpaid work, pursue hobbies, do the gardening, or in other ways keep active. GHQ scores are worse for those whose time is not fully occupied, or who have problems in filling the time, with correlations as high as ·55 (Warr, 1984). High GHQ scores are associated with spending more time sitting around at home, watching television and listening to the radio. After a long period of unemployment some individuals adapt in a way which is not very satisfying. They stay in bed late, kill time, and give up bothering to apply for jobs. And of course they watch television a lot – which was not possible during earlier economic recessions.

However, some unemployed people find more satisfying things to do than their previous work provided. A recent study described eleven people who used unemployment in an unusually positive way. They preferred their own organization of time and self-discipline to an imposed one, they had not liked hierarchical authority, and found enriched social support elsewhere, they chose their own goals in tune with their own values, they found their own identities, in one case as leader of a community project, and had as much opportunity as before for the daily exercise of competence and skill (Fryer and Payne, 1984).

Clearly it is possible to organize non-work activities in a very satisfying way. But which activities do this? Sitting around doing nothing obviously does not. Gardening, hobbies and decorating involve the same activities as certain kinds of work except that they are unpaid, they are done when and how one wants, and may not provide contacts with other people or broader goals. In order to provide satisfaction similar to that of work, leisure should have certain properties, such as commitment to long-term goals, cooperation in a group and use of skills. In Chapter 12 we will see how far leisure can provide such satisfaction.

It is clear that there are plenty of things for the unemployed to do with their time, just as there are for the young, the retired and the many women who choose to stay at home. If they succeed in working out an organized pattern of life, they enjoy a greater sense of well-being.

Another example of happy 'unemployed' people can be found among those middle-class and upper-class people of an earlier era who did not need to work. As far as we can see they were perfectly happy, in part perhaps because they had never heard of the Protestant Work Ethic. Perhaps it was also because they led a fairly ordered way of life, undertook extensive duties (such as running estates) and country pursuits.

Perception of the causes of unemployment. People hold differing theories about why they or others are out of work. The unemployed think that unemployment is mainly caused by government, trade unions or other societal factors, while the employed think it is also the fault of the unemployed (Furnham, 1982). During periods of full employment, to be out of work was mainly due to personal incompetence. In the current climate of opinion to be out of work may still be seen as a sign of failure; it is a social stigma, a form of deviance, as Kelvin (1981) found when interviewing unemployed people: 'And if you can't find any work to do, you have the feeling that you're not human. You're out of place. You're so different from all the rest of the people around you that you think something is wrong with you.'

Unemployment has now become very widespread, however, and includes people from all sections of society, including many who are highly qualified, and who have held responsible jobs in the past. Among the young, very large proportions cannot find work in some areas. Among the middle-aged, unemployment can be seen as 'early retirement'. The result is that many of the unemployed now feel less responsible for their plight, and more accepting of it. If you know many other people who are also out of work, this part of the identity problem is greatly eased. It is found that satisfaction with the self is higher when the local level of unemployment is high (Warr, 1984).

Implications of Unemployment for the Social Psychology of Work

A widely accepted theory is that unemployment is distressing because of the financial deprivation it produces, and because work meets certain basic human needs and produces some latent benefits. Jahoda (1982) suggests seven functions of work, while Warr (1987) modified this to nine 'vitamins', which he thinks must be above a certain level to avoid distress:

(1) Opportunity for control
(2) Opportunity for skill use
(3) Externally generated goals (i.e. demands for purposeful activity and structuring of time)
(4) Variety
(5) Environmental clarity (e.g. certainty about the future)
(6) Availability of money
(7) Physical security (i.e. safety)
(8) Opportunity for interpersonal contact
(9) Valued social position

Like vitamins, it is suggested, these factors have non-linear effects. Thus vitamins C and E improve health up to a point and then have no further effect; pay, physical conditions and interpersonal contact may be like this. Vitamins A and D produce an increase in health to a degree, but too much is bad for health; control, variety, clarity and workload may also be like this.

We have seen that there is evidence that temporal structure and social contacts are important, and need to be replaced for the unemployed. We saw earlier that job satisfaction is affected by exercise of skills, variety in work, and by social contacts. The practical implications of this theory, if correct, are that unemployed people need to be provided with leisure activities which can meet these needs. However, an alternative view has been put forward, which offers a different explanation of the effects of unemployment. Fryer and Payne (1986) argue firstly that the latent functions theory has not been properly verified, and secondly that some of the observed consequences of unemployment need a different theory. They cite Maslow and other psychologists who believe that individuals develop towards self-determination and autonomy, where behaviour is directed more from within than from external demands. We have seen that for those workers who have strong growth needs, job satisfaction is greater if they have the opportunity at work to achieve, and if they have enough autonomy. However, this does not apply to all workers, or even to a majority of them.

Fryer and Payne (1986) note that some unemployed people use the public library, spend more time than before on hobbies, and engage in such apparently irrational behaviour as growing flowers rather than vegetables, perhaps in an attempt to 'instil a vestige of non-material meaning in their lives'. However, looking back to the more typical activities of the out of work (Table 26), it must be admitted that these creative and autonomous activities only apply to a minority.

Retirement

The retired make an interesting comparison with the unemployed, since they too are not working. The main findings can tell us a little more about the social psychology of work.

Many people retire early or before they have to. Others continue to work after the statutory age of retirement, although the number is falling (it was 31 per cent for men in Britain in 1971) (Parker, 1982). Some of these had simply not retired, while others had taken new, often part-time jobs. Individuals are more likely to work if they have professional or other good jobs without a compulsory retirement age, if they are Type As, if they are in good health, or if they need the money for family reasons. Others retire early, mainly through ill health, or because they were made redundant, had low job satisfaction, their skills were obsolete, they felt that they had attained their occupational goals, or they expected to be well-off financially (Beehr, 1986).

Many people, in Britain as elsewhere, do not want to retire. In one survey 31 per cent said they did not feel happy to retire, in another 35 per cent were looking forward to it, while the rest were not or had mixed feelings (Parker, 1987).

How the retired spend their time. Retirement provides much more time for leisure, and most people keep up or extend their previous leisure interests, although a few take up something new. For those for whom leisure is an extension of work, this is very satisfactory: academics continue writing, while engineers may do up old cars. For those for whom leisure is a reaction to work, things are more difficult: e.g. 'violent' leisure (e.g. body-contact sports) in reaction to stressful work (Parker, 1982). However, the trend is towards more television watching, and other 'passive' leisure, and gardening, shopping and helping in the house. Naturally, there is a fall with age in most forms of active leisure – sport, meals and drinks out, dancing, bingo, and other outings (Birch, 1979). There is little increase after retirement in active leisure pursuits such as voluntary work and membership of clubs, although 48 per cent of retired men say they have time on their hands that they do not know what to do with, compared with 10 per cent of those of the same age still at work (Parker, 1987).

Some of those who take early retirement are more active than this. A study of 1,800 men who retired early and their wives produced an interesting set of activities (McGoldrick, 1982). It should be noted that these people were distinctly above average in health and wealth, in many cases having retired under favourable financial conditions. The activities fell into nine main types:

(1) Resting and relaxing – television, walking, gardening, etc.
(2) Time spent with wife and family, and on domestic jobs
(3) Hobbies – music, DIY, golf, bird-watching, fishing, philately
(4) Social life and travel

	Workers %	Retired %
The money the job brings in	48	31
The people at work	24	36
The feeling of being useful	10	10
The work itself	8	11
Things happening around	3	5
The respect of others	2	3
Other answers	5	4

Table 29. Aspects of work older workers and retired people would/did miss most (from Parker, 1980).

(5) Committees and clubs
(6) Voluntary work
(7) Further education
(8) Part-time jobs
(9) New jobs – slower and at a lower level

These people were very satisfied with their early retirement, since in many cases they had been having problems at work, such as changes in the job or in the company, had been getting tired, and wanted a healthy and active retirement. There is a great contrast between the morale and the activities of this early-retired group and most unemployed people. This is partly because the former were older, better off financially and better educated.

Income. Most retired people experience a drop in income. A British survey asked older workers and those who had retired what they would or did miss most about not working; workers felt they would most miss the money the job brought in, while retired people placed income loss second to loss of contact with people at work (Table 29). In Britain, however, the actual fall in income is not so great, especially if per capita income or expenditure are considered (Table 30). There would, however, be a noticeable fall in per capita income if the children had become independent some years before the household head retired.

A number of surveys have asked workers who planned to

	All families £	Head employed £	Head unemployed £	Head retired £
Family expenditure	162	219	129	91
Per head expenditure	62	68	44	58

Table 30. Average expenditure per week of the retired and others in the UK (Family Expenditure Survey, 1985).

carry on working why they would do so. Similar proportions said that they would work because they needed the money, and because they would be bored, liked to work, and wanted to stay active.

Happiness. Campbell *et al.* (1976) found that people over sixty-five years of age were a quarter of a standard deviation above the population mean on an index of subjective well-being. Later studies from the University of Michigan found little difference between retired men and others, although they reported less stress; however, the older individuals surveyed did have more health worries (Campbell, 1981). Warr and Payne (1982) found that 36 per cent of retired men and 35 per cent of retired women in Britain felt very pleased with things (all of the time), compared with 23 per cent and 17 per cent of those at work, and 21 per cent and 19 per cent of those unemployed and looking for work (Table 27).

On the negative side, retired people are more bored and they may be lonely, in other words they miss two of the main satisfactions of work – the activity and the social life. They may also feel useless and they may feel old; for former unskilled workers in particular their self-image is less based on occupation (Kasl, 1980).

Satisfaction with and adjustment to retirement depend on a number of factors, although several of these are predictors of satisfaction for everybody.

(1) *Health* has been found to predict satisfaction in all studies, although the effect is modest, typically ·2 to ·3.

(2) *Finance* is a predictor in most studies but had no effect in a study of retired American managers (Schmitt *et al.*, 1979).

(3) *Purpose in life*, life interest and self-esteem, was the strongest predictor in a study of retired British managers (Beveridge, 1980).

(4) *Having strong interests*, old or new, is important, as is belonging to educational, leisure or other organizations. O'Brien (1986) found that the main predictors of satisfaction were the amount of social interaction and the number of different activities, not the use of skills.

(5) *Education and social class* can predict satisfaction in retirement. Although middle-class people are giving up more interesting jobs, they have more resources and leisure interests with which to replace work. Managers find it difficult to accept the loss of responsibility, professionals can keep up their skills and interests more.

(6) Satisfaction can be predicted when retirement is *voluntary and planned*. However, the effects of pre-retirement courses are found to be negligible (Beehr, 1986).

(7) *Married women* have the least difficulty in adjusting to retirement.

In his British survey Parker (1982) found that many older workers saw retirement in positive terms – more freedom, leisure and relaxation, although it was also associated with getting old and the end of the working life. The retired people interviewed also mentioned the problem of adjustment, loss of money, boredom, loneliness and wanting to work.

Mental health. It was once widely believed that retirement was bad for people; in a well-known study of stressful life events retirement was rated at 45, where 'fired' scored 47, and getting married 50 (Holmes and Rahe, 1967). It was found that 25–30 per cent of workers have trouble in adjusting to retirement and wish they had carried on working; what they miss is the work associates, or the income, rather than the work itself (Table 29). However, most do settle down within the first twelve months or soon afterwards.

Adjustment is more difficult when retirement is involuntary, and if it is unplanned. American studies find that overall there is little difference in mental health before and after retirement (Kasl, 1980). A British survey found that 12 per cent of retired men and 14 per cent of retired women had unpleasant emotional strain the previous day, which is more than for those employed full-time, but less than for the unemployed (Table 27) (Warr and Payne, 1982).

Health. Ill health is the main reason for early or voluntary retirement – 50 per cent in two large British surveys (Parker, 1982). Does retirement also cause ill health? This is a research problem fraught with difficulties, for which a number of ingenious solutions have been designed. Comparisons have been made between the health of workers who have retired from jobs at different ages, and there have been longitudinal studies of the same workers before and after retirement. However, carefully conducted studies have found very little effect of retirement on health (Kasl, 1980). There is no immediate effect, and age of retirement has no effect on mortality rate or life expectancy; there is a slight improvement in the health of those who were in manual work, a slight decline for those in better jobs, but most show no change. Those in heavy, unskilled jobs benefit from the absence of stress and fatigue. However, health is correlated with status, and while those in unskilled jobs survive an average of three years after retirement, men in white-collar jobs last four to five years (Beehr, 1986; Kasl, 1980).

Comparison of the Effects of Retirement and Unemployment

The unemployed and the retired are both out of work, and have suffered a similar drop of income. They spend their time in similar ways – with increased leisure time, although activities are mainly of a passive kind, gardening, housework, etc. – although the retired do not go job hunting and they go out and about less than the unemployed. The retired are happier than those at work, the unemployed much less. There are some negative aspects for the retired, as some people feel bored, lonely and useless. The unemployed are depressed and generally in poor mental health, whereas the retired are not. The unemployed are in poor health, while the retired are no different from those of a similar age at work.

What is the explanation for these dramatic differences between the welfare of the unemployed and the retired? It must be because retirement is an accepted and honourable social status, while unemployment is not. Retirement is seen as a proper reward for a hard life's work, while unemployment has the implication of failure, being unwanted, a scrounger, living on charity. 'For most men being retired seems to be a rather benign condition of life; being unemployed is a disturbing and often degrading experience' (Campbell, 1981).

While most people say that they would carry on working if it was not financially necessary (p. 86), this is 'not because of any intrinsic satisfaction in work, but because society has not provided any meaningful alternative' (Kasl, 1980). The people most satisfied in retirement are those scientists, writers and other academics who can simply carry on working, with little loss of continuity from very satisfying jobs. Another group are those who discover really satisfying leisure activities, which in most cases have some of the characteristics of work.

12

THE FUTURE OF WORK

There have been profound changes in the extent and nature of work during recent years, which have led to much serious discussion, particularly by British social scientists, of how work will develop in the future. Economists and statisticians can make forecasts of how much work there will be, but there are several alternative scenarios, and social psychology has something to say about these. Increasing leisure seems to be an inevitable part of the future, and any major changes in work or leisure have important implications for education.

Decreasing Work

We have seen how unemployment in the UK rose to 13·1 per cent of the labour force in 1986, and how it has dropped since to 8·4 per cent. It is high in all other industrialized countries. The basic reason is that just as agriculture declined as a major source of employment after the Industrial Revolution, employment in the manufacturing industries has now declined too, mainly because of increased automation.

The introduction of micro-electronics can cause job losses of 40 per cent; during the 1970s 46,000 employees in Swiss watch-making were made redundant (Gill, 1985). Assembly work, of cars for example, will probably be hard hit: it was estimated that 50 per cent of these jobs would be automated by 1988 (Gill, 1985). Many of the simplest jobs created by Taylorism, lasting a few seconds, can easily be automated. Other industries are going through the same process, the latest being printing.

About 40 per cent of the British working population are in offices as administrators, professionals, technical or clerical workers. Despite the expansion of electronic office equipment, there has been an overall gain in clerical jobs. Banks, on the other hand, have shed jobs. An American bank reduced its clerical staff from 10,000 to 6,000 in the 1970s, but managed to employ those displaced in other areas of work into which the bank had expanded (Gill, 1985).

Economists predict a slow, continuing decline in employment. An OECD study in 1982 (cited in Gill, 1985) predicted that employment in the UK would *fall* as follows:

	by 1990	by 1995
optimistic assumptions	0·48 m	0·86 m
pessimistic assumptions	1·28 m	1·97 m

An analysis by the Institute of Manpower Studies predicted a decline in employment of half a million jobs between 1985–90, but an increase in self-employment of 2·7 million (Rajan and Pearson, 1986).

It has been estimated that by early in the next century in the UK 10 per cent of the population will be able to satisfy our material needs for agriculture and manufacturing (Stonier, 1983). This entails a fundamental change in the human condition – it is no longer necessary for so many people to work all the time. There has been, however, an increase in employment in services – medicine, education, domestic work, entertainment, eating and drinking, sport, travel and holidays, insurance, banking and finance – and this has led to more manufacturing of certain kinds, e.g. hotels and television sets. This increase was not anticipated by the forecasters of the 1950s, who as a result over-estimated the levels of unemployment. However, the services sector in turn has now been hit by micro-electronics, e.g. banking and insurance, with consequent loss of jobs. Could there be a fourth wave of employment to follow agriculture, manufacturing and services? It has been suggested that information technology might provide such a wave, although it is doubtful whether it could ever account for more than 10–15 per cent of jobs, and probably much less. In fact there has been more growth recently in unskilled jobs, such as those held by janitors, domestic workers, fast-food preparers and servers, and clerical staff (Frankel, 1987).

Work has declined in other ways. The average number of hours worked per week by full-time male workers has fallen from sixty in 1870 to about forty-two today. Holidays have increased from very little to 4·25 weeks per year. The average number of years at work for men has fallen a little, from 38·3 to 37·2. This all adds up to a fall in life hours of work for those at work of about 50 per cent over the last 100 years. The picture for women is quite different: their average years at work have increased from ten to twenty-three since 1931, much of it part-time and carried out by married women (Armstrong, 1984).

The increase in unemployment has produced great distress, as we have seen. Welfare payments make it very expensive, and it is a major source of political instability. Are we willing for these problems to become progressively worse, so that 90 per cent of the population is distressed and alienated?

If the need for work is innate, then jobs should be provided for all in some way. On the other hand, the need for work may be primarily due to socialization and indoctrination with ideas such as the Protestant Work Ethic. One way of providing some work for all is by job-sharing of some kind. There are two problems associated with this – those with jobs, and the trade unions who represent them, are mostly against it, since less work means less pay. In addition, economists believe that it leads to inflation (Layard, 1986). Nevertheless it is slowly happening. There are a number of ways of changing how we think about work in order to create jobs.

(1) *Banning overtime* would be politically unpopular, but could create 250,000 jobs in Britain (Department of Employment, 1983).

(2) A *shorter working week*, say thirty-five hours instead of forty-two, would have a much greater effect. We have seen that for

	Has tried %	Plans to enlarge %	Dropped or plans to drop %
Part-time work	68 (83·2)	19·4 (6·7)	7·1 (11·5)
Early or late retirement	53·9 (75·2)	27·3 (20·2)	3·9 (4·3)
Phased retirement	17·6	28·5	2·5
Shorter working week	20·2	15·5	9·4
Sabbaticals	6·8	8·2	6·6
Job-sharing	10·5	26·6	7·4

Table 31. Job sharing in Europe, with UK figures in brackets (from Clutterbuck and Hill, 1981).

many it has already become much shorter; a thirty-five-hour week is planned in France. Table 31 shows that 20 per cent of a sample of European managers had tried a shorter working week, and more planned to do so (Handy, 1984).

(3) A *shorter working life* (say from the age of twenty to fifty-eight), starting later after more education or training and ending earlier, or with a flexible retirement age, or an easier move to part-time work, could result in the creation of more jobs. (Table 31 shows that many European executives had tried earlier or flexible retirement.)

(4) *More part-time jobs*, longer holidays, and sabbaticals would 'free up' the work-force. (Table 31 shows that 68 per cent of European executives, and 83 per cent of those in Britain, had tried part-time work, and a few had tried sabbaticals.)

Even now 20 per cent of the British work-force is part-time (Handy, 1984). Surveys in Europe and the USA have found that few workers would be willing to trade shorter hours for less pay, but a small majority would choose a reduction in hours rather than an increase in pay. There was no overall preference for shorter hours, longer holidays or earlier retirement (OECD, 1982).

An alternative to job-sharing is governmental job creation, favoured by Keynsian economists. Job creation was carried out successfully in the USA in the Depression of the 1930s, and is being used in various schemes in Britain today, although it is believed to lead to inflation by some economists (Layard, 1986).

Already many Government-financed jobs in Britain are outside the market economy, and contribute nothing to manufacturing or exports (schools, colleges, scientific research, hospitals, the armed forces, police, roads), although they certainly contribute to the quality of life (Handy, 1984). But all this has to be paid for out of taxes, which are paid by those who are producing goods or services for which others will pay.

Changes in the nature of work. Automation has changed the nature of work in many ways. Routine, dirty, dangerous and heavy jobs can be eliminated, and jobs tend to be 'easier physically, harder mentally'. They are also more responsible, since one person may control a lot of expensive equipment.

However, automation can easily lead to 'de-skilling', and workers may be relegated to jobs of a lower level of skill, needing less pay and less training, than those which were done before. This, of course, leads to boredom and all the problems which were associated with Taylorism at an earlier period. However, automation can also result in higher levels of skill, for example where machine operatives carry out maintenance, set the controls, and do some of the programming of the machines. This can cause different problems – the workers start to bargain for higher pay, and work is taken away from supervisors or office staff. In practice there has to be negotiation of each technological change with the different levels of staff involved, and it is perfectly possible for management to decide to establish a higher level of skills rather than a lower one. Surveys have found a great deal of variation between firms, (Gill, 1985).

As a result, trade union pressure, management's desire to keep up motivation, job satisfaction and commitment and in some countries legislation has meant that the trend is for manual workers to use higher levels of skill (Francis, 1986). The manual worker of the future is likely to be a quite highly trained technician. Exactly what form work will take, and how the technology is designed should not only take account of human factors, but should be done in consultation with those who are going to be operating it (Blackler and Brown, 1986).

Automation in the office can result in de-skilling – no dictation, no need to lay out typing on the page, and creation of a number of routine, low-level jobs – word processing in the pool, filing and bookkeeping. On the other hand, there is some up-grading of skills, e.g. in the use of word processors instead of typewriters. There is a danger of polarization of jobs, with all the clerical work being done by women, and all the computer-related jobs by men. In fact, there are a number of alternative ways of introducing word processors into the office. At one extreme all secretaries work in a word-processing centre, at the other word processors are placed in scattered departments and there is less division between administrative work and typing.

Some professional positions are more at risk from automation than others. These include many quite high-level jobs, which may be threatened by the growth of 'expert systems', in which professional expertise is put into a computer program, e.g. for medical diagnosis. There has been extensive development of expert systems, although very often they are used, for example, to assist doctors with diagnosis, and to do *part* of their job, rather than to replace them (Berry and Broadbent, 1986). Child (1986) argues that managers of bank branches are at risk because much of their work can be easily automated, such as making loan decisions; this work gives low profits, and there are strong commercial pressures to introduce automation. On the other hand, doctors are probably not under threat, despite the development of expert systems of diagnosis: there is indefinite and changing occupational knowledge, there is high risk to the client, and doctors control the introduction of the new technology.

The people who are likely to gain most power and influence from the new technology are those most closely involved with it, those with most access to the computers (Oborne, 1985). In contrast, those who have been least affected are local government employees in parks, as street-cleaners and as refuse collectors.

There has already been a considerable growth in the number of people working at home. Already 62 per cent of European executives said they had worked at home, 40 per cent thought this would increase, and it is possible that a large proportion of workers could work from home (Clutterbuck and Hill, 1981). This return to a much earlier form of cottage industry has been made possible by telephone, computer, word processor and VDU links to head office, and by small-scale textile and other machinery. It is ideal for women with families and for the disabled, many of whom would otherwise not work at all. The jobs undertaken in the home are mainly typing, computing and sewing, but also include journalism, research, work for publishers, etc. Rank Xerox recently dispersed a number of executives to work from home (Handy, 1984). Home working has the advantages of cutting out commuting and saving office overheads. A European survey asked samples of workers whether they would prefer to work from home for all or part of the week; 40·8 per cent of those surveyed in the UK were in favour of working from home, while the response of ten European countries was averaged out at 35·5 per cent in favour (Clutterbuck and Hill, 1981). Those surveyed were not asked if they would like to work entirely from home. This would have the clear psychological disadvantage of leading to isolation from other workers, as experienced by housewives and the unemployed; this problem can be overcome by establishing neighbourhood centres with shared facilities, as has been done in France. There are considerable difficulties of supervising and motivating home workers; they probably need to come into the central office once or twice a week. There is also a danger that, as in the pre-Industrial Revolution cottage industries, there would be exploitation of home workers who would be unprotected by labour organizations. Again, the workers would be mainly women (Frankel, 1987; Clutterbuck and Hill, 1981; Handy, 1984).

While the service sector has been the main area of expansion of jobs, there have been a number of changes here as well. There has been a shift from people to machines, e.g. more domestic equipment, fewer domestic servants. Consumers provide more of the labour themselves (Gershuny, 1984).

An increasing number of people are becoming self-employed, about 7 per cent of the labour force, mainly in agriculture, forestry and fishing, building, shops, and professional and scientific services (Watts, 1983). There was a sharp increase in the number of self-employed from 1979–81, and the British Government has encouraged people to start small businesses. Self-employment offers one great psychological advantage – autonomy, which some desire more than others.

Handy (1984) has described as the 'mauve economy' the parttime and self-employed activities which develop out of hobbies. Examples are carpentry, dressmaking, tutoring, vegetable growing, decorating, typing, translating. Some may develop into fulltime work, some into larger concerns employing others. As Handy says, 'It is a sub-culture which needs nurturing because it does signal a change in the culture.' It is certainly an improvement on unemployment for most of those who do it.

The 'grey' or 'communal economy' consists of work which is done for ourselves or others but not paid for. This consists mainly of cooking and other housework, gardening, home maintenance, DIY and things done for others on the basis of friendship, neighbourliness or reciprocity. From the psychological point of view, this kind of work has the great advantage of strengthening social ties. The grey economy is generally believed to be growing in extent because of unemployment and the fewer hours spent in work. It has been estimated that 51 per cent of the total amount of work done is in the grey economy (Rose, 1983).

Finally, there is the 'black economy', work which is done without declaring it for tax purposes, much of it moonlighting by those with regular jobs. It is very difficult to estimate the size of the black economy, but it has been estimated as 7 per cent of the GNP in Britain, 10 per cent in the USA, and 20 per cent in Italy (Handy, 1984).

A lot of people do voluntary work, 'unpaid work of service to others apart from immediate family and friends'; in 1984 25 per cent of British adults did some, while about 10 per cent worked voluntarily once a week or more (Social Trends, 1984). The main recipients are children, teenagers, the elderly, the sick and disabled. This kind of work is a great source of satisfaction, providing social contacts, a feeling that something worthwhile has been done, and a feeling of being needed (Handy, 1984). However, it has been found that female volunteer hospital workers felt that their work was not really valued since it was unpaid (Naomi Clifton, personal communication).

It is clear that work involves more than working for wages, and that the balance of formal, 'grey' and voluntary work varies widely between individuals. Each of these kinds of work produces its own satisfactions. The next step may be to recognize that happiness or well-being do not depend solely or even primarily on wealth. They depend more on social relationships, and on engaging in worthwhile activities, whether or not they produce financial rewards (Argyle, 1987).

Increasing Leisure

If there is going to be less work, it follows that there will be more leisure. Can leisure produce as much satisfaction as work?

What exactly is 'leisure'? The definition is important. Some psychologists have made a sharp contrast between work as goal-directed or instrumental, and leisure as expressive, done for its own sake, for intrinsic rewards. However, the more serious forms of leisure also involve the pursuit of goals: people swim not just to splash about and have fun, but also to improve their style or speed, or to keep fit. A better approach is to define leisure as those activities which people do simply because they want to, for their own sake, for fun, entertainment, self-improvement or for goals of their own choosing, but not for material gain.

What, then, is 'work'? *Webster's Dictionary* defines work as:

to exert oneself physically or mentally for a purpose, esp. in common speech, to exert oneself thus in doing something undertaken for gain, for improvement in one's material, intellectual condition, or under compulsion of any kind, as distinct from something undertaken for pleasure, sport, or immediate gratification.

The distinction between work and leisure is quite subtle, since they may involve exactly the same activities – digging the garden, driving a car, decorating rooms, looking after other people, for example, may be either work or leisure. Some of the main differences are that leisure is more autonomous, although less when done in a group, there is little or no supervision, the product, if any, is one's own property, and there is little or no material reward. For a number of occupations there is no clear distinction between work and leisure, for example intellectual and scientific work, composing and performing in the arts. Nevertheless, the work parts tend to be more serious, to demand efficient levels of performance and have obligations to others, while the leisure parts tend to be more playful, and while some strive for prizes it does not really matter how well one does. Some recent thinkers have hoped that leisure and work would come to resemble one another more, and the division between them become less marked (e.g. Parker, 1983).

American surveys have compared the amount of satisfaction derived from work and from leisure. For those with jobs, 47 per cent derived more satisfaction from work, 19 per cent more from leisure, and 34 per cent found they were equally satisfying (Veroff *et al.*, 1981). For housewives and for single men, the level of satisfaction derived from leisure is higher. While the unemployed are average to low in life satisfaction, most of the retired report a high level of satisfaction (Warr and Payne, 1982).

In the past a great deal of leisure time was spent in rest and recuperation from the labours of the day. Now that people are working shorter hours, or no hours at all, the need for this kind of leisure is less, and more active kinds of leisure become possible (Martin and Mason, 1982).

There are already several 'leisure classes' – the unemployed, the retired, housewives and the young. One solution to the decline of work would be to establish a regular leisure class, with a guaranteed minimum wage, which might be augmented by working. There are serious problems with this idea, since it is almost inevitable that such a class would have little power and low social status. They would have to earn less than the now superior 'working class', or the less popular jobs would never be done (Watts, 1983).

However, the decline of work means that it will be necessary to bring about some change of values, so that leisure is valued as much as work. Aristotle valued leisure above work (p. 13), but leisure which was devoted to a disciplined quest for higher values and the practice of politics. In the Middle Ages, as in primitive society, work and leisure were not sharply separated, both were done in family and community groups and accompanied by colourful rituals. It was the Industrial Revolution which stripped work of leisure values, made it dull and drab, and created leisure as a reaction to work in the time left over.

The present-day thinkers who have advocated a 'leisure ethic' have pointed to the merits of various kinds of serious leisure, which have scope for achievement and the creation of a positive identity through the development of skills and pursuit of worthwhile goals, as opposed to a life of ease or conspicuous consumption (Parker, 1983; Watts, 1983; Martin and Mason, 1982).

What do members of our current leisure class actually do? Many young unemployed do very little apart from an increased amount of housework, shopping and visiting people (p. 287). There is a strong correlation between social status and social class: the more prosperous and educated take part in more leisure activities, especially active sports, hobbies and cultural pursuits (Argyle, 1987).

We have seen the characteristics of jobs which produce the most job satisfaction, and this could be a guide to the leisure activities which are likely to provide similar satisfaction. Some of the key properties of satisfying work are: using skills, being autonomous, making an impact on others (all found in intrinsically satisfying work); recognition for success (high status and pay); cohesive and supportive working groups; and supervision which is high on consideration and participation. We shall look at some of the main forms of leisure, and consider how far they might provide some of these sources of satisfaction.

Part-time, informal and voluntary work. We discussed these above. Informal work in the grey economy can be regarded either as work or leisure. 'Leisure and family life are thoroughly interwoven' (Roberts, 1983). Diary studies show that well over half an adult's spare time is spent in or around the home, although a lot of domestic activities are regarded as mixed work and leisure;

gardening is done regularly by 50 per cent of men and 39 per cent of women, house repairs and DIY by 51 per cent of men and 24 per cent of women (Young and Wilmott, 1973). Other home-based leisure activities include needlework and knitting, keeping pets, some hobbies, and various kinds of relaxation, which will be discussed later.

These activities produce material gains in the form of vegetables, clothes and home improvement; like proper work they are rewarded, although not done under the discipline of work, or the supervision of others. The skills involved may receive recognition, and some of these activities are done in a group.

Many women have very little leisure – those with jobs and children, for example. They spend more time in the house and most of their leisure is there. Some housework is regarded as being partly leisure – shopping and cooking, looking after pets and plants. Women watch television more than men, and do knitting and needlework; men do more gardening and DIY (Argyle, 1987).

A major home-based activity is looking after children, which is a combination of work and leisure. Some of it is more like leisure (going to the zoo, playing games); sometimes it is work (e.g. feeding infants in the middle of the night). It has effects on the whole pattern of life, including making other leisure activities less accessible.

At some ages, people spend more time at home. Young couples with small children, often with little money to spare, have limited leisure and as such it tends to be home based. In middle age, when children have become independent or have left home, few take the opportunity to expand their leisure. Some become active in church, politics or social clubs, or go out for meals or concerts, but more simply stay at home. After retirement, despite the need to replace work with something with similar rewards, most older people spend more time at home and watching television, although for some there is an increase in gardening and reading (Rapoport and Rapoport, 1975).

Voluntary work, such as running youth clubs and looking after old people, is very similar to a lot of paid work and, as we have seen, provides a great deal of satisfaction.

Serious leisure requiring commitment and skills. Csikszentmihalyi (1975) studied serious rock-climbers, chess-players and disco-dancers. He found that the most satisfying elements were enjoyment of the experience and use of skills, the activity itself (the pattern, the action, the world it provides), and development of personal skills. Similar conclusions came from a sociological study of amateurs in drama, archaeology and baseball, who were found to be deeply devoted to a disciplined and demanding form of activity which was the very opposite of relaxation (Stebbins, 1979). In addition to the expressive satisfaction obtained, there was gratification from the close social ties established, and in the social identity created. When skills are developed and displayed there is a lot of scope for recognition, for example in amateur music or theatre, art, writing stories or books, and other hobbies where there is some 'product'. These activities can also add to self-esteem and the self-image. In addition to the acquisition and display of skills, there may be special costumes, holding of offices in the organization, prizes or diplomas.

Educational activities, for example evening classes, also develop skills and knowledge in a group setting, and may develop interests which affect other leisure hours, providing satisfaction from studying rocks, birds, literature, and so on.

Sport and exercise. In 1980 in Britain the percentages of people engaging in outdoor sport over a four-week period were 38 per cent for men and 23 per cent for women (Stebbins, 1979). The rates are considerably higher for younger people: 60 per cent and 31 per cent respectively.

Among the more energetic sports, the most popular are swimming and walking (for both men and women), and football and golf (for men). An increasing number of people are jogging every day in order to keep fit. In the USA it is estimated that as much as 10 per cent of the population engages in regular exercise of some kind in order to keep fit or lose weight (Bammel and Bammel, 1982). Sport involves the development and use of skills, the recognition of expertise, and is done in groups. It has two other advantages. Aerobic exercise, such as swimming and running, releases endorphins, which are like anti-depressants and induce positive affect. Of course, exercise is good for general well-being, and for mental and physical health (Argyle, 1987).

Social leisure. A great deal of leisure is spent partly or primarily in the company of other people. There are considerable differences between the sexes, however. Outside the home women see friends and relatives more, go to church, dancing and bingo, but go out drinking less than men (*Social Trends*, 1985). There are also differences in the patterns of social leisure at different ages. Adolescents and young people engage in the greatest variety of leisure outside the home, experimenting with different activities and relationships, especially with the opposite sex. Some social leisure is quite serious: as well as voluntary work, there is committee work of various kinds, helping to run clubs, political activities, church services and other religious activities.

Social leisure can be very beneficial as it strengthens supportive social bonds with friends and family, which in turn improves physical and mental health. On the other hand, social leisure often involves drinking (and eating), sometimes too much, which has the opposite effect.

Television and other forms of relaxation. These kinds of leisure are the least like work. More time is spent watching television in Britain and the USA than on any other form of leisure – about four hours per weekday on average, much more at weekends, totalling about 45 per cent of free time (*Social Trends*, 1983). Another hour a day is spent listening to the radio, half an hour reading. While watching and listening people often do other things as well, such as eating, talking or knitting.

Watching television has immediate effects on the emotional state. Although people are found to be relaxed, cheerful and sociable, they are more drowsy, weak and passive than when reading or undertaking any other activity, for instance work, other leisure, eating or talking (Csikszentmihalyi and Kubey, 1981). Many people say that they watch television for 'entertainment', 'relaxation' etc., although experiments have found that when they are bored people choose exciting programmes. Probably an important factor is that once bought or rented, television costs nothing (except for the annual licence), and requires no effort, skill or risk. It does not provide a high level of satisfaction for most people: an American survey reported that while 32 per cent of those surveyed derived 'great satisfaction' from reading, only 17 per cent felt the same way about watching television (Robinson, 1977). For those who become involved with soap opera or a good book, there may be 'parasocial satisfaction', i.e. they feel that they (almost) know the characters and to some extent share in their exciting social lives.

Yet many people do not get much satisfaction from their leisure, and do not know what to do with it apart from watching television. On the other hand, some who lose their jobs find more satisfying things to do instead (p. 297). For many people at work their leisure is more satisfying and more important. How can the enjoyment of leisure be extended to others?

(1) The Protestant Work Ethic has led us to believe that leisure is not as worthwhile or as serious as work. However, some leisure is worthwhile as the individual benefits, for example growing vegetables or keeping fit. Some leisure is of service to others, e.g. voluntary work. Some leisure has a product that is appreciated by others and gives recognition, such as arts and crafts.

(2) Many sports require special facilities – swimming pools, ice rinks etc. which are not always available. The same is true of music and other arts, and of weaving and other crafts. Local authorities are increasingly making these things available.

(3) Playing the piano, ice-skating, weaving etc. will not become satisfying leisure activities unless some training or instruction is available. Educated people have an advantage as they have acquired some intellectual interests and an enjoyment of reading. Skilled people may be able to use their skills in leisure as well as work, e.g. in making things, restoring old cars, etc.

(4) The key to leisure satisfaction is developing interests in the first place. This very often results from social contacts and joining a group, and it opens the door to a complete 'leisure world'. Let us take Scottish country dancing as an example. This is very social,

it involves the use and development of skills, and is relaxing in the sense that tensions can be discharged. It is, in addition, a complete world of its own, with special costumes and rituals, and it includes the arousal of a great deal of joy, partly generated by the music.

Creating Ideal Working Conditions

At the beginning of this book we discussed some of the main problems of work as it is arranged today – widespread dissatisfaction and alienation, lack of motivation and cooperation, and difficulties of communication. This is partly a heritage of the Industrial Revolution, with its creation of large numbers of meaningless, repetitive jobs, and an unfamiliar and uncongenial social structure. These effects have been partly alleviated by the automation revolution, which has abolished some of these jobs, and may ultimately abolish many more. Social science research has played a minor but helpful role, mainly in bringing about less punitive and authoritarian styles of leadership, via training courses for supervisors and managers. It is interesting to note that the Japanese industrial revolution (p. 328ff) went much more smoothly, by making use of traditional social structures, and stepping straight into the age of automation.

From the research findings reviewed in earlier chapters it is possible to specify the optimal conditions of work, for maximizing job satisfaction, while reducing stress and keeping up productivity. Although this research was mostly done in the USA, Britain and western Europe, the findings appear to apply over a wide variety of cultural conditions.

(1) Nature of the work

(a) *Varied and meaningful work.* There is no problem about professional, managerial, craftwork or other highly skilled work; workers in these areas use skills, produce identifiable products, have an impact on others, and there is feedback on task performance. The difficulty comes with unskilled, repetitive manual and clerical work. We have seen that these jobs can be modified by job enlargement, rotation or enrichment, and that this leads to increased productivity and satisfaction. A minority of alienated workers prefer boring jobs; this is perhaps just as well since not all jobs can be improved. Improved preparation for work during the educational period should result in most people preferring interesting work. Maslow (1954) and Herzberg and his colleagues (1959) have offered a revised view of human nature; they maintain that people have potentialities for growth, and want to develop their skills and personalities. These ideas should perhaps be regarded not as empirically testable hypotheses, but rather as ideals about what work should be like. This emphasis on growth and the development of skill and personality also appears in the writings of those who have seen craftsmanship as the ideal form of work (Mills, 1951).

(b) *Freedom to choose pace and working conditions.* This is one of the main differences between 'work' and 'leisure', and one of the main obstacles to industrialization in developing countries. Such freedom is least in assembly-line and other machine-paced work. It is greater in technically less sophisticated craftwork. It is also greater under technically more sophisticated automated systems. Fortunately the jobs most easy to automate are those which require workers to behave like machines. Here the second industrial revolution is abolishing the unpleasant jobs created by the first.

(c) *Reducing stress.* Mechanization makes it possible to reduce the physical effort required, it can remove repetitive work with a short work-cycle, and sometimes takes over dangerous jobs, and those undertaken in unpleasant environments. A lot of jobs are still stressful because they are so hectic, including those of some doctors, managers, air-traffic controllers and television employees, and need to be redesigned in some way, or to have shorter hours or rotation of duties.

(d) *Work appropriate to the worker's abilities and interests.* We have seen the great importance for job satisfaction and stress of the fit between person and job. What firms do is personnel selection – which differs from guidance in looking primarily at abilities rather than interests and needs. Personnel selection could be modified to take more account of these factors, which are important sources of job satisfaction.

(2) *Incentives*

(*a*) *Sufficient pay.* Wage incentives certainly make people work but cause a lot of friction and are widely being replaced by a guaranteed wage for an agreed rate of work. Relatively high pay is an important source of job satisfaction and it reduces labour turnover, but how can everyone have it? In the kibbutzim there is equality of wages; in Japanese factories the managers only get 50 per cent more than manual workers. On the other hand, wage differentials probably act as incentives, at any rate to those with careers in which they can be promoted. It is most important that wages levels and differentials should be regarded as fair by most of those concerned.

(*b*) *Promotion prospects and security.* Relatively high status is also sought by all, and can act as an incentive. Under the organizational changes recommended below – fewer ranks and more democratic leadership – status differences would be greatly reduced.

Security is one of the most important factors in job satisfaction. It is now being sought by the unions, although it is difficult to achieve in a rapidly changing industrial scene, in view of redundancies created by automation. It has been achieved in Japan, at least in the big firms, by adopting a policy of planning the work to employ all the people on the payroll. Under some conditions such a policy would involve using human labour rather than automated equipment.

(*c*) *Intrinsic motivation.* We have seen the desirability of making use of forms of intrinsic motivation, as well as or instead of purely economic motivation. This can be done by participating in decisions, by aligning workers' goals with those of the organization, or by the strength of their identification with the community, as in the kibbutz. It can also be done when the work itself requires the use of valued skills, or offers challenging goals which will arouse achievement motivation. Under present conditions it is only managers and professional staff who are motivated in these ways. It can be done, too, when the work fits the interests and personality of the worker.

(3) Working groups

(a) *The formation of small and cohesive groups.* Workers at all levels of skill prefer to work in small cohesive groups, which allow for social interaction. This is a valuable source of mental health, since social support buffers the effects of stress and prevents burnout. Productivity is often higher too, although this varies with the task. People who are isolated are likely to leave, groups that are too large divide into sub-groups, groups that are too heterogeneous are often discontented and uncooperative.

(b) *The use of functional groups.* We saw earlier that job satisfaction and productivity are both greater in working groups that are small, cohesive, cooperative and have small status differences within them. These principles can be made use of by constructing 'functional work groups'; instead of putting people in a group because they do similar jobs (e.g. secretarial, electronics, sales), groups are formed from those people who need to cooperate because they are engaged in the same project. Such a group should be formed so that the following conditions hold: the members are able to communicate frequently in order to cooperate effectively; they must have the necessary skills to carry out the job between them; they may have different skills, but status differences must be small; the working relationships between them must be helpful and rewarding.

(4) *Supervision and management.* We saw earlier that certain styles of supervision produce much higher levels of job satisfaction, cut absenteeism and labour turnover to one quarter of that found under other supervision, and can increase output by 10–25 per cent. The optimum style of supervision is a combination of initiating structure, consideration, democratic-persuasive skills and providing social support to help with stress. Field experiments have been carried out in which the style of supervision has been changed in these ways, with very successful results.

Changes of supervisory style will change the organizational structure without changing the organization chart. They can be brought about by training supervisors accordingly, as in the Morse and Reimer study (p. 229), although this needs to be supported by appropriate changes in the behaviour of senior managers, since styles of leadership are imitated and flow downwards through an organization.

(5) *Organizational structure*

(a) *Decentralization.* Many of the problems of organizations can be solved by making the organizational units smaller – communication is easier, people can participate more in decisions, and there are fewer levels in the hierarchy; satisfaction is greater, absenteeism and turnover lower.

(b) *Reducing the number of levels in the hierarchy.* This follows from decentralization, but the number of levels can also be reduced by increasing the span of control. This has been found to be advantageous, especially in small organizations. Some degree of hierarchical structure seems to be unavoidable.

(c) *Reduce role conflict and ambiguity.* We have seen that these are common sources of stress and low job satisfaction; they should be avoided by improving job specifications and the elimination of conflicting instructions and pressure.

(6) *Preparation for work*

(a) *Education.* Many young people do not know what work is for or why they should do it, after years of education. It would be useful for such facts of life to be spelt out more clearly. This book is indeed an attempt to do it. Schools do teach some of the skills needed at work; it would be very useful if they could also give some training in the social skills needed at work.

(b) *The transition to work* from school is often found difficult. It is very desirable for young people to try out one or two jobs in vacations so that they can be initiated gradually. Employers need to handle their young employees with particular care and understanding.

(c) *Vocational guidance.* Many young people have very little idea of what different jobs are like. It would be most useful if they could see or try out for themselves the main jobs open to them in their area. Selection procedures, as well as vocational guidance, should consider the individual's personality and interests, as well as his or her abilities.

Some writers have suggested that work should be made 'more like leisure' (Parker, 1983). There are some ways in which this can be done, for example enhancing social life at work, and providing work which is intrinsically interesting and satisfying and which makes use of skills. In addition, we have seen that for a number of occupations the line between work and leisure is very blurred.

However, a number of differences between work and leisure are likely to persist. Work requires discipline – in terms of the hours worked and the standards of performance met. Leisure is freer, more relaxed and the level of performance is unimportant. This is less true of some kinds of serious leisure, such as competitive sports and group activities such as amateur music or theatricals. People at work are usually under the direction of a supervisor, and may have responsibility for subordinates. Leisure is relatively free from such hierarchical considerations, although teams do have captains and orchestras have conductors.

APPENDIX

THE JAPANESE METHOD OF WORKING

The Japanese industrial revolution started between 1929 and 1937 (when the war with China started), and began again after 1950. Japan has few raw materials, and her economic growth has been achieved by the manufacturing and processing of raw materials, as in the steel industry. The first phase of economic growth was mainly associated with a small number of large family firms, or *zaibatsu*. These firms were each owned by a family, or group of families, which demanded absolute loyalty, and which were feudal; each had a monopoly position through controlling a whole group of firms. A number of observers have said that industrialization was made easier through the adoption of traditional forms of social organization, such as the feudal hierarchy (Abegglen, 1958); others have argued that traditional structures have been harmful through delaying the introduction of democratic management techniques and other innovations (Odaka, 1963).

There was little economic growth from 1945 to 1950: much of industry was in ruins, there were large reparations to be made, and the Allied occupation suppressed the *zaibatsu* as being illiberal and monopolistic. After 1950 the situation changed: it was accepted that further reparations were impossible, the Americans paid large sums on account of bases connected with the Korean War, and there was a high rate of savings and investment in imported technology. Pressure on the *zaibatsu* was eased, and to a large extent these monopolistic family groupings of firms were reformed (Allen, 1965). Between 1953 and 1961 there was an increase in the GNP of 217 per cent.

Japanese success in the export market, mainly to the USA, has been largely due to low wages keeping prices down. The large increase in output was partly due to the very undeveloped state of Japanese industry at the end of the Second World War (*Economist*, 1963). Until about 1955 there was a relatively low rate of mechanization, the aim of management being to make use of the large labour force already on the payroll. It was estimated in 1958 that Japanese factories were running at about 20 per cent of the output per worker of equivalent American firms (Abegglen, 1958). Since 1955 there has been a great deal of capital investment in new equipment in order to increase the productivity for the export market of the labour force. It was reported in 1969 that there was actually a labour shortage (*The Times*, 1969), although this is no longer the case.

As everyone knows, Japanese industry is now extremely effective. Could we benefit by copying their methods? Many studies have been made of Japanese industry, and its main features have been established.

Selection and training. The large firms offer larger salaries, excellent welfare facilities and social prestige, so that employment is keenly sought. The educational system has been changed since the Second World War and it now provides the normal means of job selection. Depending on their final examination results, people enter more or less desirable firms and at different levels. A person with middle-school education will enter a firm as a manual worker, and cannot rise above charge-hand; a graduate enters as an assistant manager and is slowly promoted up the hierarchy. A social survey, however, found that 91 per cent of respondents did *not* think that education should determine seniority in this way (Whitehill and Tazekawa, 1961).

While there is a strong emphasis on technical training which continues throughout the career, special attention is paid to the training of graduate management trainees. They have to live for six months at a training centre under a disciplined and spartan regime, including team sports and martial arts. They are trained in leadership and other interpersonal skills as well as in technical matters (Tanaka, 1980).

Lifetime employment and commitment. The social atmosphere in the Japanese workplace has been compared to that of a hearty public school (*Economist,* 1963). There is no feeling of inferiority among manual workers despite the hierarchy of which they form the lowest rank. Instead, they have a feeling of sharing in the collective success of the firm. A very strong feeling of identification is created, since many employees spend their whole careers with the firm and live in company houses. (It has been widely reported that Japanese firms guarantee employment to the age of fifty-five. In fact this applies only to about one-third of workers, those in the leading firms, not their subsidiaries.) In some firms the day is started by singing the company hymn. Whitehill and Tazekawa (1961) found that 32 per cent of their sample thought of their company as 'very much like a big family to which he may belong until retirement' and a further 32 per cent as 'a part of his life at least equal in importance to his personal life'. The majority welcomed company involvement in their private lives in respect of providing housing and other benefits, and in arranging outings, but were not so keen on company involvement in religion or marriage – apart from offering advice. In exchange for these benefits, and especially for the high job security, employees have a high level of loyalty and commitment to the firm, and are motivated by a feeling of social responsibility to it (Whitehill and Tazekawa, 1968).

Japanese firms in the USA spend more on social and recreational facilities (Pascale and Athos, 1982). There are also extensive arrangements for sickness benefits.

Wages and promotion. Wages are kept in line with those in other firms (Dore, 1973), and depend primarily on age, length of service, education and rank in the hierarchy. Managers are paid only about 50 per cent more than manual workers. In addition to their pay, employees get free meals, low rent housing, cheap medical services, schools for children, a pension and other welfare facilities. Very little use is made of wage incentives. A monthly productivity allowance is paid, and also a twice-yearly bonus, based on the firm's efficiency, but these are fairly stable parts of the total wage, and it is doubtful whether they have any incentive effect. There is also some variation in wages based on estimates of individual efficiency, but this forms a very small part of wages (Abegglen, 1958).

Promotion in the management hierarchy depends mainly on initial education, the point of entry into the firm and length of service. Rank is closely tied to age, and a manager should not supervise an older person (apart from manual workers). At higher levels promotion does depend on ability, and incompetent managers may find that an additional person has been appointed to the same position, or that there are other managers with overlapping authority doing his job.

Functional specialization. As part of the concern for the whole person, and as part of the encouragement of collective responsibility, Japanese workers are rotated through the different functions. In Japanese firms in the USA workers are less functionally specialized than in American-owned firms.

Working groups. The traditional form of social organization in Japan is one of close interdependence in family groups. This structure is transferred to the work situation, so that work groups are very close-knit. Groups usually have about ten members, under the equivalent of a charge-hand, who is really one of the group and has little supervisory authority. Japanese workers are encouraged to feel part of a team, and supervisors are concerned with the general well-being of their subordinates. There is general acceptance of the supervisor's involvement with life off the job, including marriage; 70 per cent favour receiving advice from supervisors (Whitehill and Tazekawa, 1968).

As we saw earlier, efforts are made to increase social support by organizing the annual entering cohorts into social groups.

Supervision. Japanese first-line supervisors are definitely production-centred. They are concerned with the welfare of their workers, but they are even more concerned with exhorting them to a high standard of work, by keeping to detailed working rules (Dore, 1973; White and Trevor, 1983).

Misumi (1985) has carried out extensive research into supervision in Japan, and has developed the two 'PM' dimensions, which are similar to the Management Grid although leader scores are obtained from ratings by subordinates. P leadership is problem-solving and goal-achieving, and leads to high group performance. M leadership is directed towards maintenance of the group, and leads to group cohesion. PM, the combination of the two, is most effective, since now there is less leadership pressure, and more use of planning and expertise. In Japan supervisors are expected to provide leadership, but they do so in a special way, known as the *ringi* method; this involves a lot of informal consulting, after which the leader takes a decision (Smith, 1984). This style of leadership can be described as 'sells' rather than 'consults' (Hofstede, 1980). Relations with subordinates are handled with some subtlety, and a lot of use is made of small face-saving hints (Pascale and Athos, 1982).

There are several traditional forms of relationship with older persons in Japan. The *oyabum-kobun* relationship is a formal relation with a kind of foster parent in which the older person shows both love and protection, but also harsh authoritarian rule; the junior person shows unquestioning obedience, dependence and loyalty (Bennett and Ishino, 1963). This relationship plays a central role in Japanese society and is found to carry over to relationships with supervisors in small firms. In larger firms the rather less formal, although still paternal, relationships of the *batsu* or clique are found, in apprenticeships, between workers and supervisors, and in groups of managers from the same university (Abegglen, 1958).

Management hierarchy. In Japanese companies there is a smaller span of control, and there are more levels in the hierarchy than in comparable British or American firms. Above the supervisors come section heads, divisional managers and the board of directors. The highest level consists of members of the family who own and control the firm, and the next level consists of senior managers who may literally be adopted by that family and are expected to show a high degree of loyalty to it (Harbison, 1959). There are also many assistant managers at each level, with considerable overlapping of authority so that there is little individual responsibility. The large number of managers is partly the result of the policy of promotion by seniority and the practice of not discharging anyone.

Managers are accepted because they are known to have earned their position by years of service, educational qualifications and technical expertise; at the same time they eat in the same dining room, wear similar clothes, and do not earn a great deal more than their subordinates (Dore, 1973). Japanese research by Misumi (1960) found that the leadership style of both first-line and second-line managers was important for productivity.

Working practices. It was observed in Japanese firms in Britain that they have a distinctive style of working practice: 'A short-list of four can be discerned: an organized or orderly approach, an emphasis on detail, an over-riding priority attached to quality, and a punctilious sense of discipline' (White and Trevor, 1983).

Unions and industrial democracy. There is one union per company, to which all levels belong. There is less workshop-level conflict or confrontation than in Britain or the USA, and less disagreement with supervisors, probably because there are more detailed contracts (Dore, 1973). In one study it was found that a third of the workers thought it better to rely on management to deal with grievances rather than go through the union (Whitehill and Tazekawa, 1968).

In the past there has been little participation or industrial democracy, although this is now changing. Consultative supervision is not liked, but workers like their views to be represented by third parties – supervisors or union officials (Whitehill and Tazekawa, 1968).

Could these Japanese methods be exported successfully? Some of them reflect traditional features of Japanese society, especially the emphasis on close-knit groups and commitment to a kind of family, the strong hierarchy, and informal skills of *ringi* consultation. However, Japanese firms have established factories in Britain and America, and while these vary between themselves, most of them employ a selective, watered-down version of Japanese practices which Ouchi (1981) has called 'Theory Z'. This includes lifetime employment, slower rates of promotion, less formal leadership, concern for the whole person, less specialization, some consensual decision-making, and responsibility as a basic value. How do these firms compare in effectiveness with British- and American-managed companies? A number of comparisons between comparable firms have been carried out. The evidence suggests that in the Japanese firms productivity is probably greater, and quality certainly is, while absenteeism is less; however, job satisfaction is no higher (Smith, 1984).

Careful observation of Japanese factories in Britain suggests that the most striking differences from British-managed ones are that (1) greater care is taken with recruitment and training, in order to build up a highly skilled work-force; (2) working practices are designed to place much more emphasis on detail and quality; (3) managers demand a high degree of commitment and discipline from workers, work very hard, and provide an example of a high standard of work and involvement with production. However, there is no lifetime employment, and no particular concern with human relations or job satisfaction (White and Trevor, 1983).

It is by no means clear which, if any, of the features of Japanese factories contribute to their economic success. It appears that a high degree of motivation and commitment is generated by a quite different approach to that which has been found to be most successful in the West. Instead of wage incentives, consultation, democratic-persuasive skills and industrial democracy, the Japanese have total commitment to productivity, in which managers set the example. Motivation is aroused from a sense of responsibility to the employer and the work group.

However, there are a number of other features of Japanese industry which are at least partly responsible for their success.

(1) Many of the leading companies are family dominated, and keep up strong company philosophies.
(2) There is a cultural tradition of duty, obedience and discipline.
(3) It is normal to retire in the mid-fifties in Japan, so there are no problems with older workers, and lifetime employment is shorter.
(4) Post-war reconstruction and an efficient electronics industry have made extensive re-equipment possible.
(5) There is close cooperation between industry and government.
(6) There is a strong sense of nationalism, adding to the motivation of workers (Schein, 1981).

Could these methods become the normal practice in Britain? There are some features which look both desirable and acceptable, e.g. lifetime employment and commitment, concern for the whole person, less specialization. However, there are other features which seem much less acceptable – the hierarchical structure and obedience, strict working procedures, production-centred supervision, and control of the private life of workers.

ACKNOWLEDGEMENTS

The author wishes to thank the many authors and publishers who have given their permission for him to include the figures and tables which appear in this edition. Unless indicated below, the publishing and copyright details of the titles from which the figures and tables have been selected can be found in the list of references on p. 341ff.

Table 2   (Holland, 1966) Reproduced by special permission of the Publisher, Psychological Assessment Resources, Inc.

Table 3   (Jasso & Rossi, 1977) Reprinted by permission of the American Sociological Association and the Authors.

Table 4   (Hackman & Oldham, 1980) Reprinted by permission of Addison Wesley Publishing Co. © 1980, Addison Wesley Publishing Co. Inc., Reading, Massachusetts.

Table 5   (Goldthorpe *et al.*, 1968) Reprinted by permission of Cambridge University Press.

Table 6   (Argyle & Henderson, 1985) Reprinted by permission of the Peters Fraser & Dunlop Group Ltd and William Heinemann Ltd.

Table 8   (Webber, 1974) Reprinted by permission of Academy of Management and R. A. Webber.

Table 9   (Argyle & Henderson, 1985) Reprinted by permission of the Peters Fraser & Dunlop Group Ltd and William Heinemann Ltd.

Table 13   (Vroom & Yetton, 1973) Reprinted by permission of the University of Pittsburgh Press. © University of Pittsburgh Press, 1973.

Table 16   (Burke & Day, 1986) Reprinted by permission of the American Psychological Association and the Authors.

Table 17   (Jackson & Schuler, 1985) Reprinted by permission of Academic Press, Inc., and R. S. Schuler.

Table 19   (Wall & Lischeron, 1977) Reprinted by permission of Toby A. Wall.

Table 21   (Gurin *et al.*, 1960) Reprinted by permission of Basic Books, Inc., Publishers. © Basic Books, Inc., 1960.

Table 22   (Cooper, 1985) Reprinted by permission of Times Newspapers Ltd and Professor C. L. Cooper. © Times Newspapers Ltd, 1985.

Table 23   (Caplan *et al.*, 1975) Reprinted by permission of the Institute for Social Research, University of Michigan, Ann Arbor.

Table 25   (Sales & House, 1971) Reprinted by permission of Pergamon Journals Ltd.

Table 26   Reprinted by permission of the Controller of Her Majesty's Stationery Office.

Table 27   (Warr & Payne, 1982) Reprinted by permission of Pergamon Journals Ltd.

Table 28   (Banks & Jackson, 1982) Reprinted by permission of the Controller of Her Majesty's Stationery Office.

Table 29   (Parker, 1980) Derived from *Older Workers and Retirement*, S. Parker, OPCS (1980) Crown Copyright. Reprinted by permission of Cambridge University Press.

Table 30   Reprinted by permission of the Controller of Her Majesty's Stationery Office.

Table 31   (Clutterbuck & Hill, 1981) Reprinted by permission of David Clutterbuck.

Fig. 1   (McClelland, 1961) Reprinted by permission of Van Nostrand Reinhold.

Fig. 2   (McClelland, 1961) Reprinted by permission of Van Nostrand Reinhold.

Fig. 5   (Whyte, 1948) Reprinted by permission of Prof. William F. Whyte.

Fig. 6   (Vernon, 1964) Reprinted by permission of Methuen & Co.

Fig. 7   (Hackman & Oldham, 1980) Reprinted by permission of Addison Wesley Publishing Co. © 1980, Addison Wesley Publishing Co. Inc., Reading, Massachusetts.

Fig. 10   (Nemeroff & Cosentino, 1979) Reprinted by permission of Academy of Management and Wayne Nemeroff.

Fig. 11   (Roethlisberger & Dickson, 1939) Reprinted by permission of Harvard University Press.

Fig. 12   (Roethlisberger & Dickson, 1939) Reprinted by permission of Harvard University Press.

Fig. 15   (Fleishman & Harris, 1962) Reprinted by permission of Personnel Psychology, Inc.

Fig. 16   (Fleishman & Harris, 1962) Reprinted by permission of Personnel Psychology, Inc.

Fig. 19   (Michalos, 1980) Reprinted by permission of Kluwer Academic Publishers.

Fig. 20   (Caplan *et al.*, 1975) Reprinted by permission of the Institute for Social Research, University of Michigan, Ann Arbor.

Fig. 22   (House, 1981) Reprinted by permission of Addison Wesley Publishing Co. © 1981, Addison Wesley Publishing Co. Inc., Reading, Massachusetts.

Fig. 23   (Parkes, 1987) Reprinted by permission of the American Psychological Association and the Author.

The publishers regret that their attempts to contact the copyright holders of Table 1 (Janson, R.) and Figures 8 and 9 (Porter, L. W.) have been unsuccessful. Due acknowledgement will gladly be made in later editions if the relevant information is forthcoming.

REFERENCES

Abegglen, J. C. (1958), *The Japanese Factory*, Asia Publishing House, Bombay.

Ackrill, M. (1987), *Manufacturing Industry Since 1870*, Philip Allan, Deddington.

Acton Society Trust (1953), *Size and Morale*, Acton Society Trust, London.

Adelmann, P. K. (1987), 'Occupational complexity, control, and personal income: their relation to psychological well-being in men and women', *Journal of Applied Psychology*, **72**, 529–37.

Albrecht, P. A., Glaser, E. M. and Marks, J. (1964), 'Validation of a multiple-assessment procedure for managerial personnel', *Journal of Applied Psychology*, **48**, 351–60.

Alderfer, C. (1972), *Existence, Relatedness and Growth*, Free Press, New York.

Alfredsson, L., Spetz, C.-L. and Theorell, T. (1985), 'Type of occupation and near-future hospitalization for myocardial infarction and some other diagnoses', *International Journal of Epidemiology*, **14**, 378–88.

Allen, G. C. (1965), *Japan's Economic Expansion*, Oxford University Press, Oxford.

Allen, P. T. and Stephenson, G. M. (1983a), 'Inter-group understanding and size of organization', *British Journal of Industrial Relations*, **21**, 312–29.

Allen, P. T. and Stephenson, G. M. (1983b), 'Inter-group understanding and inter-party dispute: an example from industry', University of Kent, unpublished.

Allen, V. L. (1954), *Power in Trade Unions*, Longmans, London.

Andrews, F. M. and Withey, S. B. (1976), *Social Indicators of Well-Being*, Plenum, New York.

Andriessen, E. J. H. and Coetsier, P. L. (1984), 'Industrial democratiza-
tion', *in* P. J. D. Drenth *et al.* (eds.), *Handbook of Work and Organizational
Psychology*, Wiley, Chichester.

Andrisani, P. J. and Nestel, G. (1976), 'Internal–external control as a
contributor and outcome of work experience', *Journal of Applied Psychology*, **61**, 156–65.

Anthony, P. D. (1977), *The Ideology of Work*, Tavistock, London.

Argyle, M. (1953), 'The relay assembly test room in retrospect', *Occupational Psychology*, **27**, 98–103.

— (1969), *Social Interaction*, Methuen, London.

— (1983), *The Psychology of Interpersonal Behaviour*, 4th edn, Penguin
Books, Harmondsworth.

— (1984), 'Some new developments in social skills training', *Bulletin of
the British Psychological Society*, **37**, 405–10.

— (1987), *The Psychology of Happiness*, Methuen, London.

— (1988), *Bodily Communication*, 2nd edn, Methuen, London.

Argyle, M. and Crossland, J. (1987), 'The dimensions of positive
emotions', *British Journal of Social Psychology*, **26**, 127–37.

Argyle, M. and Furnham, A. (1983), 'Sources of satisfaction and conflict
in long-term relationships', *Journal of Marriage and the Family*, **45**,
481–93.

Argyle, M., Furnham, A. and Graham, J. A. (1981), *Social Situations*,
Cambridge University Press, Cambridge.

Argyle, M., Gardner, G. and Cioffi, F. (1958), 'Supervisory methods relating to productivity, absenteeism and labour turnover', *Human Relations*, **11**, 23–45.

Argyle, M. and Henderson, M. (1985), *The Anatomy of Relationships*,
Heinemann, London and Penguin Books, Harmondsworth.

Argyle, M., Lalljee, M. and Lydall, M., 'Selling as a social skill', unpublished (cited in Argyle, 1983).

Argyle, M., Salter, V., Nicholson, H., Williams, M. and Burgess, P. (1970),
'The communication of inferior and superior attitudes by verbal and
non-verbal signals', *British Journal of Social and Clinical Psychology*, **9**,
222–31.

Argyris, C. (1964), *Integrating the Individual and the Organization*, Wiley,
London.

Armstrong, P. J. (1984), 'Work, rest or play? Changes in time spent at
work', *in* P. Marstrand (ed.), *New Technology and the Future of Work and
Skills*, Pinter, London and Dover.

Arvey, R. D. and Begalla, M. E. (1975), 'Analysing the homemaker job using the Position Analysis Questionnaire (PAQ)', *Journal of Applied Psychology*, **60**, 513–17.

Atkinson, J. W. (ed.) (1958), *Motives in Fantasy, Action and Society*, Van Nostrand, Princeton, New Jersey.

Austin, W., McGinn, N. C. and Susmilch. C. (1980), 'Internal standards revisited: effects of social comparisons and expectancies on judgements of fairness and satisfaction', *Journal of Experimental Social Psychology*, **16**, 426–41.

Babbage, C. (1835), *On the Economy of Machinery and Manufacturers*, Kelley, New York, 1971.

Babchuk, N. and Goode, W. J. (1951), 'Work incentives in a self-determined group', *American Journal of Sociology*, **16**, 679–87.

Badin, I. J. (1974), 'Some moderator influences on relationships between consideration, initiating structure and organizational criteria', *Journal of Applied Psychology*, **59**, 380–82.

Bammel, G. and Bammel, L. L. B. (1982), *Leisure and Human Behavior*, W. C. Brown, New York.

Banks, M. H. and Jackson, P. R. (1982), 'Unemployment and risk of minor psychiatric disorder in young people: cross sectional and longitudinal evidence', *Psychological Medicine*, **12**, 789–98.

Baron, R. A. (1983, 1986), *Behavior in Organizations*, Allyn & Bacon, Boston.

Bass, B. M. (1965), *Organizational Psychology*, Allyn & Bacon, Boston.

— (1981), *Stogdill's Handbook of Leadership*, Collier Macmillan, London.

Bateman, T. S. and Organ, D. W. (1983), 'Job satisfaction and the good soldier: the relationship between affect and employee "citizenship"', *Academy of Management Journal*, **26**, 587–95.

Bateman, T. S. and Strassen, S. (1983), 'A cross-lagged regression test of the relationships between job tension and employee satisfaction', *Journal of Applied Psychology*, **68**, 439–45.

Batstone, E., Boraston, I. and Frenkel, S. (1977), *Shop Stewards in Action*, Blackwell, Oxford.

— (1978), *The Social Organization of Strikes*, Blackwell, Oxford.

Baumgartel, H. J., Reynolds, J. I. and Pathan, R. Z. (1984), 'How personality and organizational climate variables moderate the effectiveness of management development programmes: a review and some recent research findings', *Management and Labour Studies*, **9**, 1–16.

Bazerman, M. H. and Neale, M. A. (1982), 'Improving effectiveness under final offer arbitration: the role of selection and training', *Journal of Applied Psychology*, **67**, 543–8.

Beals, R. L. and Hoijer, A. (1965), *An Introduction to Anthropology*, Collier Macmillan, London.

Beck, A. T. *et al.* (1961), 'An inventory for measuring depression', *Archives of General Psychiatry*, 4, 561–71.

Beehr, T. A. (1986), 'The process of retirement: a review and recommendations for future investigation', *Personnel Psychology*, 39, 31–55.

Behrend, H. (1951), *Absence under Full Employment*, Monograph A3, Studies in Economics and Society, University of Birmingham.

Bendix, R. (1956), *Work and Authority in Industry*, Wiley, New York.

Bennett, J. W. and Ishino, I. (1963), *Paternalism in the Japanese Economy*, University of Minnesota Press, Minneapolis.

Berkman, L. F. and Syme, S. L. (1979), 'Social networks, host resistance, and mortality: a nine-year follow-up study of Alemeda county residents', *American Journal of Epidemiology*, 109, 186–204.

Berkowitz, L., Fraser, C., Treasure, F. P. and Cochran, S. (1987), 'Pay, equity, job qualifications, and comparisons in pay satisfaction', *Journal of Applied Psychology*, 72, 544–51.

Berman, F. E. and Miner, J. B. (1985), 'Motivation to manage at the top executive level: a test of the hierarchic role-motivation theory', *Personnel Psychology*, 38, 377–91.

Berry, D. C. and Broadbent, D. E. (1986), 'Expert systems and man-machine interface', *Expert Systems*, 3, 228–31, 4, 18–28.

Beveridge, W. E. (1980), 'Retirement and life significance: a study of the adjustment to retirement of a sample of men at management level', *Human Relations*, 33, 69–78.

Bhagat, P. S. (1982), 'Conditions under which stronger job performance–job satisfaction relationships may be observed: a closer look at two situational contingencies', *Academy of Management Journal*, 25, 772–89.

Bingham, W. V. (1932), 'Making work worthwhile', *Psychology Today*, 262–4, University of Chicago Press, Chicago.

Birch, F. (1979), 'Leisure patterns 1973 and 1977', *Population Trends*, 17, 2–8.

Blackler, F. and Brown, C. (1986), 'Alternative models to guide the design and introduction of the new information technologies into work organizations', *Journal of Occupational Psychology*, 59, 287–313.

Blake, R. R. and Mouton, J. S. (1964), *The Management Grid*, Gulf Publishing Company, Houston.

Blankenship, L. V. and Miles, R. E. (1968), 'Organizational structure and managerial decision behavior', *Administrative Science Quarterly*, **13**, 106–20.

Blau, P. M. (1955), *The Dynamics of Bureaucracy*, University of Chicago Press, Chicago.

Blau, P. M. and Scott, W. R. (1963), *Formal Organizations*, Routledge & Kegan Paul, London.

Blauner, R. (1960), 'Work satisfaction and industrial trends in modern society', *in* W. Galenson and S. M. Lipset (eds.), *Labor and Trade Unions*, Wiley, New York.

— (1964), *Alienation and Freedom*, University of Chicago Press, Chicago.

Blumberg, P. (1968), *Industrial Democracy: the Sociology of Participation*, Constable, London.

Boot, R. and Reynolds, M. (1984), 'Rethinking experience based events', *in* C. Cox and J. Beck (eds.), *Management Development*, Wiley, Chichester.

Booth-Kewley, S. and Friedman, H. S. (1987), 'Psychological predictors of heart disease: a quantitative review', *Psychological Bulletin*, **101**, 343–62.

Bower, S. A. and Bower, G. H. (1976), *Asserting Yourself*, Addison-Wesley, Reading, Massachusetts.

Brayfield, A. H. and Crockett, W. H. (1955), 'Employee attitudes and employee performance', *Psychological Bulletin*, **52**, 396–424.

Brenner, M. H. (1976), *Estimating the Social Costs of National Economic Policy: Implications for Mental and Physical Health and Criminal Aggression*, US Government Printing Office, Washington.

Broadbent, D. E. (1985), 'The clinical impact of job design', *British Journal of Clinical Psychology*, **24**, 33–44.

Brockner, J. and Adsit, L. (1986), 'The moderating effect of sex on the equity-satisfaction relationship: a field study', *Journal of Applied Psychology*, **71**, 585–90.

Brown, G. W. and Harris, T. (1978), *Social Origins of Depression*, Tavistock, London.

Brown, Roger (1965), *Social Psychology*, Free Press, New York.

Brown, Rupert (1978), 'Divided we fall: an analysis of relations between sections of a factory workforce', *in* H. Tajfel (ed.) (1978), *Differentiation between Social Groups*, Academic Press, London.

Brown, Rupert, Condor, S., Mathews, A., Wade, G. and Williams, J. (1986), 'Explaining intergroup differentiation in an industrial organization', *Journal of Occupational Psychology*, **59**, 273–86.

Brown, W. (1981), *The Changing Contours of British Industrial Relations*, Blackwell, Oxford.

Bruning, N. S. and Frew, D. R. (1987), 'Effects of exercise, relaxation, and management skills training on physiological stress indicators: a field experiment', *Journal of Applied Psychology*, 72, 515–21.

Buck, R. (1988), *Human Motivation and Emotion*, Wiley, New York.

Bull, R. and Horncastle, P. (1983), *An Evaluation of the Metropolitan Police Training Programme*, The Police Foundation, London.

Burke, M. J. and Day, R. R. (1986), 'A cumulative study of the effectiveness of managerial training', *Journal of Applied Psychology*, 71, 232–45.

Burke, R. J. and Greenglass, E. R. (1987), 'Work and family', *in* C. L. Cooper and I. T. Robertson (eds.), *International Review of Industrial and Organizational Psychology 1987*, Wiley, Chichester.

Burke, R. J. and Weir, T. (1980), 'Coping with the stress of managerial occupations', *in* C. L. Cooper and R. Payne (eds.), *Current Concerns in Occupational Stress*, Wiley, Chichester.

Burns, T. (1955), 'The reference of conduct in small groups: cliques and cabals in occupational milieux', *Human Relations*, 8, 467–86.

Burns, T. and Stalker, G. M. (1961), *The Management of Innovation*, Tavistock, London.

Cameron, D. (1982), 'Performance appraisal and review', *in* A. M. Bowey (ed.), *Handbook of Salary and Wage Systems*, Gower, Aldershot.

Campbell, A. (1981), *The Sense of Well-Being in America*, McGraw-Hill, New York.

Campbell, A., Converse, P. E. and Rodgers, W. L. (1976), *The Quality of American Life*, Sage, New York.

Campbell, D. P. (1971), *Handbook for the Strong Vocational Interest Blank*, Stanford University Press, Stanford.

Campbell, J. P. and Dunnette, M. D. (1968), 'Effectiveness of T-group experiences in management training', *Psychological Bulletin*, 70, 73–104.

Campbell, J. P. and Pritchard, R. D. (1976), 'Motivation theory in industrial and organizational psychology', *in* M. D. Dunnette (ed.), *Handbook of Industrial and Organizational Psychology*, Rand McNally, Chicago.

Caplan, R. D., Cobb, S., French, J. R. P., van Harrison, R. and Pinneau, S. R. (1975), *Job Demands and Worker Health*, Institute for Social Research, University of Michigan, Ann Arbor, Michigan.

Caplan, R. D. and Jones, K. W. (1975), 'Effects of work load, role ambiguity and personality Type A on anxiety, depression, and heart rate', *Journal of Applied Psychology*, 60, 713–19.

Caplow, T. (1954), *The Sociology of Work*, University of Minnesota Press, Minneapolis.

Carruthers, M. (1980), 'Hazardous occupations and the heart', *in* C. L. Cooper and R. Payne (eds.), *Current Concerns in Occupational Stress*, Wiley, Chichester.

Carsten, J. M. and Spector, P. E. (1987), 'Unemployment, job satisfaction, and employee turnover: a meta-analytic test of the Muchinsky model', *Journal of Applied Psychology*, **72**, 374–9.

Cartwright, L. K. (1979), 'Sources and effects of stress in health careers', *in* G. C. Stone, F. Cohen, N. E. Adles and associates, *A Handbook of Health Psychology*, Jossey-Bass, San Francisco.

Catalano, R., Dooley, D. and Jackson, R. (1981), 'Economic predictors of admissions to mental health facilities in a nonmetropolitan community', *Journal of Health and Social Behavior*, **22**, 284–97.

Centers, R. and Cantril, H. (1946), 'Income satisfaction and income aspiration', *Journal of Abnormal and Social Psychology*, **41**, 64–9.

Chacko, T. I. (1983), 'Job and life satisfaction: a causal analysis of their relationships', *Academy of Management Journal*, **26**, 163–9.

Chadwick-Jones, J., Nicholson, N. and Brown, C. (1982), *Social Psychology of Absenteeism*, Praeger, New York.

Chapanis, A. R. E. (1965), *Man-Machine Engineering*, Tavistock, London.

Chapple, E. D. and Sayles, C. R. (1961), *The Measure of Management*, Macmillan, New York.

Chell, F. (1986), 'The entrepreneurial personality: a review and some theoretical developments', *in* J. Curran, J. Stanworth and D. Watkins (eds.), *The Survival of the Small Firm*, Gover, Aldershot.

Chesney, M. A. and Rosenman, R. (1980), 'Type A behavior in a work setting', *in* C. L. Cooper and R. Payne (eds.), *Current Concerns in Occupational Stress*, Wiley, Chichester.

Child, J. (1976), *Organizational Design and Performance: Contingency Theory and Beyond*, University of Aston in Birmingham.

— (1984), *Organization: a Guide to Problems and Practice*, 2nd edn, Harper and Row, London.

— (1986), 'New technology and the service class', *in* K. Purcell *et al.* (eds.), *The Changing Experience of Employment*, Macmillan, London.

Child, J. and Mansfield, R. (1972), 'Technology, size and organization structure', *Sociology*, **6**, 369–93.

Child, J. and Partridge, B. (1982), *Lost Managers*, Cambridge University Press, Cambridge.

Clegg, C. W. (1983), 'Psychology of employee lateness, absence, and turnover: a methodological critique and an empirical study', *Journal of Applied Psychology*, **68**, 88–101.

Clutterbuck, D. and Hill, R. (1981), *The Re-making of Work*, Grant McIntyre, London.

Cobb, S. (1976), 'Social support as a moderator of life stress', *Psychosomatic Medicine*, **38**, 300–14.

Cobb, S. and Kasl, S. V. (1977), *Termination: the Consequences of Job Loss*, US Dept of Health, Education and Welfare, Cincinnati.

Coch, L. and French, J. R. P. (1948), 'Overcoming resistance to change', *Human Relations*, 1, 512–32.

Cofer, C. N. and Appley, M. H. (1964), *Motivation: Theory and Research*, Wiley, New York.

Constable, J. and McCormick, R. (1987), *The Making of British Managers*, British Institute of Management and Confederation of British Industry, London.

Cook, J. D., Hepworth, S. J., Wall, T. D. and Warr, P. B. (1981), *The Experience of Work*, Academic Press, London.

Cooper, C. L. (1985), 'Your place in the stress league', *Sunday Times*, 24 February.

Cooper, C. L. and Marshall, J. (1976), 'Occupational sources of stress: a review of the literature relating to coronary heart disease and mental ill-health', *Journal of Occupational Psychology*, **49**, 11–28.

— (1978), 'Source of managerial and white-collar stress', *in* C. L. Cooper and R. Payne (eds.), *Stress at Work*, Wiley, Chichester.

Cox, T. (1980), 'Repetitive work', *in* C. L. Cooper and R. Payne (eds.), *Current Concerns in Occupational Stress*, Wiley, Chichester.

Crocker, O. L., Chiu, J. S. L. and Charney, C. (1984), *Quality Circles*, Methuen, Toronto.

Crouch, A. and Yetton, P. (1987), 'Manager behavior, leadership style, and subordinate performance: an empirical extension of the Vroom–Yetton conflict rule', *Organizational Behavior and Human Decision Processes*, **39**, 384–96.

Csikszentmihalyi, M. (1975), *Beyond Boredom and Anxiety*, Jossey-Bass, San Francisco.

Csikszentmihalyi, M. and Kubey, R. (1981), 'Television and the rest of life: a systematic comparison of subjective experiences', *Public Opinion Quarterly*, **45**, 317–28.

Curran, J., Burrows, R. and Evandrou, M. (1987), *Small Business Owners and the Self-Employed in Britain*, Small Business Research Trust, London.

Cyert, R. M. and MacCrimmon, K. R. (1968), 'Organizations', *in* G. Lindzey and E. Aronson (eds.), *Handbook of Social Psychology* (2nd edn), vol. 1, Addison-Wesley, Reading, Massachusetts.

Dahrendorf, R. (1959), *Class and Class Conflict in Industrial Society*, Routledge & Kegan Paul, London.

Davidson, M. A. and Hutt, C. (1964), 'A study of 500 Oxford student psychiatric patients', *British Journal of Social and Clinical Psychology*, 3, 175–85.

Davies, R., Hamill, L., Moylan, S. and Smee, C. H. (1982), 'Incomes in and out of work', *Dept of Employment Gazette*, June, 237-43.

Davis, J. H. (1963), *Great Aspirations*, vol. 1, Chicago National Opinion Research Center, Chicago.

Davis, L. E. and Cherns, A. B. (eds.) (1975), *The Quality of Working Life*, Free Press, New York.

Davison, J. P. *et al.* (1958), *Productivity and Economic Incentives*, Allen and Unwin, London.

Dawson, S. (1986), *Analysing Organisations*, Macmillan, Basingstoke.

Deci, E. L. (1980), *The Psychology of Self-determination*, D. C. Heath, Lexington, Massachusetts.

de Jong, J. R. and Thierry, H. (1984), 'Job evaluation', *in* P. J. D. Drenth *et al.* (eds.), *Handbook of Work and Organizational Psychology*, Wiley, Chichester.

Department of Employment (1983), Statistical Series, *Employment Gazette*, 91, no. 1, January.

de Wolff, C. J. and van den Bosch, G. (1984), 'Personnel selection', *in* P. J. D. Drenth *et al.* (eds.), *Handbook of Work and Organizational Psychology*, Wiley, Chichester.

Dion, K. K. (1985), 'Socialization in adulthood', *in* G. Lindzey and E. Aronson (eds.), *Handbook of Social Psychology* (3rd edn), vol. 2, Random House, New York.

Dore, R. (1973), *British Factory Japanese Factory*, Allen and Unwin, London.

Drucker, P. F. (1954), *The Practice of Management*, Harper and Row, New York.

Dubin, R. (1958), *The World of Work*, Prentice-Hall, Englewood Cliffs, New Jersey.

Duchon, D., Green, S. G. and Taber, T. D. (1986), 'Vertical dyad linkage: a longitudinal assessment of antecedents, measures and consequences', *Journal of Applied Psychology*, 71, 56–60.

Dunnette, M. S. (1966), *Personnel Selection and Placement*, Tavistock, London.

Earley, P. C. and Kanfer, R. (1985), 'The influence of component participation and role models on goal acceptance, goal satisfaction, and performance', *Organizational Behavior and Human Decision Processes*, 36, 378–90.

Economist (1963), 'Consider Japan', Duckworth, London.

Edholm, O. G. (1967), *The Biology of Work*, Weidenfeld and Nicolson, London.

Elder, E. H. (1968), 'Adolescent socialization and development', *in* E. F. Borgatta and W. W. Lambert (eds.), *Handbook of Personality Theory and Research*, Rand McNally, Chicago.

Ellis, R. A. and Taylor, M. S. (1983), 'Role of self-esteem within the job search process', *Journal of Applied Psychology*, 68, 632–40.

Emery, F. E. and Thorsrud, E. (1969), *Form and Context in Industrial Democracy*, Tavistock, London.

Emler, N. and Dickinson, J. (1985), 'Children's representation of economic inequalities: the effects of social class', *British Journal of Developmental Psychology*, 3, 191–8.

Erikson, E. H. (1956), 'The problem of ego identity', *American Journal of Psychoanalysis*, 4, 56–121.

Etzioni, A. (1961), *A Comparative Analysis of Complex Organizations*, Free Press, New York.

Evans, C. E. and La Laseau, V. N. (1950), *My Job Contest*, Personnel Psychology Inc., Washington.

Eysenck, H. J. (1967), 'Personality patterns in various groups of businessmen', *Occupational Psychology*, 41, 249–50.

Falkenburg, L. E. (1987), 'Employee fitness programs: their impact on the employee and the organization', *Academy of Management Review*, 12, 511–22.

Family Expenditure Survey (1985), HMSO, London.

Farrell, D. (1983), 'Exit, voice, loyalty and neglect as responses to job satisfaction, a multidimensional scaling study', *Academy of Management Journal*, 26, 596–607.

Farris, G. F. (1981), 'Groups and the informal organization', *in* R. Payne and C. L. Cooper (eds.) (1981), *Groups at Work*, Wiley, Chichester.

Faucheux, C. and Moscovici, S. (1960), 'Études sur la créativité des groupes: II. Tâche, structure des communications et réussite', *Bull. CERP*, 9, 11–22.

Feather, N. T. (1982), 'Unemployment and its psychological correlates: a study of depressive symptoms, self-esteem, Protestant Ethic values, attributional style and apathy', *Australian Journal of Psychology*, 34, 309–23.

Feather, N. T. and Bond, M. J. (1983), 'Time structure and purposeful activity among employed and unemployed university graduates', *Journal of Occupational Psychology*, **56**, 241–54.

Feather, N. T. and Davenport, P. R. (1983), 'Unemployment and depressive affect: a motivational and attributional analysis', *Journal of Personality and Social Psychology*, **41**, 422–36.

Feldman, D. C. and Arnold, H. J. (1983), *Managing Individual and Group Behavior in Organizations*, McGraw-Hill, New York.

Ferris, G. R. (1985), 'Role of leadership in the employee withdrawal process', *Journal of Applied Psychology*, **70**, 777–81.

Fiedler, F. E. (1967), *A Theory of Leadership Effectiveness*, McGraw-Hill, New York.

— (1970), 'Leadership experience and leader performance – another hypothesis shot to hell', *Organizational Behavior and Human Performance*, **5**, 1–14.

Fiedler, F. E. and Chemers, M. M. (1984), *Improving Leadership Effectiveness*, Wiley, New York.

Fiedler, F. E. and Garcia, J. E. (1987), *New Approaches to Effective Leadership*, Wiley, New York.

Finlay-Jones, B. and Eckhardt, B. (1981), 'Psychiatric disorder among the young unemployed', *Australian Journal of Psychiatry*, **7**, 475–89.

Fischman, J. (1987), 'Type A on trial', *Psychology Today*, February, 42–50.

Fisher, C. D. (1978), 'The effects of personal control, competence, and extrinsic reward systems on intrinsic motivation', *Organizational Behavior and Human Performance*, **21**, 273–88.

Fleishman, E. A. (1953), 'The description of supervisory behavior', *Journal of Applied Psychology*, **37**, 1–6.

— (1965), 'The description and prediction of perceptual-motor skill learning', in R. Glaser (ed.), *Training Research and Education*, Wiley, New York.

Fleishman, E. A. and Harris, E. F. (1962), 'Patterns of leadership behavior related to employee grievances and turnover', *Personnel Psychology*, **15**, 43–56.

Forbes, R. J. and Jackson, P. R. (1980), 'Non-verbal behaviour and the outcome of selection interviews', *Journal of Occupational Psychology*, **53**, 65–72.

Ford, J. D. and Hegarty, W. H. (1984), 'Decision makers' beliefs about the causes and effects of structure: an exploratory study', *Academy of Management Journal*, **27**, 271–91.

Fottler, M. D. and Bain, T. (1984), 'Realism of occupational choice among High School seniors: implications for quality of work life', *Journal of Occupational Behaviour*, 5, 237–51.

Fox, A. (1971), *The Sociology of Work*, Collier Macmillan, London.

— (1973), 'Industrial relations: a social critique of pluralist ideology', *in* J. Child (ed.), *Man and Organization*, Allen and Unwin, London.

Francis, A. (1986), *New Technology at Work*, Clarendon Press, Oxford.

Frankel, B. (1987), *The Post-Industrial Utopias*, Blackwell, Oxford.

Fraser, R. (1947), *The Incidence of Neurosis among Factory Workers*, Medical Research Council, HMSO.

French, E. G. (1958), 'Effects of interaction of motivation and feedback on task performance', *in* J. W. Atkinson (ed.), *Motives in Fantasy, Action and Society*, Van Nostrand, Princeton, New Jersey.

French, J. R. P. and Caplan, R. D. (1970), 'Psychosocial factors in coronary heart disease', *Industrial Medicine*, 39, 383–97.

French, J. R. P., Caplan, R. D. and van Harrison, R. (1982), *The Mechanisms of Job Stress and Strain*, Wiley, Chichester.

Frese, M. (1987), 'Human-computer interaction in the office', *in* C. L. Cooper and I. T. Robertson (eds.), *International Review of Industrial and Organizational Psychology* – 1987, Wiley, Chichester.

Friedlander, F. (1986), 'The ecology of work groups', *in* J. W. Lorsch (ed.), *Handbook of Organizational Behavior*, Prentice-Hall, Englewood Cliffs, New Jersey.

Fried, Y. and Ferris, G. R. (1987) 'The validity of the job characteristics model,' *Personnel Psychology*, 40, 287–322.

Friedmann, G. (1961), *The Anatomy of Work*, Heinemann, London.

Fryer, D. and Payne, R. (1984), 'Proactive behaviour in unemployment', *Leisure Studies*, 3, 273–95.

— (1986), 'Being unemployed: a review of the literature on the psychological experience of unemployment', *in* C. L. Cooper and I. T. Robertson (eds.), *International Review of Industrial and Organizational Psychology 1986*, Wiley, Chichester.

Furneaux, W. D. (1962), 'The psychologist and the university', *Universities Quarterly*, 17, 33–47.

Furnham, A. (1982), 'Explanations for unemployment in Britain', *European Journal of Social Psychology*, 12, 335–52.

— (1984a), 'Many sides of the coin: the psychology of money usage', *Personality and Individual Differences*, 5, 501–9.

— (1984b), 'Getting a job: school leavers' perceptions of employment prospects', *British Journal of Educational Psychology*, 54, 293–305.

— (1984c), 'The Protestant work ethic: a review of the psychological literature', *European Journal of Social Psychology*, **14**, 87–104.

Furnham, A. and Lewis, A. (1986), *The Economic Mind*, Wheatsheaf, Brighton.

Furnham, A. and Schaeffer, R. (1984), 'Person-environment fit, job satisfaction and mental health,' *Journal of Occupational Psychology*, **57**, 295–307.

Gabarro, J. J. (1986), 'The development of working relationships', *in* J. W. Lorsch (ed.), *Handbook of Organizational Behavior*, Prentice-Hall, Englewood Cliffs, New Jersey.

Gage, N. L., Runkel, P. J. and Chatterjee, B. B. (1960), *Equilibrium Theory and Behavior Change: an experiment in feedback from pupils to teachers*, Bureau of Educational Research, Urbana.

Gaines, J. and Jermier, J. M. (1983), 'Emotional exhaustion in a high stress organization', *Academy of Management Journal*, **26**, 567–86.

Ganster, D. C., Mayes, B. T., Sime, W. E. and Tharp, G. D. (1982), 'Managing organizational stress: a field experiment', *Journal of Applied Psychology*, **67**, 533–42.

Georgopoulos, B. S., Mahoney, G. M. and Jones, N. W. (1957), 'A path-goal approach to productivity', *Journal of Applied Psychology*, **41**, 345–53.

Gershuny, J. I. (1984), 'The future of service employment', *in* P. M. Marstrand (ed.), *New Technology and the Future of Work and Skills*, Pinter, London and Dover.

Gilbreth, F. B. (1909), *Bricklaying System*, M. C. Clark, New York.

Gill, C. (1985), *Work, Unemployment and New Technology*, Polity Press, Cambridge.

Gilmore, D. C., Beehr, T. A. and Love, K. G. (1986), 'Effects of applicant sex, applicant physical attractiveness, type of rater and type of job on interview decisions', *Journal of Occupational Psychology*, **59**, 103–9.

Ginzberg, E. *et al.* (1951), *Occupational Choice: An Approach to a General Theory*, Columbia University Press, New York.

Glanzer, M. and Glaser, R. (1961), 'Techniques for the study of group structure and behavior: II. Empirical studies of the effects of structure in small groups', *Psychological Bulletin*, **58**, 1–27.

Glass, D. C. (1977), *Behavior Patterns, Stress and Coronary Disease*, Erlbaum, Hillsdale, New Jersey.

Goffman, E. (1956), *The Presentation of Self in Everyday Life*, Edinburgh University Press, Edinburgh.

— (1961), *Asylums*, Anchor Books, New York.

Goldberg, D. (1978), *Manual of the General Health Questionnaire*, National Foundation for Educational Research, Windsor.

Goldsen, R. K. *et al.* (1960), *What College Students Think*, Van Nostrand, Princeton, New Jersey.

Goldstein, A. P. (1981), *Psychological Skill Training*, Pergamon Press, New York.

Goldstein, A. P. and Sorcher, M. (1974), *Changing Supervisor Behavior*, Pergamon Press, New York.

Goldthorpe, J. H., Lockwood, D., Bechofer, F. and Platt, J. (1968), *The Affluent Worker: Industrial Attitudes and Behaviour*, Cambridge University Press, Cambridge.

Gooding, R. Z. and Wagner, J. A. (1985), 'A meta-analytic review of the relationship between size and performance: the productivity and efficiency of organizations and their subunits', *Administrative Science Quarterly*, 30, 462–81.

Goodman, P. S. (1967), 'An empirical examination of Elliott Jaques' concept of time-span', *Human Relations*, 20, 155–70.

Goodman, P. S., Atkin, P. S. and Associates (1984), *Absenteeism*, Jossey-Bass, San Francisco.

Gordon, M. E. and Nurick, A. J. (1981), 'Psychological approaches to the study of the unions and union-management relations', *Psychological Bulletin*, 90, 293–306.

Graen, G. B., Scandura, T. A. and Graen, M. R. (1986), 'A field experimental test of the moderating effects of growth–need–strength on productivity', *Journal of Applied Psychology*, 71, 484–91.

Greenberg, J. (1977), 'The Protestant work ethic and reactions to negative performance evaluations on a laboratory test', *Journal of Applied Psychology*, 62, 682–99.

— (1986), 'Human motivation in organizations', *in* R. A. Baron, *Behavior in Organizations*, Allyn & Bacon, Boston.

— (1987), 'Reactions to procedural injustice in payment distribution: do the means justify the ends?', *Journal of Applied Psychology*, 72, 55–61.

Greenberg, J. and Ornstein, S. (1983), 'High status job title as compensation for underpayment: a test of equity theory', *Journal of Applied Psychology*, 68, 285–97.

Greenhalgh, L. (1987), 'Interpersonal conflict in organization', *in* C. L. Cooper and I. T. Robertson (eds.), *International Review of Industrial and Organizational Psychology 1987*, Wiley, Chichester.

Grice, H. P. (1975), 'Logic and conversation', *in* P. Cole and J. L. Morgan (eds.), *Syntax and Semantics: Vol. 3. Speech Acts*, Academic Press, New York and London.

Griffin, R. W. and Bateman, T. S. (1986), 'Job satisfaction and organizational commitment', in C. L. Cooper and I. T. Robertson (eds.), *International Review of Industrial and Organizational Psychology 1986*, Wiley, Chichester.

Grove, E. A. and Kerr, W. A. (1951), 'Specific evidence on origin of halo effect in measurement of employee morale', *Journal of Applied Psychology*, 34, 165–70.

Gruneberg, M. M. (1979), *Understanding Job Satisfaction*, Halsted, London.

Guest, D. E. (1984), 'Social psychology and organizational change', in M. Gruneberg and T. Wall (eds.), *Social Psychology and Organizational Behaviour*, Wiley, Chichester.

Gurin, G., Veroff, J. and Feld, S. (1960), *Americans View their Mental Health*, Basic Books, New York.

Guzzo, R., Jette, R. D. and Katzell, R. A. (1985), 'The effects of psychologically based intervention programs on worker productivity: a meta analysis', *Personnel Psychology*, 38, 275–91.

Hackett, R. D. and Guion, R. M. (1985), 'A re-evaluation of the absenteeism – job satisfaction relationship', *Organizational Behavior and Human Decision Processes*, 35, 340–81.

Hackman, J. R. (1977), 'Work design', in J. R. Hackman and J. L. Suttle (eds.), *Improving Life at Work*, Goodyear, Santa Monica.

Hackman, J. R. and Oldham, G. R. (1976), 'Motivation through the design of work: test of a theory', *Organizational Behavior and Human Performance*, 16, 250–79.

— (1980), *Work Redesign*, Addison-Wesley, Reading, Massachusetts.

Hackman, J. R., Pearce, J. L. and Wolfe, J. C. (1978), 'Effects of changes in job characteristics on work attitudes and behaviour: a naturally occurring quasi-experiment', *Organizational Behavior and Human Performance*, 21, 289–304.

Haire, M. (1955), 'Role-perceptions in labor-management relations: an experimental approach', *Industrial Labour Relations Review*, 8, 204–16.

Hale, M. (1982), 'History of employment testing', in F. J. Landy (ed.), *Readings in Industrial and Organizational Psychology*, Dorsey, Chicago.

Hall, D. T. (1976), *Careers in Organizations*, Goodyear, Pacific Palisades, California.

Hall, J. G., Van Treuven, R. R. and Virnelli, S. (1987), 'Hardiness and health: a critique and alternative approach', *Journal of Personality and Social Psychology*, 53, 518–30.

Halpin, A. W. and Winer, B. J. (1952), *The Leadership Behavior of the Airplane Commander*, Ohio State University, Columbus.

Handy, C. (1984), *The Future of Work*, Blackwell, Oxford.

— (1987), *The Making of Managers*, Manpower Services Commission, National Economic Development Council, British Institute of Managers, London.

Harbison, F. (1959), 'Management in Japan', *in* F. Harbison and C. A. Myers (eds.), *Management in the Industrial World*, McGraw-Hill, New York.

Hartley, J. (1984), 'Industrial relations psychology', *in* M. Gruneberg and T. Wall (eds.), *Social Psychology and Organizational Behaviour*, Wiley, Chichester.

Haw, A. H. (1982), 'Women, work and stress: a review and agenda for the future', *Journal of Health and Social Behavior*, **23**, 132–44.

Hazewinkel, A. (1984), 'Organizational structure and contingency theory', *in* P. J. D. Drenth *et al.* (eds.), *Handbook of Work and Organizational Psychology*, Wiley, Chichester.

Headey, B. and Wearing, A. (1986), 'Chains of well-being, chains of ill-being', International Sociological Association Conference, New Delhi.

Heinecke, C. and Bales, R. F. (1953), 'Developmental trends in structure of small groups', *Sociometry*, **16**, 7–38.

Hemphill, J. K. (1960), *Dimensions of Executive Positions*, Bureau of Business Research Monograph 98, Ohio State University, Columbus.

Henderson, M. and Argyle, M. (1985), 'Social support by four categories of work colleagues: relationships between activities, stress and satisfaction', *Journal of Occupational Behaviour*, **6**, 229–39.

Herzberg, F., Mausner, B. and Snyderman, B. B. (1959), *The Motivation to Work*, Wiley, New York.

Hespe, G. W. A. and Little, A. J. (1971), 'Some aspects of employee participation', *in* P. B. Warr (ed.), *Psychology at Work*, Penguin Books, Harmondsworth.

Hewitt, D. and Parfit, J. (1953), 'A note on working morale, and size of group', *Occupational Psychology*, **27**, 38–42.

Hickson, D. J., Pugh, D. S. and Pheysey, D. C. (1969), 'Operations technology and organization structure: an empirical appraisal', *Administrative Science Quarterly*, **14**, 378–97.

Himmelweit, H. and Whitfield, J. (1944), 'Mean intelligence scores of a random sample of occupations', *British Journal of Industrial Medicine*, **1**, 224–6.

Hobert, R. D. (1965), 'Moderating effects in the prediction of managerial success from psychological test scores and biographical factors', University of Minnesota Ph.D. thesis, cited by Dunnette (1966).

Hobhouse, L. T., Wheeler, G. C. and Ginsberg, M. (1915), *The Material Culture and Social Institutions of the Simpler Peoples*, Routledge & Kegan Paul, London.

Hoffman, L. R. (1965), 'Group problem-solving', *Advances in Experimental Social Psychology*, **2**, 99–132.

Hofstede, G. (1980), *Culture's Consequences*, Sage, Beverly Hills.

Holland, J. L. (1966), *Making Vocational Choices: a Theory of Careers*, Prentice-Hall, Englewood Cliffs, New Jersey.

Hollander, E. P. (1958), 'Conformity, status, and idiosyncrasy credit', *Psychological Review*, **65**, 117–27.

— (1985), 'Leadership and power', *in* G. Lindzey and E. Aronson (eds.), *The Handbook of Social Psychology* (3rd edn), vol. 2, Random House, New York.

Holmes, T. H. and Rahe, R. H. (1967), 'The social readjustment rating scale', *Journal of Psychosomatic Research*, **11**, 213–18.

Hom, P. W., Griffith, R. W. and Sellaro, C. L. (1984), 'The validity of Mobley's (1977) model of employee turnover', *Organizational Behavior and Human Performance*, **34**, 141–74.

Homans, G. C. (1951), *The Human Group*, Routledge & Kegan Paul, London.

Hoppock, R. (1935), *Job Satisfaction*, Harper, New York.

House, R. J. (1971), 'A path-goal theory of leader effectiveness', *Administrative Science Quarterly*, **16**, 321–38.

House, J. S. (1981), *Work Stress and Social Support*, Addison-Wesley, Reading, Massachusetts.

Hudson, L. (1968), *Frames of Mind*, Methuen, London and Penguin, Harmondsworth.

Hulin, C. L. and Blood, M. R. (1968), 'Job enlargement, individual differences and worker responses', *Psychological Bulletin*, **69**, 41–55.

Hunter, J. E. and Hirsch, H. R. (1987), 'Applications of meta-analysis', *in* C. L. Cooper and I. T. Robertson (eds.), *International Review of Industrial and Organizational Psychology 1987*, Wiley, Chichester.

Hunter, J. E. and Hunter, R. F. (1984), 'Validity and utility of alternative predictors of job success', *Psychological Bulletin*, **96**, 72–98.

Hutchins, D. W. (1963), *Technology and the Sixth Form Boy*, Department of Education, University of Oxford, Oxford.

Hutchins, D. (1985), *Quality Circles*, Pitman, London.

Iaffaldano, M. T. and Muchinsky, P. M. (1985), 'Job satisfaction and job performance: a meta analysis', *Psychological Bulletin*, **97**, 251–73.

Industrial Democracy in Europe (IDE) (1981), Clarendon Press, Oxford.

Ingram, J. K. (1926), 'Slavery', *in Encyclopedia Britannica*, 13th edn, **25**, 216–27.

Innes, J. M. and Clarke, A. (1985), 'Job involvement as a moderator variable in the life events–stress–illness relationships', *Journal of Occupational Behaviour*, **6**, 299–303.

Ivancevich, J. M. (1986), 'Life events and hassles as predictors of health symptoms, job performance, and absenteeism', *Journal of Occupational Behaviour*, **7**, 39–57.

Jablin, F. M. (1979), 'Superior–subordinate communication: the state of the art', *Psychological Bulletin*, **86**, 1201–22.

Jackson, J. (1965), 'Structural characteristics of norms', *in* I. D. Steiner and M. Fishbein (eds.), *Current Studies in Social Psychology*, Holt, New York.

Jackson, J. H. and Keaveny, T. J. (1980), *Successful Supervision*, Prentice-Hall, Englewood Cliffs, New Jersey.

Jackson, P. R. *et al.* (1983), 'Unemployment and psychological distress in young people: the moderating role of employee commitment', *Journal of Applied Psychology*, **68**, 52.

Jackson, S. E. and Schuler, R. S. (1985), 'A meta-analysis and conceptual critique of research on role ambiguity and role conflict in work settings', *Organizational Behavior and Human Decision Processes*, **36**, 16–78.

Jahoda, M. (1982), *Employment and Unemployment*, Cambridge University Press, Cambridge.

Jahoda, M., Lazarsfeld, P. F. and Zeisel, H. (1933), *Marienthal: the Sociography of an Unemployed Community* (trans. 1972), Tavistock, London.

James, L. R. and Tetrick, L. E. (1986), 'Confirmatory analytic tests of three causal models relating job perception to job satisfaction', *Journal of Applied Psychology*, **71**, 77–82.

Janis, I. L. and Mann, L. (1977), *Decision Making: a Psychological Analysis of Conflict, Choice and Commitment*, Collier Macmillan, London.

Janman, K. (1985), 'Achievement motivation, fear of success and occupational success', D.Phil. thesis, University of Oxford, Oxford.

Janson, R. (1971), 'Job enrichment in the modern office', *in* J. Maher (ed.), *New Perspectives in Job Enrichment*, Van Nostrand, New York.

Janson, R. and Martin, J. K. (1982), 'Job satisfaction and age: a test of two views', *Social Forces*, **60**, 1089–1102.

Jaques, E. (1961), *Equitable Payment*, Heinemann, London.

Jasso, G. and Rossi, P. H. (1977), 'Distributive justice and earned income', *American Sociological Review*, **42**, 639–51.

Jemmott, J. B. and Locke, S. E. (1984), 'Psychosocial factors, immunology mediation, and human susceptibility to infectious diseases: how much do we know?', *Psychological Bulletin*, **95**, 78–108.

Jenner, D. A., Reynolds, V. and Harrison, G. A. (1980), 'Catecholamine excretion rates and occupation', *Ergonomics*, **23**, 237–46.

Johns, G. and Nicholson, N. (1982), 'The meanings of absence: new strategies for theory and research', *in* B. M. Staw and L. L. Cummings (eds.), *Research in Organizational Behavior*, **4**, 127–72.

Johnson, D. W., Maruyama, G., Johnson, R. and Skon, L. (1980), 'Effects of cooperation, competition, and individualistic goal structures on achievement: a meta-analysis', *Psychological Bulletin*, **89**, 47–62.

Kahn, R. L., Wolfe, D. M. and Quinn, R. P. (1964), *Organizational Stress: Studies in Role Conflict and Ambiguity*, Wiley, New York.

Kalleberg, A. L. and Loscocco, K. A. (1983), 'Aging, values and rewards: explaining age differences in job satisfaction', *American Sociological Review*, **48**, 78–90.

Kaplan, E. M. and Cowen, E. L. (1981), 'Interpersonal helping behavior of industrial foremen', *Journal of Applied Psychology*, **66**, 633–8.

Karasek, R. A. (1979), 'Job demands, job decision latitude, and mental strain: implications for job redesign', *Administrative Science Quarterly*, **24**, 285–308.

Karasek, R. A., Gardell, B. and Lindell, J. (1987), 'Work and non-work correlates of illness and behaviour in male and female Swedish white-collar workers', *Journal of Occupational Behaviour*, **8**, 187–207.

Kasl, S. V. (1978), 'Epidemiological contributives to the study of work stress', *in* C. L. Cooper and R. Payne (eds.), *Stress at Work*, Wiley, Chichester.

— (1980), 'The impact of retirement', *in* C. L. Cooper and R. Payne (eds.), *Current Concerns in Occupativeal Stress*, Wiley, Chichester.

— (1982), 'Strategies of research on economic instability and health', *Psychological Medicine*, **12**, 637–49.

Katz, D. and Kahn, R. L. (1952), 'Some recent findings in human relations research', *in* E. Swanson, T. M. Newcomb and E. Hartley (eds.), *Readings in Social Psychology*, Holt, Rinehart & Winston, New York.

— (1966), *The Social Psychology of Organizations*, Wiley, New York.

Katz, R. (1978), 'Job longevity as a situational factor in job satisfaction', *Human Relations*, **23**, 204–23.

Kay, E., Meyer, H. H. and French, J. R. P. (1965), 'Effects of threat in a performance appraisal interview', *Journal of Applied Psychology*, **49**, 311–17.

Keller, R. T. (1986), 'Predictors of the performance of project groups in R and D organizations', *Academy of Management Journal*, **29**, 715–26.

Kelly, J. E. (1982), *Scientific Management, Job Redesign and Work Performance*, Academic Press, London.

Kelvin, P. (1981), 'Work as a source of identity', *British Journal of Counselling and Guidance*, **9**, 2–11.

Kelvin, P. and Jarrett, J. (1985), *The Social Psychological Effects of Unemployment*, Cambridge University Press, Cambridge.

Kets de Vries, M. (1977), 'The entrepreneurial personality: a person at the crossroads', *Journal of Management Studies*, **14**, 34–57.

Kilmann, R. H. (1985), 'Corporate culture', *Psychology Today*, April, 62–8.

Kirchner, W. K. and Dunnette, M. D. (1957), 'Identifying the critical factors in successful salesmanship', *Personnel*, **34**, 54–9.

Kluckhohn, C. (1954), 'Culture and behavior', in G. Lindzey (ed.), *Handbook of Social Psychology* (1st edn), vol. 2, Addison-Wesley, Cambridge, Massachusetts.

Knowles, K. G. J. C. (1952), *Strikes – a Study of Industrial Conflict*, Blackwell, Oxford.

Kobasa, S. C. (1982), 'The hardy personality: towards a social psychology of stress and health', *in* G. S. Sanders and J. Suls (eds.), *Social Psychology of Health and Illness*, Erlbaum, Hillsdale, New Jersey.

Kohn, M. L. and Schooler, C. (1982), 'Job conditions and personality: a longitudinal assessment of their reciprocal effects', *American Journal of Sociology*, **87**, 1257–86.

Kolaja, J. (1965), *Workers' Councils: the Yugoslav Experience*, Tavistock, London.

Komaki, J. L. (1986), 'Toward effective supervision: an operant analysis and comparison of managers at work', *Journal of Applied Psychology*, **71**, 270–9.

Kondrasuk, J. N. (1981), 'Studies in MBO effectiveness', *Academy of Management Review*, **6**, 419–30.

Kornhauser, A. (1965), *Mental Health of the Industrial Worker*, Wiley, New York.

Landsberger, H. A. (1961), 'The horizontal dimension in bureaucracy', *Administrative Science Quarterly*, **6**, 299–332.

Landy, F. J. and Farr, J. L. (1983), *The Measurement of Work Performance*, Academic Press, Orlando.

Landy, F. J., Vasey, J. J. and Smith, F. D. (1984), 'Methodological problems and strategies in predicting absence', *in* P. S. Goodman, R. S. Atkin and Associates (eds.), *Absenteeism*, Jossey-Bass, San Francisco.

Latané, B., Williams, K. and Harkins, S. (1979), 'Many hands make light work: the causes and consequences of social loafing', *Journal of Personality and Social Psychology*, 37, 822–32.

Latham, G. P. and Napier, N. K. (1984), 'Practical ways to increase employee attendance', *in* P. S. Goodman, R. S. Atkin and Associates (eds.), *Absenteeism*, Jossey-Bass, San Francisco.

Latham, G. P. and Saari, L. M. (1979), 'Application of social-learning theory to training supervisors through behavioral modelling', *Journal of Applied Psychology*, 64, 239–46.

Lawler, E. E. (1971), *Pay and Organizational Effectiveness*, McGraw-Hill, New York.

Lawler, E. E. and Hackman, J. R. (1969), 'The impact of employee participation in the development of pay incentive systems: a field experiment', *Journal of Applied Psychology*, 53, 467–71.

Lawler, E. E. and Porter, L. W. (1963), 'Perceptions regarding management compensation', *Industrial Relations*, 3, 41–9.

Lawrence, P. R. and Lorsch, J. W. (1967), *Organization and Environment*, Harvard Business School, Boston.

Layard, R. (1986), *How to Beat Unemployment*, Oxford University Press, Oxford.

Lesieur, F. S. (1958), *The Scanlon Plan*, Wiley, New York.

Lew, E. A. and Garfinkel, L. (1979), 'Variations in mortality by weight among 750,000 men and women', *Journal of Chronic Diseases*, 32, 563–76.

Likert, R. (1961), *New Patterns of Management*, McGraw-Hill, New York.

Litwin, G. H. and Stringer, R. A. (1968), *Motivation and Organizational Climate*, Harvard Business School, Boston.

Locke, E. A. (1968), 'Toward a theory of task motivation and incentives', *Organizational Behavior and Human Performance*, 3, 157–89.

— (1976), 'The nature and causes of job satisfaction', *in* M. D. Dunnette (ed.), *Handbook of Industrial and Organizational Psychology*, Rand McNally, Chicago.

Locke, E. A. and Henne, D. (1986), 'Work motivation theories', *in* C. L. Cooper and I. T. Robertson (eds.), *International Review of Industrial and Organizational Psychology 1986*, Wiley, Chichester.

Loher, B. T., Noe, R. A., Moeller, N. L. and Fitzgerald, M. P. (1985), 'A meta-analysis of the relation of job characteristics to job satisfaction', *Journal of Applied Psychology*, 70, 280–9.

Lupton, T. (1968), 'Beyond payment by results', in D. Pym (ed.), Industrial Society, Penguin Books, Harmondsworth.

Luthans, F. and Martinko, M. (1987), 'Behavioral approaches to organizations', in C. L. Cooper and I. T. Robertson (eds.) International Review of Industrial and Organizational Psychology 1987, Wiley, Chichester.

Maas, A. and Clark, R. D. (1984), 'Hidden impact of minorities', Psychological Bulletin, 95, 428–51.

McClelland, D. C. (1961), The Achieving Society, Van Nostrand, New York.

— (1962), 'On the psychodynamics of creative physical scientists', in H. E. Gruber et al. (eds.), Contemporary Approaches to Creative Thinking, Atherton Press, New York.

McClelland, D. C. and Boyatzis, R. E. (1982), 'Leadership motive pattern and long-term success in management', Journal of Applied Psychology, 67, 737–43.

McClelland, D. C. and Winter, D. G. (1969), Motivating Economic Achievement, Free Press, New York.

McClelland, D. C. et al. (1953), The Achievement Motive, Appleton-Century-Crofts, New York.

McCormick, E. J. and Ilgen, D. (1985), Industrial and Organizational Psychology (8th edn), Allen and Unwin, London.

McEvoy, G. M. and Cascio, W. F. (1985), 'Strategies for reducing employee turnover: a meta-analysis', Journal of Applied Psychology, 70, 342–53.

McGoldrick, A. (1982), 'Early retirement: a new leisure opportunity', in Leisure Studies Association Series, Work and Leisure, 15, 73–89.

McGregor, D. (1960), The Human Side of Enterprise, McGraw-Hill, New York.

McGuire, W. J. (1969), 'The nature of attitudes and attitude change', in G. Lindzey and E. Aronson (eds.), Handbook of Social Psychology (2nd edn), vol. 3, Addison-Wesley, Reading, Massachusetts.

Macholowitz, M. (1980), Workaholics, Addison-Wesley, Reading, Massachusetts.

Mackay, C. and Cooper, C. L. (1987), 'Occupational stress and health: some current issues', in C. L. Cooper and I. T. Robertson (eds.), International Review of Industrial and Organizational Psychology 1987, Wiley, Chichester.

McShane, S. L. (1983), 'Job satisfaction and absenteeism: a meta-analytic re-examination', in G. Johns (ed.), Proceedings of the Annual Conference of the Administrative Science Association of Canada, Administrative Science Association of Canada, Ottawa.

Mahoney, T. A., Jerdee, T. H. and Carroll, S. I. (1965), 'The job(s) of management', *Industrial Relations*, **4**, 97–110.

Maier, N. R. F. (1958), *The Appraisal Interview*, Wiley, New York.

Maier, N. R. F. and Solem, A. R. (1952), 'The contribution of a discussion leader to the quality of group thinking: the effective use of minority opinion', *Human Relations*, **5**, 277–88.

Mangoine, T. W. and Quinn, R. P. (1975), 'Job satisfaction, counter productive behaviour and drug use at work', *Journal of Applied Psychology*, **60**, 114–16.

Mann, F. C. (1957), 'Studying and creating change: a means to understanding social organization', *Research in Industrial Human Relations*, **17**, 146–67.

Mann, F. C. and Baumgartel, H. J. (1953), *Absences and Employee Attitudes in an Electric Power Company*, Institute for Social Research, Ann Arbor, Michigan.

Mann, J. W. (1963), 'Rivals of different rank', *Journal of Social Psychology*, **61**, 11–28.

March, J. G. (1954), 'Group norms and the active minority', *American Sociological Review*, **19**, 733–41.

March, J. G. and Simon, H. A. (1958), *Organizations*, Wiley, New York.

Marcia, J. A. (1966), 'Development and validation of ego-identity status', *Journal of Personality and Social Psychology*, **3**, 551–8.

Marriott, R. (1968), *Incentive Payment Systems*, Staples, London.

Marsh, R. M. and Mannari, H. (1981), 'Technology and size as determinants of the organizational structure of Japanese factories', *Administrative Science Quarterly*, **26**, 33–57.

Marshall, J. and Cooper, C. L. (1979), *Executives Under Stress*, Macmillan, London.

— (eds.) (1981), *Coping with Stress at Work*, Gower, Andover.

Martin, W. H. and Mason, S. (1982), *Leisure and Work: the Choices for 1991 and 2001*, Leisure Consultants, Sudbury, Suffolk.

Maslach, C. and Jackson, S. E. (1982), 'Burnout in health professions: a social psychological analysis', *in* G. S. Sanders and J. Suls (eds.), *Social Psychology of Health and Illness*, Erlbaum, Hillsdale, New Jersey.

Maslow, A. H. (1954), *Motivation and Personality*, Harper, New York.

Massie, J. L. (1965), 'Management theory', *in* J. G. March (ed.), *Handbook of Organizations*, Rand McNally, Chicago.

Masumoto, Y. S. (1970), 'Social stress and coronary heart disease in Japan: a hypothesis', *Milbank Memorial Fund Quarterly*, **48**, 9–36.

Mathias, P. (1983), *The First Industrial Nation*, 2nd edn, Methuen, London.

Matteson, M. T. and Ivancevich, J. M. (1983), 'Note on tension discharge rate as an employee health status predictor', *Academy of Management Journal*, **26**, 540–5.

Maxwell, G. M. and Pringle, J. K. (1986), 'Social skills training for managers', *New Zealand Journal for Business*, **8** (December), 28–39.

Mayo, E. (1933), *The Human Problems of an Industrial Civilization*, Macmillan, New York.

— (1945), *The Social Problems of an Industrial Civilization*, Harvard University Graduate School of Business Administration, Boston.

Melhuish, A. H. (1981), 'The doctor's role in educating managers about stress', *in* J. Marshall and C. L. Cooper (eds.), *Coping with Stress at Work*, Gower, Andover.

Merton, R. K. (1957), *Social Theory and Social Structure*, Free Press, Glencoe, Illinois.

Merton, R. K., Reader, G. G. and Kendall, P. L. (1957), *The Student-Physician*, Harvard University Press, Cambridge, Massachusetts.

Metzner, H. and Mann, F. C. (1953), 'Employee attitudes and absence', *Personnel Psychology*, **6**, 467–85.

Michalos, A. C. (1980), 'Satisfaction and happiness', *Social Indicators Research*, **8**, 385–422.

Miller, C. S. and Schuster, M. (1987), 'A decade's experience with the Scanlon Plan: a case study', *Journal of Occupational Behaviour*, **8**, 167–74.

Miller, K. I. and Monge, P. R. (1986), 'Participation, satisfaction, and productivity: a meta-analytic review', *Academy of Management Journal*, **29**, 727–53.

Mills, C. W. (1951), *White Collar*, Oxford University Press, New York.

Miner, J. B. and Smith, J. R. (1982), 'Decline and stabilization of managerial motivation over a 20-year period', *Journal of Applied Psychology*, **67**, 297–305.

Minsky, M. *et al.* (1968), 'Machines like men', *Science Journal*, **4**, no. 10.

Mintzberg, H. (1973), *The Nature of Managerial Work*, Prentice-Hall, Englewood Cliffs, New Jersey.

Mirels, H. and Garrett, J. (1971), 'Protestant ethic as a personality variable', *Journal of Consulting and Clinical Psychology*, **36**, 40–4.

Mischel, W. (1969), *Personality and Assessment*, Wiley, New York.

Misumi, J. (1960), 'A field study of human relations in Japanese small sized enterprises', *Industrial Training*, **6** (3) 2–12, (4) 2–13.

— (1985), *The Behavioral Science of Leadership*, University of Michigan Press, Ann Arbor, Michigan.

Mitchell, T. W. and Klimoski, R. J. (1982), 'Is it natural to be empirical? A test of methods for scoring biographical data', *Journal of Applied Psychology*, **67**, 411–18.

Mobley, W. H. (1977), 'Intermediate linkages in the relationship between job satisfaction and employee turnover', *Journal of Applied Psychology*, **62**, 237–40.

— (1982), *Employee Turnover: Causes, Consequences and Control*, Addison-Wesley, Reading, Massachusetts.

Mobley, W. H., Griffith, R., Hand, H. and Meglino, B. (1979), 'A review and conceptual analysis of the employee turnover process', *Psychological Bulletin*, **62**, 493–522.

Modern Industry (April 1946), 'Pay plans for higher production', p. 51 f. cited by Viteles (1954).

Mohrman, S. A. *et al.* (1986), 'Quality of work life and employee involvement', *in* C. L. Cooper and I. T. Robertson (eds.), *International Review of Industrial and Organizational Psychology 1986*, Wiley, Chichester.

Moon, G. G. and Hariton, T. (1958), 'Evaluating an appraisal and feedback training program', *Personnel*, **35**, 34–41.

Morley, I. (1981), 'Negotiation and bargaining', *in* M. Argyle (ed.), *Social Skills and Work*, Methuen, London.

Morley, I. E. and Hosking, D. M. (1984), 'Decision-making and negotiation', *in* M. Gruneberg and T. Wall (eds.), *Social Psychology and Organizational Behaviour*, Wiley, Chichester.

Morris, L. W. (1979), *Extraversion and Introversion: an Interactional Perspective*, Wiley, New York.

Morrison, A. and McIntyre, D. (1971), *Schools and Socialization*, Penguin Books, Harmondsworth.

Morrison, R. F., Owens, W. A., Glennon, J. R. and Albright, L. E. (1962), 'Factored life history antecedents of industrial research performance', *Journal of Applied Psychology*, **46**, 281–4.

Morrow, P. (1983), 'Concept redundancy in organizational research: the case of work commitment', *Academy of Management Review*, **8**, 486–500.

Morse, N. C. and Reimer, E. (1956), 'The experimental change of a major organizational variable', *Journal of Abnormal and Social Psychology*, **52**, 120–29.

Moscovici, S. (1985), 'Social influence and conformity', *in* G. Lindzey and

E. Aronson (eds.), *Handbook of Social Psychology* (3rd edn), vol. 2, Erlbaum, Hillsdale, New Jersey.

Moser, K. A., Fox, A. J. and Jones, D. R. (1984), 'Unemployment and mortality in the OPCS longitudinal study', *Lancet*, 2, 1324–9.

Motowidlo, S. J., Packard, J. S. and Manning, M. R. (1986), 'Occupational stress: its causes and consequences for job performance', *Journal of Applied Psychology*, 71, 618–29.

Mowday, R. T. (1979), 'Equity theory predictions of behavior in organizations', *in* R. M. Steers and L. W. Porter (eds.), *Motivation and Work Behavior*, McGraw-Hill, New York.

Mowday, R. T., Porter, L. W. and Steers, R. M. (1982), *Employee–Organization Linkages*, Academic Press, New York.

Moylan, S., Millar, J. and Davies, R. (1984), *For Richer for Poorer: DHSS Study of Unemployed Men*, HMSO, London.

Muchinsky, P. M. (1986), 'Personnel selection methods', *in* C. L. Cooper and I. T. Robertson (eds.), *International Review of Industrial and Organizational Psychology 1986*, Wiley, Chichester.

Mulder, M. (1960), 'Communication structure, decision structure and group performance', *Sociometry*, 23, 1–14.

— (1971), 'Power equalization through participation?', *Administrative Sciences Quarterly*, 16, 31–8.

Mulder, M., de Jong, R. D., Koppelaar, L. and Verhage, J. (1986), 'Power, situation, and leaders' effectiveness: an organizational field study', *Journal of Applied Psychology*, 71, 566–70.

Mulford, H. A. and Salisbury, W. W. (1964), 'Self-conceptions in a general population', *Sociological Quarterly*, 5, 35–46.

Murphy, L. R. (1984), 'Occupational stress management: a review and appraisal', *Journal of Occupational Psychology*, 57, 1–15.

Murray, O. (1986), 'Life and society in classical Greece', *in* J. Boardman *et al.* (eds.), *The Oxford History of the Classical World*, Oxford University Press, Oxford.

National Institute for Occupational Safety and Health (NIOSH) (1987), *Stress Management in Work Settings*, NIOSH, Cincinatti.

National Institute of Industrial Psychology (1952), *Joint Consultation in British Industry*, Staples, London.

Nealey, S. M. and Blood, M. R. (1986), 'Leadership performance of nursing supervisors at two organizational levels', *Journal of Applied Psychology*, 52, 414–22.

Nealey, S. M. and Fiedler, F. E. (1968), 'Leadership functions of middle managers', *Psychological Bulletin*, 70, 313–20.

Near, J. P., Rice, R. W. and Hunt, R. G. (1980), 'The relationship between work and nonwork domains', *Academy of Management Review*, **5**, 415–29.

Near, J. P., Smith, C., Rice, R. W. and Hunt, R. G. (1983), 'Job satisfaction and nonwork satisfaction as components of life satisfaction', *Journal of Applied Psychology*, **13**, 126–44.

Neff, W. S. (1985), *Work and Human Behavior*, 3rd edn, Aldine, New York.

Nemeroff, W. F. and Cosentino, J. (1979), 'The benefits of combining feedback and goal setting', *Academy of Management Journal*, **22**, 566–76.

Norris, D. R. and Cox, J. F. (1987), 'Quality circle programmes: volunteering for participation', *Journal of Occupational Behaviour*, **8**, 209–17.

Oborne, D. J. (1985), *Computers at Work*, Wiley, Chichester.

O'Brien, G. E. (1981), 'Age and job satisfaction', *Australian Psychologist*, **16**, 49–61.

— (1986), *Psychology of Work and Unemployment*, Wiley, Chichester.

Odaka, K. (1963), 'Traditionalism and democracy in Japanese industry', *Industrial Relations*, **3**, 95–103.

Organization for Economic Co-operation and Development (OECD) (1982), *Growth Constraints and Work Sharing*, OECD, Paris.

Ortega, D. F. and Pipal, J. E. (1984), 'Challenge seeking and the type A coronary-prone behavior pattern', *Journal of Personality and Social Psychology*, **46**, 1328–34.

Osborne, A. F. (1957), *Applied Imagination*, Scribner, New York.

Osgood, C. E. (1960), *Graduated Reciprocation in Tension Reduction: a Key to Initiative in Foreign Policy*, Institute of Communication Research, University of Illinois, Illinois.

Ostberg, O. and Nilsson, C. (1985), 'Emerging technology and stress', *in* C. L. Cooper and M. J. Smith (eds.), *Job Stress and Blue Collar Work*, Wiley, Chichester.

Ouchi, W. (1981), *Theory Z*, Addison-Wesley, Reading, Massachusetts.

Palmore, E. (1969), 'Predicting longevity: a follow-up controlling for age', *The Gerontologist*, **9**, 247–50.

Parker, S. (1980), *Older Workers and Retirement*, HMSO, London.

— (1982), *Work and Retirement*, Allen and Unwin, London.

— (1983), *Leisure and Work*, Allen and Unwin, London.

— (1987), 'Retirement in Britain', *in* K. S. Markides and C. L. Cooper (eds.), *Retirement in Industrialized Societies*, Wiley, Chichester.

Parkes, K. (1982), 'Occupational stress among student nurses: a natural experiment', *Journal of Applied Psychology*, **67**, 784–96.

— (1983), 'Smoking as a moderator of the relationship between affective state and absence from work', *Journal of Applied Psychology*, **68**, 698–708.

— (1984), 'Locus of control, cognitive appraisal, and coping in stressful episodes', *Journal of Personality and Social Psychology*, **46**, 655–68.

— (1986), 'Coping in stressful episodes: the role of individual differences, environmental factors, and situational characteristics', *Journal of Personality and Social Psychology*, **51**, 1277–92.

— (1987), 'Relative weight, smoking, and mental health as predictors of sickness and absence from work', *Journal of Applied Psychology*, **72**, 275–86.

Parkinson, C. N. (1957), *Parkinson's Law*, Murray, London.

Pascale, R. T. and Athos, A. G. (1982), *The Art of Japanese Management*, Penguin, Harmondsworth.

Pasmore, W., Francis, C. and Haldeman, J. (1984), 'Sociotechnical systems: a North American reflection on empirical studies of the seventies', *Human Relations*, **35**, 1179–1204.

Patchen, M. (1960), 'Absence and employee feelings about fair treatment', *Personnel Psychology*, **13**, 349–60.

Payne, R. and Cooper, C. L. (eds.) (1981), *Groups at Work*, Wiley, Chichester.

Pearce, J. J., Stevenson, W. B. and Perry, J. L. (1985), 'Managerial compensation based on organizational performance: a time-series analysis of the effects of merit pay', *Academy of Management Journal*, **28**, 261–78.

Pearlin, L. I. and Schooler, C. (1978), 'The structure of coping', *Journal of Health and Social Behavior*, **19**, 2–21.

Pelz, D. C. (1952), 'Influence: a key to effective leadership in the first-line supervisor', *Personnel*, **3**, 209–17.

Perrow, C. (1970), *Organizational Analysis: a Sociological View*, Tavistock, London.

Perry, C., MacArthur, R., Meredith, G. and Cunnington, B. (1986), 'Need for achievement and locus of control of Australian small business owner–managers and super-entrepreneurs', *International Journal of Small Business*, summer issue.

Peters, R. K. and Benson, H. (1978), 'Time out from tension', *Harvard Business Review*, **56**, 120–24.

Pettigrew, A. M. (1979), 'On studying organizational climates', *Administrative Science Quarterly*, **24**, 570–81.

Petty, M. M., McGee, G. W. and Cavender, J. W. (1984), 'A meta-analysis of the relationships between individual job satisfaction and individual performance', *Academy of Management Review*, **9**, 712–21.

Phelps Brown, H. (1977), *The Inequality of Pay*, Oxford University Press, Oxford.

Platt, S. (1984), 'Unemployment and suicidal behaviour: review of the literature', *Social Science and Medicine*, **19**, no. 2, 93–115.

— (1986), 'Recent trends in parasuicide ("attempted suicide") and unemployment among men in Edinburgh', *in* S. Allen *et al.* (eds.), *The Experience of Unemployment*, Macmillan Education, Basingstoke.

Podsakoff, P. M., Toder, W. D., Grover, R. A. and Huber, V. L. (1984), 'Situational moderators of leader reward and punishment behaviors: fact or fiction?', *Organizational Behavior and Human Performance*, **34**, 21–63.

Pollard, S. (1965), *The Genesis of Modern Management*, Arnold, London.

Porter, L. W. (1964), *Organizational Patterns of Managerial Job Attitudes*, American Foundation for Management Research, New York.

Porter, L. W. and Lawler, E. E. (1965), 'Properties of organization structure in relation to job attitudes and job behavior', *Psychological Bulletin*, **64**, 23–51.

— (1968), *Managerial Attitudes and Performance*, Homeword, Illinois.

Porter, L. W., Steers, R., Mowday, R. and Boulian, P. (1974), 'Organizational commitment, job satisfaction, and turnover among psychiatric technicians', *Journal of Applied Psychology*, **59**, 603–9.

Poulton, E. C. (1978), 'Blue collar stresses', *in* C. L. Cooper and R. Payne (eds.), *Stress at Work*, Wiley, Chichester.

Prawer, J. and Eisenstadt, S. N. (1968), 'Feudalism', *International Encyclopedia of the Social Sciences*, **5**, 393–402.

Price, J. L. (1977), *The Study of Turnover*, Iowa State University Press, Ames, Iowa.

Pritchard, R. D. and Curtis, M. I. (1973), 'The influence of goal setting and financial incentives on task performance', *Organizational Behavior and Human Performance*, **10**, 175–83.

Pritchard, R. D., Dunnette, M. D. and Jorgenson, D. O. (1972), 'Effects of perceptions of equity and inequity on worker performance and satisfaction', *Journal of Applied Psychology*, **56**, 75–94.

Pruitt, D. (1976), 'Power and bargaining', *in* B. Seidenberg and A. Snadowsky (eds.), *Social Psychology: an Introduction*, Free Press, New York.

— (1983), 'Strategic choice in negotiation', *American Behavioral Scientist*, **27**, 167–94.

Pugh, D. S. and Hickson, D. J. (1976), *Organizational Structure in its Context*, Saxon House, Farnborough.

Pugh, D. S., Hickson, D. J. and Hinings, C. R. (1969), 'An empirical taxonomy of structures of work organizations', *Administrative Science Quarterly*, 14, 115–26.

Rackham, N. and Carlisle, J. (1978, 1979), 'The effective negotiator', *Journal of European Industrial Training*, 2, no. 6, 6–11, no. 7, 2–5.

Rackham, N. and Morgan, T. (1977), *Behavior Analysis and Training*, McGraw-Hill, New York.

Rae, D. (1981), *Equalities*, Harvard University Press, Cambridge, Massachusetts.

Rajan, A. and Pearson, R. (1986), *UK Occupation and Employment Trends to 1990*, Butterworths, London.

Randolph, W. A. and Dess, G. G. (1984), 'The congruence perspective on organization design: a conceptual model and multivariate research design', *Academy of Management Journal*, 9, 114–27.

Rapoport, R. and Rapoport, R. N. (1975), *Leisure and the Family Life Cycle*, Routledge & Kegan Paul, London.

Rawls, J. (1972), *A Theory of Justice*, Harvard University Press, Cambridge, Massachusetts.

Reeves, T. K. and Woodward, J. (1970), 'The study of managerial control', *in* J. Woodward (ed.), *Industrial Organization: Theory and Practice*, Oxford University Press, Oxford.

Reilly, R. R. and Chao, G. T. (1982), 'Validity and some alternative employee selection procedures', *Personnel Psychology*, 35, 1–62.

Remitz, U. (1960), *Professional Satisfaction among Swedish Bank Employees*, Munksgaard, Copenhagen.

Revans, R. W. (1958), 'Human relations, management and size', *in* E. M. Hugh-Jones (ed.), *Human Relations and Modern Management*, North-Holland Publishing, Amsterdam.

Rhodes, S. R. (1983), 'Age-related differences in work attitudes and behavior: a review and conceptual analysis', *Psychological Bulletin*, 93, 328–67.

Rice, A. K. (1958), *Productivity and Social Organization: The Ahmedabad Experiment*, Tavistock, London.

Riesman, D., Glazer, N. and Denney, R. (1950), *The Lonely Crowd*, Yale University Press, New Haven.

Rivera, A. N. and Tedeschi, J. T. (1976), 'Public versus private reactions to positive inequity', *Journal of Personality and Social Psychology*, 34, 895–900.

Roberts, K. (1983), *Leisure* (2nd edn), Longman, London.

Robertson, I. T. and Makin, P. J. (1986), 'Management selection in Britain: a survey and critique', *Journal of Occupational Psychology*, **59**, 45–57.

Robinson, J. P. (1977), *How Americans Use Time*, Praeger, New York and London.

Rodgers, R. C. and Hunter, J. E. (1986), 'The impact of management by objectives on organizational productivity', cited by J. E. Hunter and H. R. Hirsch (1987).

Roe, A. (1964), 'Personality structure and occupational behavior', *in* H. Borow (ed.), *Man in a World of Work*, Houghton Mifflin, Boston.

Roethlisberger, F. J. and Dickson, W. J. (1939), *Management and the Worker*, Harvard University Press, Cambridge, Massachusetts.

Rose, R. (1983), *Getting by in Three Economies*, Centre for the Study of Public Policy, University of Strathclyde, Glasgow.

Rosenberg, M. (1957), *Occupations and Values*, Free Press, Glencoe, Illinois.

Rosse, J. G. and Miller, H. E. (1984), 'Relationship between absenteeism and other variables', *in* P. S. Goodman, R. S. Atkin and Associates (eds.), *Absenteeism*, Jossey-Bass, San Francisco.

Rotter, J. B. (1966), 'Generalised expectancies for internal versus external locus of control of reinforcement', *Psychological Monographs*, **80**.

Roy, D. (1955), 'Efficiency and "the fix": informal intergroup relations in a piece-work machine shop', *American Journal of Sociology*, **60**, 255–66.

— (1959), 'Banana time: job satisfaction and informal interaction', *Human Organization*, **18**, 158–68.

Runciman, W. G. (1966), *Relative Deprivation and Social Justice*, Routledge & Kegan Paul, London.

Runyon, W. (1978), 'The life course as a theoretical orientation: sequences of person–situation interaction', *Journal of Psychiatry*, **46**, 569–93.

Rusbult, C. E. and Farrell, D. (1983), 'A longitudinal test of the investment model: the impact on job satisfaction, job commitment, and turnover of variations in rewards and costs, alternatives and outcome', *Journal of Applied Psychology*, **68**, 429–38.

Rushing, W. A. (1966), 'Organizational size, rules, and surveillance', *Journal of Experimental Social Psychology*, **2**, 11–26.

Salancik, G. R. (1977), 'Commitment and the control of organizational behavior and belief', *in* B. M. Staw and G. R. Salancik (eds.), *New Directions in Organizational Behavior*, St Clair Press, Chicago.

Salancik, G. R. and Pfeffer, J. (1977), 'An examination of need–satisfaction models of job attitudes', *Administrative Science Quarterly*, **22**, 427–56.

— (1978), 'A social information processing approach to job attitudes and job design', *Administrative Science Quarterly*, **23**, 224–53.

Sales, S. M. and House, J. (1971), 'Job dissatisfaction as a possible risk factor in coronary heart disease', *Journal of Chronic Diseases*, **23**, 861–73.

Sayles, L. R. and Strauss, G. (1966), *Human Behavior in Organizations*, Prentice-Hall, Englewood Cliffs, New Jersey.

Scanlon, J. N. (1948), 'Profit-sharing under collective bargaining: three-case studies', *Industrial and Labour Relations Review*, **2**, 58–75.

Scheflen, K., Lawler, E. and Hackman, J. (1971), 'Long term impacts of employee participation in the development of pay incentive plans: a field experiment revisited', *Journal of Applied Psychology*, **55**, 182–6.

Schein, E. H. (1978), *Career Dynamics: Matching Individual and Organizational Needs*, Addison-Wesley, Reading, Massachusetts.

— (1981), 'Does Japanese management style have a message for American managers?', *Sloan Management Review*, autumn issue, 55–68.

Schermerhorn, J. R., Hunt, J. G. and Osborn, R. N. (1985), *Managing Organizational Behavior*, Wiley, New York.

Schmidt, F. L., Hunter, J. E., Croll, P. R. and McKenzie, R. C. (1983), 'Estimation of employment test validities by expert judgement', *Journal of Applied Psychology*, **68**, 590–601.

Schmidt, F. L., Hunter, J. E., McKenzie, R. C. and Muldrow, T. W. (1979), 'Impact of valid selection procedures on work-force productivity', *Journal of Applied Psychology*, **64**, 609–26.

Schmidt, F. L., Hunter, J. E. and Pearlmen, K. (1982), 'Assessing the economic impact of personnel programs on workforce productivity', *Personnel Psychology*, **35**, 333–47.

Schmitt, N. and Bedeian, A. G. (1982), 'A comparison of LISREL and two-stage least squares analysis of a hypothesised life–job satisfaction reciprocal relationship', *Journal of Applied Psychology*, **67**, 806–17.

Schmitt, N., Gooding, R. Z., Noe, R. D. and Kirsch, M. (1984), 'Meta-analyses of validity studies published between 1964 and 1982 and the investigation of study characteristics', *Personnel Psychology*, **37**, 407–22.

Schmitt, N. and Noe, R. (1986), 'Personnel selection and equal opportunity employment', *in* C. L. Cooper and I. T. Robertson (eds.), *International Review of Industrial and Organizational Psychology 1986*, Wiley, Chichester.

Schmitt, N., White, J. K., Coyle, B. W. and Rauschenberger, J. (1979), 'Retirement and life satisfaction', *Academy of Management Journal*, 22, 282–91.

Schriesheim, C. A. (1978), 'Job satisfaction, attitudes towards unions, and voting in a union representation election', *Journal of Applied Psychology*, 61, 548–52.

Schriesheim, C. A. and Hosking, D. (1978), review essay of Fiedler, F. E., Chemers, M. M. and Mahar, L. 'Improving leadership effectiveness: the leader match concept', *Administrative Science Quarterly*, 23, 496–505.

Schuchman, A. (1957), *Codetermination: Labor's Middle Way in Germany*, Public Affairs Press, Washington.

Schultz, D. P. (1982), *Psychology and Industry Today*, Collier Macmillan, London.

Schwab, D. P., Olian-Gottlieb, J. D. and Heneman, H. G. (1979), 'Between subjects expectancy theory research: a statistical review of studies predicting effort and performance', *Psychological Bulletin*, 86, 139–47.

Scott, W. D., Clothier, R. C. and Spriegel, W. R. (1960), *Personal Management*, McGraw-Hill, New York.

Seashore, S. E. (1954), *Group Cohesiveness in the Industrial Work Group*, Institute for Social Research, University of Michigan, Ann Arbor, Michigan.

Seashore, S. E., Indik, B. P. and Georgopoulos, B. S. (1960), 'Relationship among criteria of job performance', *Journal of Applied Psychology*, 44, 195–202.

Shaffer, G. S. (1987), 'Patterns of work and nonwork satisfaction', *Journal of Applied Psychology*, 72, 115–24.

Shaw, A. G. and Pirie, D. S. (1982), 'Payment by time systems', *in* A. M. Bowey (ed.), *Handbook of Salary and Wage Systems*, Gower, Aldershot.

Shaw, M. E. (1981), *Group Dynamics*, 3rd edn, McGraw-Hill, New York.

Shikiar, R. and Freudenberg, R. (1982), 'Unemployment rates as a moderator of the job dissatisfaction-turnover relation', *Human Relations*, 10, 845–56.

Shirom, A., Eden, D., Silberwasser, S. and Kellerman, J. J. (1973), 'Job stresses and risk factors in coronary heart disease among occupational categories in Kibbutzim', *Social Science and Medicine*, 7, 875–92.

Short, J., Williams, E. and Christie, B. (1976), *The Social Psychology of Telecommunications*, Wiley, Chichester.

Shostak, A. B. (1982), 'Work meanings through Western history: from Athens to Detroit and beyond', *in* S. H. Akabas and P. A. Kurzman (eds.), *Work, Workers, and Work Organizations*, Prentice-Hall, Englewood Cliffs, New Jersey.

Sidney, E. and Argyle, M. (1969), *Selection Interviewing*; films and training kit distributed by Mantra Ltd.

Siegel, J., Dubrovsky, V., Kiesler, S. and McGuire, T. W. (1986), 'Group processes in computer-mediated communication', *Organizational Behavior and Human Decision Processes*, 37, 157–87.

Smith, B. B. (n.d.), *Evaluating a Leadership Training Program*, Kepner-Tregoe, Princeton, New Jersey.

Smith, P. B. (1984), 'The effectiveness of Japanese styles of management: a review and critique', *Journal of Occupational Psychology*, 57, 121–36.

Smith, P. C., Kendall, L. M. and Hulin, C. L. (1969), *The Measurement of Satisfaction in Work and Retirement*, Rand McNally, Chicago.

Smith, R. (1985–6), 'Occupationless health', *British Medical Journal* (11 articles), 12 October–25 January.

Social Trends (1982–7), vols. 12–17, HMSO, London.

Sofer, C. (1970), *Men in Mid-Career*, Cambridge University Press, Cambridge.

Spector, P. E. (1985), 'Higher-order need strength as a moderator of the job scope–employee outcome relationship: a meta analysis', *Journal of Occupational Psychology*, 58, 119–27.

— (1986), 'Perceived control by employees: a meta-analysis of studies concerning autonomy and participation at work', *Human Relations*, 11, 1005–16.

Spence, J. T. and Helmreich, R. L. (1983), 'Achievement-related motives and behaviors', *in* J. T. Spence (ed.), *Achievement and Achievement Motivation*, W. H. Freeman, San Francisco.

Spencer, D. G. (1986), 'Employee voice and employee retention', *Academy of Management Journal*, 29, 488–502.

Stafford, E. M., Jackson, P. R. and Banks, M. H. (1980), 'Employment, work involvement and mental health in less qualified young people', *Journal of Occupational Psychology*, 53, 291–304.

Stebbins, R. A. (1979), *Amateurs*, Sage, Beverly Hills.

Steers, R. M. (1975), 'Effect of need achievement on the job performance–job attitude relationship', *Journal of Applied Psychology*, 60, 678–82.

Steers, R. M. and Rhodes, S. R. (1984), 'Knowledge and speculation about absenteeism', *in* P. S. Goodman, R. S. Atkin and Associates (eds.), *Absenteeism*, Jossey-Bass, San Francisco.

Stephan, W. G. (1985), 'Intergroup relations', *in* G. Lindzey and E.

Aronson (eds.), *Handbook of Social Psychology* (3rd edn), vol. 2, Random House, New York.

Stewart, R. (1967), *Managers and their Jobs*, Macmillan, London.

— (1976), *Contrasts in Management*, MacGraw-Hill, London.

Stokols, D., Novaco, R. W., Stokols, J. and Campbell, J. (1978), 'Traffic congestion, Type A behavior, and stress', *Journal of Applied Psychology*, 63, 467–80.

Stonier, T. (1983), *The Wealth of Information*, Methuen, London.

Suinn, R. M. (1982), 'Intervention with Type A behaviors', *Journal of Consulting and Clinical Psychology*, 50, 933–49.

Sundstrom, E. (1986), *Work Places*, Cambridge University Press, Cambridge.

Super, D. E. (1957), *The Psychology of Careers*, Harper, New York.

Super, D. E. and Overstreet, P. L. (1960), *The Vocational Maturity of Ninth-grade Boys*, Bureau of Publications, Teachers' College, Columbia University, New York.

Tajfel, H. (1978), *Differentiation between Social Groups*, Academic Press, London.

Tanaka, H. (1980), 'The Japanese method of preparing today's graduate to become tomorrow's manager', *Personnel Journal*, 59, 109–12.

Tavris, C. and Offir, C. (1977), *The Longest War*, Harcourt Brace Jovanovich, New York.

Tawney, R. H. (1926), *Religion and the Rise of Capitalism*, Penguin Books, Harmondsworth.

Taylor, D. W., Berry, P. C. and Block, C. H. (1958), 'Does group participation when using brainstorming facilitate or inhibit thinking?', *Administrative Science Quarterly*, 3, 23–47.

Taylor, F. W. (1911, 1947), *Scientific Management*, Harper, New York.

Taylor, M. (1979), *Coverdale on Management*, Heinemann, London.

Temporal, P. (1984), 'Helping self-development to happen', *in* C. Cox and J. Beck (eds.), *Management Development*, Wiley, Chichester.

Tharenou, P. (1979), 'Employee self-esteem: a review of the literature', *Journal of Vocational Behavior*, 15, 316–46.

Thomas, E. J. and Fink, C. F. (1963), 'Effects of group size', *Psychological Bulletin*, 60, 371–84.

Thomas, J. and Griffin, R. (1983), 'The social information processing model of task design: a review of the literature', *Academy of Management Review*, 8, 672–82.

Thomas, K. (1964), 'Work and leisure in pre-industrial society', *Past and Present*, 29, 50–66.

Thorndike, R. L. and Hagen, E. (1959), *Ten Thousand Careers*, Wiley, New York.

Thurley, K. and Wirdenius, H. (1973), *Supervision: a Reappraisal*, Heinemann, London.

Tiger, L. (1969), *Men in Groups*, Nelson, London.

Tiggemann, M. and Winefield, A. H. (1984), 'The effects of unemployment on the mood, self-esteem, locus of control, and depressive affect of school leavers', *Journal of Occupational Psychology*, **57**, 33–42.

The Times, Japan's golden combination, Sept. 29th (1969).

Tjoswold, D. (1985), 'Power and social context in superior–subordinate interaction', *Organizational Behavior and Human Decision Processes*, **35**, 281–93.

Tjoswold, D., Wedley, W. C. and Field, R. H. G. (1986), 'Constructive controversy, the Vroom-Yetton model, and managerial decision-taking', *Journal of Occupational Behaviour*, **7**, 125–38.

Trist, E. L., Higgin, G. W., Murray, H. and Pollock, A. B. (1963), *Organizational Choice*, Tavistock, London.

Tubbs, M. E. (1986), 'Goal-setting: a meta-analytic examination of the empirical evidence', *Journal of Applied Psychology*, **71**, 474–83.

Turner, A. N. and Lawrence, P. (1966), *Industrial Jobs and the Worker*, Harvard Graduate School of Business Administration, Cambridge, Massachusetts.

Tziner, A. (1983), 'Correspondence between occupational rewards and occupational needs and work satisfaction: a canonical redundancy analysis', *Journal of Occupational Psychology*, **56**, 49–56.

Tziner, A. and Eden, D. (1985), 'Effects of crew composition on crew performance: does the whole equal the sum of its parts?', *Journal of Applied Psychology*, **70**, 85–93.

Udy, S. H. (1959), *The Organization of Work*, Human Relations Area Files, New Haven.

Ulrich, L. and Trumbo, D. (1965), 'The selection interview since 1949', *Psychological Bulletin*, **63**, 100–116.

Urwick, L. (1929), *The Meaning of Rationalisation*, Nisbet, London.

Van de Vliert, E. (1984), 'Conflict-prevention and escalation', *in* P. J. D. Drenth *et al.* (eds.), *Handbook of Work and Organizational Psychology*, Wiley, Chichester.

Van Dijkhuizen, N. (1981), 'Towards organizational coping with stress', *in* J. Marshall and C. L. Cooper (eds.), *Coping with Stress at Work*, Gower, Andover.

Van Harrison, R. (1978), 'Person–environment fit and job stress', *in* C. L. Cooper and R. Payne (eds.), *Stress at Work*, Wiley, Chichester.

Van Zelst, R. H. (1951), 'Worker popularity and job satisfaction', *Personnel Psychology*, **4**, 405–12.

— (1952), 'Validation of a sociometric regrouping procedure', *Journal of Abnormal and Social Psychology*, **47**, 299–301.

Vecchio, R. P. (1981), 'An individual-differences interpretation of the conflicting predictions generated by equity theory and expectancy theory', *Journal of Applied Psychology*, **66**, 470–81.

— (1985), 'Predicting employee turnover from leader-member exchange: a failure to replicate', *Academy of Management Journal*, **28**, 478–85.

Veen, P. (1984a), 'Characteristics of organizations', *in* P. J. D. Drenth *et al.* (eds.), *Handbook of Work and Organizational Psychology*, Wiley, Chichester.

— (1984b), 'Organization theories', *in* P. J. D. Drenth *et al.* (eds.), *Handbook of Work and Organizational Psychology*, Wiley, Chichester.

Veness, T. (1962), *School Leavers*, Methuen, London.

Vernon, P. E. (1950), 'The validation of Civil Service Selection Board procedures', *Occupational Psychology*, **24**, 75–95.

— (1964), *Personality Assessment*, Methuen, London.

Veroff, J., Douvan, E. and Kulka, R. A. (1981), *The Inner American*, Basic Books, New York.

Viteles, M. S. (1954), *Motivation and Morale in Industry*, Staples, London.

Vroom, V. H. (1960), *Some Personality Determinants of the Effects of Participation*, Prentice-Hall, Englewood Cliffs, New Jersey.

— (1964), *Work and Motivation*, Wiley, New York.

Vroom, V. H., Grant, L. D. and Cotton, T. S. (1969), 'The consequences of social interaction in group problem-solving', *Organizational Behavior and Human Performance*, **4**, 77–95.

Vroom, V. H. and Jago, A. G. (1978), 'On the validity of the Vroom-Yetton model', *Journal of Applied Psychology*, **63**, 151–62.

Vroom, V. H. and Yetton, P. W. (1973), *Leadership and Decision-making*, University of Pittsburgh Press, Pittsburgh.

Walker, C. R. and Guest, R. H. (1952), *The Man on the Assembly Line*, Harvard University Press, Cambridge, Massachusetts.

Wall, T. D. and Clegg, C. W. (1981), 'A longitudinal study of group work redesign', *Journal of Occupational Behaviour*, **2**, 31–49.

Wall, T. D., Clegg, C. W. and Jackson, D. R. (1978), 'An evaluation of the job characteristics model', *Journal of Occupational Psychology*, **51**, 183–96.

Wall, T. D., Kemp, N. J., Jackson, P. R. and Clegg, C. W. (1986), 'Outcomes of autonomous workgroups: a long-term field experiment', *Academy of Management Journal*, **29**, 280–304.

Wall, T. D. and Lischeron, J. A. (1977), *Worker Participation*, McGraw-Hill, London.

Wall, T. D. and Martin, R. (1987), 'Job and work design', *in* C. L. Cooper and I. T. Robertson (eds.), *International Review of Industrial and Organizational Psychology 1987*, Wiley, Chichester.

Wall, T. D., Stephenson, G. M. and Skidmore, C. (1971), 'Ego-involvement and Herzberg's two-factor theory of job satisfaction: an experimental field study', *British Journal of Social and Clinical Psychology*, **10**, 123–31.

Warnous, J. P. (1980), *Organizational Entry: Recruitment, Selection and Socialization of Newcomers*, Addison-Wesley, Reading, Massachusetts.

Warr, P. B. (1978), 'A study of psychological well-being', *British Journal of Psychology*, **69**, 111–21.

— (1982), 'A national study of non-financial employment commitment', *Journal of Occupational Psychology*, **55**, 297–312.

— (1983), 'Job loss, unemployment and psychological well-being', *in* E. van de Vliert and V. Allen (eds.), *Role Transitions*, Plenum, New York.

— (1984), 'Work and unemployment', *in* P. J. D. Drenth *et al.* (eds.), *Handbook of Work and Organizational Psychology*, Wiley, Chichester.

— (1987), *Work, Unemployment, and Mental Health*, Clarendon Press, Oxford.

Warr, P. B., Cook, J. and Wall, T. D. (1979), 'Scales for the measurement of some work attitudes and aspects of well-being', *Journal of Occupational Psychology*, **52**, 129–48.

Warr, P. B. and Jackson, P. R. (1984), 'Men without jobs: some correlations of age and length of unemployment', *Journal of Occupational Psychology*, **57**, 77–85.

— (1985), 'Factors influencing the psychological impact of prolonged unemployment and of re-employment', *Psychological Medicine*, **15**, 795–807.

Warr, P. B. and Payne, R. (1982), 'Experience of strain and pleasure among British adults', *Social Science and Medicine*, **16**, 1691–7.

— (1983), 'Social class and reported changes in behavior after job loss', *Journal of Applied Psychology*, **13**, 206–22.

Warr, P. B. and Routledge, T. (1969), 'An opinion scale for the study of managers' job satisfaction', *Occupational Psychology*, **43**, 95–109.

Watts, A. G. (1983), *Education, Unemployment and the Future of Work*, Open University Press, Milton Keynes.

Weaver, C. N. (1980), 'Job satisfaction in the United States in the 1970s', *Journal of Applied Psychology*, **65**, 364–7.

Webber, R. A. (1974), 'The relationship of group performance to the age of members in homogeneous groups', *Academy of Management Journal*, **17**, 570–4.

Weber, M. (1904), *The Protestant Ethic and the Spirit of Capitalism*, Scribner, New York.

— (1923), *General Economic History*, Allen & Unwin, London.

Webster, E. C. (1964), *Decision-making in the Employment Interview*, McGill University Industrial Relations Centre, Montreal.

— (1982), *The Employment Interview*, SIP Publications, Schomberg, Ontario.

Werts, C. E. (1968), 'Parental influence on career choice', *Journal of Counseling Psychology*, **15**, 48–52.

Wexley, K. N. (1984), 'Personnel training', *Annual Review of Psychology*, **35**, 519–51.

Wexley, K. N. and Latham, G. P. (1981), *Developing and Training Human Resources in Organizations*, Scott, Foresman & Co., Glenview, Illinois.

White, M. and Trevor, M. (1983), *Under Japanese Management*, Heinemann, London.

Whitehill, A. M. and Tazekawa, S. (1961), *Cultural Values in Management–Worker Relations: Gimu in Transition*, University of North Carolina School of Business Administration, North Carolina.

— (1968), *The Other Worker*, East–West Center Press, Honolulu.

Whitehorn, C. (1984), 'Whistle while you work', *Observer* colour supplement, 21 October, 91–2.

Whyte, W. F. (1948), *Human Relations in the Restaurant Industry*, McGraw-Hill, New York.

— (1957), *The Organization Man*, Simon & Schuster, New York and Penguin Books, Harmondsworth.

Wilkins, L. T. (1950–51), 'Incentives and the young male worker', *International Journal of Opinion and Attitude Research*, **4**, 540–61.

Williams, L. J. and Hazer, J. T. (1986), 'Antecedents and consequences of satisfaction and commitment in turnover models: a reanalysis using latent variable structural equations', *Journal of Applied Psychology*, **71**, 219–31.

Wilson, J. R. and Rutherford, A. (1987), 'Human interfaces with advanced manufacturing processes', *in* C. L. Cooper and I. T. Robertson (eds.), *International Review of Industrial and Organizational Psychology 1987*, Wiley, Chichester.

Wish, M., Deutsch, M. and Kaplan, S. J. (1976), 'Perceived dimensions of interpersonal relations', *Journal of Personality and Social Psychology*, 33, 409–20.

Wolpin, J. and Burke, R. J. (1985), 'Relationships between absenteeism and turnover: a function of the measures?', *Personnel Psychology*, 38, 57–74.

Woodman, R. W. and Sherwood, J. J. (1980), 'The role of team development in organizational effectiveness: a critical review', *Psychological Bulletin*, 88, 166–86.

Woodward, J. (1965), *Industrial Organization: Theory and Practice*, Oxford University Press, Oxford.

Wyatt. S. (1934), *Incentives in Repetitive Work*, Industrial Health Research Board, Report No. 69, HMSO, London.

Yoder, D. and Staudohar, P. D. (1982), *Personnel Management and Industrial Relations*, Prentice-Hall, Englewood Cliffs, New Jersey.

Young, M. and Wilmott, P. (1973), *The Symmetrical Family*, Routledge & Kegan Paul, London.

Zajonc, R. B. (1965), 'Social facilitation', *Science*, 149, 269–74.

Zimbardo, P. G. (1973), 'A Pirandellian prison', *The New York Times Sunday Magazine*, 8 April, 38–60.

AUTHOR INDEX

Abegglen, J. C.   328, 329, 331, 332
Ackrill, M.   26
Action Society Trust   211
Adelmann, P. K.   244
Adsit, L.   95
Albrecht, P. A.   73
Albright, L. E.   83
Alderfer, C.   56
Alfredsson, L.   266
Allen, G. C.   328
Allen, P. T.   135, 142
Allen, V. L.   217
Andrews, F. M.   247
Andreissen, E. J. H.   223
Andrisani, P. J.   59
Anthony, P. D.   17
Appley, M. H.   87, 105
Argyle, M.   40, 57, 59, 69, 116, 118, 126–7, 128, 129, 138, 139, 140, 149, 151, 153–4, 155, 156, 157, 172, 176, 188, 190, 196, 207, 233, 236, 238, 242, 243, 244, 248, 264, 277, 281, 295, 315, 317, 318, 320, 321
Argyris, C.   208–9
Armstrong, P. J.   309
Arnold, H. J.   137, 141, 144, 146
Arvey, R. D.   98
Athos, A. G.   330, 332
Atkin, P. S.   255
Atkinson, J. W.   67

Atkinson, J. W.   292
Austin, W.   97

Babbage, C.   30
Babchuck, N.   90
Badin, I. J.   162
Bain, T.   67
Bales, R. F.   198
Bammel, G.   319
Bammel, L. L. B.   319
Banks, M. H.   286, 291, 292
Baron, R. A.   56, 86, 96, 111, 162, 219, 220, 260, 268
Bass, B. M.   158, 159, 161, 163, 167, 190, 193, 205, 206, 217, 230
Bateman, T. S.   110, 245, 246, 248, 256
Batstone, E.   141, 217, 218
Baumgartel, H. J.   120, 186, 257
Bazerman, M. H.   180, 188
Beals, R. L.   10
Bechofer, F.   56, 125–6, 134, 240, 241
Beck, A. T.   274
Bedeian, A. G.   247
Beehr, T. A.   172, 301, 304, 305
Begalla, M. E.   98
Behrend, H.   250
Bendix, R.   23, 25
Bennett, J. W.   332
Benson, H.   278
Berkman, L. F.   275

Berkowitz, L. 239
Berman, F. E. 104
Berry, D. C. 312
Berry, P. C. 144
Beveridge, W. E. 304
Bhagat, P. S. 245
Bingham, W. V. 108
Birch, F. 301
Blackler, F. 311
Blake, R. R. 162, 221
Blankenship, L. V. 166
Blau, P. M. 131, 140, 205
Blauner, R. 45, 234, 237
Block, C. H. 144
Blood, M. R. 167, 236
Blumberg, P. 222, 224, 225, 231
Bond, M. J. 291
Boot, R. 194
Booth-Kewley, S. 280
Boraston, I. 141, 217, 218
Boulian, P. 110
Bower, G. H. 192
Bower, S. A. 192
Boyatzis, R. E. 55, 102–3
Brayfield, A. H. 244
Brenner, M. H. 294
Broadbent, D. E. 262, 265, 279,
312
Brockner, J. 95
Brown, C. 252, 253, 254, 311
Brown, G. W. 260, 296
Brown, Roger 19, 20
Brown, Rupert 141, 142
Brown, W. 217
Bruning, N. S. 280
Buck, R. 103
Bull, R. 190
Burgess, P. 153
Burke, M. J. 185
Burke, R. J. 253, 271, 279, 281,
283
Burns, T. 47, 138, 212, 213
Burrows, R. 265

Cameron, D. 91
Campbell, A. 244, 246, 288, 289,
303, 306

Campbell, D. P. 68
Campbell, J. 268
Campbell, J. P. 87, 193
Cantril, H. 93
Caplan, R. D. 242, 246, 261, 262–
3, 265, 268, 271, 273, 274, 275,
276, 278
Caplow, T. 242
Carlisle, J. 180
Carroll, S. I. 166
Carruthers, M. 267
Carsten, J. M. 256
Cartwright, L. K. 269
Cascio, W. F. 256
Catalano, R. 293
Cavender, J. W. 244
Centers, R. 93
Chacko, T. I. 247
Chadwick-Jones, J. 251, 252, 253,
254
Chao, G. T. 76
Chapanis, A. R. E. 37
Chapple, E. D. 47–8
Charney, C. 226
Chatterjee, B. B. 190
Chell, F. 55
Chemers, M. M. 158
Cherns, A. B. 35
Chesney, M. A. 271
Child, J. 49, 156, 157, 210, 212,
213, 214, 312
Chiu, J. S. L. 226
Christie, B. 51
Cioffi, F. 149, 190
Clark, R. D. 147
Clegg, C. W. 245, 251, 284
Clothier, R. C. 89, 257
Clutterbuck, D. 51, 310, 313
Cobb, S. 242, 262–3, 265, 268,
271, 273, 274, 275, 276, 278,
294, 296
Coch, L. 231
Cochran, S. 239
Coetsier, P. L. 223
Cofer, C. N. 87, 105
Condor, S. 141–2
Consentino, J. 108

Constable, J. 184
Converse, P. E. 244, 246, 289, 303
Cook, J. 236
Cook, J. D. 234, 293
Cooper, C. L. 118, 246, 262–3, 265, 266, 277, 282, 284
Cowen, E. L. 242, 278
Cox, J. F. 226
Cox, T. 267
Coyle, B. W. 304
Crocker, O. L. 226
Crockett, W. H. 244
Croll, P. R. 77
Crossland, J. 236
Crouch, A. 162
Csikszentmihalyi, M. 236, 237, 319, 320
Cunnington, B. 55
Curran, J. 265
Curtis, M. I. 109
Cyert, R. M. 201, 204

Dahrendorf, R. 216
Davenport, P. R. 293
Davidson, M. A. 65
Davies, R. 288, 293
Davis, J. H. 69
Davis, L. E. 35
Davison, J. P. 89
Dawson, S. 46, 214, 215
Day, R. R. 185
Deci, E. L. 100
de Jong, J. R. 173
de Jong, R. D. 162
Denney, R. 64
Dess, G. G. 214
Deutsch, M. 125, 155
de Wolff, C. J. 77–8
Dickinson, J. 97
Dickson, W. J. 115–17, 137, 150, 207
Dion, K. K. 69
Dooley, D. 293
Dore, R. 330, 332, 333
Douvan, E. 112, 316
Drucker, P. F. 220

Dubin, R. 30
Dubrovsky, V. 50
Duchon, D. 165
Dunnette, M. D. 73, 193
Dunnette, M. S. 74

Earley, P. C. 109
Eckhardt, B. 292
Eden, D. 123, 268
Edholm, O. G. 23
Eisenstadt, S. N. 17
Elder, E. H. 62, 66
Ellis, R. A. 59
Emery, F. E. 231
Emler, N. 97
Erikson, E. H. 60, 62
Etzioni, A. 109, 113, 199
Evandrou, M. 265
Evans, C. E. 243
Eysenck, H. J. 67, 100

Falkenburg, L. E. 281
Farr, J. L. 174
Farrell, D. 110, 258
Farris, G. F. 138
Faucheux, C. 45
Feather, N. T. 291, 292, 293
Feld, S. 237
Feldman, D. C. 137, 141, 144, 146
Ferris, G. R. 236
Fiedler, F. E. 3, 158, 164, 167, 190
Field, R. H. G. 164
Fink, C. F. 147
Finlay-Jones, B. 292
Fischman, J. 271
Fisher, C. D. 100
Fitzgerald, M. P. 235, 236
Fleishman, E. A. 54, 149–50, 159–61
Forbes, R. J. 172
Ford, J. D. 204
Fottler, M. D. 67
Fox, A. 26, 216
Fox, A. J. 294
Francis, A. 311
Francis, C. 44

Frankel, B. 309, 313
Fraser, C. 239
Fraser, R. 251
French, E. G. 54, 108
French, J. R. P. 173–4, 231, 242, 246, 261, 262–3, 265, 268, 271, 273, 274
Frenkel, S. 141, 217, 218
Frese, M. 50
Freudenberg, R. 257
Frew, D. R. 280
Fried, Y. 236
Friedlander, F. 140
Friedman, H. S. 280
Friedmann, G. 31
Fryer, D. 285, 286, 295, 296, 297, 300
Furneaux, W. D. 77
Furnham, A. 64, 93–4, 111, 112, 154, 156

Gabarro, J. J. 125
Gage, N. L. 190
Gaines, J. 270
Ganster, D. C. 279, 280
Garcia, J. E. 164
Gardell, B. 261
Gardner, G. 149, 190
Garfinkel, L. 281
Garrett, J. 111
Georgopoulos, B. S. 73, 104
Gershunny, J. I. 313
Gilbreth, F. B. 31
Gill, C. 36, 48, 49, 307, 308, 311
Gilmore, D. C. 172
Ginsberg, M. 11
Ginzberg, E. 60, 61
Glaser, E. M. 73
Glass, D. C. 271
Glazer, N. 64
Glennon, J. R. 83
Goffman, E. 120, 201
Goldberg, D. 262, 291
Goldsen, R. K. 68
Goldstein, A. P. 186, 187, 192
Goldthorpe, J. H. 56, 125–6, 134, 240, 241

Goode, W. J. 90
Gooding, R. Z. 76, 85, 211
Goodman, P. S. 99, 255
Gordon, M. E. 209
Graen, G. B. 100, 164
Graen, M. R. 100, 164
Graham, J. A. 154
Green, S. G. 165
Greenberg, J. 95, 98, 111
Greenglass, E. R. 271
Greenhalgh, L. 181
Grice, H. P. 153
Griffin, R. 249
Griffin, R. W. 110, 248, 256
Griffith, R. 256, 257, 258
Griffith, R. W. 258
Grove, E. A. 239
Grover, R. A. 161
Gruneberg, M. M. 244, 252
Guest, D. E. 219
Guest, R. H. 32, 266
Guion, R. M. 251
Gurin, G. 237
Guzzo, R. 89, 101, 218, 220

Hackett, R. D. 251
Hackman, J. R. 33–4, 55, 89, 100–101, 112, 146, 235, 236, 248, 256
Hagen, E. 66
Haire, M. 217
Haldeman, J. 44
Hale, M. 82
Hall, D. T. 64, 66
Hall, J. G. 273
Halpin, A. W. 159, 162
Hamill, L. 288
Hand, H. 256
Handy, C. 184, 310, 311, 313, 314
Harbison, F. 333
Hariton, T. 175
Harkins, S. 119
Harris, E. F. 149–50
Harris, T. 260, 296
Harrison, G. A. 264
Hartley, J. 215, 216, 218

Haw, A. H. 261
Hazer, J. T. 256
Hazewinkel, A. 213
Headey, B. 243
Hegarty, W. H. 204
Heinecke, C. 196
Helmreich, R. L. 103
Henderson, M. 69, 118, 126–7, 129, 157, 196, 242, 277
Heneman, H. G. 87
Henne, D. 100, 102
Hepworth, S. J. 234, 293
Herzberg, F. 3, 100, 104, 236, 240, 242, 247–8, 323
Hespe, G. W. A. 232
Hewitt, D. 135
Hickson, D. J. 47, 212
Hill, R. 51, 310, 313
Himmelweit, H. 66
Hinings, C. R. 212
Hirsch, H. R. 73, 79, 235, 255, 259
Hobert, R. D. 77
Hobhouse, L. T. 11
Hoffman, L. R. 177–8
Hofstede, G. 332
Hoijer, A. 10
Holland, J. L. 68, 274
Hollander, E. P. 138, 161, 163
Holmes, T. H. 304
Hom, P. W. 258
Homans, G. C. 124
Hoppock, R. 233
Horncastle, P. 190
Hosking, D. 158
Hosking, D. M. 180
House, J. 238, 246, 264
House, J. S. 275, 276, 283
House, R. J. 162
Huber, V. L. 161
Hudson, L. 64
Hulin, C. L. 234, 236
Humble, J. W. 167
Hunt, J. G. 245
Hunt, R. G. 247
Hunter, J. E. 73, 76, 77, 79, 82, 83, 85, 220, 235, 255, 259

Hunter, R. F. 76, 82, 83, 85
Hutchins, D. 226
Hutt, C. 65

Iaffaldano, M. T. 244
Ilgen, D. 72, 87, 89, 98
Indik, B. P. 73
Ingram, J. K. 15
Ishino, I. 332
Ivancevich, J. M. 220, 251, 273

Jablin, F. M. 132
Jackson, D. R. 245
Jackson, J. 121
Jackson, J. H. 175
Jackson, P. R. 172, 286, 291, 292, 295, 296
Jackson, R. 293
Jackson, S. E. 202–3, 269, 270
Jago, A. G. 164
Jahoda, M. 235, 286, 299
James, L. R. 236
Janis, I. L. 145
Janman, K. 65, 69
Janson, R. 33–4, 244
Jaques, E. 99
Jarrett, J. 286, 295
Jasso, G. 97
Jemmott, J. B. 276
Jenner, D. A. 264
Jerdee, T. H. 166
Jermier, J. M. 270
Jette, R. D. 89, 101, 218, 220
Johns, G. 252
Johnson, D. W. 119
Johnson, R. 119
Jones, D. R. 294
Jones, K. W. 268
Jones, N. W. 104
Jorgenson, D. O. 95, 96

Kahn, R. L. 120, 202, 225, 268, 272
Kalleberg, A. L. 244
Kanfer, R. 109
Kaplan, E. M. 242, 278
Kaplan, S. J. 125, 155

Karasek, R. A.   261, 265
Kasl, S. V.   246, 260, 265, 267, 294, 296, 303, 305, 306
Katz, D.   120, 225
Katzell, R. A.   89, 101, 218, 220
Kay, E.   173-4
Keaveny, T. J.   175
Keller, R. T.   119
Kellerman, J. J.   268
Kelly, J. E.   31, 32-3, 44, 45, 256
Kelvin, P.   286, 295, 298
Kendall, L. M.   234
Kendall, P. L.   63
Kerr, W. A.   239
Kets de Vries, M.   55
Kiesler, S.   50
Kilmann, R. H.   122
Kirchner, W. K.   73
Kirsch, M.   76, 85
Klimoski, R. J.   83
Kluckhohn, C.   9
Knowles, K. G. J. C.   216
Kobasa, S. C.   272
Kohn, M. L.   59
Kolaja, J.   224
Komaki, J. L.   160
Kondrasuk, J. N.   220
Koppelaar, L.   162
Kornhauser, A.   263
Kubey, R.   320
Kulka, R. A.   112, 316

La Laseau, V. N.   243
Lalljee, M.   151, 190
Landsberger, H. A.   130
Landy, F. J.   174, 251
Latané, B.   119
Latham, G. P.   186, 189, 190, 255
Lawler, E.   89
Lawler, E. E.   146, 238
Lawrence, P.   34
Lawrence, P. R.   213
Layard, R.   309, 310
Lazarsfeld, P. F.   286
Lesieur, F. S.   92, 226
Lew, E. A.   281
Lewis, A.   292

Liem, R.   292
Likert, R.   148-9, 160, 207, 208
Lindell, J.   261
Lischeron, J. A.   227-30
Little, A. J.   232
Litwin, G. H.   122
Locke, E. A.   100, 102, 105, 236, 242, 245, 249
Locke, S. E.   276, 277
Lockwood, D.   56, 125-6, 134, 240, 241
Loher, B. T.   235, 236
Lorsch, J. W.   213
Loscocco, K. A.   244
Love, K. G.   172
Lupton, T.   90, 91
Luthans, F.   101
Lydall, M.   151, 190

Maas, A.   147
MacArthur, R.   55
McClelland, D. C.   15, 20-22, 55, 62, 67, 102-3
McCormick, E. J.   72, 87, 89
McCormick, R.   184
MacCrimmon, K. R.   201, 204
McEvoy, G. M.   256
McGee, G. W.   244
McGinn, N. C.   97
McGoldrick, A.   301
McGregor, D.   3, 168, 174
McGuire, T. W.   50
McGuire, W. J.   181
Macholowitz, M.   111
McIntyre, D.   64, 70
MacKay, C.   266
McKenzie, R. C.   77, 79
McShane, S. L.   251
Mahoney, G. M.   104
Mahoney, T. A.   166
Maier, N. R. F.   173, 177-8
Makin, P. J.   85
Mangoine, T. W.   245
Mann, F. C.   120, 252, 257
Mann, J. W.   142
Mann, L.   145
Mannari, H.   212

Manning, M. R.   262
Mansfield, R.   210
March, J. G.   122–3, 259
Marcia, J. A.   60
Marks, J.   73
Marriott, R.   90, 91, 92
Marsh, R. M.   212
Marshall, J.   246, 265, 277, 282, 284
Martin, J. K.   244
Martin, W. H.   316, 317
Martinko, M.   101
Maruyama, G.   119
Maslach, C.   269, 270
Maslow, A. H.   3, 34, 56, 87–8, 105, 300, 323
Mason, S.   316, 317
Massie, J. L.   206
Masumoto, Y. S.   283
Mathias, P.   24, 25
Matteson, M. T.   273
Matthews, A.   141–2
Mausner, B.   100, 104, 236, 240, 242, 248, 323
Maxwell, G. M.   190
Mayes, B. T.   279, 280
Mayo, E.   207
Meglino, B.   256, 257, 258
Melhuish, A. H.   281
Meredith, G.   55
Merton, R. K.   63, 206
Metzner, H.   252
Meyer, H. H.   173–4
Michalos, A. C.   249
Miles, R. E.   166
Millar, J.   293
Miller, C. S.   226
Miller, H. E.   251, 254
Miller, K. I.   229, 230
Mills, C. W.   323
Miner, J. B.   104, 184
Minsky, M.   37
Mintzberg, H.   165
Mirels, H.   111
Mischel, W.   57
Misumi, J.   332, 333
Mitchell, T. W.   83

Mobley, W. H.   256, 257, 258, 259
Moeller, N. L.   235, 236
Mohrman, S. A.   110
Monge, P. R.   229, 230
Moon, G. G.   175
Morgan, T.   194
Morley, I.   181
Morley, I. E.   180
Morris, L. W.   57
Morrison, A.   64, 70
Morrison, R. F.   83
Morrow, P.   109, 233
Morse, N. C.   229, 231, 325–6
Moscovici, S.   45, 144, 147
Moser, K. A.   294
Motowidlo, S. J.   262
Mouton, J. S.   162, 221
Mowday, R.   110, 255, 256
Mowday, R. T.   96–7
Moylan, S.   288, 293
Muchinsky, P. M.   80, 81, 82, 83, 84, 244
Mulder, M.   44, 162, 232
Muldrow, T. W.   79
Mulford, H. A.   105
Murooka, H.   194
Murphy, L. R.   279
Murray, O.   13

Napier, N. K.   255
Neale, M. A.   180, 188
Nealey, S. M.   167
Near, J. P.   247
Neff, W. S.   14, 16, 62, 63, 105
Nemeroff, W. F.   108
Nestel, G.   59
Nicholson, H.   153
Nicholson, N.   251, 252, 253, 254
Nilsson, C.   266
Noe, R.   78, 80, 81, 82, 84
Noe, R. A.   235, 236
Noe, R. D.   76, 85
Norris, D. R.   226
Novaco, R. W.   268
Nurick, A. J.   209

Oborne, D. J.   312

O'Brien, G. E.   59, 267, 304
Odaka, K.   328
Offir, C.   261
Oldham, G. R.   33–4, 55, 100–101, 248, 256
Olian-Gottlieb, J. D.   87
Organ, D. W.   245
Ornstein, S.   95
Ortega, D. F.   56
Osborn, R. N.   245
Osborne, A. F.   144
Osgood, C. E.   181
Ostberg, O.   266
Ouchi, W.   334
Overstreet, P. L.   61
Owens, W. A.   82

Packard, J. S.   262
Palmore, E.   246, 264
Parfit, J.   135
Parker, S.   300, 301, 302, 304, 305, 316, 317, 327
Parkes, K.   261, 272, 273, 281, 282
Parkinson, C. N.   206
Partridge, B.   156, 157
Pascale, R. T.   330, 332
Pasmore, W.   44
Patchen, M.   254
Pathan, R. Z.   186
Payne, R.   118, 285, 286, 287, 288, 290, 295, 296, 297, 300, 303, 305, 316
Pearce, J. J.   92
Pearce, J. L.   236
Pearlin, L. I.   71
Pearson, R.   308
Pelz, D. C.   161, 229
Perrow, C.   47
Perry, C.   55
Perry, J. L.   92
Peters, R. K.   278
Pettigrew, A. M.   122
Petty, M. M.   244
Pfeffer, J.   248, 249
Phelps Brown, H.   98
Pheysey, D. C.   47

Pinneau, S. R.   242, 262–3, 265, 268, 271, 273, 274, 275, 276, 278
Pipal, J. E.   56
Pirie, D. S.   91
Platt, J.   56, 125–6, 134, 240, 241
Platt, S.   293
Podsakoff, P. M.   161
Pollard, S.   19
Porter, L.   255, 256
Porter, L. W.   93, 105–6, 110, 238
Poulton, E. C.   267
Prawer, J.   17
Price, J. L.   257
Pringle, J. K.   190
Pritchard, R. D.   87, 95, 109
Pruitt, D.   180, 181
Pugh, D. S.   47, 212

Quinn, R. P.   202, 245, 268, 272

Rackham, N.   180, 194
Rae, D.   95
Rahe, R. H.   304
Rajan, A.   308
Randolph, W. A.   214
Rapoport, R.   318
Rapoport, R. N.   318
Rauschenberger, J.   305
Rawls, J.   98
Reader, G. G.   63
Reeves, T. K.   46
Reilly, R. R.   76
Reimer, E.   229, 231, 325–6
Remitz, U.   238
Revans, R. W.   211
Reynolds, J. I.   186
Reynolds, M.   194
Reynolds, V.   264
Rhodes, S. R.   244, 250, 251, 252, 255
Rice, A. K.   38, 43
Rice, R. W.   247
Riesman, D.   64
Rivera, A. N.   97
Roberts, K.   317
Robertson, I. T.   85

Robinson, J. P.   321
Rodgers, R. C.   220
Rodgers, W. L.   244, 246, 289, 303
Roe, A.   60
Roethlisberger, F. J.   115–17, 137, 150, 207
Rose, R.   314
Rosenberg, M.   65, 67, 70
Rosenman, R.   271
Rosse, J. G.   251, 254
Rossi, P. H.   97
Rotter, J. B.   59
Routledge, T.   235
Roy, D.   90, 120, 128
Runkel, P. J.   190
Runyon, W.   71
Rusbult, C. E.   110, 258
Rutherford, A.   49

Saari, L. M.   186
Salancik, G. R.   110, 248, 249
Sales, S. M.   238, 246, 264
Salisbury, W. W.   105
Salter, V.   153
Sayles, C. R.   47–8
Sayles, L. R.   32, 130
Scandura, T. A.   100, 164
Scanlon, J. N.   92, 225, 226, 231
Schaeffer, R.   243, 248, 274
Scheflen, K.   89
Schein, E. H.   64, 71, 335
Schermerhorn, J. R.   245
Schmidt, F. L.   77, 79
Schmitt, N.   76, 78, 80, 81, 82, 84, 85, 247, 304
Schooler, C.   59, 71
Schriesheim, C. A.   158, 247
Schuchman, A.   224
Schuler, R. S.   202–3
Schultz, D. P.   37
Schuster, M.   226
Schwab, D. P.   87
Scott, W. D.   89, 257
Scott, W. R.   205
Seashore, S. E.   73, 120, 122
Sellaro, C. L.   258

Shaffer, G. S.   247
Shaw, A. G.   91
Shaw, M. E.   144
Sherwood, J. J.   135
Shikiar, R.   257
Shirom, A.   268
Short, J,   51
Shostak, A. B.   19, 20
Sidney, E.   172
Siegel, J.   50
Silberwasser, S.   268
Sime, W. E.   279, 280
Simon, H. A.   259
Skidmore, C.   248
Skon, L.   119
Smee, C. H.   288
Smith, B. B.   164
Smith, C.   247
Smith, F. D.   251
Smith, J. R.   104
Smith, P. B.   332, 334
Smith, P. C.   234
Smith, R.   285–6, 287, 293, 295
Snyderman, B. B.   100, 104, 236, 240, 242, 248, 323
Sofer, C.   71, 174
Solem, A. R.   177–8
Sorcher, M.   186
Spector, P. E.   235, 236, 256
Spence, J. T.   103
Spencer, D. G.   258
Spetz, C. L.   266
Spriegel, W. R.   89, 257
Stafford, E. M.   286
Stalker, G. M.   47, 212, 213
Staudohar, P. D.   184
Stebbins, R. A.   319
Steers, R.   110, 255, 256
Steers, R. M.   243, 250, 251, 252, 255
Stephan, W. G.   142
Stephenson, G. M.   135, 142, 248
Stevenson, W. B.   92
Stewart, R.   125, 165–6
Stokols, D.   268
Stokols, J.   268
Stonier, T.   308

Strassen, S. 246
Strauss, G. 32, 130
Stringer, R. A. 122
Suinn, R. M. 280
Sundstrom, E. 133
Super, D. E. 61
Susmilch, C. 97
Syme, S. L. 275

Taber, T. D. 165
Tajfel, H. 142
Tanaka, H. 329
Tavris, C. 261
Tawney, R. H. 20
Taylor, D. W. 144
Taylor, F. W. 31, 204
Taylor, M. 194
Taylor, M. S. 59
Tazekawa, S. 329, 330, 331, 333
Tedeschi, J. T. 97
Temporal, P. 195
Tetrick, L. E. 236
Tharenou, P. 59
Tharp, G. D. 279, 280
Theorell, T. 266
Thierry, H. 173
Thomas, E. J. 147
Thomas, J. 249
Thomas, K. 12, 17, 24
Thorndike, R. L. 66
Thorsrud, E. 231
Thurley, K. 156
Tiger, L. 11
Tiggemann, M. 289
Tjoswold, D. 156, 164
Toder, W. D. 161
Treasure, F. P. 239
Trevor, M. 332, 333, 334
Trist, E. L. 42
Trumbo, D. 80
Tubbs, M. E. 107, 109
Turner, A. N. 34
Tziner, A. 123, 248

Udy, S. H. 13
Ulrich, L. 80

Urwick, L. 205
van den Bosch, G. 77–8
Van de Vliert, E. 218, 219
Van Dijkhuizen, N. 283
van Harrison, R. 242, 246, 261, 262–3, 265, 268, 271, 273, 274, 275, 276, 278
Van Treuven, R. R. 273
Van Zelst, R. H. 119, 241
Vasey, J. J. 251
Vecchio, R. P. 96
Veen, P. 209
Veness, T. 64
Verhage, J. 162
Vernon, P. E. 75, 84
Veroff, J. 112, 237, 316
Virnelli, S. 273
Viteles, M. S. 88, 239
Vroom, V. H. 65, 66, 70, 86, 100, 103, 104, 163, 164, 189, 191, 229

Wade, G. 141–2
Wagner, J. A. 211
Walker, C. R. 32, 266
Wall, T. D. 43, 227–30, 234, 236, 245, 248, 284, 293
Warnous, J. P. 259
Warr, P. B. 86, 234, 235, 236, 264, 266, 267, 286, 287, 288, 289, 290, 291, 292, 293, 294, 295, 296, 297, 299, 303, 305, 316
Watts, A. G. 313, 316, 317
Wearing, A. 243
Weaver, C. N. 234
Webber, R. A. 144–5
Weber, M. 12, 15, 19, 21, 204
Webster, E. C. 170, 172
Wedley, W. C. 164
Weir, T. 279, 281, 283
Werts, C. E. 70
Wexley, K. N. 186, 190, 193
Wheeler, G. C. 11
White, J. K. 304
White, M. 332, 333, 334
Whitehill, A. M. 329, 330, 331, 333

Whitehorn, C.   234
Whitfield, J.   66
Whyte, W. F.   40–41, 82
Wilkins, L. T.   239
Williams, E.   51
Williams, J.   141–2
Williams, K.   119
Williams, L. J.   256
Williams, M.   153
Wilmott, P.   318
Wilson, J. R.   49
Winefield, A. H.   289
Winer, B. J.   159, 162
Winter, D. G.   103
Wirdenius, H.   156
Wish, M.   125, 155

Withey, S. B.   247
Wolfe, D. M.   202, 268, 272
Wolfe, J. C.   236
Wolpin, J.   253
Woodman, R. W.   135
Woodward, J.   45, 46, 212
Wyatt, S.   112

Yetton, P.   162
Yetton, P. W.   163–4, 189, 191
Yoder, D.   184
Young, M.   318

Zajonc, R. B.   119
Zeisel, H.   286
Zimbardo, P. G.   200

SUBJECT INDEX

abilities 66ff
absenteeism 120, 250ff
  causes of 251ff
  theories of 253ff
  managing 254
achievement motivation 15, 55,
  67, 101ff
adolescents 61ff
age, and satisfaction 244
agriculture 11ff, 23
alienation 3ff
animals 7ff
appraisal 91ff
  interview 172ff
aptitude tests 81ff
assembly lines 31ff
assessment centres 84
authoritarianism 58, 195
authority, types of 199
automation 48ff, 311
autonomous groups 43ff

Bank Wiring Observation
  Room 117, 138ff
black economy 314
buffering, of stress 275ff
bureaucracy 204ff
burn-out 269ff

capitalism 19ff
careers 70ff
chairing a committee 177ff

children 60
church, influence of 16ff
civilizations, ancient 13ff
classical organization theory 204ff
coal-mining 42
commitment, organizational 109ff
committees 143ff
  chairmanship 177ff
conflict, industrial 5, 140ff, 215ff
consideration 161ff
contingency theories 163ff, 213ff
continuous process technology 46
control 266
cooperation, over task 38ff
corporate climates 122
craft
  guilds 19
  workers 45ff
creativity, in groups 144
culture 9ff

de-skilling 311
division of labour 13
doctors 63, 270
domestic system 18
dual-career family 69

Economist (1963) 329, 330
educational methods of
  training 191ff
entrepreneurs 23
equity 94ff

evolution   7ff
exercise   280ff, 319ff
expectancy theory   65
expert systems   312
extroversion   57, 67

factories, early   24ff
fair wages   97ff
Family Expenditure Survey   303
feedback see knowledge of results
feudalism   16ff
friends at work   126ff

gender differences   11, 68, 102ff,
     244
Germany, West   224
goal-setting   105ff
Greece   13ff
groups
     working, 41ff, 114ff
     cohesiveness   119ff, 132ff, 142
     creativity   144
     decision-taking   143ff
     flexible   43ff
     formation of   124
     groupthink   144ff
     informal   117
     internal structure   138ff
     methods of training   193ff
     new technology and   50
     norms   120ff, 135ff
     productivity   118ff
     riskiness   144ff
     satisfaction in   240ff
growth need strength   55ff

happiness   246ff, 288ff, 303ff
hardiness   272
Hawthorne effects   159
health   245ff, 264, 293ff
     habits   281
home working   313
Human Relations movement   206ff

identity achievement   60ff
incentives   86
industrial democracy   223ff

Industrial Democracy in Europe   232
Industrial Revolution   21ff
informal communication   47ff,
     129ff
initiating structure   160ff
integration of employees and
     organization   208ff
intelligence   53ff, 66, 81, 164
interaction, social   126ff
inter-group conflict   140ff
internal–external control   59
interviews   79ff, 168ff

Japan   26, 226, 328ff
jobs
     analysis   72
     characteristic model   100ff
     design   30ff
     enlargement   32ff
     enrichment   32ff
     learning on the   189ff
     redesign, effects of   45
     satisfaction   31, 229ff; causes of
          235; effects of   244ff, 251, 255;
          measurement   233ff; theories
          247ff
     sharing   310
     status   263ff
     success   73
joint consultation   223
judgement   54

knowledge of results   101, 107ff

labour turnover   120, 255ff
     causes of   255ff
     managing   259ff
     models of   258ff
leaders, informal   139
leadership hierarchy   198
leisure   297ff, 301ff, 315ff

Management by Objectives
     (MBO)   167, 220ff
     grid   221
     self-development   194ff
managers   165ff

man-machine systems 36ff
mathematicians 3, 234
mechanistic structures 47
mental health 245ff, 291ff, 304
merchant capitalism 18ff
Michigan, University of 207
micro-electronics 307ff
minority views 146ff
Modern Industry 1946 89
money 88ff, 93ff
moratorium 61
motivation 4, 54ff, 86ff
  achievement 15, 55, 67, 101ff
  economic 88ff
  incentive schemes 89ff
  intrinsic 99
  occupational choice and 67
  power 103
  promotion 104
  self-fulfilment 105ff
motor skills 54

National Institute for Occupational
  Safety and Health, 1987 278
National Institute of Industrial
  Psychology 223, 231
negotiation 179ff
neuroticism 57ff
new technology 48ff, 311ff
non-verbal communication 153ff,
  172

occupations
  choice of 59ff
  job satisfaction 235, 237ff
  perception of, stereotypes 64ff
  stress 262ff
office automation 49, 312
organic structures 47
Organization for Economic
  Cooperation and
  Development (OECD) 1982, 310
organizations 4f, 197ff
  change 283ff
  commitment to 109
  conflict 215ff
  contingency theories 213ff

  design of 214ff
  different kinds 199, 210ff
  ideas about 204ff
  shape 211ff
  size 210ff
organizational development
  (OD) 219ff

Parkinson's Law 206
participation
  in goal-setting 108ff
  and leadership 163ff
part-time work 310
path-goal theory 162ff
pay, and satisfaction 238
person–job fit 67ff, 243, 273ff
personality 52ff, 65ff, 82
personnel
  interview 175ff
  selection 71ff
Position Analysis
  Questionnaire 72
power, need for 55
presenting skills 181ff
primates 8ff
productivity 118ff, 149, 244
Protestant Work Ethic (PWE) 20ff,
  111ff, 321
Protestantism 19ff
psychologists 2, 64

quality circles 226
Quality of Working Life
  movement 35

reality shock 64
relationships, working 125f, 155,
  277
Relay Assembly Test Room 115ff,
  207ff
restaurant 40ff
retirement 300ff
  v. unemployment 305
riskiness, in groups 144ff
role 200ff
  ambiguity 202
  conflict 201ff, 268ff

differentiation 199ff
-playing 186ff
Roman Empire 14ff
rules, social 129, 154ff
Russia 26, 98

Scandinavia 35ff
Scanlon Plan 225ff
security 239
selection
    personnel 71ff
    classical model 77
    fairness 78
    methods 80ff
    utility 79
    validity 73ff
service sector 313
slaves 14ff
social
    anxiety 57ff, 195
    interaction 128ff
    organizations, see organizations
    skills 54, 148ff, 195; training
        183ff
    support 274ff, 282ff, 296
Social Trends 1982–7 278, 281,
    285, 287, 288, 289, 314, 320
socialization for work 9ff, 61ff
socio-technical systems 381
sport and exercise 280ff, 319ff
steam power 22ff, 29
stress 67ff, 260ff
    management 278ff
    personality factors 271ff
    prevention 278
    social support 274ff, 282ff, 296
    sources of 263ff
strikes, 216ff
Strong-Campbell inventory 68, 82
supervision 155ff, 277ff
    rules 157
    satisfaction 242
    skills 39, 149ff
    technology and 51

Tavistock Institute of Human
    Relations 41ff

Taylorism 27, 31ff
technological change 5ff
technology 21, 29ff
    new 48ff, 311ff
    organization and 45ff, 212
tests see aptitude tests; intelligence;
    personality
textile industry 43
Theory Z 334
time-span of responsibility 99
trade unions 27, 98, 215ff
    leaders 217
    representation 222
T-groups 192ff
Type A personality 56, 271ff
typists 33ff

unemployment 285ff
    effects of 286ff
    future of 308ff
    perception of causes 298ff
USA 26ff, 33ff

vertical integration 32ff
village communities 11ff
vitamins 299
voluntary work 314ff

wages, fair 97ff
women
    fear of success 69
    occupational choice 68ff
    wages 98
    see also gender differences
work
    definition of 315
    future of 307
    history of 7ff
    learing how to 39ff
    purpose of 1
    socialization for 62ff
    voluntary 317ff
worker-directors 224ff
workers' councils 223ff
working conditions, ideal 322ff

Yugoslavia 223ff

READ MORE IN PENGUIN

In every corner of the world, on every subject under the sun, Penguin represents quality and variety – the very best in publishing today.

For complete information about books available from Penguin – including Puffins, Penguin Classics and Arkana – and how to order them, write to us at the appropriate address below. Please note that for copyright reasons the selection of books varies from country to country.

In the United Kingdom: Please write to *Dept. JC, Penguin Books Ltd, FREEPOST, West Drayton, Middlesex UB7 OBR.*

If you have any difficulty in obtaining a title, please send your order with the correct money, plus ten per cent for postage and packaging, to *PO Box No. 11, West Drayton, Middlesex UB7 OBR*

In the United States: Please write to *Consumer Sales, Penguin USA, P.O. Box 999, Dept. 17109, Bergenfield, New Jersey 07621-0120.* VISA and MasterCard holders call 1-800-253-6476 to order all Penguin titles

In Canada: Please write to *Penguin Books Canada Ltd, 10 Alcorn Avenue, Suite 300, Toronto, Ontario M4V 3B2*

In Australia: Please write to *Penguin Books Australia Ltd, P.O. Box 257, Ringwood, Victoria 3134*

In New Zealand: Please write to *Penguin Books (NZ) Ltd, Private Bag 102902, North Shore Mail Centre, Auckland 10*

In India: Please write to *Penguin Books India Pvt Ltd, 706 Eros Apartments, 56 Nehru Place, New Delhi 110 019*

In the Netherlands: Please write to *Penguin Books Netherlands bv, Postbus 3507, NL-1001 AH Amsterdam*

In Germany: Please write to *Penguin Books Deutschland GmbH, Metzlerstrasse 26, 60594 Frankfurt am Main*

In Spain: Please write to *Penguin Books S. A., Bravo Murillo 19, 1° B, 28015 Madrid*

In Italy: Please write to *Penguin Italia s.r.l., Via Felice Casati 20, I–20124 Milano*

In France: Please write to *Penguin France S. A., 17 rue Lejeune, F–31000 Toulouse*

In Japan: Please write to *Penguin Books Japan, Ishikiribashi Building, 2–5–4, Suido, Bunkyo-ku, Tokyo 112*

In Greece: Please write to *Penguin Hellas Ltd, Dimocritou 3, GR–106 71 Athens*

In South Africa: Please write to *Longman Penguin Southern Africa (Pty) Ltd, Private Bag X08, Bertsham 2013*

READ MORE IN PENGUIN

PSYCHOLOGY

Introduction to Jung's Psychology Frieda Fordham

'She has delivered a fair and simple account of the main aspects of my psychological work. I am indebted to her for this admirable piece of work' – C. G. Jung in the Foreword

Child Care and the Growth of Love John Bowlby

His classic 'summary of evidence of the effects upon children of lack of personal attention ... presents to administrators, social workers, teachers and doctors a reminder of the significance of the family' – *The Times*

Recollections and Reflections Bruno Bettelheim

'A powerful thread runs through Bettelheim's message: his profound belief in the dignity of man, and the importance of seeing and judging other people from their own point of view' – *Independent*. 'These memoirs of a wise old child, candid, evocative, heart-warming, suggest there is hope yet for humanity' – *Evening Sta..lard*

Female Perversions Louise J. Kaplan

'If you can't have love, what do you get? Perversion, be it mild or severe: shopping, seduction, anorexia or self-mutilation. Kaplan charts both Madame Bovary's "perverse performance" and the more general paths to female self-destruction with a grace, determination and intellectual firmness rare in the self-discovery trade. A most remarkable book' – Fay Weldon

The Psychology of Interpersonal Behaviour Michael Argyle

Social behaviour and relationships with others are one of the main sources of happiness, but their failure may result in great distress and can be a root cause of mental illness. In the latest edition of this classic text, Michael Argyle has included the latest research on non-verbal communication, social skills and happiness, and has extensively revised and updated the text throughout.

READ MORE IN PENGUIN

PSYCHOLOGY

Psychoanalysis and Feminism Juliet Mitchell

'Juliet Mitchell has risked accusations of apostasy from her fellow feminists. Her book not only challenges orthodox feminism, however; it defies the conventions of social thought in the English-speaking countries ... a brave and important book' – *New York Review of Books*

The Divided Self R. D. Laing

'A study that makes all other works I have read on schizophrenia seem fragmentary ... The author brings, through his vision and perception, that particular touch of genius which causes one to say "Yes, I have always known that, why have I never thought of it before?"' – *Journal of Analytical Psychology*

Po: Beyond Yes and No Edward de Bono

No is the basic tool of the logic system. *Yes* is the basic tool of the belief system. Edward de Bono offers *Po* as a device for changing our ways of thinking: a method for approaching problems in a new and more creative way.

The Informed Heart Bruno Bettelheim

Bettelheim draws on his experience in concentration camps to illuminate the dangers inherent in all mass societies in this profound and moving masterpiece.

The Care of the Self Michel Foucault
The History of Sexuality Vol 3

Foucault examines the transformation of sexual discourse from the Hellenistic to the Roman world in an inquiry which 'bristles with provocative insights into the tangled liaison of sex and self' – *The Times Higher Education Supplement*

Mothering Psychoanalysis Janet Sayers

'An important book ... records the immense contribution to psycho-analysis made by its founding mothers' – Julia Neuberger in the *Sunday Times*